THE BRITISH POLITICAL TRADITION

VOLUME ONE
THE RISE OF COLLECTIVISM

THE BRITISH POLITICAL TRADITION
in four volumes

THE BRITISH POLITICAL TRADITION

W.H. GREENLEAF

VOLUME ONE

THE RISE OF COLLECTIVISM

ROUTLEDGE

First published in 1983 by
Methuen & Co. Ltd
11 New Fetter Lane, London EC4P 4EE
First published as a University
Paperback in 1988 by Routledge

© 1983 W.H. Greenleaf

Printed in Great Britain
at the University Press, Cambridge

British Library Cataloguing in Publication Data

Greenleaf, W.H.
The British political tradition.
Vol. 1: The rise of collectivism
1. Great Britain – Politics and government –
19th century   2. Great Britain – Politics and
government – 20th century
I. Title
320.941   JN216

ISBN 0-415-00709-7

We construct our world as an interpretation which attempts to restore the unity which the real has lost by our making its diversity explicit.

B. BOSANQUET, *Logic*, II.ix.1 (i)

p. [xiv] lines 7 and 9	'Record'
p. 29 n. 75	'R. Com. Rep., 1973–4' (also p. 172 n. 276)
pp. 49–50	'Technological change, the accumulation of capital, and the expansion of productive capacity have fundamentally altered the form of war.'
p. 125 n. 122	'(Berlin, 1986)'
p. 191 line 7	'Board-schools'
p. 284 line 14	'Dostoevsky'
p. 334	'University Grants Committee 194'

CONTENTS

FIGURES AND TABLES

ABBREVIATIONS

ACAS	Advisory, Conciliation, and Arbitration Service
C., Cd., Cmd., Cmnd.	Command Paper
CPC	Conservative Political Centre
DNB	*Dictionary of National Biography* (Compact edition, Oxford, 1975)
GNP	Gross National Product
H.C. Deb.	House of Commons Debates
IEA	Institute of Economic Affairs
ILP	Independent Labour Party
KCA	*Keesing's Contemporary Archives*
LGAO	Local Government Act Office
LPDL	Liberty and Property Defence League
NUA	National Unionist Association
OED	*Oxford English Dictionary* (Compact edition, Oxford, 1971)
Parl. Deb.	Parliamentary Debates
PEP	Political and Economic Planning
PRO	Public Record Office
PSBR	Public Sector Borrowing Requirement
R. Com.	Royal Commission
Rep.	Report
Sel. Cttee	Select Committee
TLS	*The Times Literary Supplement*
Trans. R. Hist. S.	*Transactions of the Royal Historical Society*

GENERAL PREFACE

The present study of the British Political Tradition will be published in four volumes. The first two appear together; the third will come out shortly; while the fourth will, I hope, be ready in due course. The purpose is fourfold. The overall intention is to suggest a particular point of view about the study of politics; and though this is no more than sketched at the outset it is subsequently exemplified at large, albeit indirectly. The second aim (pursued in the first volume) is to provide a certain historical perspective in the context of which the development of our modern politics may be seen. Then, given this prospect, a survey is offered (in volumes two and three) of both our political ideas and institutions. And I must confess that though the review of governmental and allied machinery is (if not profound) reasonably complete within the limits imposed, the examination of the doctrines is no more than illustrative. I suspect this is partly because there is little secondary literature to provide an obvious general guide or point of departure. I fear also that Michelet's ideal of showing how institutions and ideas react on and co-operate with one another has been too little pursued. But I did not master the material sufficiently well to attempt this exercise, supremely valuable though it would be. The final object is to consider (in the same general perspective) the overseas dimension of our affairs, foreign and imperial policy and administration, and ideas about them. These exotic elements have had a not inconsiderable effect on the growth of the collectivist state and will be reviewed in the fourth volume under the title 'The World Outside'.

The approach is in many ways determinedly old-fashioned. At the same time the work as a whole hardly constitutes a simple account of the British Constitution in the conventional way not being (for all its length) detailed or comprehensive enough for that in certain important respects; as well, it wanders rather far from the traditional institutional high road. In any case, there are already very many admirable surveys which provide a review of the system of government as such. Nor could I claim, despite all the references, citations, and similar paraphernalia, that this is a work of fundamental research. Apart from anything else I am very much aware how greatly the archival dimension has been neglected especially in respect of the institutional studies. I dipped a toe in this vast ocean and hastily, and guiltily, retreated. Moreover I have to confess (with Dicey) that the theme came first and then the task of illustrating or substantiating it. So I suppose one might say that for all its length and detail the entire study is really little more than an extended essay.

I embarked on an apparently limited task some years ago; as I now realize rather foolishly. What has been done was achieved with a growing sense of inadequacy as the array of potential evidence increased before my eyes to astonishing and quite unmanageable proportions. Of course, I should have known better at the outset and have anticipated this. And I suppose I might have avoided at least part of the difficulty by filling in one of those absurdly vast questionnaires and with a bit of luck got a massive grant from the Social Science Research Council and employed a brace of research assistants to do all the spadework for me, subsequently feeding the data expensively through a computer or two. But I have never fancied that way of working, regarding it (apart from anything else) as rather a cheat and believing it essential to brood over the details oneself so far as possible and not at second-hand. However, the actual result is (or so it frequently seems to me now) often little more than a sciolistic sketch of a matter both deep and complex, and revealing at best a kind of 'encyclopaedic half-knowledge' (I think Günter Grass uses this apt phrase somewhere). Contemplating the result so far, I can only reach for Peer Gynt's lame excuse:

> You think my enterprise transgressed
> the bounds of what's permissible?
> Yes, I felt that myself – most keenly,
> and in the end I came to hate it.
> But once one's started, as you know,
> it's hard to extricate oneself . . .

Even so, I like to think the thing has a recognizable identity as a piece of historical retrospection; and that the generalizations, if crass, may nevertheless have some educative or pedagogic value and help the student of politics (or of other aspects of social study even) to make connexions between topics which are still too often sundered in academic presentation, and this is not unimportant; nor is the set of categories I propose which cuts across the usual misleading polarities of right and left. One thing I have tried to avoid is making this too much of a polemical tract. I have my own prejudices in these matters like anyone else and (to reveal at once where the bias lies) often wanted not to let the collectivist dogs get the better of it; but I have tried to be impartial (if not indifferent) and trust I have not succumbed unduly to such partisan promptings as stirred me from time to time. To give way in this respect is easy and constitutes the ultra-crepidarian indulgence, all too common I fear, of the academic, teaching (as Burke had it) the humour of the professor rather than the principles of the science. Certainly, I had no intention of meddling directly with questions of contemporary politics or of trying to peer too far into the future. I know my place, hope I have kept to it on the whole, and will be satisfied if I have adequately reviewed the developments of the recent past without taking sides too much and without asking too assertively where it is all leading.

My intellectual obligations are many and no doubt very obvious. I owe most, of course, to the works of Spencer, Dicey, and Halévy and, at a quite different level, of Michael Oakeshott. Specific indications of source and authority are given in the footnotes. No doubt these are too profuse for some tastes though I confess that, for myself, I rather revel in them in other people's books and papers and hope that here they may sometimes act as a kind of fingerposts pointing to the luring pathways beyond. Full details of publication are given at the first reference in each section; subsequent use in that section of the same work is normally noted by author and short title only or by the usual contractions. Given that the notes are fairly extensive I did not think it worthwhile to include a bibliography as well.

My thanks are due to the Principal and Council of the University College, Swansea, for granting me leave for most of the session 1977–8 so that I might tackle the penultimate stages of composition; also to the Nuffield Foundation for generous financial aid enabling me to visit libraries and repositories during that period to consult material not available in Swansea and also in respect of some typing costs. I am grateful, too, for particular help received from the staff of the University College Library, from Mr G. D. M. Block of the Conservative Research Department, and from the South Wales Miners' Library, Swansea. Mr John Naylor of Methuen has shown a degree of patience much, much beyond the point of proper indulgence. With exemplary stoicism, Mrs E. Evans, Mrs B. Langford, Mrs P. Rees, Mrs A. Watkins, and Mrs P. Yates have (among others concerned) coped with reams of authorial scribble often resembling an ancient and many-layered palimpsest; my thanks are owed to them all and especially to Mrs Yates who has lately borne the main burden of the typing.

May 1982   W. H. GREENLEAF
                                                                Swansea

ACKNOWLEDGEMENTS

Some of the material used here has previously appeared in the pages of *Public Administration, Parliamentary Affairs*, and the *British Journal of Political Science*. I have also used some passages from my chapter in R. Benewick *et al.*, *Knowledge and Belief in Politics* (Allen & Unwin, London, 1973) and from my inaugural lecture *The World of Politics* (University College, Swansea, 1968). I acknowledge with thanks the permission of the Clerk of the Records, the House of Lords Records Office, to cite from materials in his charge. Crown copyright records in the Public Records Office are cited by permission of the Controller of Her Majesty's Stationery Office as are passages from official publications of various sorts.

W.H.G.

*   *   *

The author and publishers would also like to thank the following for their kind permission to use copyright material:

Basil Blackwell Publisher for material from B. Keith-Lucas, *The English Local Government Franchise: a Short History*, for inclusion in Table 8. Crowell Collier & Macmillan (Publishers) Ltd for material from S. Gordon, *Our Parliament*, for inclusion in Table 9. Lloyds Bank for material from *The British Economy in Figures, 1981*, for inclusion in Table 7. Macmillan, London and Basingstoke, for material from D. Butler and A. Sloman, *British Political Facts 1900–1979*, for inclusion in Tables 6 and 9 and Figure 2. National Bureau of Economic Research, Inc. for material from M. Abramowitz and V. Eliasberg, *The Growth of Public Employment in Great Britain* (Princeton University Press, 1957), for inclusion in Table 3. Professor A. T. Peacock and Professor J. Wiseman for material from *The Growth of Public Expenditure in the United Kingdom* (Allen & Unwin, 1967), for inclusion in Tables 1 and 2 and Figure 1. Yale University Press for permission to reproduce extracts from R. H. Tawney, *The British Labor Movement* (1925).

PART ONE
THEME AND CONTEXT

To what tune danceth this Immense?
Semi-Chorus in T. HARDY, *The Dynasts*,
1904–8; repr. 1965, p. 524

I
THE CHARACTER OF MODERN
BRITISH POLITICS

I' th' commonwealth I would by contraries
Execute all things; . . . .
The Tempest, II.i.143–4

THE STUDY OF BRITISH POLITICS

'Nothing here but trees and grass', thinks the traveller, and marches
on. 'Look,' says the woodsman, 'there is a tiger in that grass.'
R. G. COLLINGWOOD, *An Autobiography*, 1939, p.100

W H E N Phineas Finn wrote home to say he had been invited to stand for
Parliament he justified his acceptance of the nomination by confessing,
'"I own that I am fond of politics, and have taken great delight in their
study"'. '"Stupid young fool!" his father said to himself as he read this'.[1]
Quite so: for concern is inevitably and properly aroused at so curious an
interest and eccentric an ambition not least because the motives for such
intimate political engagement are rarely happily considered or appropriate. Nevertheless the value and attractions of the study itself
(however ill-conceived the precise grounds or occasions involved) have
by now been deemed sufficiently strong for the subject to be introduced in
one form or another in most if not all of our universities. And for obvious
reasons consideration of British affairs in particular has bulked large in
these academic pursuits. There have become established, too, specific
ways of examining these matters, various categories of approach that
between them comprise the possibilities currently explored by university
departments when their attention is directed to the domestic political
scene; and this in addition to the usual array of comment and review of
different sorts and levels by politicians themselves, journalists, and other
professional publicists.

First, there is what might reasonably be called the traditional manner,

1 A. Trollope, *Phineas Finn, The Irish Member* (1869; Panther, 1975), p.28.

the conventional and most long-established kind of inquiry into the British Constitution. It takes three forms which, though they may in practice be interwoven, are notionally distinct. One consists in studies of constitutional law. Here there is naturally a substantial though never exclusive emphasis on the framework of convention, statute, and case-law relating to our political institutions and practices. And certain aspects of our concerns that may otherwise receive scant attention (such as military or electoral law, Parliamentary privilege, public liability, administrative justice, the Privy Council, and the courts) are in this legal context usually given treatment in some depth. The manner of discussion, which may be highly technical, is easily familiar to readers of such well-established authorities as Keir and Lawson or Wade and Phillips, recent studies of the same kind such as that of Professor de Smith, and, as well, specialized works like Rogers on elections or Edwards on the law officers of the Crown. The second traditional style is that of constitutional history, a discipline concerned, of course, to examine the past and development of our public offices either as a whole or in respect of some specific topic relating to a given period, issue, department, or procedure; nor are the individual persons neglected who have played some significant role. A good many of the earlier accounts of our politics took this form though the emphasis or interest could vary notably as the contrast between, say, the work of Hallam and Maitland makes quite clear. Very often there is a close and natural connexion with the history of the law as in Sir William Holdsworth's great and masterly volumes.

However, these two kinds of study of our constitution are usually stronger in other departments of universities than those which deal explicitly with politics. There the remaining traditional fashion flourishes, constituting, I fancy, the greater part of the output of academic students of British political affairs. It is institutional rather than legal or historical in nature and, though it may contain perhaps quite substantial elements of these other sorts, it need not do so. It involves a notable concentration on official structure and procedure and offers a more or less detailed examination of the formal machinery of government and the way it works. Of course, there are, again, varieties of emphasis and nuance and even of omission – some recent general textbooks curiously fail to consider such matters as local authorities or the nationalized industries which are hardly insignificant channels of public power. But, within this general mode, descriptions are invariably provided of government departments and their operation, the functioning of parties, the role and procedure of Parliament, how Cabinet business is arranged, and so on; or a chosen aspect of the system may be looked at closely to examine, say, the conduct of a single election, the passage of a particular piece of legislation, the organization of some office or agency, or the origin and implementation of a given act of policy. All such accounts draw on a range of sources from newspapers and government reports to biographies and histories of one kind or another; and though participants may be interviewed where this is possible, it is still rather unusual for archival material to be tapped especially in the broader surveys, partly I imagine because these primary data may be inaccessible in respect of more recent times. Obviously there is a wide spectrum of work of this type in which the institutional concern shades into the contemporary interest. There is often, indeed, a high premium placed on current relevance and tendency, and consequently the expression of critical opinion, even partisan bias, is not always avoided. It is, in truth, easy to see how an academically inappropriate tendentiousness can creep into this sort of commentaries: that statute is against the national interest and ought not to have become law but another implemented in its stead; this institution is inefficient or this procedure is unfair and should be reformed; such and such a policy or influence is ideologically suspect and should be withdrawn or contained. The temptation is obvious, and I must quickly repeat what I said in the Preface that in respect of the present essay I would not claim to be completely immune to the lure though I have tried to resist it. In any event, this entire genre is manifestly well-established and it has changed relatively little over the years. It is true that of late the range of consideration has extended somewhat to include an increasing amount of material on the social context of political matters and especially on such topics as elections, the process of socialization, the influence of the media, and the activities of pressure groups. Nevertheless, for all the differences of scope and treatment, the similarity is remarkable between an early exemplar such as Sir Sidney Low's *The Governance of England* (1904) and a modern review like, say, Professor Peter Bromhead's *Britain's Developing Constitution* (1974) and this despite the lapse of three-quarters of a century. And what follows here certainly and inevitably owes a very great deal to this basic tradition of writing about British politics.

Secondly, there is the sociological view or approach, in some ways a latter-day development or, rather, rediscovery. It naturally tends to concentrate on matters that especially suit its emphasis either to examine particular segments of the general political scene (the role of special interests, the formation of opinions and values, the class background of élites, the social basis of party affiliation, themes such as participation and communication, and so forth) or to focus attention on particular localities for intensive study (Glossop or Banbury, for instance). The purely Marxist literature apart, however, and with the possible exception of a winsome yet ultimately forlorn attempt by Professor Richard Rose, I think there is no general account of British politics premeditated on this sort of basis. Nor is the deficiency surprising because the reach of this style of analysis, though immensely powerful within its range, is limited in scope. It can list what schools ministers and their advisers went to and the like and draw conclusions, though necessarily of a limited kind, from such evidence; but it cannot really help us all the way or all that much when we want to know, say, the whys and wherefores of specific Cabinet decisions or particular institutional arrangements. It can purport to describe precisely, to a couple of decimal points, what percentage of subjectively working-class Conservatives think it is better to be ruled by an old Etonian than by a grammar-school boy (or girl) but it does not tell us a great deal about the political role of the Prime Minister. At its best this approach can be a powerful searchlight; but we often need a flare. And even where its questions are politically relevant or significant the information necessary to deal with them may be unavailable and in any case open to a wide variety of interpretation.

A *fortiori* this kind of narrowness or irrelevance is also the case with the fashionable worship of naturalistic gods: the pursuit of laws, taxonomies, causal or functional relationships, the use of aggregate analysis, regression coefficients, systemic models, and all that. On the whole these exercises are very long on technique and very short on concrete political content. What they reveal to us of scientific significance I am unable to say and really rather indifferent, though I suspect the work is merely imitative: no real scientists ever seem to be interested in it. But the failure so far to add much to our detailed understanding of British politics – the field with which we are here concerned – is pretty clear and results from the procedures employed being inappropriate to that grasp of practical, moral, and historical confusion which is a crucial feature of political life. The point made so forcibly by Keynes about 'pseudo-mathematical methods' in economics is most apt. Too much of what results, he suggested, is mere concoction, as imprecise as the initial assumptions it rests on; and the great danger involved is that it allows 'the author to lose sight of the complexities and interdependencies of the real world in a maze of pretentious and unhelpful symbols'. In respect of this scholar's fairyland, I incline myself to the opinion of Mr Ramboat in H. G. Wells's *Tono-Bungay*: 'There's a lot of this Science about nowadays, . . . but I sometimes wonder a bit what good it is'. Equally, books and papers fashioned in this style, 'following along the path of solemn unintelligibility', will no doubt continue to pour out for some while yet until the fad fades away.[2]

Of course, the work comprised by these different kinds of endeavour (always with the exception of the last) constitutes an impressive and

2 J. M. Keynes, *The General Theory of Employment, Interest and Money* (1936; London, 1942), pp.297–8; H. G. Wells, *Tono-Bungay* (1909; Penguin, 1946), p.114. The last phrase cited is from H. Brogan, *Tocqueville* (Fontana, 1973), p.10.

invaluable foundation for the study of British politics. One could only hope to advance by building on it. Yet improvement is required for, despite its extent and amount, the general corpus of inquiry may none the less leave a certain sense of narrowness or incompletion that needs to be supplied. Three deficiencies in particular seem manifest. First, there is almost always a neglect of the ideological dimension of our political life, of the doctrines and ideas that constitute in fact so crucial an aspect of this experience. It was indeed an utter disgrace that for so long there was not simply no good account but no recent account at all of modern British political thought. There have, of course, been studies of particular doctrines, especially Socialism, or of particular writers. And an attempt at a complete survey was made in 1925 by an American graduate student Lewis Rockow in his *Contemporary Political Thought in England*; but until just the other day this had no successor and naturally in some respects began after a while to show its age. There is now Dr Rodney Barker's admirable conspectus which covers the whole ground most swiftly and expertly.[3] But it is significant that it stands out and stands alone. Then, secondly, there is often no attempt to relate foreign and imperial affairs to the conduct of domestic politics and the development of institutions and ideas. It is true that these exotic matters may receive specialized attention of a most extensive and detailed kind from students of international affairs whether these be historians or political scientists. But the latter tend often to take a vulgarly naturalistic view of their professional preoccupations; and neither is necessarily concerned to integrate the external to the home dimension of our political tradition. Then, thirdly, the study of British politics not unusually lacks an explicit organizing perspective of an adequate historical kind: there is thus no 'Gestalt in the beholder's eye' in the context of which the mass of political detail presented may assume order and meaning.[4] In consequence, general examination of our politics too often takes the form of a series of almost discrete studies of specific topics or institutions with little or no attempt to present an overall framework of analysis and review. In this connexion, I am reminded of a tale told in the prologue to Harold Macmillan's memoirs. After 1945, he writes, Winston Churchill, as Leader of the Opposition, was 'in the habit of entertaining his colleagues in the Shadow Cabinet to fortnightly luncheons at the Savoy Hotel. At one of these there was brought in a rather equivocal and shapeless pudding, which he viewed with some distaste. He called the waiter, "Pray take away this pudding. It has no theme".' I have, adds Macmillan, always remembered this incident, 'a warning to authors as well as to

3 R. S. Barker, *Political Ideas in Modern Britain* (London, 1978).
4 The phrase cited is Lord Balogh's: see his 'Theory and Policy Making', *TLS* (9 July 1976), p. 857.

cooks'.[5] It is indeed an admonition that should be heeded by anyone trying to describe a subject so wide-ranging in scope and diverse in its particulars as the nature and development of British political life over the past century or so, which is my object here.

What is required is intimated, however, by two types of book. The first is the kind which aims precisely both to present a general view of institutions and to relate this to cognate developments in political thought. There are too few of these studies of recent note but they are admirable and point the way and, like everyone working in this field, I must acknowledge my very great indebtedness to them. I have in mind four particular works: A. H. Birch on *Representative and Responsible Government* (1964), S. H. Beer's *Modern British Politics* (1965), T. A. Smith's analysis of *Anti-Politics* (1972), and his later *The Politics of the Corporate Economy* (1979). Like Bacon these serve the office of bell-ringers, first up to call others to church. Then there are the historical exercises (under which heading I make bold to include some of the better institutional and sociological inquiries): detailed accounts based not only on secondary sources but on the primary material in the public records and private archives and dealing with the origin and development of particular institutions, practices or events, or of the personalities involved in them. One learns so much more of British politics from this sort of studies than from the rash of stuff on computer simulation or causal models of voting behaviour. Even so, in the end, attention here naturally tends to be confined to the limited task in hand; and the broader constitutional histories themselves are often strongly legal or insti-tutional in cast. But this historical work, too, is a crucial part of the basis on which more general accounts of British political life and thought must build.

How, then, should we proceed? What better prospect can be offered? It is necessary that, amid the inevitable mass of detail both institutional and ideological, some unifying identity should be discerned, a generaliz-ing and synthetic theme lurking in the particulars and which marshals them and reveals their significance. The problem is how to recognize and establish the concept involved. So, by way of further preamble, I shall first say something about the idea of character for, as may be surmised, the term was not included in the title of this chapter for no reason at all and bears closely on the way I believe this problem should be tackled.

THE CONCEPT OF A POLITICAL TRADITION

It is good to be often reminded of the inconsistency of human nature. . . .
LORD MACAULAY, 'Warren Hastings', in *Essays*, 1889, p.666

5 H. Macmillan, *Winds of Change, 1914–1939* (London, 1966), p.29.

The general rule of analysis adopted here is by no means new. It derives in particular from the work of some historians and from that of the philosophical idealists. For instance, there is a passage in one of T. H. Green's lay sermons which briefly summarizes the idea involved, that of unity in diversity:

> An assertion of identity . . . not only admits of but implies difference or change. . . . When we speak of the identity of the body in youth and age, we have in view the sameness of organisation determining a constant flux of material. Wherever unity of principle or law runs through any process of change, there the different objects which result from the process at its several stages have a real identity with each other, though they be as different as the oak from the acorn or the complete animal from the embryo; and on the recognition of the difference depends the significance of the assertion of identity.[6]

The problem of characterization is thus one of making a feasible unity out of a range of varying tendency and to do so without ignoring any ambivalences, differences, or alterations that the evidence to hand may suggest. A sceptical Mr Justice Holmes, no Hegelian, nevertheless admitted on one occasion the 'sometimes profitable dodge of uniting disparates'.[7] The question is, What is involved?, or, How to do it?

In principle there are two ways of going about this exercise whether the disposition in question is that of one person or of a society as a whole. And it is helpful here to stand Socrates on his head and look for the key to political understanding in the individual rather than the other way round.[8]

Tristram Shandy believed that the animal spirits in a person's make-up tread the same steps over and over again making 'a road of it as plain and as smooth as a garden walk', a well-worn course which not even the Devil can easily divert.[9] Certainly, one way of establishing the nature of an individual is to look for just such uniformity, for the single thread to lead us safely through the labyrinth of data about a personality, for the dominating feature which suffuses the form throughout. This is perhaps the obvious and easy course; but it proves too simplistic to be

---

6 T. H. Green, 'The Word is Nigh Thee', *Works*, ed. R. L. Nettleship (London, 1885–8), iii.225. An unpublished paper by Professor Oakeshott, 'The Idea of "Character" in the Interpretation of Modern Politics' (1954) is of particular importance in this context. See also his *On Human Conduct* (Oxford, 1975), part III, 'On the Character of a Modern European State'.

7 Holmes to Laski (12 September 1916), M. D. Howe (ed.), *Holmes-Laski Letters: the Correspondence of Mr. Justice Holmes and Harold J. Laski, 1916–1935* (London, 1953), i.18.

8 Cf. *Republic*, 368d–369a.

9 L. Sterne, *The Life & Opinions of Tristram Shandy, Gentleman* (1759–67; Everyman, 1924), p. 3.

satisfactory. And the reason is that no one aspect of temperament is likely always and adequately to sum up the whole of what a person is, except in the case of a saint or a madman perhaps. It may be urged that an individual is, say, wholly unselfish but it is likely, even inevitable, that a close examination of his behaviour will reveal a more chequered picture. Someone can be a good parent but unsociable to his neighbours; honest in his work but not above being less than straightforward in the matter of a tax return; tolerant on some moral issues but quite bigoted about others. Chesterton recalls an acquaintance, 'an extreme Radical', who was a champion of liberty everywhere except at home.[10] And, of course, a person's manner can change over time as he gets older or as his circumstances alter: in this sense, character is a process and an unfolding. So in ordinary experience we find no one is ever so uniform in behaviour that a single crucial feature of his make-up permeates all he is or does. The old wisdom of the law has always recognized this: *unus homo plures personas sustinet*. In a recent volume of biographical sketches, Arnold Toynbee observed the point (and directly rebutted the Shandyan view) when he suggested there is 'a mixture of motives and a tangle of contradictions in the conduct and character of the most single-minded and self-consistent human being. Any single track interpretation . . . is therefore unlikely to hit the whole truth.' Chesterton, again, was fond of asking people who expressed an admiration for David Lloyd George, 'Which George do you mean?', because the politician had worn so many colours.[11] A literary instance may provide other illustration.[12] In George Eliot's *Middlemarch*, Dorothea urges that Lydgate cannot be guilty of the accusation levelled against him because his disposition would not permit such an action. Her interlocutor in this conversation, Mr Farebrother, is more worldly-wise: he smiles gently at her ardour and says, 'But, my dear Mrs. Casaubon, . . . character is not cut in marble – it is not something solid and unalterable. It is something living and

10 G. K. Chesterton, *Autobiography* (1936; London, 1937), p. 28.

11 A. Toynbee, *Acquaintances* (London, 1967), p.86; M. Ward, *Gilbert Keith Chesterton* (London, 1944), p.2.

12 In the course of what follows in these pages I cite several times works of fiction as witness to attitudes or events; and, by a harsh empiricist or some aesthetic purist, this might be thought unreasonable or improper. Yet for a careful and stimulating statement of the case that the novel may provide important insight and evidence useful to the student of politics and administration, see D. Waldo, *The Novelist on Organization & Administration: an Inquiry into the Relationship between Two Worlds* (Berkeley, Calif., 1968) which contains an extensive, annotated bibliography. For two recent comments, see G. Watson, *The English Ideology: Studies in the Language of Victorian Politics* (London, 1973), pp.2–9; and R. A. W. Rhodes, 'Wilting in Limbo: Anthony Trollope and the Nineteenth Century Civil Service', *Public Administration*, li (1973), esp. pp.207–8.

changing'.[13] A personality is rather to be seen, therefore, as a continual tergiversation: and every person portrays many parts. A little while ago, a leading contemporary actor said that if he had any professional philosophy it was that, like other people, he had within himself 'the potential for doing everything' as 'all the opposites are within us': in the Whitmanesque phrase, we contain multitudes, even contradictions.[14]

But all this does not mean that character is unrecognizable or that its nature cannot be grasped; it simply implies that it is more complex, diffuse, vacillant, even contrarious than is suggested by the search for an unmixed universal emphasis. So we need to look to the alternative possibility which rests explicitly on the recognition of ambivalence in disposition, thus anticipating coherence (which admits diversity) rather than uniformity (which excludes it). We must acknowledge that to describe or understand character it is necessary to get clear not the quality that is presumed to feature in every action but rather the habitual – and more or less varied and incompatible – inclinations that indicate the extremes of conduct of which an individual is capable and to which he is urged alike by an undecided will, a tangled heredity, and a changing and perhaps confusing environment. To act in character is to act not in the same or in a constant way but to move within certain limits; and the task of characterization involves, first, the establishment of these confining tendencies and then the observation of their diverse fusion throughout the entire range of specific aspects of thought and action.

Of course, there have (as already intimated) been many observations of these 'incongruities of sentiment and belief' that may be manifested within a single psyche.[15] One's desultory reading can produce an extensive and varied catalogue of instances but I limit myself to three further witnesses only of the point in mind. The first is the young Macaulay writing a letter about the famous Scottish lawyer and critic, Lord Jeffrey. He describes his subject's rapid changes of manner and says: 'A person who had seen him in only one state would not know him if he saw him in another.' He goes on to elaborate the assemblage of dissimilar qualities involved and concludes: 'I can easily conceive that two people who had seen him on different days might dispute about him as travellers in the fable disputed about the chameleon.'[16] The second statement is from the stimulating and controversial study of Thomas Jefferson by Professor Leonard Levy who suggests that the received view

13 G. Eliot, *Middlemarch* (1871–2; Everyman, 1969), ii.273–4.
14 Ian McKellen, cited in *Woman's Journal* (May 1976), p.20; Whitman's *Leaves of Grass*, 'Song of Myself', §51.
15 The phrase cited is Herbert Spencer's from *The Study of Sociology* (1873; Ann Arbor, Mich., 1961), p.270.
16 Sir G. O. Trevelyan, *The Life and Letters of Lord Macaulay* (1876; 2nd edn, London, 1889), pp.106–7.

of his subject as a uniform and consistent apostle of freedom is misleading for there is another, very different, aspect of the matter. He puts the problem of describing the President's character in this way:

> Historians have been fascinated with him as a figure of contradictions and ambiguities. The incandescent advocate of natural rights was a slaveholder; the strict constructionist of constitutional powers purchased Louisiana and adopted the embargo; the philosopher wrote the *Manual of Parliamentary Practice*; the aristocrat championed democracy; and the democrat never introduced a proposal for universal manhood suffrage.[17]

(This is a theme, too, which has lately received a fascinating fictional presentation in Gore Vidal's novel *Burr* [1973].) My final example is culled from a recent study of Lord Nelson and the Trafalgar campaign by the eminent military historian John Terraine. He notes, for instance, that the Admiral could be gentle and considerate but that he was also nervous, highly-strung, vain, and capable of the most intense hatred. And there is the startling transformation of Nelson's manner described by Wellington on the only occasion on which the two men met. Nelson then appeared both as a silly charlatan and as a most sensible man of affairs and, said the Duke, 'a more sudden and complete metamorphosis I never saw'. Terraine comments: 'So it is by a study of contrasts and opposites, not by following a single consistent thread, that we approach an understanding of Nelson.'[18] What might (in imitation of contemporary jargon) be called the Jekyll and Hyde syndrome seems to a degree to be characteristic of every individual.

And as it is thus with a single personality so it is even more with groups of people, their ideas and institutions. A family, an association, or a political society as a whole, are not to be described by reference to nuclear attributes. A grasp of their diathesis (or constitutional disposition) has to be achieved out of what Herbert Spencer called 'a chaos of conduct and of opinion' and is indicated by the antithesis of extreme features within which limits their behaviour falls.[19] These contrasts define a typical style or way of acting. And all their various aspects do not share a common quality but, within the range in question, are related to one another in many different ways; they reflect perhaps highly confused and varied combinations of the contrasting tendencies. The identity is real enough but a description of it, while it necessarily summarizes, must take account of the manifold, the dissemblances as well as the

---

17 L. W. Levy, *Jefferson & Civil Liberties: The Darker Side* (Cambridge, Mass., 1963), p. 16.
18 J. Terraine, *Trafalgar* (London, 1976), p. 52.
19 Spencer, op. cit., p. 131.

similarities, and must, in addition, not be indifferent to the process of change involved in such a living variety of connexions. This is why it is not inappropiate to talk of a 'tradition' of political activity because this concept implies just such a unity in diversity: a complex amalgam of different forces and opposing choices, and therefore of internal tensions, which is at the same time in a continual state of flux and development but which nevertheless constitutes a recognizable and acknowledged whole.

It is this kind of elucidation which is attempted in the present study. Professor Oakeshott once said that a tradition of behaviour is 'a tricky thing to get to know'.[20] But this is not really true in the sense that, though a lot of work is involved and a mass of diverse detail has somehow to be grasped and brought together, it is fairly clear as a matter of scholarly principle what it is necessary to attempt. And in the case in question, that of the British political tradition as it has developed in modern times, it is appropriate to see it as constituted by a dialectic between the two opposing tendencies which, taken together, constitute the limits within which the possibilities of that politics freely range. It is a case-study in the analysis of political androgyny. Nor is the student of this task by any means without experienced guidance for he may wisely and safely set his steps to follow the commentaries of a long line of ancestors as varied as de Tocqueville and Spencer, Dicey and Redlich, Lowell and Halévy, and a good many others.

Thus the specific political compass to be suggested rests on the designation of two strains within the tradition which (following a long-established usage) may be conceptualized as 'libertarianism' and 'collectivism'; and it supposes a diverse interplay between them concretely observed in the practice of British political life. As Winston Churchill said many years ago, it 'is not possible to draw a hard-and-fast line' between these concepts. 'No man can be a collectivist alone or an individualist alone. He must be both. . . . The nature of man is a dual nature. The character of the organisation of human society is dual'; though he added, too, that the dominant tendency of affairs was 'towards the multiplication of . . . collective functions'.[21] These are indeed the 'conflicting facets of any advanced social morality'; and any specific institution and the way it works is to be interpreted in terms of the mutual interaction of these two notional tendencies.[22] Of course, the relationship is never unchanging and at any given moment different areas of political activity will not reflect this connexion in exactly the same

20 M. Oakeshott, *Rationalism in Politics and Other Essays* (London, 1962), p.128.
21 Speech at Glasgow, 11 October 1906, in *Liberalism and the Social Problem*, 2nd edn (London, 1909), pp.79–80.
22 The phrase cited is from W. B. Gallie, *Philosophy and the Historical Understanding* (London, 1964), p.182.

way or proportion. Similarly, our political ideologies are not so much uniform doctrines built on a constant core of ideas but are rather varied combinations of different, indeed opposing, intellectual propensities affined to the paradigms mentioned. The overall view premeditated on this basis would, at its best, offer what Ezra Pound once claimed for a certain kind of poetic image: it would present in 'an instant of time' an entire complex of thoughts and emotions and, in so doing, might perhaps give a liberating sense of a new perspective. Or, more pragmatically, it will enable me to share something of Dicey's hope to be able to present British politics as a whole without going through the whole of British politics.[23] Naturally there are difficulties in this approach not least the dangers of anachronism and, above all, of being too Procrustean. But dealing with such an array of testimony as is involved in the study of an entire constitutional ethos, one desperately needs to educe what F. R. Leavis calls 'the lines of significant organization', the major 'axes of reference'.[24]

I have in mind, then, an impressionistic working hypothesis of an historical kind with which to provide some sort of consistency to a mass of otherwise irregular and fragmentary activities, to pull together and place within a common framework the diverse strands of British political life, its practices and ideas, as these have developed over the past century or so: that is, to establish its character or identity.

THE FRAMEWORK: LIBERTARIANISM AND COLLECTIVISM

> O whether devil planned or no,
> Life here is ambushed, this our fate,
> That road to anarchy doth go
> This to the grim mechanic state.
> 'Æ' (G. W. RUSSELL), 'The Iron Age', in *Collected Poems*, 2nd
> edn, 1926, pp. 267–8

The character of a form of political life is, then, to be established by indicating the full range of activity to which it is confined. In this way, modern British politics may be portrayed in terms of the two contrasting extremes which manifest the potential it has revealed. Its institutions and ideas are to some degree or other a fusion of the extreme types: there is a contention or interplay between these poles that makes our politics what it is. Or, in the terms used by Spencer, men's emotions create 'antagonist social tendencies' the conflict between which creates an alternating

---

23 E. Pound, 'A Few Don'ts by An Imagiste', *Poetry: A Magazine of Verse*, i (1912–13), pp. 200–1; A. V. Dicey, *Lectures on the Relation between Law & Public Opinion in England during the Nineteenth Century* (1905; 2nd edn, London, 1920), p. vii.

24 F. R. Leavis, *Mill on Bentham and Coleridge* (London, 1959), pp. 5, 6.

'rhythm'; and 'the institutions of any given age exhibit the compromise made by these contending moral forces at the signing of their last truce.'[25] And though neither of these limits is ever fully realized or is by itself adequate to define that politics, nor is anything ever beyond the pale. Furthermore, it must be emphasized that these concepts are not mere abstractions or figments: they emerge from, or rather are immanent in, the concrete historical reality itself and the contrast they represent has permeated, indeed constitutes, the entire course of British politics in modern times. Nor is the phenomenon of merely domestic occurrence but of European and even world-wide scope; any modern state is to be understood as a more or less unresolved tension between two irreconcilable dispositions of this sort.[26]

What, then, is entailed by the terms libertarianism and collectivism and the idea of their fusion and antithesis? The basic contrast, in the form influentially deployed by Elie Halévy (notably in his study of *The Growth of Philosophic Radicalism*) is that between, on the one hand, the notion of a natural harmony in society achieved without recourse to state intervention and, on the other, the idea of an artificial identification of human interests resulting from legislative or other political regulation.[27] But it is necessary to elaborate the meaning of the two key concepts a little more fully. Not, of course, that the particular watchwords chosen are necessarily satisfactory. But they have long been in use for this purpose and, as an earlier analyst of these matters said, the 'happy discoverer of a new pair of opposed terms' which will satisfy all the requirements entailed 'will lay us all under a heavy obligation'.[28]

By libertarianism I mean four things.

It involves in the first place a stress on the basic importance of individuality, that is, on the rights of the individual and his freedom from both social supervision and arbitrary political control. Disciplined self-realization, the achievement of what was sometimes called 'authenticity', is only possible where individuality is thus fully acknowledged.[29] As one mid-nineteenth-century commentator put it, 'personal

---

25 H. Spencer, *The Study of Sociology* (1873; Ann Arbor, Mich., 1961), p. 164; *Social Statics* (1851; Farnborough, Hants, 1970), p. 428.

26 e.g. F. E. Lawley, *The Growth of Collective Economy* (London, 1938), esp. vol. ii, chs. II, VI; M. Oakeshott, *On Human Conduct* (Oxford, 1975), pp. 200–1.

27 For discussion of Halévy's 'paradox', see J. B. Brebner, 'Halévy: Diagnostician of Modern Britain', *Thought*, xxiii (1948), pp. 101–13; C. C. Gillispie, 'The Work of Elie Halévy: a Critical Appreciation', *Journal of Modern History*, xxii (1950), pp. 232–49, esp. pp. 234–5, 246; and M. Chase, *Elie Halévy: an Intellectual Biography* (New York, 1980), esp. ch. two. De Tocqueville had earlier intimated the same contrast: see *Democracy in America* (1835–40; Fontana, 1968), ii. 924 note Y.

28 Sir R. K. Wilson, *The Province of the State* (London, 1911), p. viii.

29 Cf. M. Berman, *The Politics of Authenticity: Radical Individuality and the Emergence of Modern Society* (London, 1971), introduction.

freedom is the chief end of society', and 'the English idea of liberty is independence, jealousy of interference, and the security of certain spheres and conditions of life from all public inquiry and interference of government'.[30] Traditionally in Britain these claims have been regarded not as abstract demands but as actual privileges long recognized and preserved. For instance, in 1689 the Bill of Rights did not profess to make new law but to vindicate and assert various 'ancient rights and liberties'.[31] In the same vein, Burke invariably spoke of the freedom of Englishmen as a patrimony, an inheritance derived from their forefathers and enshrined in the 'prejudice' or 'prescription' of the ancient constitution of the realm.[32] In the following century, radical businessmen like Cobden who asserted the cause of free trade, and legal publicists such as Toulmin Smith who declared against the growing power of the central state, alike invoked the liberties of our Saxon ancestors as an argument of contemporary warrant appropriate to be applied in defence of the freedom and due of the individual.[33] Even those who used another, more rationalistic, language of exposition – theorists such as Locke and Paine – were really doing no more than translating into the speculative discourse they favoured an abridgement of the customary claims made by and for Englishmen under the venerable and common law of the realm. These included, for instance, the right to be tried only by due process of law; to be taxed only after a Parliament (in which there was freedom of debate) had consented to the imposition; to be able freely to elect representatives to that Parliament; to petition the Crown (a matter at one time of considerable importance) and, what this implied, the further right of private persons to meet publicly and in association to discuss and prepare a submission in defence of their interests; and so on. These are all what might be called political or civil rights. But perhaps the most crucial and fundamental of these claims may be subsumed under a right pertaining to economic and social matters, that of the individual to acquire, use, and dispose of his property

30 R. Simpson, 'The Individual, the Corporation and the State', *The Rambler*, n.s., vi (1861–2), pp. 437, 444. For discussion, see K. W. Swart, '"Individualism" in the Mid-nineteenth Century (1826–1860)', *Journal of the History of Ideas*, xxiii (1962), pp. 77–90, from which I originally took this reference.

31 Text in E. N. Williams (ed.), *The Eighteenth-Century Constitution, 1688–1815: Documents and Commentary* (Cambridge, 1960), p. 28. Cf. ibid., p. 30.

32 e.g. E. Burke, *The Works* (World's Classics, 1906–7), iv. 34–5. And see J. G. A. Pocock's definitive analysis in *The Ancient Constitution and the Feudal Law* (Cambridge, 1957) and 'Burke and the Ancient Constitution' (1960) in *Politics, Language and Time* (London, 1972), ch. 6.

33 e.g. Cobden's *Speeches on Questions of Public Policy*, ed. J. Bright and J. E. T. Rogers (London, 1878), pp. 191, 558; J. Toulmin Smith, *Government by Commissions Illegal and Pernicious* (London, 1849), pp. 47, 61–2, and *Local Self-Government and Centralization . . .* (London, 1851), pp. 17–18.

including his labour. It was not for nothing that John Locke encapsulated his doctrine of natural law in the telling claim to 'property', that is, to life, liberty, and estate. Nor, for Locke and his followers, was the possession or exercise of any such title formally dependent on the discharge of any function or service to society as a whole. It was anterior to and independent of any such relationship or responsibility. A pre-Lockeian statement indeed – an anonymous pamphlet of 1644 – sums up the doctrine. Let us, it says, 'who are English subjects . . . blesse God for his guidance who hath . . . made us absolute proprietors of what we enjoy, so that our lives, liberties and estates, doe not depend upon, nor are subject to, the sole breath or arbitrary will of our Soveraigne'.[34]

The second feature of libertarianism is now clearly dictated. For if the individual thus has an inalienable title to a free realm of self-regarding action (for that is what the claim to a series of rights involves) then it follows that the role of government or cognate authority must, in principle, be limited. It may not properly interfere in (or at least permanently eliminate) this sphere of individuality; indeed it exists to sustain it. The great and chief end of men's submission to civil government, said Locke, 'is the Preservation of their Property', by which he meant the sum total of their rights as individuals. Similarly, for Blackstone in the eighteenth century and for Herbert Spencer in the next, the business of the state was to sanction and defend men's rights.[35] And in a classic formulation that looks to the problem of restricting the ambit of government and social pressure in a democratic community, J. S. Mill urged as indispensable the maintenance of a limit to permissible interference with individual autonomy. Of course, it is difficult in practice to draw the line but the principle or intention is clear. Bagehot, again, commented on the English people as one which had a 'natural impulse' to resist authority and which possessed a spirit of 'inbred insubordination'. 'We look on State action', he said, 'not as our own action but as alien action; as an imposed tyranny from without, not as the consummated result of our own organised wishes.'[36]

Moreover, it is recognized – and this is the third point – that any high concentration of power is likely to be dangerous to this sacrosanct zone of individual choice and activity. So it is deemed desirable to establish or maintain a situation in which there is a diffusion of decision and

34 *England's Monarch, or a Conviction and Refutation of those False Principles . . . of Albericus* (1644) cited in H. Perkin, *The Origins of Modern English Society 1780–1880* (1969; London, 1972), pp. 52–3.

35 Locke, *Of Civil Government*, §124; Sir W. Blackstone, *Commentaries on the Laws of England* (1765–9; 6th edn, Dublin, 1775), i. 47–8, 52, 124–5, 129ff; H. Spencer, *The Man Versus the State* (1884; Penguin, 1969), p. 167.

36 J. S. Mill, 'On Liberty', in *Collected Works*, ed. J. M. Robson et al. (London, 1963ff), xviii. 220; W. Bagehot, *The English Constitution* (2nd edn, 1867; Fontana, 1966), pp. 262–3.

authority. In a perceptive essay, the Spanish writer José Ortega y Gasset observed that 'liberty and plurality are Reciprocal'; and Lord Acton similarly remarked that 'Liberty depends on the division of power.'[37] Therefore, it seemed to be entailed that the force of government must never be unnecessarily great and any accretions of authority had to be jealously watched. The doctrine of the separation of powers acquired special force in this context as one of the traditional means whereby the matchless constitution sustained the liberties of the people. Further, devolution of authority is highly desirable. Local or regional self-government is no mere administrative convenience but an essential principle of libertarian society. Similarly it is appropriate that government should be faced with extra-political foci of influence and interest – churches, trade unions, associations and corporations of all kinds – to act as countervailing centres of action. This pluralist idea was, like the concept of individual rights to which it was related, implicit in the old constitution of the realm by which the country was governed rather through Quarter Sessions and the County Meeting than by London. This was the polity often praised by commentators, as by Disraeli in the famous *Vindication* which he published in 1835 and in which he extolled the many great and varied 'national institutions' on which the security of British freedom depended.[38] Not surprisingly, from this point of view the centralizing tendencies of Chadwick and his like were seen as wholly improper and inexpedient as well, as indeed was the growing public control exercised over various aspects of industry.[39] To maintain a proper dispersion of power even an acknowledged administrative confusion was not too high a price to pay, a theme familiar, for instance, to students of the British system of military administration. The various armed forces were supervised by fifteen or more different offices and thereby, at least in part deliberately, kept in a state of organizational disarray. This was why, to take one instance, the army was for so long without its own transport system: its mobility (and so its effectiveness) depended not only on the prior approval of the civilian Secretary-at-War but also on the goodwill and assistance of the civil authorities of the areas through which the soldiers passed. It was with this state of affairs in mind that Halévy himself argued that English liberties rested above all on

37   J. Ortega y Gasset, 'The Unity and Diversity of Europe', in *History as a System and other Essays Toward a Philosophy of History* (1941; New York, 1962), p.58; *The Letters of Lord Acton to Mary Gladstone* (London, 1904), p.124.

38   W. Hutcheon (ed.), *Whigs and Whiggism: Political Writings by Benjamin Disraeli* (London, 1913), p.215. Cf. Simpson, art. cit., pp.441, 449–50, on the importance to this end of the group and the corporation.

39   W. C. Lubenow, *The Politics of Government Growth: Early Victorian Attitudes toward State Intervention, 1833–1848* (Newton Abbot, 1971), *passim*.

the inefficiency of native institutions.[40] An anonymous writer of the early 1840s summarized the case against the 'centralisation system', as destructive of English character and freedom, by linking the concepts of Gothic liberty, dispersion of power, and the notions of initiative and progress; and he did so in the terms commonly used by those whom Dr Redlich called the 'Constitutional Romanticists':

> Alfred's system, that under which England flourished so long, great and free, and by which the Saxon race were reared up in that hardy spirit of self-dependence which has emboldened them to march forth the conquerors of the world, the Saxon system was to multiply the centres of government, so that the energies of all were called into play . . . . We hold all centralisation to be objectionable, and only to be tolerated in cases of absolute necessity.[41]

Finally, libertarianism demands (as a crucial embodiment of these anti-statist sentiments) the Rule of Law, a doctrine classically expounded in 1885 by Dicey who regarded it as 'the distinguishing characteristic of English institutions'.[42] A version of the older notion of a fundamental law by which the world's affairs should be guided and assessed and which sets limits to legitimate acts of government, the concept (as Dicey describes it) has three related aspects. The first is that there must be no arbitrary power of constraint and that no one may be punished or made to suffer in body or goods except for a distinct breach of the regular law established in the usual way before the ordinary courts of the land. A wide discretionary authority in the hands of government is, therefore, excluded and uncertainty on the part of the citizen avoided. Secondly, there is the principle of equality before the law which is to say that no person or class of persons is above it. Everyone, of what rank or condition soever, is amenable to the jurisdiction of the courts. Dicey meant this especially to apply to public functionaries of all kinds. 'With us', he said, 'every official, from the Prime Minister down to a constable or a collector of taxes, is under the same responsibility for every act done without legal justification as any other citizen.' Consequently he objected to any system in which persons in their official capacity were to a degree 'exempted from the ordinary law of the land, protected from the

---

40 On all this, see C. M. Clode, *The Military Forces of the Crown; Their Administration and Government* (London, 1869), still the standard work on the legal and constitutional history of these matters. For Halévy's view, see Chase, op. cit., p. 105.

41 'Delenda est Carthago. The Poor Law Commission Must be Determined', *Fraser's Magazine*, xxiii (1841), pp. 387–8. For Redlich's phrase, see B. Keith-Lucas, *The English Local Government Franchise: a Short History* (Oxford, 1952), p. 6.

42 A. V. Dicey, *Introduction to the Study of the Law of the Constitution* (1885; 10th edn, London, 1964), p. 187.

jurisdiction of the ordinary tribunals, and subject in certain respects only to official law administered by official bodies.' In the same vein, he criticized the Trades Disputes Act of 1906 for making a trade union 'a privileged body exempted from the ordinary law of the land'.[43] Thirdly, it was urged that the rights of the individual are inherent, recognized and protected by the courts but not created by them, let alone by Parliament or by government. Nor do they depend merely on some abstract statement of claim. It follows that these rights cannot be taken away or superseded without a general revolution of affairs. Dicey here urged the crucial importance of means of protecting and enforcing these rights, a matter indeed to which much recent attention has been given.[44] And with this emphasis the principles of the Rule of Law join hands with the stress on individuality and its demands mentioned at the outset. Thus formulated the doctrine appears to exclude as improper the delegation of any legislative or judicial powers to officials, extensive executive discretion, or the creation of administrative tribunals separate from the ordinary courts.[45] It is no wonder that, as Professor E. C. S. Wade noted, Dicey's work has served as a crucial text for those who are opposed to the extending activities of the modern state.[46]

Collectivism is simply the tendency in British political life which stands in contrast to this stress on individuality. It is the direction of affairs that in the last century was often described as 'functionarism', 'officialism', and less pejoratively as 'empiricism' or simply 'construction'.[47]

One of its dominant features is a concern with the public good. If a libertarian point of view emphasizes the privileges of the individual and especially the protection of his liberty to do as he will with his own, a collectivist attitude brings to the fore rather the interests of the community which are regarded as primary claims morally superior to any individual demand. Thus a society is seen as 'something more than the sum of its members' and as having 'a life and health distinguishable from those of its individual atoms.' And there will be created 'an order of

43 ibid., pp. 193, 195; idem, Lectures on the Relation between Law & Public Opinion in England during the Nineteenth Century (1905; 2nd edn, London, 1920), introduction to 2nd edn, p. xlvi.

44 Dicey, The Law of the Constitution, pp. 195–203, 286–7. For the recent attention, see e.g. Lord MacDermott, Protection from Power under English Law (London, 1957), esp. pp. 7–8, on the preference of the Rule of Law for the individual rather than the state.

45 Of course, since Dicey first wrote, these developments have in fact taken place on a vast scale as described in volume iii, A Much-Governed Nation, ch. 6.

46 Dicey, The Law of the Constitution, introduction, p. cxvii.

47 For examples of the older terminology, see pp. 32, 217, 227; and vol. ii, The Ideological Heritage.

social life, in which the common good overrules individual caprice'.[48] Of course, libertarian opinion always paid some regard to general concerns, in the matter of defence for example. The difference is that the collectivist tends on any matter to look first at the public will and interest and to want this established and used as the criterion of conduct and policy. There is a vital contrast of emphasis and priority here. The apposition is, in fact, nicely illustrated by the provisions of article 43 of the Irish constitution of 1937. Following earlier papal encyclicals this says that the state acknowledges, in virtue of man's rational being, his 'natural right, antecedent to positive law, to the private ownership of external goods' and affirms that no law will be passed attempting to abrogate this right or that of bequest and inheritance. Yet it is also provided that the exercise of property right is to be regulated for 'the common good' and in accordance with 'the principles of social justice.'[49]

This last phrase uses the concept – social justice – in terms of which the public weal is invariably seen. Herbert Spencer, an extreme libertarian, feared there was abroad in his time 'a notion . . . that all social suffering is removable, and that it is the duty of somebody or other to remove it.'[50] The object was held to involve the creation of uniform conditions of both equality and security as a means of preventing or mitigating that suffering. Instead of the competitive play of individuality, with all the variations that this might bring as a result of differences of ability and opportunity, instead of an emphasis on freedom of contract and the like, collectivism stresses the importance of achieving security for all in equal conditions of security of at least a minimum or basic kind. This may be a matter of principle on the argument perhaps that a theoretical equality before the law presupposes a genuine and effective social parity, in particular a greater uniformity in the possession of wealth and similar advantages. But there is also a question of administrative convenience involved which leads in the direction of universal treatment, for, in the execution of complex and large-scale public functions, it is easier not to have to make distinctions or to tolerate the rivalry of substantial private or sectional initiative. Moreover, as the tendency to uniformity gathers strength any remaining dissimilarities seem increasingly unacceptable. Equality of opportunity is not enough: the object becomes 'equality of

---

48 S. Webb, *The Difficulties of Individualism*, Fabian tract no. 69 (London, 1896), p. 17; A. Marshall, *Principles of Economics* (1890; 8th edn, London, 1930), Appendix A, p. 752.

49 Dr D. G. Boyce drew my attention to these contrasting provisions, for which see A. J. Peaslee, *Constitutions of Nations* (3rd edn rev., The Hague, 1968), iii. 492. For the terms of the encyclicals of 1891 and 1931, see H. Bettenson (ed.), *Documents of the Christian Church* (1943; 2nd edn, London, 1963), pp. 387–93.

50 H. Spencer, *The Man Versus the State*, p. 83.

outcome'.[51] It follows also that decentralization of authority to intermediate or local offices and assemblies that are anything other than mere
agencies will be part of the collectivist anathema.[52] The concept of liberty
is redefined, too, in the process of pursuing social justice: from being
conceived as the absence of legislative or social restraint it is revealed as
requiring the attainment of a complete and reasonable life as that which
above all the proper organization of society requires.[53]

And, of course, to secure these goals action on the part of public
authority is essential and increasingly acceptable to the democratic
citizen. He may be reluctant to obey his neighbour whom he regards
merely as his equal; but the state excites no envy and ensures the common
dependence of all on the same master.[54] So increasing supervision, the
idea of positive government, is a third mark of collectivism. Dicey
asserted that its 'fundamental principle . . . is faith in the benefit to be
derived by the mass of the people from the action or intervention of the
State'.[55] Public bodies, whether central or local, do more and more for
the individual or on his behalf. They supervise or manage economic life,
provide extensive social welfare services and the like, all of which is seen
to be necessary for the general good and is so justified. Government, it is
held, must act to create a harmony which does not exist naturally,
subordinating individual claims to social need on the largest possible
scale and doing so not as an incidental but as a permanent feature of
political action. There is necessarily entailed in all this a further tendency
which Halévy called 'fiscalism', an attitude to the public revenues which
permits increasingly heavy taxation to establish welfare schemes and so
forth and which thus involves a substantial redistribution of wealth.[56]

A particularly perceptive and early recognition of these collectivist
tendencies, one so acute indeed that it requires special mention, is to be
found in de Tocqueville's pages. The passages concerned occur in Part IV
of the second volume (1840) of his *Democracy in America*, especially
chapter 2 where he discusses the way in which democratic ideas favour

---

51 Cf. de Tocqueville, *Democracy in America*, ii. 873–4. For the phrase cited in the text,
see M. and R. Friedman, *Free to Choose: a Personal Statement* (Penguin, 1980),
pp. 166ff.

52 G. Langrod, 'Local Government and Democracy', *Public Administration*, xxi (1953),
pp. 28–9.

53 Cf. B. Bosanquet, *The Civilization of Christendom and Other Studies* (London,
1893), pp. 379–80.

54 de Tocqueville, op. cit., ii. 873.

55 Dicey, *Law & Public Opinion*, p. 259. See also J. A. Hobson, *The Crisis of
Liberalism: New Issues of Democracy* (London, 1909), p. 114.

56 E. Halévy, *The Era of Tyrannies: Essays on Socialism and War* (1938; trans., London,
1967), pp. 196–7.

the concentration of political power.[57] Democracies, he says, have the vision of a great nation 'in which every citizen resembles one set type' and which is 'controlled by one single power'. There is, too, 'uniform legislation' which eliminates the 'slightest privileges' or differences between people so that individuals are 'lost in the crowd'. Men thus naturally acquire

> a very high opinion of the prerogatives of society and a very humble one of the rights of the individual. They will easily admit that the interest of the former is everything and that of the latter nothing. They also freely agree that the power which represents society has much more education and wisdom than any of the men composing it and it is its duty, as well as its right, to take each citizen by the hand and guide him.

De Tocqueville goes on to indicate the growth of state power entailed: 'the idea of intermediate powers is obscured and obliterated. The idea of rights inherent in certain individuals is rapidly disappearing from men's minds; the idea of the omnipotence and sole authority of society at large is coming to fill its place.' All parties and persons begin to think that 'the government ought constantly to act and interfere in everything.' The result is that all modern political systems share one striking feature, the 'unity, ubiquity, and omnipotence of the social power and the uniformity of its rules'. In such circumstances, sovereigns easily 'acquire new conceptions about the scope of their action and duties.' They 'learn that the central power which they represent can and should administer directly according to a uniform plan all affairs and all men.' Thus while men may argue about who should have the sovereign power they readily agree about its rights and duties, all of them thinking of the government 'as a sole, simple, providential, and creative force.' 'Everywhere', he concludes, the state eliminates any rival foci of power and 'increasingly takes control of the humblest citizen and directs his behaviour even in trivial matters.' De Tocqueville's prescience as to the future course of events is amazing.

Beyond all this it will be apparent that both sets of principles, the libertarian and collectivist alike, entail wide-ranging theories of economic, social, and political organization. Yet, as definitions of an abstract kind, they do not by any means tell the whole story. One important thing is that neither position is uniform in every respect. They are not simply extreme and opposing paradigms; there is in reality an array of

57 Citations which follow in this paragraph are from de Tocqueville, op. cit., ii. 867–70, 883.

intermediate possibilities, varying responses to the matter of the proper role and office of government.[58]

Thus libertarian opinion on this question varies from a complete *laissez faire* or even anarchist attitude to a point of view that shades into a collectivist way of thinking. Presupposing an evolving harmony or progressive equilibrium immanent in the nature of things – a concept reflected, for instance, in the 'invisible hand' of William Paley and Adam Smith – a few libertarians were disposed to urge that individual advantage and public benefit alike were best achieved in the almost complete absence of state interference. The cogency of such a view derived at least in part from the corruption and inefficiency of contemporary government: industrial and commercial progress was seen as the result not of communal action but of private initiative which would be unduly hampered by attempts at public intervention bound to be both incompetent and costly. The doctrine of evolution and natural selection also seemed to suggest that advance was only achieved by unhindered competitive struggle and the freest adaptation to environmental necessity. As Lord Keynes said, in the light of this grand conception collective interference came to seem 'not merely inexpedient, but impious, . . . calculated to retard the onward movement of the mighty process by which we ourselves had risen like Aphrodite out of the primeval slime of Ocean.'[59] This context of ideas was sustained, too, by vulgarized versions of classical political economy and by the contemporary moral belief in self-help as the only proper means of improvement in character. The widest view of the function of government that could be entertained on these terms was that it should (in Lassalle's contemptuous phrase) simply act as night-watchman: that is, provide the basic services of external defence and, to a small degree, domestic police; set up a system of law courts to punish and deter criminals and adjudicate in civil disputes between citizens; and precious little else. Carlyle pithily described this proposed state of affairs as anarchy with only the street constable in the middle of it.[60] And J. S. Mill, writing of the eighteenth century in this country, described how government was then regarded as an evil which should 'make itself as little felt as possible. The cry of the people was not "help us," "guide us," "do for us the things we cannot do, and instruct us, that we may do well

---

58 For an early review of this variety of response, see W. S. M'Kechnie, *The State & the Individual: an Introduction to Political Science, with Special Reference to Socialistic and Individualistic Theories* (Glasgow, 1896), part II, esp. ch. XII on 'The Problem of the Province of Government'.

59 J. M. Keynes, *The End of Laissez-Faire* (London, 1926), p. 14.

60 T. Carlyle, 'Latter-Day Pamphlets' (1850), in *The Works* (People's edn, 1871–4), XX.25.

those which we can" – ... the cry was "let us alone." '[61] I suppose it was Herbert Spencer who drew all the threads together and articulated the fullest and most sophisticated statement of such an extreme individualist, indeed anarchist, creed.

But this theoretical position was an ideal; although it may sometimes have had considerable importance as a kind of watchword or myth, it hardly reflected any state of affairs that ever actually existed in this country (except perhaps during the 1700s to some extent when the remaining elements of effective mercantile policy largely concerned the control only of foreign trade).[62] Even the term *laissez faire* itself seems to have been less used than is often supposed: it has been shown, for example, that it does not occur even once in the 1,500 double-column pages of Hansard which report the debate on free trade in 1846.[63] And, as if in recognition of the illusion of the extreme paradigm, libertarians adopted not infrequently a modified and it might seem more realistic position which construed more positively, though often in a hesitant and limited way, the role of government as umpire to the play of affairs.[64] In addition to the normal acknowledgement of the part the state must play in defence, the maintenance of public order, and dealing with emergencies, it might seem proper for the legislature to regulate commercial practices or industrial situations inimical to individual choice and incompatible with the maintenance of competitive enterprise. This was why a good many of those otherwise hostile to state intervention were prepared to advocate it to hinder any monopolistic tendencies. Similarly, exceptional treatment in this regard might be conceded to help infant industries or give temporary patent protection. Further, there was a sphere of public regulation, increasing greatly as time went on, that came under the heading of protection or guidance and which involved attempts to equalize the advantages enjoyed by individuals.[65] Unless they

---

61   J. S. Mill, 'Coleridge' (1840), in *Collected Works*, x.143. Mill is here reporting a view often expressed by Bentham that in economic matters government ought in general to '*Be quiet*', e.g. *Works*, ed. Bowring (1838–43; New York, 1962), iii.33.

62   J. Brebner, 'Laissez Faire and State Intervention in Nineteenth-Century Britain', *Journal of Economic History*, suppl., viii (1948), pp.59–60. See also A. J. Taylor's monograph of the same title (London, 1972); Perkin, op. cit., pp.65–7; and G. Watson, *The English Ideology: Studies in the Language of Victorian Politics* (London, 1973), ch. 5, '*Laissez-faire* and the State'. The best brief account of the origin and development of the doctrine is J. Viner, 'The Intellectual History of Laissez Faire', *Journal of Law and Economics*, iii (1960), pp.45–69.

63   D. H. Macgregor, *Economic Thought and Policy* (London, 1949), p.56.

64   R. L. Crouch distinguishes 'crude' and 'refined' versions of the doctrine in 'Laissez-Faire in Nineteenth Century Britain: Myth or Reality?', *The Manchester School*, xxxv (1967), pp.199–215.

65   Dicey, *Law & Public Opinion*, pp.262–6.

were of the extreme school represented by Spencer, libertarians would invariably, or at least often, admit that some classes of people (like children or mad persons and perhaps women) could not properly look after themselves and needed the special aid of the community. Again, it might be accepted as dishonest to hold that an individual could fulfil himself and make the best use of his rights and freedom if he were, say, illiterate or otherwise disadvantaged and incapable of knowing and pursuing his best interests. And some essential goods and services, it might be acknowledged, were unlikely to be effectively provided through the market mechanisms. Given this kind of considerations, a libertarian could think it proper for the state to help stimulate the provision of educational facilities or to impose some degree of regulation on the use of labour in factories. Such steps would be seen as limited, indeed abnormal, concessions merely, restricted to special cases and circumstances, and to be particularly justified on humanitarian or prudential grounds. Thus public action to relieve distress was seen, for instance, as preventing consequences incompatible with the maintenance of social peace on which the fulfilment of individuality depended. One famous example of all this is Macaulay who, while normally hostile to government intervention, accepted that it might be necessary in respect of education, public health, the labour laws, and control of the railways because these were spheres where commercial considerations had to give way to higher interests.[66] In some such fashion the edge of the collectivist wedge was more and more firmly inserted into the libertarian position as precedents of this kind increased.[67] As well there were some libertarians, like Toulmin Smith, who were prepared to condone or even encourage an extensive degree of action by *local* authorities, men acting collectively in their counties, towns, or parishes, but who would fight tooth and nail to resist any centralizing tendency, any intervention by government department or quasi-government board in London, because this would leave no room for individual choice or initiative. But either this local effort was ineffective in dealing with a problem; or if it did work it thereby created a foundation for desirable further policy conceived on a larger scale or applied elsewhere. And in either case central involvement was ultimately invited.

Equally, there are similar differences of degree or manner in the collectivist attitude to the role of government. As an American student of politics said at the beginning of this century, 'Collectivism can be applied in small doses as well as large; it can come by imperceptible steps as well as by revolutionary cataclysms; there is such a thing as conservative as

---

66 See e.g. his speech on Fielden's Factory Bill (1846), in *The Miscellaneous Writings and Speeches* (London, 1889), pp. 718–29.
67 Cf. de Tocqueville, op. cit., ii. 872–3 n.1.

well as radical collectivism.'[68] Dicey believed that in Britain the process began in an 'unsystematic' way, a simply piecemeal intervention to deal with specific practical frictions and because there was some scepticism about the supposedly natural healing processes of the social organism.[69] But there is a cumulative effect even to such hesitant or *ad hoc* intrusions.[70] There is first permissive and then compulsory legislation and of increasing scope and amount. In a most useful and interesting paper, Professor Harold Perkin has recently distinguished a number of phases or aspects of collectivism which constitute an important part of the 'continuum' of attitudes involved. Clearly there is some overlap with what I have here suggested are modifications of libertarianism but the features he has in mind are: the prevention of obvious nuisances or dangers; the enforcement of minimum standards; financial help to aid private action; direct public provision of various kinds; state monopoly of essential services; and nationalization.[71] But there must come a time in this process of extending public interest when there emerges a challenge to the individualist system as such and the community may then embark on a deliberate search on a national scale for what is thought to be a more humane or efficient alternative, one organized through the power and authority of its governing bodies. An extreme note of this kind can perhaps be detected in the purposes of the statute of 1947 intended to extend the earlier Supplies and Services (Transitional Powers) Act (1945) and which were to sustain the government in its treatment of the contemporary crisis and impending difficulties. The authority granted was to embrace such goals as promoting the productivity of industry, commerce, and agriculture; controlling external trade; and generally 'ensuring that the whole resources of the community are available for use, and are used, in a manner best calculated to serve the interests of the community'.[72] These are the authentic accents of a deliberate collectiv-

---

68 E. Kelly, *Government or Human Evolution* (London, 1900–1), vol. ii, p. vii. This book is the most extensive single study of the antithesis between libertarianism and collectivism I have seen: its principal aim is 'to destroy the doctrine of Herbert Spencer' (ibid., ii.249), and to expound the moral and practical superiority of the collectivist state.

69 Dicey, *Law & Public Opinion*, p. 399.

70 For an interesting minor example of how the growth of government spending could, simply in itself, have important effects on economic structure and activity, see B. W. E. Alford, 'Government Expenditure and the Growth of the Printing Industry in the Nineteenth Century', *Economic History Review*, 2s., xvii (1964–5), pp. 96–112.

71 H. Perkin, 'Individualism Versus Collectivism in Nineteenth-Century Britain: a False Antithesis', *Journal of British Studies*, xvii (no. 1, 1977–8), esp. pp. 114–116 where these different meanings or aspects of collectivism are stated and exemplified. Cf. a brief preliminary review in *The Origins of Modern English Society 1780–1880*, pp. 437–8.

72 10 & 11 Geo. 6, c. 55, §1 (I) (a)–(c), in *Public General Acts and Measures of 1947*, ii. 1933.

ism, the antithesis of that near-anarchist view to be found at the other extreme.

There is, then, revealed over the past century or so a whole range of views covering the spectrum between the contrasting theories of anti-statist libertarianism and directorial collectivism. But before taking the exposition on to the next stage, one other very crucial point needs to be made. This is that these two strains or tendencies in our political life are most definitely not to be equated simply with specific political parties or ideologies: we must not, warned Dicey, 'confound the accidental division of parties with essential differences of political faith'.[73] There has been, and may still be, a temptation to equate libertarianism with a Liberal or a Conservative point of view, and collectivism with the Labour or Socialist position. Nothing could be more misleading. Each partisan doctrine is, in this respect, ambivalent, a kind of 'living oxymoron' reflecting a range of libertarian and collectivist attitudes. Moreover, as a matter of historical fact, supporters of Conservatism and Liberalism have contributed more to the actual development of collectivism (as here broadly defined) than have exponents of Socialism, in the Labour Party or out of it. Nor is this surprising because the former parties have been in office for longer periods over the past century and a half. As Ivor Jennings noted some decades ago, the 'policies which *all* parties have accepted during the past fifty years imply intervention by public authorities in social and economic affairs.'[74] This ideological and party diversity will receive detailed attention in later volumes; the proviso is simply made here to avoid initial confusion.

THE GROWTH OF COLLECTIVISM: INDICATORS

> Thundering and bursting
> In torrents, in waves –
> Carolling and shouting
> Over tombs, amid graves –
> See! On the cumber'd plain
> Clearing a stage,
> Scattering the past about,
> Comes the new age.
>
> MATTHEW ARNOLD, 'Bacchanalia; or, the New Age', 1867

Since about 1800 the dialectic between the libertarian and collectivist tendencies has assumed the aspect of a diverse but growing dominance of

---

73 Dicey, *Law & Public Opinion*, p. 409.
74 W. I. Jennings, *Parliamentary Reform* (London, 1934), p. 25 (my italics). Cf. ibid., p. 140; also a similar and much earlier comment on the non-partisan development of state interference, S. Low to T. Leak (15 November 1909), in D. Chapman-Huston, *The Lost Historian: a Memoir of Sir Sidney Low* (London, 1936), p. 231. I am grateful to Mr F. Field, MP, for the timely gift of a copy of Jennings's book.

the latter in all areas of political activity. At the beginning of the last century the role of central government was relatively slight and by modern standards impinged little on the life of the people. It had important functions in respect of external affairs and defence, the regulation of overseas trade, the maintenance of law and order, and, of course, the raising of the revenue necessary to sustain this business. And there were the relics of what Halévy called 'the administrative socialism' of a bygone age represented, for instance, by the old Poor Law and the Statute of Labourers. There was, too, the variety of tasks which fell to the different local authorities. Yet, by and large, the attitude to most domestic concerns was passive and non-interventionist, and people were left to run their own affairs. Britain could thus be described, and with only a little exaggeration, as 'a country without officials and without police'. Its national executive was weaker than that of any other major European power; its administrative arrangements were, even by the standards of the day, primitive and inefficient. Matthew Arnold for one saw this as a matter not for congratulation but for complaint, urging that in this country we had not grasped the concept of the state so familiar to the ancient world and on the continent, the idea of 'the nation in its collective and corporate character, entrusted with stringent powers for the general advantage, and controlling individual wills in the name of an interest wider than that of individuals.'[75]

Of course, this condition of affairs has by now been radically altered as a result of the gradual and sporadic but ultimately massive extension of government functions which has taken place in the interim. During this period agencies of public ownership and control have increased in number and extended their scope into many areas of social and economic life from which they had previously been excluded. As early as the mid-1840s, *The Times* noticed in a famous passage that 'Session after session we are amplifying the province of the Legislature, and asserting its moral prerogatives. Parliament aspires to be the *pater patriae*, and is for laying aside the policeman, the gaoler, and the executioner, in exchange for the more kindly and dignified functions of the father, the schoolmaster, and the friend.'[76] It was a phenomenon the significance of which was increasingly recognized and which excited both wonderment and perturbation. Among the many comments of the day, one may stand as illustration, a passage from a well-known pamphlet by G. J. Goschen who, while observing the force of these developments, viewed them with

---

75 M. Arnold, *Culture and Anarchy* (1869; Cambridge, 1960), p.75. Halévy's phrases cited above come from *A History of the English People in the Nineteenth Century* (1913–46; 2nd trans. edn, London, 1961), i.379–80; vol.i., pp.v, vi. For a recent statement of the quondam libertarian position, see The Constitution, R.Com.Rep., 1972–3 (vol.xi), Cmnd.5460, p.75 §227.

76 *The Times* (4 May 1847), p.5.

some diffidence. He summarized the process under way as follows:

> among all the complicated social and economical phenomena of the
> present day, none appears more interesting or of deeper importance . . .
> than the changes which have occurred and are daily occurring in the
> relations between the State and individual liberty. . . . We see narrower
> and narrower limits assigned to the application of the principle of
> 'Laissez-faire,' while the sphere of Government control and inter-
> ference is expanding in ever widening circles.

The extension of State action to new and vast fields of business, such
as telegraphy, insurance, annuities, postal orders, and parcels post, is
not the most striking feature. What is of far deeper import is its
growing interference with the relations between classes, its increased
control over vast categories of transactions between individuals, and
the substitution in many of the dealings of trade and manufacture, of
the aggregate conscience and moral sense of the nation, for the
conscience and moral sense of men as units. The parent in dealing with
his child, the employer in dealing with his workmen, the shipbuilder in
the construction of his ships, the shipowner in the treatment of his
sailors, the houseowner in the management of his house property, the
landowner in his contracts with his tenants, have been notified by
public opinion or by actual law that the time has gone by when the cry
of 'Laissez-nous faire' would be answered in the affirmative. The State
has determined what is right and wrong, what is expedient and
inexpedient, and has appointed its agents to enforce its conclusions.
Some of the highest obligations of humanity, some of the smallest
businesses of everyday life, some of the most complicated transactions
of our industrial and agricultural organisations have been taken in
hand by the State. Individual responsibility has been lessened.
National responsibility has been heightened. Reliance is being placed
on the efficiency of new forces, and on the application of new
principles. The attitude of the public towards 'Laissez-faire' on the one
hand and State action on the other has entirely changed.[77]

This transformation was not, at least initially, deliberately induced.
Rather it rested for a long time on what Sidney Webb used to call the
unconscious permeation of an overtly individualist society by a contrary
principle. Although, he said, 'the advocates of each particular change
intend no further alteration, the result is nevertheless an increasing social
momentum' in a collectivist direction.[78] The cumulative, incremental

77 G. J. Goschen, . . . Laissez-Faire and Government Interference (London, 1883), pp. 3–4.
78 S. Webb, Socialism in England (London, 1890), pp. 8, 16; Towards Social De-
    mocracy? A Study of Social Evolution During the Past Three-Quarters of a Century
    (London, 1916), pp. 3, 39. Webb has an amusing and triumphant account of the
    extent of public functions already undertaken even before the end of the nineteenth
    century in Socialism in England, ch. 7, esp. pp. 116–17, cited below, p. 100.

effect of these piecemeal reforms was indeed considerable. Yet as late as the mid-1920s J. M. Keynes, writing about the decline of individualism, could still assert that, although a change was in the air, we did 'not dance even yet to a new tune.'[79] A few years later, however, the Macmillan Committee on Finance and Industry provided yet another comment on the 'growing preoccupation' of government, 'irrespective of party, with the management of the life of the people' and acknowledged that the function of the state had thereby been radically transformed. It recognized the libertarian problem, too, for the Committee's report went on to say that this

> new orientation has its dangers as well as its merits. Between liberty and government there is an age-long conflict. It is of vital importance that the new policy, while truly promoting liberty by securing better conditions of life for the people of this country, should not, in its zeal for interference, deprive them of their initiative and independence which are the nation's most valuable assets.[80]

That was half a century and a world war ago. Since that day things have moved on apace.

In what ways, then, is it possible to show the rate and extent of the change in the scale of government activity that has occurred? A number of separate, though related, indicators may be used to mark the scale of this 'Silent Revolution'.[81]

Public expenditure

Unless prices fall an extension of government activity is certain to cost more, so an obvious reflector of the rise of collectivism is an increase in public expenditure and, therefore, of revenue and taxation; and early attempts were made to give some precise indication of this. In 1869, for example, the proceedings of the Royal Statistical Society of London included a paper examining the recent growth in the main heads of civil expenditure and anticipating, indeed, that because of public demand the tendency observed would continue.[82] Ardent libertarians in particular always recognized the (as they saw it) malign significance of this increase, taking such fiscal tendencies to mark a loss of essential freedom. For instance, an article in *The Parliamentary Remembrancer* in 1859 similarly noted the substantial rise in estimates that had occurred since

79 J. M. Keynes, *The End of Laissez-Faire* (London, 1926), p. 5.
80 Finance and Industry, R. Com. Rep., 1931–2 (vol. xiii), Cmd. 3897, pp. 4–5 §8.
81 The phrase comes from a leading article in *The Times* (25 March 1935), p. 15.
82 H. Mann, 'On the Cost and Organization of the Civil Service', *Journal of the Royal Statistical Society of London*, xxxii (1869), pp. 38–60.

the 1830s: 'The meaning of this is, that those in power have used their power to extend, under every sort of pretence, the growth of Functionarism in England; by which . . . the things which the people ought to do for themselves . . . are done for them by paid officials, set over them by the Ministers of the Crown, but who are paid for out of the pockets of the people.'[83] In 1895 *The Economist* still sustained the conventional libertarian view that government expenditure was growing and ought to be diminished:

> The increase of expenditure of the State is the one invariable element in the Budget . . . . No one runs any danger of being proved wrong if he assumes that next year the total expenditure will be larger than that of the year before.
>
> If we analyse this growth of expenditure, we shall find that it is largely due to the growth of Government action in the various departments of civil life . . . . Little by little, and year by year, the fabric of State expenditure and State responsibility is built up like a coral island, cell on cell. Every year half-a-dozen Acts of Parliament are passed which give the State new powers and new functions . . . .

And this entails more inspectors and officials and 'the expenditure of more money', often on 'a most lavish scale'. It means, as a result, the imposition of more taxation and more interference with individual action, more waste and more inefficiency as well as an untoward impact on the vital processes of wealth production. It was quite clear, therefore, that this 'evil' of 'State interference in the dominion of civil life and with the machinery of production' was reflected in growth of expenditure.[84] Others have regarded these developments more complacently and have even seen them as an inevitable tendency inherent in the growing prosperity of industrialized nations. The nineteenth-century German economist Adolph Wagner formulated a so-called Law of Expanding State Activity on this assumption. The argument was that as the general income increases so does the capacity and demand for the provision of goods and services by public authority to which is diverted, therefore, an increasing proportion of national output. This is so, not only in respect of administrative and protective functions concerning the regulation of the greater complexities of a more populous and urbanized society, but also in regard to cultural and welfare objectives. It is further induced by the greater economic involvement demanded by the growing scale of investment needed for technological change.[85]

83 *The Parliamentary Remembrancer*, ii (1859), p. 75. The article is anonymous but may confidently be attributed to Toulmin Smith.
84 'State Interference', *The Economist*, liii (25 May 1895), p.679.
85 See the interesting series of articles on Wagner's Law in *Public Finance*, xxvi (1971), pp. 1–105.

There has indeed been an enormous increase in the amount of money spent by central and local government in this country over the past century and a half, the degree of growth being very clear even when allowance is made for the march of inflation by expressing the sums concerned in terms of a common price index. On the latter basis, total government expenditure increased by a factor of more than fifty between 1870 and 1979. The same trend is confirmed, though of course much less decisively, when this expenditure is calculated as a percentage of the gross national product. Here the factor of increase during the same period is under six but this shows nevertheless that public expenditure has been rising significantly faster than the national output of goods and services. And by the mid-1970s, when economic growth was relatively stagnant, public expenditure continued to grow in real terms until it was absorbing almost the same proportion of national resources as during the Second World War (though by the end of the decade there had been a slight fall). Of course, these comparisons are rough and ready in some respects (and I am no statistician) but they indicate without any shadow of doubt both the broad levels of public expenditure involved and its general direction of change. The relevant data are given in Table 1.

Table 1   Growth in government expenditure (central and local), 1792–1979[86]

Year	Total government expenditure (£m)		Total government expenditure as a percentage of GNP
	At current prices	At 1900 prices	
1792	22	17	11
1831	63	48	16
1870	93	74	9
1890	131	133	9
1900	281	281	14
1910	272	264	13
1920	1,592	565	26
1930	1,145	602	26
1940	3,905	—	60
1950	4,539	1,195	39
1960	9,400	1,927	41
1970	20,896	2,925	47
1979	84,906	3,820	52

86 Extracted from A. T. Peacock and J. Wiseman, *The Growth of Public Expenditure in the United Kingdom* (1961; new edn, London, 1967), Tables 1, A-5; *Annual Abstract of Statistics*, no. 117 (1981), Tables 14.1, 14.18. For the period 1946–74 official figures

The main reason for this great, long-term increase has been the expansion in economic and welfare services, expenditure on which has risen at nearly twice the rate of government activity as a whole. By comparison, defence spending has simply kept pace with the general rate of growth though it is also true (as will be seen in due course) that war has had the most dramatic or intense effect on collectivist development. The matter is complicated by various hidden subsidies in respect of military expenditure and by the quondam existence of imperial costs borne elsewhere but the broad nature of the trend is indicated in Table 2:

Table 2   Public expenditure on defence and social functions, 1890–1979[87]

	Percentage of total public expenditure		Percentage of GNP	
Year	Defence	Social, economic, and environmental services	Defence	Social, economic, and environmental services
1890	26.7	35.7	2.4	3.2
1910	27.3	52.0	3.5	6.7
1928	11.4	53.3	2.8	12.9
1950	18.5	60.8	7.2	23.7
1979	10.7	80.7	5.5	41.8

The continuing momentum, then, that drives public expenditure forward is very clear; and it is a force that has acted through all governments. From the record of recent times it is impossible to distinguish a high- and a low-spending party, and almost all political groups have agreed that 'the social and environmental services should be pressed forward hard, with not very much regard for the implications for the national economy . . . of the rate of their development.'[88]

(which differ only marginally from those given here) are to be found in a written Parliamentary answer, 904 H.C. Deb. 5s., 2 February 1976, col. 453; see also the table in Sir R. Clarke, 'Parliament and the Public Expenditure', *Political Quarterly*, xliv (1973), p.139, and *idem, Public Expenditure Management and Control: the Development of the Public Expenditure Survey Committee (PESC)* (London, 1978), p.148, as well as the comment at p.147, §396 on the validity of such figures. And for some international comparisons covering the period 1958–65, see the chart in 'The Rise of Government Expenditure', *Barclay's Bank Review*, xlii (no.2, May 1967), p.27.

87 Based on Peacock and Wiseman, op. cit., Tables 9, A-17; *Annual Abstract of Statistics*, no.117 (1981), Tables 14.1, 14.18. Cf. the somewhat similar figures relating to defence in Clarke, *Public Expenditure Management and Control*, p.23, n.6.

88 Clarke, 'Parliament and Public Expenditure', loc. cit., pp.141–2.

Similar indications of growth are given by other aspects of public sector finance. The rise in the national debt, for instance, reflects not merely increasing government expenditure but also marks the extent to which this is being sustained by borrowing and so by passing on the cost to future generations. During the nineteenth century the national debt rose relatively slowly from about £520 millions to £690 millions; but in 1978 it was nearly £80,000 millions.[89] Of course, a substantial proportion of this enormous expansion is due to the inflation that has occurred; and it is true that latterly the debt has considerably declined as a percentage of GNP.[90] But the broad increase is still undoubted; and to it has to be added the equally substantial debt of both local authorities and public corporations. The former alone, for example, amounted in 1979 to over £36,400 millions.[91]

In a recent review of these matters, Professor T. E. Chester summarized the present position as follows:

> The Government controls the flow of more than 50 per cent of the gross national product, it contributes more than 40 per cent of all new investment, employs 27 per cent of the working population, pays about one-third of all wages and salaries and owns nearly half the national fixed assets. This, moreover, leaves out of account the manifold indirect influences on the economic decisions of the private sector, such as price controls and industrial development certificates.[92]

This state of affairs clearly indicates a substantial degree of collectivism as compared with a century or so ago. And the contemporary pressures which have assisted the continuation and even intensification of this tendency are manifest to all.[93]

The employment of labour by public authorities

Another index is the number of people in public employment for, again, as government activity grows so will the size of its labour force. Of course, the relationship is not necessarily steady or proportionate but the

---

89 Totals from 1900 to 1978 are available in D. Butler and A. Sloman, *British Political Facts, 1900–1979*, 5th edn (London, 1980), pp. 356–7.

90 'Anatomy of the National Debt: the Decline in its Relative Significance', *Midland Bank Review* (November 1972), esp. pp. 9–10 and Table 4.

91 *Annual Abstract of Statistics*, no. 117 (1981), Table 16.31.

92 T. E. Chester, 'The Public Sector – its Dimensions and Dynamics', *National Westminster Bank Quarterly Review* (February 1976), p. 36. This interesting paper briefly touches on and summarizes many of the matters raised here; as does Lord Diamond, *Public Expenditure in Practice* (London, 1975), esp. ch. 1.

93 See the excellent analysis in D. Galloway, *The Public Prodigals: the Growth of Government Spending and How to Control It* (London, 1976), esp. the summary on p. 75.

statistics do have the advantage of reflecting more or less accurately the growth in the public use of real resources without having to allow for the effect of inflation. During most of the nineteenth century the various levels of British government markedly increased their absorption of labour though probably this did not then outstrip the rise in the population itself. But towards the end of the century the pace of government growth hastened and the fraction of the labour force employed by the state increased rapidly.[94] Table 3 shows how the situation developed over a 120-year period.

Table 3   Total public employment and working population, 1851–1976[95]

Year	(a) Numbers employed in the armed forces and civil central and local government (millions)	(b) Total working population (millions)	(c) (a) as a percentage of (b)
1851	0.25 (approx.)	10.5	2.4
1891	0.55 (approx.)	14.7	3.7
1901	0.96 (approx.)	16.6	5.8
1911	1.27	18.5	6.9
1921	1.96	19.6	10.0
1931	2.06	21.3	9.7
1938	2.24	22.6	9.9
1951	3.38	23.3	14.5
1961	3.56	24.7	14.4
1971	4.96	25.1	19.8
1976	5.79	25.5	22.7

The numbers employed by government since the mid-nineteenth century have thus increased well over twenty times and represent also a larger proportion of the growing work-force available – nearly 23 per cent instead of less than 3 per cent. Moreover the figures in Table 3 do not include the numbers of those who work for the public corporations. If these are added the contrast with earlier years is even more startling. The totals in column (a) rise to 6.17 millions for 1951 and 7.80 millions for

94 M. Abramowitz and V. F. Eliasberg, *The Growth of Public Employment in Great Britain* (Princeton, N.J., 1957), p.24.

95 Based on Abramowitz and Eliasberg op. cit., p.19, n.21, Table 1, p.25; Department of Employment and Productivity, *British Labour Statistics: Historical Abstract 1886–1968* (London, 1971), Tables 152–3, p.298; Department of Employment, *British Labour Statistics Year Book 1976* (London, 1978), Table 88; *Annual Abstract of Statistics*, no. 89 (1952), Table 121; ibid., no. 117 (1981), Table 6.1. The figures for 1851 are not strictly comparable with the rest of the table but are adequate for purposes of general indication. See also Figure 2, p.65 below.

1976 and in column (c), for the same two years, to 26.5 per cent and 30.6 per cent respectively. The general trend is manifest. The working population during the whole period since 1851 grew by some 143 per cent but the number in public service increased fifteen times as fast and well over twenty times as fast if the public corporations are included. Another way of putting this is to note that whereas in the 1850s one worker in forty-two was employed by a public agency of some kind, a century and a quarter later it was more than one in four. Moreover the tendency has intensified of late. For instance, by 1975 there were a million more local government employees than twelve years earlier. In fact the numbers in this field of public employment doubled between 1952 and 1975.[96]

As with expenditure, the pattern of public employment has also changed over the years; and again it is the great development in the regulatory and welfare functions of government that has completely transformed the picture. During the latter half of the last century, the chief responsibility of British government, as measured by manpower, was national defence: roughly one in two of all persons employed by government was in or working for the armed forces. During the next seventy or so years the total number of persons concerned in this activity increased but their relative significance fell notably: in 1974 only one in ten of government employees was so categorized. The increase in civilian central and local government manpower has, therefore, been very much more marked.[97] The nature of the civil services of the Crown was also altering. Defence apart, it was dominated at the beginning of this century by the GPO, the Inland Revenue, the Customs, and similar traditional offices. But the assumption of responsibility on an increasing scale for such matters as employment, health insurance, education, housing, and the like has obviously had a major effect: the percentage of civilian central government workers dealing with 'modern services' rose from 9.5 to 25.1 between 1914 and 1950.[98] Similarly, at one time the most significant single local government responsibility so far as manpower was concerned was police; but this is now notably outweighed by the various social services, in particular education.[99]

96 M. Wright (ed.), *Public Spending Decisions: Growth and Restraint in the 1970s* (London, 1980), p.1, p.10 Table 2.1.
97 Abramowitz and Eliasberg, op. cit., p.26; *Annual Abstract of Statistics*, no.113 (1976), Table 181, p.188.
98 Abramowitz and Eliasberg, op. cit., Charts 3 and 4, pp.46–7.
99 ibid., Chart 6, p.73.

The machinery of government

As government has assumed many new tasks concerning welfare and economic management, there has necessarily been a considerable extension and adaptation of the institutions of administration. Even at a very early stage of collectivist growth, between 1825 and 1860, sixteen new government agencies were created. By the 1880s, Maitland could write that, 'We are becoming a much governed nation, governed by all manner of councils and boards and officers, central and local, high and low, exercising the powers which have been committed to them by modern statutes'.[100] Many aspects of this development are reviewed in detail in volume iii of the present work, *A Much-Governed Nation*.

Table 4   Major government offices created since 1851[101]

Date	Office	Date	Office
1851	Commission of Works	1942	Ministry of Fuel, Light and Power
1871	Local Government Board		
1885	Scottish Office	1943	Ministry of Town and Country Planning
1889	Board of Agriculture		
1899	Board of Education	1944	Ministry of National Insurance
1916	Ministry of Pensions		
1916	Ministry of Labour	1944	Ministry of Civil Aviation
1916	Department of Scientific and Industrial Research	1951	Ministry of Housing and Local Government
1917	Air Ministry	1954	Ministry of Welsh Affairs
1917	Overseas Trade Department	1964	Ministry of Overseas Development
1919	Ministry of Transport		
1920	Mines Department	1964	Ministry of Technology
1925	Dominions Office	1968	Civil Service Department
1939	Ministry of Food	1972	Northern Ireland Office
1939	Ministry of Supply	1974	Ministry of Prices and Consumer Protection

100 D. Roberts, *Victorian Origins of the British Welfare State* (1960; Archon, 1969), Appendix, pp. 327–33; F. W. Maitland, *The Constitutional History of England* (1908; Cambridge, 1974), p. 501.

101 The table is perhaps impressionistic rather than strictly accurate because there are numerous, and obvious, omissions. The object of the list is simply to show when offices were first set up to deal with major areas of policy. No attempt is made to indicate the more ephemeral departments (e.g. the early Food Control Office, 1917–21, or the Ministry of Materials, 1951–4) or changes of title or amalgamations (as involved in the creation of the Ministry of Health in 1919 or of the recent omnibus departments such as Defence or the Environment). For complete details, see e.g. F. M. G. Willson, *The Organization of British Central Government 1914–1964*, 2nd edn (London, 1968), esp. Appendix C; also the regular annual reviews appearing in *Parliamentary Affairs*.

Here it is simply appropriate to note a few major changes. For example, there is the increase in the quasi-government field, not only the public corporations, great and small, from the Electricity Council to the British Airports Authority, but also a very wide range of semi-independent institutions from the scientific research organizations to such bodies as the Countryside Commission and the Horserace Totalisator Board. There is a host of such establishments which has been created mainly in modern times to meet a need for public supervision, initiative, or aid without direct departmental control or operation. Similarly, many new departments of government have themselves been set up. Of the twenty or so major government offices now in existence, over half has been created in the last fifty to seventy years. Something of the tendency is indicated in Table 4.

It is not, of course, that the entire range of functions represented by these offices is always completely new. But even so the departmental formalization and the extent of responsibility involved indicate a considerable institutional enhancement. Further, the traditional departments as well as these new creations have invariably acquired a growing range of tasks. For instance, the Treasury has, in addition to its conventional duty of financial control, assumed some responsibility for overall economic management; and the Home Office has acquired new functions concerning community programmes and equal opportunities including race relations. Naturally this situation is continually changing: the temporary proliferation during time of war was particularly great. It is the case, too, that some functions and agencies are shed from time to time as in the aftermath of imperial decline. But the general tendency is one of augmentation. There is also the elaborate development of regional and local offices and the complex phenomenon of the specialist classes in the Civil Service to bear in mind in this context. As well there is the extensive proliferation of both the judicial functions of departments and a whole array of administrative tribunals. Further there has been a parallel process of centralization reflected in the relative weakening of local government and its increasing dependence on national aid. The change in the nature of Parliamentary questions also reveals something of this same general tendency. The Crowther-Kilbrandon Commission, searching for ways of illustrating the immense widening of the responsibilities of central government that has occurred, examined a series of questions, both oral and written, which were answered in one week in June 1971 'to see how far it would have been appropriate to put them at the beginning of the century.' There were 718 questions in all and it was estimated that 'between 80 and 90 per cent of them could not have been tabled in 1900 since they related to matters which were not then of government concern.'[102]

102 The Constitution, R.Com. Rep., p.76 §231.

The volume of legislation

One final indicator of the growing pressure of government business is the amount of legislation which is passed through Parliament. Initially, in the century after 1750, this took the form of an increase in the number of local bills introduced, for the immediate legislative result of the economic and social changes we know as the Industrial Revolution was a relative surge of private legislation as individuals, groups, and communities attempted to cope with the problems of the transition and sought new powers to do so.[103] In time, and for various reasons, public legislation of a general character came to supersede these earlier efforts; and this not simply in respect of the number of statutes but also of their size and complexity. If the actual total of public general Acts passed is considered then more were put on the statute-book between 1866 and 1869 than during any other comparable period since. But in terms of statute length, this rate of legislation was indeed subsequently surpassed though not until the late 1930s and after. There was thus a decline from the mid-nineteenth-century level of lawmaking; but since the beginning of this century the rate of enactment has again shown a steady tendency to increase as measured by the size of the annual statutory output. This is shown in Table 5.

Table 5   The volume of legislation (public general Acts), 1866–1979[104]

Year	Average number of statutes per year	Average number of statute-book pages per year
1866–9	128.8	1073.3
1870–9	91.7	652.4
1880–9	66.7	378.2
1890–9	59.1	419.7
1900–09	48.3	267.9
1910–19	66.2	367.3
1920–9	57.9	697.7
1930–9	63.7	1036.9
1940–9	58.6	1236.0
1950–9	62.0	1063.0
1960–9	71.5	1563.2
1970–9	68.7	1936.6
Overall average	70.3	891.0

103 F. H. Spencer, *Municipal Origins: an Account of English Private Bill Legislation Relating to Local Government, 1740–1835* . . . (London, 1911), pp.1–3.
104 Based on figures derived from *Public General Statutes*, *Public General Acts and Measures*, and *Chitty's Annual Statutes*. For the period 1940–9, the figures cover an average of eight years only, viz., 1940–1 and 1944–9.

The average annual number of statute-book pages between 1936 and 1939 was 1326; and it exceeded 2000 for the first time in 1947. The annual average for the period 1946–9 was 1882.6, a figure not matched for another twenty years. Between 1970–9 it reached an annual average of 1936.6 with a peak of 2800 in 1975.

A cognate indication of government involvement is the growth that has occurred in the amount of subordinate or delegated legislation. The data are given in Table 6 which shows that the annual total has more than doubled since the beginning of the century and, for the past forty years, has been sustained at this high level.

Table 6   The number of statutory instruments, 1900–77[105]

Year	Annual total	General	Local
1900	995	174	821
1910	1368	218	1150
1920	2475	916	1559
1929	1262	391	871
1940	2222	1626	596
1950	2144	1211	933
1960	2495	733	1762
1970	2044	1040	1004
1977	2202	1168	1034

*   *   *

It is this tendency towards government growth which has often and so rightly been seen as an increasingly dominant, though of course never exclusive, feature of our political life over the past century and a half: politically it is the crucial sesquicentennial fact. Dicey may most appropriately be permitted a last word at this point. In an auto-biographical fragment written towards the end of his life (he died in 1922), he commented on this development describing it as both 'indisputable' and 'very important'. During the last fifty years or so, he went on, 'a more fundamental revolution in the beliefs, in the habits, and in the life of England, has taken place than has ever been achieved within so short a period in any other civilized country known to us from history.'[106]

105 Butler and Sloman, *British Political Facts 1900–1979*, p.190, gives figures for every ten years 1900–77. The statistics given may not, in fact, be complete as a substantial number of local rules escaped being recorded. As well, in 1948 the system of registration changed and the figures before and after that date may not be strictly comparable. On the increase of delegated legislation between 1947 and 1974, see the memorandum by the academic members of the Study of Parliament Group in Procedure, Sel. Cttee 1st Rep., 1977–8 (vol.xviii), HC 588-III, Appendix 1, p.5.
106 R. S. Rait (ed.), *Memorials of Albert Venn Dicey, Being Chiefly Letters and Diaries* (London, 1925), p.2.

The emergence of collectivism is indeed unmistakable: but why has it occurred? Why, in Britain, has a libertarian, individualist society sustaining a limited conception of government been in so many ways and to such a degree replaced by the positive state pursuing explicit policies of widespread intervention in the name of social justice and the public good? This is the next question to be explored as a necessary preliminary to the detailed study of ideas and institutions.

PART TWO
THE GREAT CHANGE

Collectivism will spread, but it will spread from no one centre.
B. WEBB, Diary (17 September 1893), in *Our Partnership*,
1948, p. 39

PROEM

I glance but at a few conspicuous marks,
Leaving ten thousand others, ...
WILLIAM WORDSWORTH, *The Prelude*, 1805,
VII. 566–7

Macaulay began a famous chapter in his *History* by observing that since
the end of the seventeenth century a change had taken place in Britain for
which the old world furnished no parallel. How much more, then, has the
process of alteration advanced in the years that have elapsed since his
own day? It has in so many ways intensified, cumulated its effects, and
thus become ever more profound and extensive in its scope. Nor has it
been of merely domestic significance: something got hold of the entire
world that was destined to alter the form and scale of every human affair.
The following chapters in this volume will sketch, often in a merely
impressionistic way, some of the factors and occasions related to this
great change so far as Great Britain is concerned and do so with a
view to indicating how the role of public authority has as a result been
notably augmented. Most of the matters touched on are perhaps of pretty
obvious relevance though a few may not at first glance be quite so
striking in their bearing on this development. No doubt, too, there are
errors, omissions, and misinterpretations: the account is hardly definitive
and every reader will have amendments and additions to make to the
catalogue of considerations proposed. But although I have only an
amateur familiarity with the vast array of historical and other literature
involved, I like to think all the same that the main forces and cardinal
moments which have in recent times been part of, or contributed to, the
transformation of our political life are here at least briefly or cursorily
indicated. Nor is one without skilled and perceptive guidance as to the
main forces entailed: to mention no other source, de Tocqueville alone
offers a superb analysis.[1] And even if the particular account which
follows is deemed deficient, it is none the less the case that in principle
students of modern British politics ought always to attempt a grasp of
this wider metamorphosis as in no other way is it possible to achieve a
proper conception of those correlative changes in government and in

---

1 See esp. his *Democracy in America* (1835–40; Fontana, 1968), vol. ii, part IV, ch. 5.

political policy and ideas in which they are primarily interested. Without some perspective of this sort their special study will proceed in a kind of vacuum and be found in consequence to be wanting in important respects.

No really vital significance attaches to the order of exposition adopted. I did at one stage of composition try to separate practical and intellective considerations but found, inevitably perhaps, that it was impossible to sustain a clear distinction. As the arrangement now stands, I review and exemplify in varying detail a series of general categories of influence: military; economic and social; political; scientistic; and philanthropic. Of course, the specific political ideologies and the impact of foreign and imperial affairs are also of great importance in this context; but these doctrinal and exotic matters are the special concern of other volumes of this work and so are omitted here save for some inevitable incidental reference.

THE GRIM HARBINGER

... war – the supreme expression of state-intervention ....
H. J. LASKI, *The State in Theory and Practice*, 1935; repr.1941, p.230

THE SIGNIFICANCE OF WAR

Everywhere, and at all times, chronic war generates a militant type of
structure, not in the body of soldiers only but throughout the community
at large.
H. SPENCER, 'From Freedom to Bondage', in T. Mackay (ed.), *A
Plea for Liberty*, 2nd edn, 1891, p.8

AT THE conclusion of his epic account of the world crisis of 1914–18,
Churchill wrote that the whole story of the human race is war.[1] And, of
course, the intimate connexion between war and politics has long been
recognized. To reach back no further, Hobbes discerned in conflict and
its avoidance both the natural propensities of man and the very
formation of the state, while for Hume it is in the military camp that the
advantages of political leadership and control are first developed and
learned. Hegel acknowledged an intensification of the link with his
understanding that in modern war the maintenance of the state's
independence requires the sacrifice of property, life, opinion, and all else.
Equally de Tocqueville observed (in his most acute study of the factors
tending in his day to the centralization of political power) that it is above
all in war that people wish, and need, to increase the prerogatives of
government.[2] It is a point that has subsequently been realized *à outrance*
in experience and reflection alike. Even if we reject the extreme
Sombartian thesis that the nature of the economic and social process is
basically determined by war and preparation for it, it is none the less true
that nowadays we understand almost instinctively that war has been a

---

1 W. S. Churchill, *The World Crisis* (London, 1923–9), v.451.
2 Hobbes, *Leviathan*, I.xiii, ii.xvii; Hume, *A Treatise of Human Nature*, III.ii.8;
  Hegel, *Philosophy of Right*, §324; de Tocqueville, *Democracy in America*, II.iv.4.

crucial, perhaps the most vital, factor in the history of our time.[3] And the point of relevance here is that war inevitably tends to augment the role of government, specifically that changes in the nature of its conduct and form in recent times have led to a very considerable growth of public intervention indeed. In the inspired phrase used by the translator of Halévy's commentaries on this matter, war has been 'the grim harbinger' of collectivism.[4]

Britain has always prided itself on the protection of old-established liberties. Even so, when national necessity called, these could easily be brushed aside as with the impressment of seamen for naval service. But this was a great and scandalous exception though it did perhaps intimate the possibilities that later permitted not only much wider forms of conscription but also such practices as internment without trial and so forth. Yet the potential thus revealed took time to appear and has only fully emerged in the period since 1789. Hegel's opinion (cited above) was, of course, a theoretical expression of what was implicit in French Revolutionary experience as with the attempts of Carnot and his associates to create the controlled economy necessary to sustain the Nation in Arms. Wellington insisted to Earl Stanhope that revolutionary France 'was constituted upon a military basis. All its institutions were framed for the purpose of forming and maintaining its armies'.[5] The new France was indeed a grand and awful portent of the future in this as in so many other respects. Later the Crimean War was an equally important turning-point for it brought home to this country in an especially acute way the lesson that heroism and the traditional ideal of aristocratic leadership were not enough for the effective conduct of hostilities. This required organization of a kind hitherto unrealized in order to deploy effectively the material and human resources involved. And if the achievement of this goal was, at that time, definitely and most often associated with the practices of private commerce and not with the routine of public departments, this proved but a stage in the journey that led to a growing role for government as the limitations of the man of business and his procedures became apparent.[6] The same trend was also

3 For Sombart's view, see J. M. Winter's introduction to the symposium he edited, *War and Economic Development* (Cambridge, 1975), pp. 4–6. This volume of essays is dedicated to the memory of David Joslin. I would like to snatch this marginal opportunity to express my gratitude for his great kindness on the too few occasions I was fortunate enough to meet him.

4 C. Bouglé's Preface to E. Halévy, *The Era of Tyrannies: Essays on Socialism and War* (1938; trans. R. K. Webb, London, 1967), p. xix.

5 Memorandum (18 September 1836) in Earl Stanhope, *Notes of Conversations with the Duke of Wellington. 1831–1851* (1886; 2nd edn, London, 1888), p. 81.

6 O. Anderson, *A Liberal State at War: English Politics and Economics during the Crimean War* (London, 1967), pp. 104, 108, and ch. 3 *passim* on the contemporary mood.

starkly revealed (if an exotic precedent may be admitted) in the war between the American states. The South was, in particular, dedicated to the proposition that the best government is that which governs least and, given the circumstances in which the Confederacy was founded and the notable emphasis there on states' rights, its political machinery was established on the assumption that the general government should have a minimal range of responsibilities. Here was a situation in which there was always bound to be substantial resistance to the growth of war powers. Yet, despite this inevitable opposition, the administration of President Davis was increasingly driven not only to conscription but also to the control of foreign commerce (including the vital blockade-running enterprise), the railways, and manufacturing industry; in addition it was led to the institution of such welfare schemes as that for the relief of soldiers' families. This sort of regulation meant high and discriminatory taxation and resulted, too, in a substantial bureaucratic growth.[7] Of course, all this was primitive and did not go very far by later standards. Nevertheless, in inauspicious political and geographical circumstances, the germ can be seen in the Confederate States of America of the kind of wartime executive power that has since become increasingly familiar and obvious. In this as in other respects the American conflict may plausibly be called the first of the modern wars. Nor did tendency of this sort when revealed closer to home escape the criticism of libertarian observers. For the later nineteenth century, Herbert Spencer discerned even in contemporary Britain the extension of 'militant' characteristics derived from the growth of centralized administration and compulsory regulation caused by preparation for hostilities.[8] And very recently Professor Oakeshott has described how, in the long perspective of the developing European state, what he calls the managerial element in government comes decisively to the fore in the context of modern war.[9]

The basic reason for the close link between war and the intensification of collectivism in modern times is the development of industrialism which indeed war itself has, in turn, so often stimulated. As an official memorandum put it early in 1941, 'war is now a highly mechanized form of economic activity, requiring very heavy capital investment. It is now waged on a "totalitarian" scale, involving a diversion of the entire national economy to a single purpose.'[10] Technological change, the

7 L. B. Hill, *State Socialism in the Confederate States of America* (Charlottesville, Va, 1936); F.E. Vandiver, *Jefferson Davis and the Confederate State* (Oxford, 1964), esp. pp.8, 17–20.
8 See e.g. Spencer's *The Principles of Sociology* (1876ff; 3rd edn, London, 1885), i.570
9 M. Oakeshott, *On Human Conduct* (Oxford, 1975), pp.272–4. Cf. ibid., pp.146–7.
10 PRO, CAB 117/39, memorandum on economic demobilization (19 February 1941), p.1.

fundamentally altered the form of war and its impact on the communities involved. Specifically, the *matériel* used is much more complex and costly and the rate of its consumption has quickened. Not to mention technical improvement in weapons themselves, consider, for instance, the effect on preparation for and the conduct of battle of the coming of the railway, steam navigation, the ironclad ship, the electric telegraph, and later such crucial developments as the invention and large-scale production of the internal combustion engine and the wireless. The Boer Wars knew neither of the latter;[11] in the Great War the motor-car, lorry, tank, radio, and aeroplane played an important but usually still subsidiary role (though the Marne and Verdun alike showed how vital mechanical transport could be). During the Second World War, all this was crucial as was the use of such additional innovations as radiolocation, wireless interception and signal intelligence, beam-navigation, and other forms of electronic wizardry. Since then nuclear physics, satellites, rocket technology, jet propulsion, and so on have transformed still further the nature and cost of national defence. None of these advances would have been possible without a sophisticated and extensive industrial base. Moreover, in the circumstances thus created, it became essential in fighting and preparation for it to mobilize more resources and to do so more swiftly and thoroughly than ever before. E. H. Carr for one noted 'the indispensability of a planned economy for national efficiency' in war. And this outcome is inevitable not only for the obvious military reasons, such as the production and supply of munitions, but also to deal with the many shortages and other incidental problems that the direct demands of war create. Conflict between the highly industrialized communities of the present day necessarily results in what Correlli Barnett recently called 'total strategy'. War can no longer be simply a military matter; it is only possible as a confrontation of entire societies, their resources, technology, and personnel (which is what a people becomes), the fighting services being no more than 'the cutting edge' of a nation at war. And, in Churchill's phrase (echoing no doubt unconsciously the Hegelian theme), capital and labour alike 'cast aside their interests, rights, and customs and put them into the common stock.'[12]

Above all, then, a belligerent nation in the circumstances of modern

---

11 Or so I thought when I wrote this. But I have since read that 'wireless telegraphy' was used on an experimental basis though with inadequate results and so abandoned. See L. S. Amery (ed.), *The Times History of the War in South Africa 1899–1902* (London, 1900–9), vi. 361.

12 E. H. Carr, *The New Society* (1951; London, 1965), p. 35; Correlli Barnett, *Strategy and Society* (Manchester, 1975), p. 8; 361 H. C. Deb. 5s., 4 June 1940, col. 793. For the origin of the phrase about the armed forces being only the 'cutting edge' of the nation, see Winter op. cit., pp. 4 and 9 n. 27.

war turns over to a system of control in which a major proportion of its productive capacity and economy, indeed its life as a whole, comes in one way or another under public supervision; and the role of government is thus greatly augmented.[13]

And of all such phases of modern experience, it is the war of 1914–18 which constitutes the great watershed, the event of most traumatic significance. It was widely recognized as such both at the time and subsequently.[14] The day after Britain entered the war, Henry James wrote in a letter of the 'plunge of civilization' into an 'abyss of blood and darkness', a tragic and treacherous denial of what the whole long age of 'bettering' had meant.[15] Certainly if the intensity of a period of hostilities and its impact may be measured by the casualties incurred then, relative to the population involved, the Great War was over eight times the average prevailing since the seventeenth century.[16] As, against original expectations, the fighting dragged on to the Somme and Third Ypres it seemed indeed to be fulfilling James's prophecy, to have drawn the shades decisively on the glad confident morning of progress which had for so many people been heralded by the preceding era: 'Never such innocence again' in Philip Larkin's sad line.[17] Another contemporary poet, Vernon Scannell, who was wounded in the second war, wrote during its course some verses in which he says that it is not the conflict in which he himself fought that he recalls whenever war is mentioned,

> But the one called Great
> Which ended in a sepia November
> Four years before my birth.

'The war that was called Great invades the mind'.[18]

If this ordeal seemed for so many to have destroyed the foundation of things, to have broken the front held by civilization against barbarism, then it did so significantly – to come to the political point – because it meant, in Jules Romains' phrase, the onset of despotism. Ernest Benn, an ardent libertarian who much admired both Spencer and Halévy, believed with the latter that the traditional liberty of England died on 2 August

13 For some comparisons of a variety of national experience, cf. A. S. Milward, *War, Economy and Society 1939–1945* (London, 1977).

14 See the detailed and definitive account in A. Marwick, *The Deluge: British Society and the First World War* (1965; Penguin, 1967).

15 P. Lubbock (ed.), *The Letters of Henry James* (New York, 1920), ii. 384, in P. Fussell, *The Great War and Modern Memory* (1975; London, 1977), p. 8.

16 Q. Wright, *A Study of War* (1942; Chicago, 1959), Appendix XXI, Table 54, Fig. 40, i. 660–1. Though for cautionary analysis of the statistics of this matter, see J. Terraine, *The Smoke and the Fire: Myths and Anti-Myths of War 1861–1945* (London, 1980), chs. III–V.

17 P. Larkin, 'MCMXIV', in *The Whitsun Weddings* (London, 1964), p. 28.

18 Scannell's lines are cited in Fussell, op. cit., pp. 319, 322–3.

1914, the day that marks the introduction of the Defence of the Realm Act which gave so much power to government to deal with the emergency.[19]

Nor was what impended in the need for extensive government control unrecognized upon the occasion, although at the outset the point was grasped only by a few. In September 1914, only one month after the outbreak of fighting, Admiral Sir Charles Ottley (who had been Secretary to the Committee of Imperial Defence from 1907 to 1912) wrote for his successor in that post, Colonel Maurice Hankey, a long memorandum about the future conduct of the war. In this he stressed the need for someone to be appointed 'with plenary powers to commandeer the entire manufacturing potentialities of the Empire, and more particularly of Great Britain'. Thus early in the conflict, before even the Marne had been fought and the race to the sea begun and while, therefore, the harsh stalemate of trench warfare and the long attrition of human and other resources were barely foreseen, Admiral Ottley discerned that the war would entail gearing up the entire economy under a control in some respects almost dictatorial. Kitchener was another who was equally or even more prescient in this respect.[20] Again, consider the evidence of a foreign observer, the Spanish journalist Ramiro de Maeztu, who had been living in England for some years. Of radical propensity, he had been involved with the Guild Socialists and the circle that gathered around Alfred Orage, editor of *The New Age*, and in 1915 began to publish in that journal a series of articles which in the following year appeared in book form. These studies constituted in large part a series of reflections on the impact of the war thus far on British society. And the great increase in the powers of government was one of the features which Maeztu singled out for attention: the overcoming of 'subjective rights' like those involved in private property and freedom of contract; the control assumed over the railways, capital, investment, and trade; the way in which factories had been taken over; the high taxation, especially of profits, and the redistribution of income involved; the mobilization of labour even to the point of conscription.[21] A 'new principle of economic organization under public authority' was thus emerging on the British scene.[22]

19 E. Benn, *Happier Days: Recollections and Reflections* (London, 1949), pp.212–13.
20 Admiral C. L. Ottley to M. Hankey (2 September 1914), Kitchener Papers, PRO 30/57/81, in S. Roskill, *Hankey: Man of Secrets* (London, 1970–4), i.149. For Kitchener's far-sightedness, see P. Magnus, *Kitchener: Portrait of an Imperialist* (1958; Grey Arrow, 1961), pp.273–4; and Sir G. Arthur, *Life of Lord Kitchener* (London, 1920), iii.9–11.
21 R. de Maeztu, *Authority, Liberty and Function in the Light of the War* (London, 1916), pp.204, 207–8.
22 F. E. Lawley, *The Growth of Collective Economy* (London, 1938), vol. i, p.ix.

H. G. Wells may be taken as a final preliminary witness to these matters. Always a perceptive analyst of contemporary tendencies, he had long foreseen that in the twentieth century war would in many crucial respects be quite different from that of the past and would require in particular control and guidance of a totally new order. In 1901 he had written:

> a practical realization of socialistic conceptions will quite inevitably be forced upon the fighting State. The State that has not incorporated with its fighting organization all its able-bodied manhood and all its material substance, its roads, vehicles, engines, foundries, and all its resources of food and clothing . . . will be at an overwhelming disadvantage against a State which has emerged from the social confusion of the present time, got rid of every vestige of our present distinction between official and governed, and organized every element in its being.

Three decades later, Wells still recurred to this theme of the way in which, as never before, militancy had begun to invade and modify the texture of normal life through conscription, unprecedented monetary levies, indemnities, taxes, and the like: 'The New Warfare, it was already being remarked by 1918, was a war of whole populations'.[23] The microcosmic parallel to these generalizations was revealed, in fictional form, in *Mr. Britling Sees It Through* (1916). In this novel, the increasing, and in the end tragic, impact of the war is shown as it affected a small group of people in Essex and, more particularly, one human life and brain. The war was 'an immense thing, it would touch everybody'; and the symbolically named Mr Britling reflected the collectivist spirit aroused. He imagined the British people saying to the government: '"Here we are at your disposal. This is not a diplomatist's war nor a War Office war; this is a war of the whole people. We are willing and ready to lay aside our usual occupations and offer our property and ourselves. Whim and individual action are for peace time. Take us and use us as you think fit. Take all we possess."'[24] Germany had long been a militaristic nation absorbed in the army and its administration. Britain had not: much or most of its life had lain outside the public sphere. Now this life was challenged by the war and was weak because of the 'insufficiency of direction' it embodied. Everything had to alter: 'Suddenly all the underlying ideas of that outer, greater English life beyond politics, beyond the services, were challenged

23 H. G. Wells, *Anticipations of the Reaction of Mechanical and Scientific Progress upon Human Life and Thought* (1901; rev. edn, London, 1914), p.185; *The Shape of Things to Come* (1933; Corgi, 1967), pp.164–5.
24 H. G. Wells, *Mr. Britling Sees It Through* (1916; London, 1933), pp.132, 144–5.

..., its freedom, and its irresponsibility.' '"One thing after another in the country is being pulled up by its roots", reflected Mr. Britling.'[25]

The war thus became universal not simply in its geographical but in its domestic scope. It was not a matter to be left simply to the specialists in violence; it enlisted almost all human activities in its train. Its aim was destruction; but in pursuit of this goal it needed everything man could produce. In consequence, the nature of modern war is such that it requires the mobilization and use of the entire resources of a belligerent country; and this necessarily means a vast extension of government functions and agencies. Total war alone has not, of course, created this development; the process had been long under way. But it has substantially and dramatically strengthened it, more perhaps than any other individual factor.

WAR AND THE ROLE OF GOVERNMENT

Ideas that have ruled life . . . are being chased and slaughtered in the streets. The rights of property, for example, the sturdy virtues of individualism . . . vanished suddenly . . . leaving . . . Collectivism in possession.
H. G. WELLS, *The War That Will End War*, 1914, p. 58[26]

There is no doubt at all, then, that nowadays government activity increases particularly swiftly and extensively in war. As this is reflected in the growth of expenditure and the employment of manpower, something of its nature is to be observed in Tables 1–3 (pp. 33–6). But its pattern in this particular respect is more clearly revealed perhaps in graphic form. In Figure 1 the shape of the government expenditure curve, taken in conjunction with that showing the growth of the GNP, visually confirms the general point that public expenditure as a whole is absorbing an increasing proportion of national resources. But something more specific than this is manifest. There is a clearly defined pattern of peaks and plateaux and the sharp rises coincide with the second Anglo-Boer War (1899–1902), the two world wars, and the Korean War (1950–3).

This wartime expansion of government reflects the assumption of new functions and powers and the parallel proliferation of new offices and agencies. For one thing, government becomes the chief consumer of the nation and sets itself up as the final arbiter of production and distribution.[27] Again it was the Great War which marked a sea-change in these matters and which saw an alteration in respect of government

---

25 ibid., pp. 150–2, 219.
26 My colleague, Dr R. Taylor, kindly drew my attention to this passage.
27 Cf. E. Halévy, *The Era of Tyrannies: Essays on Socialism and War* (1938; trans., London, 1967), p. 86.

Figure 1 Total government expenditure and gross national product, at current prices, 1890–1955[28]

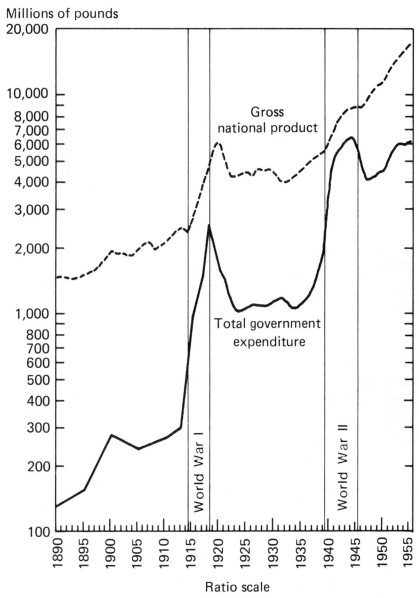

Millions of pounds

Ratio scale

28 Reproduced from A. T. Peacock and J. Wiseman, *The Growth of Public Expenditure in the United Kingdom* (1961; new edn London, 1967), p. 43. When allowance is made for the inflation of prices over the period concerned, the general shape of the curves remains the same, although their steepness is reduced, ibid., p. 47. Cf. the similar graph in A. J. P. Taylor, *English History, 1914–1945* (1965; Penguin, 1970), Figure 7, p. 793.

control of a degree that beforehand would have seemed quite impossible and would have met with invincible opposition if suggested. Reflecting after the end of hostilities on the impact of the war, William Beveridge wrote that as a result of the stress it entailed, 'We have. . . made practical discoveries in the art of government almost comparable to the immense discoveries made at the same time in the art of flying.'[29] Of course, there was a great deal of psychological and moral resistance even amid the perils of war to the extension of government activities required by its exigencies, so strong was the predisposition and commitment to individualism and free trade. Ministers, many of whom had spent their political careers attacking what they saw as the fallacies of protection and other forms of collectivism, found it difficult to adjust to the need for extensive state intervention. Officials – Beveridge himself being an obvious exception – were by and large of a similar mind, having had little or no experience that could serve as a guide to the conduct of administration on the tremendously augmented scale required. Nor were proposals for government interference with industry and its practices always welcomed by organized labour, while managers and owners in industry were, of course, invariably diffident to say the least.[30] Given this, there was no deliberate policy of state control carefully thought out and applied; it was increasingly seen to be necessary only because of the force of circumstances. This sort of pressures and the extent of the administrative response must be indicated in detail to show the nature of the change that occurred.

A good example of what happened concerns the supply of munitions.[31] At the beginning of the war, the Army Contracts Department, following the policy laid down by the Murray Committee on Government Factories and Workshops and (the output of the Ordnance establishments apart) used to relying for its requirements on private enterprise and competitive tendering, assumed, despite the lessons of the Boer War, that an adequate flow of shells would be forthcoming if specialist suppliers were

29 W. H. Beveridge, *The Public Service in War & Peace* (London, 1920), p. 5.
30 J. Harris, *William Beveridge: a Biography* (Oxford, 1977), pp. 203ff; C. Wrigley, 'Liberals and the Desire for Working-Class Representatives in Battersea, 1886–1922', in K. D. Brown (ed.), *Essays in Anti-Labour History: Responses to the Rise of Labour in Britain* (London, 1974), pp. 152–3.
31 There is a good account in E. M. H. Lloyd, *Experiments in State Control at the War Office and the Ministry of Food* (Oxford, 1924), chs. I–III, XXI on which I draw here. The weapon and ammunition problems and the steps taken to meet them are also succinctly described in the official histories compiled by J. E. Edmonds: *Military Operations, France and Belgium, 1914* (London, 1923–5), ii. 11–17; and the volumes dealing with 1915 (London, 1927), i. 37–58. The best single volume survey is S. J. Hurwitz, *State Intervention in Great Britain: a Study of Economic Control and Social Response, 1914–19* (1949; London, 1968) which treats seriatim different industries and issues of mobilization. See also Harris, op. cit., pp. 206ff.

induced to produce more in response to greater demand and increased prices.[32] So in October 1914 the War Office did not seriously consider a proposal that the government should take over the big armaments firms and operate them as a public service so as to make sure of supplies and protect itself against exploitation. But it soon became apparent that the speed of response to the great demands of modern war of both individual contractors and the armaments industry as a whole had been overestimated, and the following year there was a critical shortage of shells which made it clear something drastic and different had to be done. A Ministry of Munitions was created to deal with the problem: 'National organization and centralized control were found to be more effective than high prices and *laisser-faire* in stimulating supply.'[33] Existing factories were commandeered; new ones were built by the government; raw materials were monopolized and distributed at fixed prices, block foreign orders being placed where appropriate; regulation was extended back to the steel industry and so to the production of iron ore; shipping space and foreign currency were controlled and allocated according to need. The diversion of resources caused shortages and high prices and these had to be dealt with too: manufacturers were required to produce at prices based on cost and told how to do it. Not least, collective bargaining, restrictive practices, and the use of the strike weapon had to be limited in the interests of war production. Something of the scale of administrative change involved is indicated by the growth in the size of the organization concerned: in August 1914 twenty clerks in the Army Contracts Department dealt with the purchase of munitions; by November 1918 this had become a staff of over 65,000 (and this covered only part of the army's requirements).[34] A similar scale of action had to be taken to deal with the shortage of sandbags required for the new trench warfare. Again the need for 'optical munitions' (rangefinders, field-glasses, and the like) for the supply of which the country had been largely dependent on German production, led to government aid for the development of the home industry.[35]

The organization of food supplies reflected similar phases of development. Despite the fact that in 1914 some two-thirds of Britain's food was

32 On the 'Business as Usual' attitude that prevailed and the forms of initial intervention, see Hurwitz, op. cit., ch. II. For the similarly acute problems which arose during the Boer War, see C. Trebilcock, 'War and the Failure of Industrial Mobilisation: 1899 and 1914' in J. M. Winter (ed.), *War and Economic Development* (Cambridge, 1975), esp. pp. 143–51. On the Murray Committee, ibid., pp. 152–4.
33 Lloyd, op. cit., p. 23. Cf. Trebilcock, loc. cit., pp. 155–6.
34 Lloyd, op. cit., p. 24.
35 For the two cases mentioned, see Hurwitz, op. cit., pp. 157–9; and R. and K. Macleod, 'War and Economic Development: Government and the Optical Industry in Britain, 1914–18', in Winter, op. cit., ch. 8.

imported, the new President of the Board of Trade Walter Runciman, who was opposed to state interference, refused to introduce statutory control on the outbreak of war. For more than two years the import, manufacture, and distribution of food (with the major exception of sugar which had to be treated differently because pre-war supplies had largely been drawn from enemy countries) were left almost entirely to private enterprise. But then there was increasing pressure for wider state control: prices had been rising fast, troops and munitions were competing for cargo space, the submarine campaign was beginning to bite, speculation and hoarding were on the increase, and so on. Runciman was forced to retreat from his non-interventionist position and in mid-November 1916 the Board of Trade acquired power over the production, price, and distribution of food supplies. When George became Prime Minister the following month a new department, the Ministry of Food, was specifically created for this purpose. Even so, Beveridge, one of the senior civil servants transferred to the new Ministry, found that reluctance to introduce extensive measures of control still persisted. But again the course of events and the growth of public discontent forced a change of both minister and policy; rationing and price regulation were introduced followed by such measures as the bulk purchase of imports and control of wholesale supplies.[36]

What was happening in many such areas of public interest may also be indicated by another instance, the key example of the coal industry. Of course, this had, even before the war, been subject to some regulation, as by the series of Acts (mainly concerning safety) from 1842 on, by the Eight Hours Act of 1908, the Minimum Wage Act of 1912, and suchlike. But after 1915 the position was cumulatively transformed by the introduction of a new system of control intended to maintain and increase output, prevent famine prices, and avoid trade disputes. R. H. Tawney, who was very familiar with the industry and its problems, described the sequence of events in a way that specifies in drab administrative detail how the grip of the state was tightened:

> In February, 1915, the Coal-mining Organization Committee was established, and in May, 1915, the Coal Exports Committee. In July, 1915, the Price of Coal (Limitation) Act was passed, which fixed pit-head prices at a maximum of 4s. per ton over pre-war prices, at the same time giving the Board of Trade power to vary the maximum by order, but did not interfere with retail prices. In December, 1915, the Central Coal and Coke Supplies Committee was set up to regulate supply and distribution, and in June, 1916, power was taken under a Defence of the Realm Regulation to make orders as to priority of

36 On these matters, see Harris, op. cit., pp.232–9.

supplies. In November, 1916, another Defence of the Realm Regulation gave the State power to assume complete control of all coal mines and of enterprises connected with them, and an order was issued at once applying control to South Wales. In February, 1917, the whole of the coal mines of Great Britain were brought under control, and a Coal Controller's Department was established, in which was merged the Coal Mining Organization Committee and the Central Coal and Coke Supplies Committee, while an Advisory Board, composed of an equal number of miners and coal-owners was appointed to assist the Controller. In February, 1918, the Coal Mines Agreement Confirmation Act was passed, which gave statutory sanction to an agreement reached between the Coal Controller and the mineowners in July, 1917.[37]

This precise catalogue of controls and agencies shows how, bit by bit, government regulation was advanced first over one thing then over another to the point of virtual nationalization such that, on the basis of what was done to meet the war emergency, public ownership did not, by the end of hostilities, seem so *outré* that it could not appeal at least to the Sankey Commission then looking into coal-mining problems. Some other industries were in a similar situation. Shipping, for example, was so extremely regulated, and for obvious reasons, that by the beginning of 1917 practically all the mercantile fleet was under requisition and the Cabinet considered outright nationalization.[38] As well, the consequences of the shortage of shipping space indicate the cumulative nature of the development involved: it led in turn to the licensing of imports and this to the rationing of materials and food and so to the control of home production especially agriculture.

A final example of the extension of control, one drawn from a different but related aspect of affairs, is the wide delegation of lawmaking power that occurred during the years of the Great War. The initial Parliamentary legislation required on the outbreak of hostilities was slight, simply a pronouncement that His Majesty in Council had power to issue regulations for securing the public safety and the defence of the realm. When the Home Secretary submitted a brief Bill to the House of Commons for this purpose, he made a speech that takes up not much more than a couple of columns of Hansard broadly indicating the desirability of having some speedy way of dealing with such offences as

37 R. H. Tawney, *The British Labor Movement* (New Haven, Conn., 1925), pp. 69–70. Cf. Tawney's comments in S. J. Chapman (ed.), *Labour and Capital after the War* (London, 1918), p. 123.
38 PRO, CAB 23/1, 46 (12 and Appendices II, III), 26 January 1917; CAB 23/2, 121(13), 17 April 1917.

tapping wires or blowing up bridges.'[39] 'From this grain of mustard seed', commented Sir Cecil Carr, 'sprang a goodly forest of regulations.' And these, in time, went much beyond what was originally envisaged to embrace such matters as the acquisition of factories, the appropriation of materials, the control of food supply and production, the disposal of securities, the felling of timber, the taking over of industries, prohibiting the holding of dog-shows, the sale of opium, or the whistling for cabs in London – 'all in the name of the Defence of the Realm'.[40]

It was, of course, the expanding possibilities (indicated by the examples cited) that so worried many people at the outset and, in the end, even some who were ardent collectivists. For instance, Beatrice Webb wrote at the outbreak of war that it would mean 'an increase of corporate feeling and collective action in all directions'. And while she herself welcomed this sort of development she noted, a little while after, that there was to be detected in the country at large a notable fear of the growth in bureaucratic and militant tendencies that was afoot. By 1916 she was commenting on the possibly untoward implications of the extensive regulations that had been promulgated, the proposed introduction of conscription, control of the press, and the like. With all this, and more that was envisaged, the 'Servile State will have been established', she thought.[41] The following year Keynes recognized, too, how far the sphere of government control had been extended, 'far beyond what would have been believed possible' a short time before.[42] With little accurate information or previous experience and with few trained administrators, a system of 'war socialism' was thus created.[43]

Consider, in summary, the following official account of what had been done after three years of hostilities:

> In common with all belligerents, . . . this country has, since August, 1914, moved steadily along the road of an ever-extending State control of industry. . . . Section after section of industry was taken over, and in wages, prices and profits, from raw material to finished product, was placed under Government control. The process of extending State control, taking over more works and applying it to an always widening range of products continued unbroken right up to the end of

39 65 H.C. Deb. 5s., 7 August 1914, cols.2191–3.

40 C. T. Carr, *Delegated Legislation: Three Lectures* (Cambridge, 1921), p.18.

41 M. Cole (ed.), *Beatrice Webb's Diaries 1912–1924* (London, 1952), pp.29, 32, 52. Cf. the similar fear expressed by Harold Laski in 'The New Liberalism', *The Daily Herald* (21 November 1914) cited in J. Weeks, 'The Politics of Pluralism', *Bulletin of the Society for the Study of Labour History* (no.32, Spring 1976), p.61 n.7.

42 J. M. Keynes, *Collected Writings*, xvi.262, cited in R. Skidelsky, 'The Reception of the Keynesian Revolution', Milo Keynes (ed.), *Essays on John Maynard Keynes* (London, 1975), p.103.

43 A. J. P. Taylor, *English History, 1914–1945* (1965; Penguin, 1970), pp.99, 113.

1916 . . . . Industries essential to war needs had been taken under Government control, while industries serving the civil population were still left in private hands.

Then a further qualitative change occurred and 1917 itself was referred to as 'the year in which State control was extended until it covered not only national activities directly affecting the military effort but every section of industry – production, transport and manufacture.'[44] The result of this intensifying process – described euphemistically as strengthening 'the organic life of the community' – was catalogued as follows:

the vast majority of the people are now working directly or indirectly on public service. If they are not in the Army, the Navy or the Civil Service, they are growing food, or making munitions, or engaged in the work of organising, transporting or distributing the national supplies. On the other hand, the State has taken control for the period of the war over certain national industries, such as the railways, shipping, coal and iron mines, and the great majority of engineering businesses. It has also made itself responsible for the securing of adequate quantities of certain staple commodities and services, such as food, coal, timber and other raw materials, railroad and sea transportation, and for distributing the available supplies justly as between individual and individual in the national interest. The Government has further had to regulate prices and prevent profiteering. It has done so partly by controlling freights, fixing maximum prices to the home producer, and regulating wholesale and retail charges, and partly by its monopoly of imported supplies . . . . Thus the war, and especially the year 1917, has brought about a transformation of the social and administrative structure of the State, much of which is bound to be permanent.[45]

Indeed something of the collectivist wrack left by the tide of the Great War did remain; though not so much as many wished. Then there was the impact of the inter-war depression and the continuing growth of social services. So that when the second even greater conflict broke out, only two decades after the end of the first, it began at a higher·level altogether and proceeded much farther. The grip of government was not only tighter and more extensive but also applied sooner and more deliberately and systematically. In the early stages, there was some criticism about the lack of effective co-ordination and control of the

44 'Report for the Year 1917', The War Cabinet, 1918 (vol. xiv), Cd. 9005, p. 130.
45 ibid., pp. xv–xvi.

economy.[46] But the subsequent state of affairs is well symbolized by a single, extreme piece of legislation. On 21 May 1940, Neville Chamberlain presided over a Cabinet committee which, despite a certain hesitancy on the part of C. R. Attlee, agreed to the proposition that, in the emergency, all the resources of the community should be placed at the disposal of the state.[47] The War Cabinet agreed and, the following day, an Emergency Powers (Defence) Bill was passed through both Houses and enacted in that one day. It was sometimes referred to as the 'Everything and Everybody Act' for it extended the government's rule-making power to cover 'provision for requiring persons to place themselves, their services, and their property at the disposal of His Majesty' so far as appeared necessary or expedient for securing the public safety; and so on. In effect this statute gave to the government powers to take control of all persons and property in the country. For instance, with this authority labour could be directed to any task, industrial or military, thought necessary for the defence of the realm; hours and conditions of work could everywhere be prescribed; commercial and industrial establishments could be taken over or closed down. This Act was surely the most remarkable example in our history of the extent of the sovereignty of Parliament. Certainly it was also, as Sir Cecil Carr said, the high-water mark of the voluntary surrender of liberty: for, of course, this surge of power was assumed and a siege-economy created with the general consent of the realm. But the authority thus taken was nevertheless complete and was used to control a vast mass of people, resources, and opinions.[48] The very high degree of mobilization achieved in Britain during the Second World War has been well documented.[49] Retailing the extending activities of the government in the summer of 1940 Tawney told the American public:

> Powers are conferred on the Government amounting, in effect, to *carte blanche* to nationalise any industry and property if and when the national interest so requires. In ordinary circumstances the storm

46 P. Addison, *The Road to 1945: British Politics and the Second World War* (London, 1975), pp. 65–9, 73.
47 D. Dilks, 'The Twilight War and the Fall of France: Chamberlain and Churchill in 1940', *Trans. R. Hist. S.* 5s., xxviii (1978), p. 81.
48 For the Bill and its enactment, see *KCA* (1937–40), p. 4063A. Also C. K. Allen, *Law and Orders* (1945; 3rd edn, London, 1965), p. 53; and Sir C. Carr, *Concerning English Administrative Law* (New York, 1941), pp. 19–20. An excellent short account of the use of emergency powers (largely from the civil liberties viewpoint) is J. Eaves, *Emergency Powers and the Parliamentary Watchdog: Parliament and the Executive in Great Britain, 1939–51* (London, 1957).
49 For an early official survey, see *Statistics Relating to the War Effort of the United Kingdom*, 1943–4 (vol. viii), Cmd. 6564. And for a summary, there is A. J. P. Taylor's account of the 'siege economy', *English History, 1914–1945*, pp. 618–23.

raised would have been tremendous. Hardly a murmur is heard.

There is nothing very novel in war collectivism of this kind. What is striking is the rapidity with which . . . it is now being carried through.[50]

And one is reminded of the remark made after the war by Albert Speer (the German Minister for War Economy) that although Britain started behind Germany in using its resources for conflict it was, in the end, much more successful in this enterprise: 'You won because you made total war and we did not.' There seems little doubt that the economy of wartime Britain was subjected to a greater degree of state supervision than that of Nazi Germany.[51]

The kinds of control and influence were numerous: rationing, conscription and manpower budgeting, subsidies, price controls, allocation of raw materials, and so on. As the kind of progression involved has been fully exemplified in respect of the Great War, one further instance only (among many that might be given) must suffice as to the effect of the Second World War on the economic life of the nation and the development of government control. It relates to the growth in the work of the Ministry of Supply. This department was first set up in the summer of 1939 shortly before the outbreak of hostilities. When the Churchill Coalition government took office in May 1940, Harold Macmillan became Parliamentary Secretary and served a succession of Ministers until February 1942. In his memoirs he has given an impression of the expansion of the Supply Ministry's task. To deal with the provision of arms, equipment, and warlike stores it had, for example, to control the supply of scrap metal and other raw material, cope with the machine-tool problem, deal generally with difficulties about industrial capacity, establish priorities, schemes of allocation, and the like. The theme is summarized in the following passage:

As the war went on and the demands of production began to outstrip the productive capacity of the nation, even with the building and adaptation of factories, the mobilisation and purchase of tools, and the recruiting and training of labour, it was clear that some system of central planning must be devised to meet the conditions of a world where money was losing its importance and a price mechanism could no longer operate. The Government was becoming more and more the sole purchaser and it must find a method of regulating its own demands.[52]

50 R. H. Tawney, 'Why Britain Fights' (1940), in *The Attack and Other Papers* (London, 1953), p. 79.
51 Cited by S. H. Beer in B. Crick (ed.), *Essays on Reform, 1967: a Centenary Tribute* (London, 1967), p. 100. Cf. A. Harrison, *The Framework of Economic Activity. The International Economy and the Rise of the State in the Twentieth Century* (London, 1967), pp. 73–4.
52 H. Macmillan, *The Blast of War 1931–1945* (London, 1967), p. 96. Cf. ibid., ch. V *passim*, esp. pp. 87–95, 119–20.

Thus in the interests of efficient war production, it was sometimes necessary to install a government controller in place of the existing management of a factory or to use compulsory powers to acquire the equity of a firm.[53]

In 1930 G. B. Shaw wrote ironically of the fact (as he saw it) that a British government, under the pressures of the Great War and stimulated by a German bayonet at its throat, 'could perform with precipitous celerity and the most satisfactory success all the feats of national organization it had declared impossible and Utopian when they were pressed on it by nothing sharper than the arguments of the Fabians and the votes of the Socialists in the country'.[54] A *fortiori* this was true of the Second World War.

It all necessarily required new offices and agencies (sometimes called 'mushroom ministries'), the extension of the duties of existing departments, and the proliferation of machinery to co-ordinate the growing range of government functions. Asquith's intention at the beginning of the Great War, given that he (and many others) expected it to be of short duration, was to run affairs through the usual centre of the government machine with such few additions as might be necessary. But the inexorable pressures led to many and radical changes to produce a more vigorous and effective war directorate. In time, for instance, ten new ministries and 160 new boards and commissions came into existence.[55] And the early days of the Second World War saw the establishment of ministerial offices dealing with supply, economic warfare, information, home security, food, shipping, war production, town and country planning, and aircraft production. By March 1941 the War Cabinet alone had twelve principal committees dealing with such civil affairs as production, raw materials, industrial capacity, manpower, food policy, and export surpluses.[56] This was, of course, in addition to the military

53 ibid., p.115. On the Ministry of Supply, see also the detailed summary of one aspect of its work in O. Franks, *Central Planning and Control in War and Peace* (London, 1947), pp.9–15.

54 G. B. Shaw, 'Preface to the 1931 Reprint', *Fabian Essays* (1889; Jubilee edn, London, 1950), p.ix.

55 C. L. Mowat, *Britain Between the Wars, 1918–1940* (1955; London, 1968), p.28. There are detailed studies of many aspects of the machinery of control in the twenty-four volumes comprising the British series produced under the aegis of the Carnegie Endowment for International Peace. The best brief summary is in F. E. Lawley, *The Growth of Collective Economy* (London, 1938), i.33–78. For a succinct and recent account of the institutional changes, see P. Fraser, 'The Impact of the War of 1914–18 on the British Political System', in M. R. D. Foot (ed.), *War and Society: Historical Essays in Honour and Memory of J. R. Western 1928–1971* (London, 1973), pp.123–39.

56 Details in J. R. M. Butler, *Grand Strategy* (London, 1957), vol. ii (September 1939–June 1941), Appendix VII; S. S. Wilson, *The Cabinet Office to 1945*, PRO Handbook no. 17 (London, 1975), pp.103–9.

committees. As well, there was a massive creation of similar bodies at lower and departmental level.[57] And all this was naturally reflected in a great increase in the number of public employees, a graphic representation of which shows indeed the same pattern of wartime expansion as public expenditure. Figure 2 plots the growth in the number of non-industrial civil servants that has occurred in the first three-quarters of the present century. Of course, the broad upward tendency over the whole period is largely the result of the long-term increase in welfare, economic, and environmental services: this is observable before 1914, in the interwar years, and especially since the 1940s.[58] But the specific and enormous impact of the two world wars is also clearly visible. Nor, as is also obvious, has the collectivist advance induced by war ever substantially receded: 'what is learned in war is remembered when hostilities subside.'[59]

Figure 2 Numbers of non-industrial civil servants, 1914–77[60]

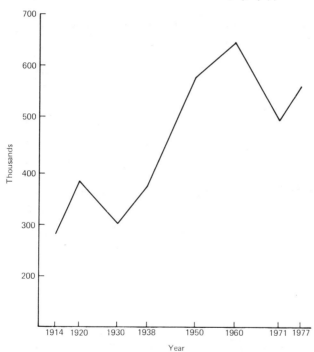

57 Something of the number and range of these bodies is indicated by the list in Wilson, op. cit., Annex 11, Part 3, pp. 220–39.
58 See also Table 3, p. 36 above.
59 M. Oakeshott, *On Human Conduct* (Oxford, 1975), p. 274.
60 Based on figures in D. Butler and A. Sloman, *British Political Facts 1900–1979*, 5th edn (London, 1980), p. 264. It is stressed (ibid., p. 263) that these statistics are not strictly commensurable and so must be used with great caution: but the overall tendencies are clear enough.

GOVERNMENT IN THE AFTERMATH OF WAR

War lays a burthen on the reeling state,
And peace does nothing to relieve the weight . . . .
W. COWPER, 'Expostulation', 1782, ll. 306–7, in *The Poems*, 1980, i. 305

Of course, with the coming of peace many offices will be abolished and
the level of government functions be substantially cut back.[61] Yet the
enduring impact of war on collectivist development is clearly indicated
because the reversion is never to the *status quo ante bellum*, departments
which have grown during the war inevitably wishing to quarter their
enlarged staffs on the public when peace returns.[62] This was clearly
recognized after the Great War in an official discussion of reconstruction
problems:

> During the war the entire field of production and distribution was
> more or less controlled by the State. Since the end of the war efforts
> have been made to relax these controls and demobilise the staffs as
> rapidly as possible. But there must be a certain permanent residuum of
> the policy necessitated by the exigencies of the war. . . .

Moreover 'the principles and methods of the public service' would
equally require 'fundamental reconsideration and readjustment . . . to
meet the new conditions created by the experience of the war.'[63] And
though the war collectivism of 1914–18 did not perhaps bite deeply in
any intellectual or emotional way, or at least sufficiently radically to
change social habits, it is the case that (as intimated in the previous section)
a substantial effect remained.[64] Figure 1 (p. 55) shows that although there
is at the end of hostilities a decline from the extreme heights of government expenditure reached during the war itself, this fall stops at a level
higher than that prevailing during the pre-war period. A substantial
residue of the increased wartime activity remains. This is instanced, too,
by the level of legislation which after 1945 never returned to that prevailing before the war.[65] This phenomenon has, in its important financial

---

61 For the abolition of offices and control after 1918, see C. L. Mowat, *Britain Between
the Wars, 1918–40* (1955; London, 1968), pp. 28–9.

62 The latter phrases derive from a Churchillian minute of 1943 concerning a proposal
for an enlarged intelligence service: see F. H. Hinsley *et al.*, *British Intelligence in the
Second World War: Its Influence on Strategy and Operations* (London, 1979 ff), ii. 16.

63 Ministry of Reconstruction, *The Business of Government II: the Work of the
Departments* (London, 1919), pp. 26–7; op. cit., *I: The Central Machinery*, p. 2.

64 On the vulnerability of wartime collectivism, see R. H. Tawney, 'The Abolition of
Economic Controls, 1918–1921', *Economic History Review*, xiii (1943), p. 7.

65 See Tables 5 and 6, pp. 40–1 above; also the comments of Sir Cecil Carr to the Select
Committee on Delegated Legislation, Minutes of Evidence, 1952–3 (vol. iv),
Cmd. 310-I, p. 20 qq. 91–2.

manifestation, been called the 'displacement effect'.[66] This appears to result from the operation of three factors. First, there is an obvious and continuing impact in respect of debt commitments, payment of war pensions, and the like. Secondly, there are the important fiscal effects of war concerning the level of taxation which is acceptable. And thirdly, there is a general loosening of restrictions hitherto imposed on government activity.

The first point requires no elaboration. So far as the second is concerned, it is manifest that during a war the tax base will be broadened and revenue expectations and possibilities increased. New types of tax are introduced and everyone gets used to a higher level of payment than was previously thought possible or desirable. In the week of Dunkirk the rate of duty on excess war profits was raised from 60 to 100 per cent, a step made both feasible and necessary by the new political climate.[67] But the classic example is, of course, income tax. Originally introduced as a merely temporary impost during the wars against Napoleonic France, it none the less became a regular part of the tax system by the mid-nineteenth century; and since 1916 it has been the most important single source of government revenue.[68] In 1902 the Chancellor of the Exchequer was most concerned that income tax would possibly have to remain at 1s.2d in the £; yet by 1919 it had risen to 6s.0d.[69] And the connexion between income tax and the extension of the peacetime, welfare functions of the state is indicated by an observation made by Shaw. He was, he wrote to Henry Salt, an enthusiastic supporter of the Boer War because it had shaken the country out of its mercenary commercial preoccupations: it had, he said, 'put 4d on the income tax . . . so that old age pensions will be within reach' in the not too distant future.[70] Similarly purchase tax was introduced in October 1940 with the object (restriction of spending apart) of tapping a new source of revenue to help in financing the war: it has (in one form or another) been with us ever since. Again a post-1945 Budget has involved a tax burden that would have been unthinkable to a pre-war electorate or government. But the social disturbance caused by the Second World War had created a

---

66 In A. T. Peacock and J. Wiseman, *The Growth of Public Expenditure in the United Kingdom* (1961; new edn, London, 1967), *passim* esp. p.xxxiv.

67 P. Addison, *The Road to 1945: British Politics and the Second World War* (London, 1975), p.116.

68 See the table of the main sources of government revenue in D. Butler and A. Sloman, *British Political Facts 1900–1979*, 5th edn (London, 1980), pp.354–5 (though the significance of customs and excise duties has increased substantially since the 1940s).

69 ibid., p.348; J. L. Garvin and J. Amery, *The Life of Joseph Chamberlain* (London, 1932–69), iv.395–6.

70 Cited in A. Fremantle, *This Little Band of Prophets: the British Fabians* (1959; Mentor, 1960), p.146.

new set of norms which were broadly accepted by all citizens and parties. It is these changed fiscal anticipations which, without necessarily any proportionate increase of productivity, make feasible the higher rate of public expenditure involved by a surge of increased government action.[71] Speaking in 1943 in support of his report on social insurance, Sir William Beveridge, with respect to the cost of his proposals, said it meant simply that present taxes would to that extent be lowered less when war spending stops.[72] Further, the impact of war in this way has to be seen against the background of long-term changes in attitudes towards the public finances. The old idea of retrenchment and the saving of candle-ends, the traditional canons of so-called 'Gladstonian' finance, have been replaced by different concepts which demonstrate a lesser degree of practical stringency and which accept the positive economic value of government spending.[73]

This increased revenue potential combines with the prospect that wartime conditions permit an easy relaxation of limits previously imposed on government action; and both relate to the growing confidence in the efficacy of state intervention that success in war produces. This constitutes the nub of the third point relating to the loosening of restrictions imposed on the public sphere. Various factors are at work here.

It is the case that the pressures and strains of war will not simply draw attention to deficiencies in the social order but also create circumstances in which the public will demand a remedy through official action. Tawney expressed the attitude of the social reformer when he wrote in 1918 that the Great War did not create the problems which had to be dealt with but was rather 'the lightning which revealed them', a phenomenon which Peacock and Wiseman have appropriately called the 'inspection effect'.[74] A specific instance will indicate the process at work. The medical examination of recruits will obviously provide useful information about the state of health of many of the nation's young men, especially those coming from the growing urban areas where conditions of living so often left much to be desired. Even during the Crimean War concern was aroused about the physical fitness and illiteracy of those coming forward.[75] But a major crisis of confidence in this regard was precipitated by the experience of the second Anglo-Boer War which brought to light

---

71 On the psychological effect of the vast wartime expenditures, cf. E. Bridges, *Treasury Control* (London, 1950), p. 9.

72 Cited in 'Celticus' [A. Bevan], *Why Not Trust the Tories?* (London, 1944), p. 44.

73 Some aspects of these changes of attitude are reviewed in vol. iii, *A Much-Governed Nation*, ch. 4.

74 R. H. Tawney, 'The Conditions of Economic Liberty' (1918), in *The Radical Tradition* (1964; Penguin, 1966), p. 102; Peacock and Wiseman, op. cit., p. xxxiv.

75 O. Anderson, *A Liberal State at War: English Politics and Economics during the Crimean War* (London, 1967), p. 179.

the appallingly low standard of many of the men flocking to the colours. Of 11,000 examined for the army in 1899 in Manchester (admittedly the worst area) 8000 were rejected at once and only 1200 were found to be completely fit and this despite a lowering of standards. An inquiry set up as a result of the ensuing public furore also revealed that in the whole decade prior to 1902 nearly 35 per cent of volunteers were rejected on medical examination in addition to the further unknown, but very large, number not even considered worth this inspection. The inter-departmental committee established to investigate the causes of this 'physical deterioration' in the male population attributed it to such factors as bad housing conditions and the underfeeding of school-children.[76] And these revelations helped to create the climate of public opinion in which provision for the housing of the working classes was enhanced and arrangements made, by an order of 1905, for the Poor Law Guardians to feed necessitous schoolchildren. In fact, in regard to the latter improvement, the Guardians proved unable to cope so, under Labour pressure, the Liberal government of the day passed an Act allowing other local authorities to take on the task. This was followed in 1907 by a statute authorizing school medical inspection designed to prevent detectable incapacity as early as possible. Though only permissive, these measures were, in fact, quite important as marking a new beginning in British social legislation for they signalled that the state was intervening in matters previously considered to be primarily the responsibility of the family. Nor did the matter end there. Experience during the Great War was similarly taken to show an appalling record of public health as witnessed, for instance, by the facts that only three out of nine men medically examined for military service were held to be perfectly fit and that certain communities and classes of people were particularly deprived.[77] By 1939 there had, of course, been a considerable improvement in this regard. But cognate problems were disclosed. For example, the condition of health and education of evacuated schoolchildren similarly seemed to indicate the problems of poverty that existed in the great cities and to call for raised standards of social service.[78] Neville

76 'Physical Unfitness of Men Offering Themselves for Enlistment in the Army', Memorandum, 1903 (vol. xxxviii), Cd. 1501, pp. 5–6; 'Physical Deterioration', Inter-departmental Committee Report, 1904 (vol. xxxii), Cd. 2175, Part II.

77 C. L. Mowat, *Britain Between the Wars, 1918–1940* (1955; London, 1968), p. 512. And for detailed, critical discussion of the data, see J. M. Winter, 'Military Fitness and Civilian Health in Britain during the First World War', *Journal of Contemporary History*, xv (1980), pp. 211–44.

78 Mowat, op. cit., pp. 512–13; R. A. Butler, *The Art of the Possible* (London, 1971), p. 92; A. Marwick, *Britain in the Century of Total War: War, Peace and Social Change, 1900–1967* (1968; Penguin, 1970), pp. 266–8. See also R. M. Titmuss, *Problems of Social Policy* (London, 1950), pp. 101–36, 142–82, and his 'War and Social Policy', in *Essays on 'The Welfare State'* (London, 1958), ch. 4.

Chamberlain, who as Minister of Health had done substantial work in the welfare field, nevertheless confessed in a private letter written in 1939 that evacuation had revealed conditions such as he never knew existed, and he added, 'I feel ashamed of having been so ignorant of my neighbours. For the rest of my life I mean to try to make amends by helping such people to live cleaner and healthier lives'.[79] Certainly the wartime innovations, such as the large-scale emergency health measures, provided a basis for later peacetime growth in this field of welfare provision not least because the war had revealed the maldistribution of medical services that existed. There was substantial recognition that the war would (as Anthony Eden put it) 'bring about changes which may be fundamental and revolutionary in the economic and social life of this country.' And Robert Boothby wrote to George in 1939 that 'You cannot hope to go through a world convulsion of this magnitude without fundamental changes in the social as well as the economic structure'.[80] Necessarily the government 'stepped in to plug the worst gaps in the services that the war caused or revealed'.[81] It is, of course, no accident that educational planning and advance have so often coincided with war as with the major statutes of 1902, 1918, and 1944; nor that a large surge of council house building occurred after both world wars.

Further, as Henry James remarked somewhere, any substantial invasion of our usual routine of life accustoms us to the vital habit of breaking habits. And war certainly produces a period of major ferment in social conditions and ideas and creates a new environment of opinion and expectations.[82] J. L. Hammond the historian, who served in the army during the Great War, put this point in a paper he published in 1919: 'The soldier who returns has broken through the strongest force in our nature, the customary standard, the habit of accepting the world as he finds it . . . . This is a new moral force in our society: the presence of a great mass of men, conscious of sacrifices and services, who look at the world with new

79 Neville to Hilda Chamberlain (17 September 1939), Chamberlain Papers, in Addison, op. cit., p. 72.
80 A. Eden, *Freedom and Order: Selected Speeches 1939–1946* (London, 1947), p. 48; Boothby, memorandum on war aims (7 November 1939), in Lloyd George Papers, LG G/3/13. Both in Addison, op. cit., p. 72. Cf. R. A. Butler, *The Art of the Possible*, p. 91.
81 S. Fergusson and H. Fitzgerald, *Studies in the Social Services* (London, 1954), p. 8.
82 The story of the impact of modern war on political ideas and doctrines in Britain has been too much neglected. Olive Anderson's *A Liberal State at War* is a crucial pioneering study; and J. M. Winter's recent work, although deliberately restricted to a consideration of Socialism, is also valuable in this respect: *Socialism and the Challenge of War: Ideas and Politics in Britain 1912–18* (London, 1974), esp. ch. 9. P. Addison's *The Road to 1945* is vital on the Second World War.

eyes.'[83] But, of course, only government can meet the new demands and this by the continuation, appropriately modified or extended, of the administrative machine and policies created for the purposes of war. In this way the system of price-fixing and regulation that had been built up during the war impressed many politicians and men of affairs who recommended its continuance after the armistice.[84] Similarly, the establishment of a wartime nutrition policy confirmed the idea of minimum standards of food consumption necessary to the national health. And because a modern war has to be fought on a basis of social unity, its conduct demands policies involving a sense of co-operation between different classes. The general restriction of personal expenditure and the specific imposition of rationing, the redistribution of income (through increased progressive taxation and the course of inflation) together with the classless sacrifice of combat all help to create a climate of increased social equality that it is difficult not to extrapolate into the post-war era. A. E. Zimmern wrote in 1918 that 'Men who have breathed the larger air of common sacrifice are reluctant to return to the stuffy air of self-seeking.'[85] Another mark of the same social tendency was the way in which the officers of the British Expeditionary Force had, by the end of the war, ceased to be a socially exclusive group.[86] Equally (and as already intimated) the war tends to eliminate thoughts of cost, a state of affairs symbolized by the diminished role of the Treasury in government and the relaxation of normal limits on spending. If tanks and bombers can be produced in many respects regardless of expense, why should not this later be the case with schools, hospitals, and houses? Certain groups (women, for instance) emerge to new political and economic significance and establish demands of their own. The co-operation of trade unions has to be sought in the abatement of traditional industrial practices that seem to stand in the way of an intensified war effort. The price is a fairer distribution of the nation's wealth as well as specific concessions such as the creation, under government aegis, of more effective machinery for consultation, bargaining, and conciliation, the establishment of minimum standards of amenity, and the like. Thus the shop steward

83 J. L. Hammond, 'The War and the Mind of Great Britain', *Atlantic Monthly*, cxxiii (March 1919), p. 356, in Winter, op. cit., pp. 180–1 n. 38. For Tawney's similar view, see *The Radical Tradition*, pp. 103–4.
84 E. M. H. Lloyd, *Stabilisation: an Economic Policy for Producers & Consumers* (London, 1923), pp. 25–6.
85 A. E. Zimmern, *Nationality & Government with other War-time Essays* (London, 1918), p. 245.
86 See J. Keegan, *The Face of Battle* (London, 1976), pp. 272–3. A fictional (and semi-autobiographical) account of one lower-middle-class 'temporary gentleman' is graphically provided in the fascinating volumes of Henry Williamson's *A Chronicle of Ancient Sunlight*.

movement and the establishment of Whitley Councils date from the Great War; just as the acceptance by government of a peacetime commitment to full employment and a more or less comprehensive system of social insurance grew (somewhat haphazardly perhaps) out of the Second World War.[87] The war effort itself nowadays requires (as a means of bolstering the morale of the armed forces and civilians alike) a concern with war aims such as plans for post-war social reconstruction, a better world for heroes to live in, 'fit to fight, fit to vote', and so on. And this envisages not simply the undoing of the chaos created by hostilities or the restoration of the pre-war situation but of building positively a new social order. In one of his broadcasts in 1940, J. B. Priestley emphasized the point that the huge collective effort demanded by the war 'is compelling us to change not only our ordinary, social and economic habits, but also our habits of thought'. And he went on to specify that, in particular, a sense of community was growing that would serve not only as a defence against Nazi aggression but also as a means to guide us to a better world.[88]

In an essay which Halévy wrote in 1922, he described his impression of the effect of wartime developments on opinion about how the economy should be run in peacetime:

> When peace came, the state was monopolizing the nation's commerce; it decided what exports and what imports could be allowed; it restricted civilian consumption; it operated all the coal mines; it ran all the railways and the entire merchant fleet; it manufactured munitions and controlled all the industries that affected the conduct of the war in any degree. Was this admirable work of organization by which victory had been won to be abruptly broken off? Because there was peace, was that a reason to return to the old anarchy? The workers did not think so, nor did the intellectuals. And the Prime Minister . . . seemed . . . to have intended . . . to prolong that formidable *étatisme* of war on which victory had just conferred so much prestige.[89]

Or again, as E. M. H. Lloyd wrote in 1924, the main effect of the Great War was to stimulate the transformation of the old economic system into one that was more efficient and less wasteful. Having admitted to a

---

87 Dr J. Harris has shown the rather indirect way in which the Coalition government came to accept these policies; see her 'Social Planning in War-time: Some Aspects of the Beveridge Report', in J. M. Winter (ed.), *War and Economic Development* (Cambridge, 1975), ch. 11.

88 J. B. Priestley, *Postscripts* (London, 1940), p. 38, in Addison, op. cit., p. 118.

89 'The Present State of the Social Question in England', in *The Era of Tyrannies: Essays on Socialism and War* (1938; trans., London, 1967), pp. 141–2. Cf. ibid., pp. 192–3 and J. M. Keynes, *The End of Laissez-Faire* (London, 1926), p. 35. For one such intellectual response, see H. J. Laski, *The Foundations of Sovereignty and Other Essays* (London, 1921), pp. 99–100.

prejudice in favour of 'personal freedom and private property', he nevertheless went on to say:

> I am disinclined to admit that *all* the measures of industrial and commercial organization adopted during the war, which are commonly lumped together under the term State control, were merely necessary evils to be got rid of as soon as possible and never to be thought about again. A considerable extension of co-operative and collective enterprise seems to me probable and desirable in times of peace; and I believe there is something to be learnt from the experiments in State control during the war which may be of positive value in the difficult times ahead.[90]

Of course, this lesson or tendency of belief had a special effect on the Labour Party. This had been before 1914 little more than an extended Parliamentary Committee of the TUC. But during and after 1914–18 its position changed in the manner described by Halévy. The state had come to control directly or indirectly a great part of the economic process; the enormous wealth and taxable capacity of modern industrial society now stood revealed. Why should these possibilities not be exploited to abolish poverty? The wartime extension of state regulation of economic activity seemed to suggest that for crucial purposes public ownership or supervision was more effective than unalloyed capitalism: witness the letters published in *The Times* in 1916 which spoke of the need for a 'systematic national plan' in peacetime.[91] It was in such a context that, at one of its 1918 Conferences, the party formally and for the first time committed itself firmly to the Socialist goal of public ownership of the means of production, distribution, and exchange.[92] Similarly on a previous occasion, W. F. Purdy, giving the chairman's opening address, said that if, 'during the War and in the national interest it has been found necessary to control the railways, canals, mines, shipping, shipyards, etc., then after the War the Labour Party must insist on their being owned and controlled for the people as a whole.'[93] The general view was that in the steps taken to wage effective war there lay the vindication of

90 E. M. H. Lloyd, *Experiments in State Control at the War Office and the Ministry of Food* (Oxford, 1924), p. xi. Cf. ibid., pp. 5, 387, and ch. xxx *passim*. See also another contemporary assertion of the need to maintain and advance the sense of community and collective effort created by the war in V. Branford and P. Geddes, *Our Social Inheritance* (London, 1919), p. xiv.

91 *The Times* (June–July 1916). Written by H. G. Wells, these letters were republished as *The Elements of Reconstruction* (London, 1916): the phrase cited in the text is at p. 27. Cf. L. Dickson, *H. G. Wells: His Turbulent Life and Times* (1969; Penguin, 1972), p. 318.

92 See e.g. the debate on social and economic reconstruction, Labour Party, *Report of the Eighteenth Annual Conference* (London, 1918), pp. 42ff.

93 Labour Party, *Report of the [Seventeenth] Annual Conference* (London, 1918), p. 97.

Socialism. Harold Laski noted in 1925, *vis-à-vis* public intervention in economic affairs, that 'the record of war-control of industry in the period from 1914 to 1918' provided a mass of detailed experience and material about 'the necessary mechanisms of regulation'; and, a little later, he added that the English working class 'learned in the years of war what organization can effect for a declared objective; and it does not see why the effort should be different in terms of peace.' He continually reiterated these themes, too, during and after the Second World War in such tracts as *Where Do We Go From Here?* (1940) and *Reflections on the Revolution of our Time* (1943).[94] Herbert Morrison likewise, in a major speech made after joining the War Cabinet in 1942, said that 'much of the social control of production which we have learnt to accept and to value during the war will need to be continued during the peace'.[95] And as things turned out he was able to see that it did.

But such reactions and sentiments were by no means confined to Socialist or Labour circles. From other quarters, too, there were a number of expressions during the Great War of the belief that the days of limited government were numbered and that in existing conditions the idea was 'a dangerous guide'.[96] One instance of the interventionist kind of thinking by both Liberals and Conservatives was the proposals, canvassed in 1918–19, to revitalize British transport in the post-war period and which entailed its reorganization into a single system under state supervision. As it happened this particular scheme foundered but it revealed how far some industrialists like Sir Eric Geddes and their political associates such as D. L. George were themselves prepared to go in peacetime in the direction of state control to achieve efficiency and 'rationalization'.[97] *A fortiori* this was the kind of idea common during the Second World War and on that occasion more effectively carried through: in the outcome a great deal of the machinery of wartime control was simply continued after the end of the war or became the basis for subsequent nationalization proposals. Reflecting on this, the Liberal, Sir William Beveridge, wrote in 1942 (with specific respect to the abolition of the 'Giant Idleness' and the maintenance of full employment):

94 H. J. Laski, *A Grammar of Politics* (1925; 5th edn, London, 1948), pp. 489–90; 'England in 1929', *The Yale Review*, xviii (1928–9), p. 433. Cf. a very similar passage about the Second World War in *Reflections on the Revolution of our Time* (London, 1943), pp. 148, 163, 168–9; and cf. *Will Planning Restrict Freedom?* (Cheam, n.d. [1944]), p. 1: 'it is ... obvious that our society must plan the use of its resources in peace not less than in war.'

95 H. Morrison, *Prospects and Policies* (Cambridge, 1943), pp. 8–9.

96 Cf. W. H. Dawson (ed.), *After-War Problems* (London, 1917), esp. pp. 10, 119–20; W. C. Dampier Whetham, *The War and the Nation: a Study in Constructive Politics* (London, 1917), pp. v, 9–10, 16–36.

97 See the account by P. K. Cline, 'Eric Geddes and the "Experiment" with Businessmen in Government, 1915–22', in K. D. Brown (ed.), *Essays in Anti-Labour History: Responses to the Rise of Labour in Britain* (London, 1974), esp. pp. 90–3, 103–4.

In times of total war adjustment of resources to needs is carried out by complete state planning. Shall the aftermath of this war be treated by the former methods of peace or by the methods of war? On the face of it, the experience of 1920–39 suggests that the former methods of peace are unlikely to accomplish the object in view with even tolerable success. . . .

It followed, he concluded, that the 'maintenance of productive employment after the war' would depend substantially if not entirely on a system of 'national planning' and control like that developed for the purposes of war.[98]

In this regard the wartime coalition was probably the most radical reforming administration since the Liberal governments of the years before 1914. By 1943 there had been introduced a scheme of social security for all, family allowances, and a universal and free health service; educational changes were in view as was a commitment to full employment, to closer relations between government and industry, and to Keynesian budgetary techniques; wholesale town and country planning was envisaged; and so forth. One official history put the general point this way:

> There existed, so to speak, an implied contract between Government and people; the people refused none of the sacrifices that the Government demanded from them for the winning of the war; in return, they expected that the Government should show imagination and seriousness in preparing for the restoration and improvement of the nation's well-being when the war had been won. The plans for reconstruction were, therefore, a real part of the war effort.[99]

Certainly, too, by 1945 public opinion (as revealed in the polls of the day) approved of the general direction by the state of the transition from war to peace.[100] All parties entered the election in 1945 committed to principles of social and economic reconstruction which had been endorsed and initiated by the Grand Coalition.[101] The Labour Party proved to be the favoured legatee; and, as Aneurin Bevan wrote with reference to one specific aspect of this bequest, the government of 1945 'inherited from the war a system of war-time controls and disciplines which could not have been realised in normal conditions without

---

98 W. Beveridge, 'Reconstruction Problems: Five Giants on the Road', revised draft (25 June 1942), Beveridge Papers, VIII.45, in J. Harris, *William Beveridge: a Biography* (Oxford, 1977), pp. 432–3.
99 W. K. Hancock and M. M. Gowing, *British War Economy* (London, 1949), p. 541.
100 Addison, op. cit., p. 264.
101 ibid., p. 14.

something approaching a revolution.'[102] Not, of course, that everyone was sanguine about all this. Bevan's fellow Welshman, the nationalist Saunders Lewis, warned in the early 1940s of the way in which 'war and the demands of war' had firmly enthroned in Britain what he called Nazism, that is, a system of state planning and control, and of the danger or even inevitability of this becoming the permanent basis of society after the end of hostilities not least in order to meet the economic and social problems that would arise.[103] But this was a minority, and an extremist, opinion. At the crucial official level, it is clear that in 'determining the constitutional framework of the Welfare State, the improvisations made to conduct the war were almost more important than the reconstruction policies themselves or the Labour party's programme.'[104] The civil servants of the day tended to be very dubious about such slogans as those concerned to urge that enterprise should be set free and controls abolished; rather the official view was that the national interest demanded imperatively the continuance of at least some degree of regulation to deal with shortages, to try to iron out fluctuations of trade, and to promote industrial rationalization and efficiency.[105] The wartime inquiry into the machinery of government was indeed a vital element in adjusting the administrative machinery to the intense level of activity which would be required to face the problems of post-war reconstruction.[106]

In general, then, the two world wars – really a single struggle broken by a truce – in which Britain has been so closely involved in this century have (in these ways) stimulated the development of collectivism and conditioned many people to believe that planned effort under government control, extending supervision on a broad scale, is required for the achievement of national goals and social justice: 'As the war was managed, so would the peace be achieved.'[107] Perhaps paradoxically, war may be the real paradigm of the welfare state and managed economy of peacetime.

It remains only to mention what might be called the 'preparation effect'. If war thus conditions the peacetime which follows it, anticip-

---

102 A. Bevan, *In Place of Fear* (London, 1952), p. 10. Cf. M. Foot, *Aneurin Bevan: a Biography* (London, 1962–73), ii. 18–19.

103 S. Lewis, *Wales after the War* (1941–2; n.p. [Caernarvon], n.d. [1945?]), pp. 3, 12–13.

104 J. M. Lee, *Reviewing the Machinery of Government: 1942–1952. An Essay on the Anderson Committee and its Successors* (n.p. [London], 1977), p. 149. Cf. ibid., pp. 1, 3, 83 on the lessons and consequences of the war in this respect.

105 PRO, PREM 4 88/2, a series of letters and memoranda on controls and their peacetime function: see esp. pp. 356ff.

106 Lee, op. cit., pp. 139, 143.

107 ibid., p. 7.

ation of its coming and provision for its conduct can mould, in a very substantial way, the period that precedes its formal outbreak and constitute, therefore, a powerful reinforcement of the secular collectivist trend. Hobbes was referred to at the beginning of this chapter and may appropriately help to conclude it: for he appositely remarked that war 'consisteth not in Battell onely, or the act of fighting . . . but in the known disposition thereto'.[108]

108 Hobbes, *Leviathan*, I. xiii.

3
ECONOMIC AND SOCIAL ASPECTS

It is economic and social forces . . . which are most influential in
determining the practical operation of political institutions, and it is
economic and social relations that create the most urgent of the internal
problems confronting industrial communities.
R. H. TAWNEY, *Equality*, 1931; 4th edn, 1964, p.78

INDUSTRIAL TRANSFORMATION

In the modern nations of Europe there is one great cause . . . which
constantly aids the growth of government activity and extends its
prerogatives, . . . the development of industry . . . .
A. de TOCQUEVILLE, *Democracy in America*, 1835–40; Fontana, 1968, ii.888

AS ALREADY intimated by the primacy attached in this survey to the
impact of modern war, Professor Tawney's remark (cited as general
epigraph to this chapter) may not be wholly true. Nevertheless the march
of collectivism has undoubtedly been most powerfully stimulated by the
sort of factors he had in mind including some of the most obvious and
certainly not the least significant features of recent times: the development of industry and the relative decline of agriculture; the increase of
population and the urban growth that accompanied it; and the social and
environmental consequences attendant on the movement of this jug-
gernaut car of modern history. The implications of these and cognate
matters as they bear on the question of government intervention will be
considered in this chapter; and certainly, unless one is familiar with the
framework of economic and social history involved, it is hardly possible
effectively to understand the present position and why and how it has
developed. De Tocqueville, acutely perceptive in this as in so much else
that was afoot in his day, outlined the main theme in a passage an initial
fragment of which is cited at the head of this section. He continues:

Industry generally brings together a multitude of men in the same
place and creates new and complex relations among them. These men
are exposed to sudden great alternations of plenty and want, which
threaten public peace. Work of this sort may endanger the health, even
the life, of those who make money out of it or who are employed

therein. Therefore the industrial classes, more than other classes, need rules, supervision, and restraint, and it naturally follows that the functions of government multiply as they multiply.[1]

Britain is a small country but was the first to experience in a nation-wide way the full and rapid effects of industrialization. Of course, even in the so-called pre-industrial period there were already important and often well-established pockets of manufacturing activity in some places, as with the cloth production of the West Riding of Yorkshire or the collieries and iron furnaces of South Wales; and as well quite a number of people were occupied with foreign trade and the provision of services. There was, too, a substantial capital stock which proved adequate for the early stages of expansion and, for the time, an advanced technology which equally helped to make growth possible. It is none the less true that in the late eighteenth century the population, which was then something under ten million, was still substantially rural, the basis of the world's leading agricultural output, and that the domestic workshop continued to be the most common unit of industrial production. A hundred years later it was all quite different. There were nearly four times as many inhabitants largely concentrated in the growing towns and, as Dr Kitson Clark said, this demographic development by itself would have ensured that Victorian Britain was 'decisively different' from its Georgian predecessor: it was indeed 'one of the most startling facts' in our history and most likely the trigger which set off and the force which then sustained the process of industrial growth.[2] The area of arable land had fallen substantially; there had been a considerable rise in the size, complexity, and variety of industrial production; new machines and processes had appeared in profusion; improved communications made the movement of people and goods cheap and swift; and it all happened relatively quickly in this quite small area. Something of the scale of things involved may be gleaned from a few statistical generalizations.[3] During the nineteenth century the density of population more than trebled; between 1800 and the early 1870s textile output went up by fourteen times; coal production increased tenfold in the same period and then more than doubled in the next forty years; pig-iron output grew by a factor of nearly thirty between the end of the Napoleonic Wars and the eve of the Great War; and if by mid-century there were over 6000 miles of railway, sixty years later the total had risen to more than 23,000.

1 A. de Tocqueville, *Democracy in America* (1835–40; Fontana, 1968), ii. 888.
2 G. K. Clark, *The Making of Victorian England* (1962; London, 1968), pp. 65–6.
3 These are based on data in S. Pollard and D. W. Crossley, *The Wealth of Britain, 1085–1966* (London, 1968), p. 191; and in B. R. Mitchell and P. Deane, *Abstract of British Historical Statistics* (1962; Cambridge, 1971), *passim*.

Industrial production as a whole may have grown fourteenfold during the century.

It is hardly necessary and would not be appropriate here to describe in any detail this process of demographic and industrial expansion or to explore the question of its precise origins and form. But its impact altered the face of the land and closely affected the condition of the people working in the new factories and living in the mushrooming towns. Three contemporary comments on these changes must suffice as evidence of the transformation under way and of the impression it created. The first is the verses about 'the Manufacturing spirit' in Wordsworth's *The Excursion*, a long narrative poem which appeared in 1814. 'I have lived to mark', says the Wanderer, a 'new and unforeseen creation rise from out the labours of a peaceful Land'. The subsequent description, whether hyperbolical or not, is both succinct and vivid:

> . . . at Social Industry's command,
> How quick, how vast an increase! From the germ
> Of some poor hamlet, rapidly produced
> Here a huge town, continuous and compact,
> Hiding the face of earth for leagues – and there,
> Where not a habitation stood before,
> Abodes of men irregularly massed
> Like trees in forests, – spread through spacious tracts,
> O'er which the smoke of unremitting fires
> Hangs permanent, and plentiful as wreaths
> Of vapour glittering in the morning sun.
> And wheresoe'er the traveller turns his steps,
> He sees the barren wilderness erased,
> Or disappearing; . . . .

In an interesting note on these passages Wordsworth declared he was reacting against the optimism then prevalent about the potential influence of these industrial tendencies. Truth, he said, compelled him to dwell rather on 'the baneful effects arising out of an ill-regulated and excessive application of powers so admirable in themselves'.[4] The invitation to control the forces thus unleashed is clear and intimates the collectivist developments which were to follow. The second observation of these changes dates from the same period but is, I imagine, little known. The source is a history and description of South Wales published not long after the end of the Napoleonic Wars. Of Abercraf, in the upper Swansea Valley, it is said that since the opening of the canal connecting the area with the sea the aspect and character of the vicinity has 'greatly

---

4 W. Wordsworth, *The Excursion*, VIII. 89–91, 117–30; *The Poetical Works* (Oxford, 1964), p. 733, note to p. 682.

changed'. The 'stillness of rural life, which within the last twenty years reigned over the whole district, has been succeeded by the bustle of mining, manufacturing, and commercial activity'; and, the author continues, the consequence of this alteration 'has been an increase of population, and the deterioration of manners, which forms the bane of all manufacturing districts'.[5] The last comment to be cited is later and is interesting because of its source. It is an uncharacteristically sentimental, not to say nostalgic, passage from Herbert Spencer's autobiography which he began to write in the mid-1870s and in which he recalls the house in Derby where he passed his boyhood (he was born in 1820):

> At that time its neighbourhood differed widely from that now existing. It was one of a newly-built row . . . . Opposite was a large unoccupied space over which the town was seen; and behind stretched fields, instead of the streets and detached villas which now cover the surface. Not only the immediate surroundings are transformed, but also the region further away, where my boyish excursions were made, has had its rural beauty changed into the ugliness of a manufacturing suburb. Places where I gathered flowers and gazed with interest at the catkins of the hazel, have now become places covered with iron-works, where steam-hammers make their perpetual thuds, and through which railway-sidings everywhere ramify. Quiet lanes in which, during early boyhood, I went with a companion trying to catch minnows with a hand-net in a clear little stream running by the hedge, have been transformed into straight roads between land-allotments, with scattered houses built by artizans. And where I picked blackberries, factories now stand.[6]

There are indeed many other places in the literature and commentary of modern times in which accounts occur of how fringes and pockets of industrial life crept out across a rural landscape and finally engulfed a great part of it, a process encapsulated in Ivor Gurney's line, 'Villas are set up where sheepfolds were'.[7]

This could not occur without cost and unhappiness, the Industrial Revolution's 'Burden of Evil' as it was once called.[8] But, as well, great wealth was produced and this country became richer than ever before. It has been estimated that gross national income at current prices more

5 T. Rees, *A Topographical and Historical Description of South Wales* (London, n.d. [1815]), p.180. For a better known and somewhat later comment on South Wales, see Carlyle's description of the transformation of Merthyr Tydfil written in 1850, in J. A. Froude, *Thomas Carlyle: a History of his Life in London, 1834–1881* (1884; London, 1897), ii.54–5.
6 H. Spencer, *An Autobiography* (London, 1904), i.70.
7 I. Gurney, 'Changes', *TLS* (13 October 1978), p.1136.
8 V. Branford and P. Geddes, *Our Social Inheritance* (London, 1919), p.xxv.

than doubled between 1801 and 1851 and then trebled again over the next fifty years; and, too, that average real wages also increased during the latter period by as much as 80 per cent and this, it must be remembered, in respect of a growing population.[9] But these are matters of controversy among those learned in the arcana of economic history (both old and new) and the layman ventures on the field with trepidation. It used to be the fashion in the style of Toynbee the Elder and the Hammonds to bewail the awfulness and depravity of what happened; and those of the pessimistic school (usually also of radical political persuasion) still put their feet in the steps of these moralizing forefathers where they feel they can neither wander nor stumble. Others, more adventuresome or sanguine in nature perhaps, while not denying the hardship and suffering involved for many people and admitting, too, some shift in the distribution of the national income away from wages, feel there has been a tendency to exaggerate the untoward features of the period and a failure properly to recognize the improvements and advances achieved as compared with the often abysmal and stagnating conditions of life that prevailed before industrialization. Having in some idle moments pondered these bitter and ardent quarrels – from Hobsbawm to Hartwell as it were – my own tentative impression (though it may be, who knows, no more than wicked prejudice having its way) is that the meliorists have it, at least so far. Consequently I would want to say, in summary, that the great change brought enormous material and other advantages such that a buoyant secular trend was established for many decades. As well, I cannot see that every evil which aroused the humanitarian spirit of the day is simply to be laid at the door of the factory system and the introduction of power-driven machines. And it is clear beyond doubt that the woeful predictions of cumulative working-class misery that were so often paraded were not borne out. It may have taken a long time for the benefits of industrial growth to seep through the various layers of society and to reach the poor in the worst urban and rural slums. Even so, Sir John Clapham's verdict appears to be sane and just: that some recent historians have 'stressed the worsenings and slurred over or ignored the betterings'.[10]

Yet the frictions of change were bound to be considerable and to be

9 Mitchell and Deane, op. cit., pp. 343–4, 366; and see e.g. the substantial body of recent literature cited by N. McKendrick, 'Home Demand and Economic Growth' in the symposium he edited, *Historical Perspectives: Studies in English Thought and Society* (London, 1974), pp.174–5 and nn.; also A. J. Taylor, *The Standard of Living in Britain in the Industrial Revolution* (London, 1975).

10 Sir J. Clapham, *An Economic History of Modern Britain: the Early Railway Age, 1820–1850* (1926; 2nd edn, Cambridge, 1967), preface, p.ix. Cf. the interesting discussion of this whole question in H. Perkin, *The Origins of Modern English Society 1780–1880* (1969; London, 1972), pp.134–49, 417, 421–3.

seen as such. With no traditional protector to turn to in the new towns, many sections of society felt and suffered from the economic and social pressures at work. There were lags and deficiencies in the redeployment of resources not least the labour that was displaced by technical advance or foreign competition. There were social demands and environmental problems of many kinds to be tackled. Moreover any deficiency was so much more obvious being on a larger scale and more widely publicized than before. In addition difficulties occurred in due time to undermine the initial buoyancy and to create the less certain and more depressing economic scene increasingly familiar over the past fifty or more years.

In any event, fundamental changes of this sort could not but affect patterns of political thought and behaviour, specifically the pace and nature of government action and views about its responsibilities. In theory it was held by many, in the libertarian way, that public authority ought simply to keep the ring and not interfere with industry and commerce, intervene in industrial disputes, or attempt to mitigate the social and environmental consequences of technical change: it was simply beyond the power of government to do anything effective about such matters and the attempt would only bring harm. Nevertheless in practice this principle was more and more disregarded as a distinction came to be drawn between interference as a matter of general policy (which was widely held to be improper or inexpedient) and special action with a view to remedying particular evils. Viscount Howick (later 3rd Earl Grey) expressed this distinction in a debate on the Factory Bill of 1844. There is, he said, an important difference to be perceived 'between restrictions imposed upon industry, with the visionary hope of increasing a nation's wealth, or with the unjust design of taxing one class for the benefit of another, and those of which the aim is to guard against evils, moral or physical, which it is apprehended that the absence of such precautions might entail upon the people.'[11] And the likely overall impact of even this limited kind of concession was equally clearly discerned at the time. J. S. Mill wrote in 1845 that

> the Legislature, which seldom concerns itself much with new ten-
> dencies of opinion until they have grown too powerful to be safely
> overlooked, is invited, in each Session with increasing urgency, to
> provide that the labouring classes shall earn more, work less, or have
> their lot in some other manner alleviated; and in each Session yields
> more or less cheerfully, but still yields, though slowly yet increasingly,
> to the requisition.

He went on to observe, too, that the new schemes of benevolence were conceived by many of their proponents not merely as *ad hoc* acts of

11 74 Parl. Deb. 3s., 3 May 1844, col. 643.

sympathy but as something more, as 'instalments of a great social reform' leading to what he called, in one place, 'le système du gouvernement charitable'.[12] Involved in all this there was the increasing disciplinary power being taken by the state over property and a growing measure of intervention in economic life to regulate, rationalize, and even own the industrial and commercial resources of the nation. In this country, as so often elsewhere, an organized national economy became in time the order of the day. And if the many difficulties arising in the course of the economic and social changes had, at least in the first instance, to be dealt with by local officers, central government or its agencies nevertheless assumed an increasingly significant role of superintendence that often led to supersession as (in the words of one involved observer, a Poor Law Inspector) 'statesmen began to take note of the requirements of the period.'[13] Thus the great change produced problems inviting government intervention even as it created the wealth and facilities that made that regulation possible.

The impact of these industrial and cognate developments and their cumulative and intensified aftermath may be conveniently discerned with more particularity in three phases or aspects of euthenic mediation on the part of public authority. The distinctions involved are broadly clear though there is inevitably some overlap of chronology and manner because each disposition once initiated has, like the layers of a palimpsest, remained a continuing feature of the scene so that at any recent time all might be discerned present in complex interconnexion. The three stages or motives relevant here may be distinguished as: (a) intervention to protect the public, or sections of it, from the effects of urban concentration and industrial development; (b) intervention to preserve industry from inimical tendencies and to help it become more efficient; and (c) intervention to control industry and manage the economy as a whole in the general interest. Each will now be looked at in more detail so that the extending collectivist response of public authority is clear. In a final section of this chapter something will be said, too, about some other of the more significant social aspects of this transformation.

INTERVENTION TO PROTECT THE PUBLIC

The state almost exclusively undertakes to supply bread to the hungry, assistance and shelter to the sick, work to the idle, and to act as the sole reliever of all kinds of misery.
A. de Tocqueville, *Democracy in America*, 1835–40; Fontana, 1968, ii. 884

12 J. S. Mill, 'The Claims of Labour' (1845), *Collected Works*, ed. J. M. Robson *et al.* (London, 1963 ff), iv. 365–6; Mill to Auguste Comte (17 May 1847), ibid., xiii. 716.
13 J. Lambert, *Modern Legislation as a Chapter in Our History* (London, 1865), p. 5.

The dominant belief of the day was that if every man followed his own interest then the maximum public benefit would also be achieved. This pursuit required the absence of restrictions on the free competitive action of equal industrial and individual units. But it was quickly perceived that in practice these were far from being on a level and that there was indeed a vital range of inequalities to be observed. This had important political consequences. As Maitland put it, 'The attempt, characteristic of modern times, to protect the economically weaker classes has given rise to statutes which bristle with powers'.[14] This treatment of what was often called 'the condition of England question' had two main aspects. These concerned, first, the improvement of working conditions in factory and mine; and, secondly, the amelioration of conditions of living in the growing industrial towns.

Conditions of work and the protection of labour

In his essay on 'The New Downing Street' (1850) which reviews the prospect of a society regenerated by wise policy, Carlyle said that 'in the course of long strenuous centuries' he could 'see the State become what it is actually bound to be, the keystone of a most real "Organisation of Labour"'.[15] And, in fact, a great deal in this regard was achieved in his own lifetime.

It was inevitable that the humanitarian impulse should often find an outlet in attempts to improve the environment in which people worked and the terms on which they were employed. Moreover, issues concerning the health and safety of the worker might be seen as affecting the Queen's peace generally and, as a matter of public order, thus be a proper subject for legislation.[16] From the beginning of the nineteenth century and even before, therefore, there was a series of varied – and variously effective – measures to control onerous, dangerous, or unhealthy conditions of work.[17] Initially these laws concerned themselves primarily with the prevention of harm only to working children and young persons; then the position of women received attention; and, finally, regulation was extended to cover workers in general. In this way labour

14 F. W. Maitland, *The Constitutional History of England* (1908; Cambridge, 1974), p. 410.
15 Carlyle, 'Latter-Day Pamphlets' (1850), in *Works* (People's edn, 1871–4), xx.135.
16 Cf. L. T. Hobhouse, *The Labour Movement* (London, 1893), p. 7.
17 On these measures, see e.g. M. W. Thomas, *The Early Factory Legislation: a Study in Legislative and Administrative Evolution* (Leigh-on-Sea, 1948); J. T. Ward, *The Factory Movement, 1830–1855* (London, 1962) and *The Factory System* (Newton Abbot, 1970), ii.67ff. There is an excellent summary and analysis of this legislation in the first half of the nineteenth century in O. MacDonagh, *Early Victorian Government, 1830–1870* (London, 1977), chs. 2–4.

became the care of the state and Parliament which in consequence were to be seen, according to one episcopal peer who took part in the discussion of the Cotton Factories Bill in 1818, as 'the natural guardian of the unprotected'.[18] The *Westminster Review* declared in 1842 that, as the community had long accepted the duty to preserve any of its members from 'absolute destitution', so it ought also to recognize a responsibility to exempt children at least from any labour that might impede their moral, intellectual, and physical development; and factory legislation was thus justified not least because it marked 'a new era in our social life' brought about by the increased use of machinery.[19] There was opposition, of course. For instance, in the 1840s Cobden was much concerned at the 'socialistic' implications of this sort of legislation; during the same period (and in his usual shrill and effective way) Toulmin Smith inveighed against the centralized powers involved; and in 1855, while accepting that intervention to aid women and children might be legitimate, Palmerston (then Prime Minister) declared that any attempt to limit the freedom of adult male workers to make their own bargains was based on a 'vicious and wrong' principle.[20] Nor was it always accepted that the consequences which followed this sort of legislative intervention would necessarily be to the advantage of the groups whose interest it was intended to protect. A. J. Munby was one of those who believed that, on the contrary, the effects were often unfortunate. Thus Shaftesbury's Act of 1842, which forbade women to work below ground in the mines even if they wanted to, caused a great deal of financial distress which it made no attempt to alleviate. Nor did his hostility (or that, if he is to be believed, of the workers affected) abate with the years. Munby was a curious but acute and learned man; for his opinions in such matters there were perhaps special reasons. But he was a close and perceptive observer who carefully reported views no doubt widely shared.[21]

There was indeed a prolonged controversy. As Dicey said, the factory movement was a major battlefield of collectivism against individualism.[22] But the process of intervention continued notwithstanding the

---

18   38 Parl. Deb. 1s., 19 May 1818, col. 794. Cf. the impassioned speech of Lord John Manners on the Ten Hours Bill, 86 Parl. Deb. 3s., 13 May 1846, cols. 496–504; also Macaulay's comments in *The History of England* (1849–61; London, 1889), i. 205, 208; and A. V. Dicey's in *Lectures on the Relation between Law & Public Opinion in England during the Nineteenth Century* (1905; 2nd edn, London, 1920), pp. 238–9.

19   'First Report of the Children's Employment Commissioners: Mines and Collieries', *Westminster Review*, xxxviii (1842), pp. 86–7.

20   J. Morley, *The Life of Richard Cobden* (London, 1881), i. 302–3; J. T. Smith, *Government by Commissions Illegal and Pernicious* (London, 1849), esp. bk. II, chs. I–II; for Palmerston's opinion, see 137 Parl. Deb. 3s., 15 November 1855, col. 616.

21   D. Hudson, *Munby: Man of Two Worlds. The Life and Diaries of Arthur J. Munby 1828–1910* (1972; Abacus, 1974), pp. 75–7, 291, 328 n. 2.

22   Dicey, *Law & Public Opinion*, p. 237.

hostility and the practical difficulties of implementing reform in a little-governed society. The latter sort of problem is easily illustrated by reference to a statute of 1833 which prohibited the employment in certain factories of children under nine years of age. However, as there was then no formal registration of births much depended on the judgement of the surgeon issuing the certificate required; but nor was there yet any clear professional identity or any organization to establish who was a qualified medical man. It was hardly surprising that in these circumstances Home Office advice was also rather vague.[23] As well, the laws, such as those requiring dangerous machinery to be guarded, were frequently neither observed by employers nor always rigorously enforced by the magistrates responsible.[24]

Nevertheless much of the opposition was in time overridden and the difficulties surmounted not least through the creation of inspectorates to enforce legislative provision; and in a parade of statutes dating from 1802 onwards, applying to a growing range of industries, and culminating in the great Consolidation Acts of 1878 and 1901, it was clearly established as a firm principle that one of government's major concerns was the regulation of the conditions of labour. The supervision entailed was to some degree quite novel in the sense of involving state interference on private premises and in relations between an employer and his workers. It was, too, of increasing effectiveness and wide and detailed in scope concerning a range of matters from ventilation and sanitation to the restriction of hours of labour of various categories of worker. John Morley's classic comment on this legislative tendency brings out the very close nature of the control involved and what it implied for the general question of social organization. 'We have today', he wrote in 1881,

> a complete, minute, and voluminous code for the protection of labour; buildings must be kept pure of effluvia; dangerous machinery must be fenced; children and young persons must not clean it while in motion; their hours are not only limited but fixed; continuous employment must not exceed a given number of hours, varying with the trade, but prescribed by the law in given cases; a statutable number of holidays is imposed; the children must go to school, and the employer must every week have a certificate to that effect; if an accident happens, notice must be sent to the proper authorities; special provisions are made for bakehouses, for lace-making, for collieries, and for a whole schedule of other special callings; for the due enforcement and vigilant supervision of this immense host of minute prescriptions, there is an immense host of inspectors, certifying surgeons, and other authorities,

23 N. McCord, 'Some Limitations of the Age of Reform' in H. Hearder and H. R. Loyn (eds), *British Government and Administration* (Cardiff, 1974), p. 200.

24 See e.g. the case cited in E. J. Evans, *Social Policy 1830–1914: Individualism, Collectivism and the Origins of the Welfare State* (London, 1978), pp. 55–6.

whose business is 'to speed and post o'er land and ocean' in restless guardianship of every kind of labour, from that of the woman who plaits straw at her cottage door, to the miner who descends into the bowels of the earth, and the seaman who conveys the fruits and materials of universal industry to and fro between the remotest parts of the globe. But all this is one of the largest branches of what the most importunate Socialists have been accustomed to demand; and if we add to this vast fabric of Labour legislation our system of Poor Law, we find the rather amazing result that in the country where Socialism has been less talked about than any other country in Europe, its principles have been most extensively applied.[25]

This kind of control, which has of course continued and intensified during the present century, undoubtedly constitutes interference by the state in the economic process, restriction of the rights of property, and regulation of the administration of capital in the interest of the labourer. In a comment published within a few years of John Morley's remarks, Shaw accurately assessed the general significance of this legislation for the libertarian point of view when he wrote that the 'Factory Acts swept the anarchic theory of the irresponsibility of private enterprise out of practical politics' making employers 'accountable to the State' for the well-being of their workers.[26]

In fact, the ambit of state intervention was later also extended, albeit somewhat slowly and haphazardly, into the two cognate spheres of wage regulation and industrial conciliation.

A policy of the state regulation of wages can, of course, appeal to some very old precedents indeed going back, for instance, to the powers given by the Elizabethan statute of 1563 which, still operative in the late-seventeenth century, itself invoked 'a great number' of even older Acts. Nevertheless it was the widespread view in the nineteenth century that, as Ricardo expressed it in his *Principles*, wages should, like all other contractual matters, 'be left to the fair and free competition of the market, and should never be controlled by the interference of the legislature'. Hence his opposition to the old Poor Law as it had come to operate which in his belief tried to do just this to the detriment of all.[27] What is directly important here is that, despite such views, the state nevertheless increasingly intervened, in a kind of new Speenhamland system, to assist in the determination of wages where it was held that for some reason the normal processes of bargaining were not effective or the

25   Morley, op. cit., i. 303.
26   G. B. Shaw, 'Transition' in G. B. Shaw *et al.*, *Fabian Essays* (1889; Jubilee edn, London, 1950), p.171.
27   D. Ricardo, *The Principles of Political Economy and Taxation* (1817; Everyman, 1969), p.61.

workers concerned were exploited. The development of the so-called new unionism towards the end of the century, which brought many unskilled workers into the labour movement, led increasingly not merely to the formulation of demands for a just or living wage as a first claim on industrial costs but the addressing of these demands to the state itself rather than simply to the employer. In this context it was urged that the duty of government was to fix a minimum wage and establish, too, other reforms such as a limitation of hours and a system of workmen's compensation. This kind of pressure was sustained by the presence in the House of Commons of the Lib-Lab MPs and then, after 1906, by the Labour Party itself. The result was seen, for instance, in the way in which in 1912 the government intervened to settle a national strike in the mining industry on the basis of a district minimum; also in the Trade Board Acts of 1909 and 1918 which were intended to suppress sweating and provide machinery for the fixing of minimum wages in certain industries. There was similar legislation, as well, applying to coal-mining, road haulage, and agriculture.[28] More recent examples of the tendency for government to intervene in this sphere are the Acts (which date from 1938) providing for holidays with pay, and the post-war establishment of wages councils in some industries. The Equal Pay Act of 1970 is a still further instance while, of course, a more extensive manifestation of this propensity to regulate earnings (albeit with the addition of a quite different purpose) is reflected in the various institutional experiments of recent years: the Council on Productivity, Prices, and Incomes; the National Incomes Commission; the Prices and Incomes Board; declarations of intent; the Social Contract; and all the schemes to freeze or control incomes with which we have latterly become so familiar. In all its forms this sort of policies, whether resting on political persuasion merely or on statute, involves the claim that (as Dicey put it long ago) wages can be fixed by the government and not by 'the mere haggling of the market.'[29]

Similarly the state began quite early to take an interest in industrial consultation and conciliation procedures, at first perhaps to protect the more weakly organized workers, but then increasingly to safeguard industry and the national interest from the effects of numerous or prolonged stoppages. Traditionally, administrations were reluctant to intervene as reflected in Gladstone's attitude to the mining lock-out of 1893, though in the end he was persuaded to set up a conference under

28 E. E. Barry, *Nationalisation in British Politics: the Historical Background* (London, 1965), pp.123–4; R. C. K. Ensor, *England, 1870–1914* (1936; Oxford, 1968), pp.515–16; D. Sells, *The British Trade Boards System* (London, 1923) and *British Wages Boards: a Study in Industrial Democracy* (Washington, DC, 1939).

29 Dicey, *Law & Public Opinion*, p.xlix n.4.

Rosebery's chairmanship to attempt arbitration. One obvious factor in overcoming his diffidence was that this was the first clear occasion on which the unions had deliberately followed the tactic of inflicting shortage on the public at large (rather than directly on the employers' interests simply) in order to compel government intervention. It is no accident that the first really effective legislation followed three years later making provision for intervention by the Board of Trade and the establishment of conciliation boards to inquire into the causes of disputes.[30] The tendency to authoritative if informal action by government was further reinforced by George's settlement of the rail strikes of 1907 and 1911 and the later mining dispute of 1912. Such intervention became more common and systematic and took place at an earlier stage of disputes. The formal machinery itself proliferated during the Great War and after as with the Industrial Court and the Whitley Council. Writing in 1933 Harold Laski said that 'Every important conflict between capital and labour increasingly involves the intervention of the government' which 'is no longer permitted the rôle of passive spectator; it is expected to attempt . . . the provision of means of accommodation.' And it will be especially prompted to mediate if the industry or service is an important one or if there is public support for the claim being made. Nothing, he continued, 'indicates quite so strongly the degree to which the popular mind has abandoned the dogma of *laissez-faire* as this attitude' to the role of government in economic and union affairs.[31] The process reached a peak with the arrangements for compulsory arbitration established during the Second World War and with the attempts of recent years to control unions and industrial relations by an extension of the law. There is, too, the elaborate advisory, conciliation, and arbitration service of the present day. Similarly the earlier Liberal precedents of government involvement and personal intervention were confirmed by inter-war experience and in an especially dramatic way by the events of the General Strike; while nowadays no industrial disagreement of any note can avoid involving the government of the day in some way or other: and there was a time, not too long ago, when it seemed that refreshments and bargaining round the table in the Cabinet room was a practice likely to become standard in the settlement of major industrial disputes.[32]

30 For details, see G. Howell, *Labour Legislation, Labour Movements and Labour Leaders* (London, 1902), ch. xxxix. Perkin, *The Origins of Modern English Society*, pp. 399–404 reviews the earlier attempts (which date back to 1800) to establish arbitration machinery. Cf. V. L. Allen, 'The Origins of Industrial Conciliation and Arbitration', *International Review of Social History*, ix (1964), pp. 237–54. For the events of 1893, see Ensor, *England 1870–1914*, pp. 298–9.

31 H. J. Laski, *Democracy in Crisis* (London, 1933), p. 200.

32 A convenient brief review of recent developments in the sphere of industrial conciliation and the like is J. H. Bescoby and C. C. Hanson, 'Continuity and Change in Recent Labour Law', *National Westminster Bank Quarterly Review* (May 1976), pp. 7–19.

One obvious factor stimulating this tendency to state intervention in the labour field generally was the growth of trade unionism which itself owed much to sympathetic legislation. Having been in the early nineteenth century illegal conspiracies of little account, trade unions were, a hundred years later, bodies of some political significance with a membership of well over two million, that is, getting on for 15 per cent of the total labour force. Of course, during that period of expansion the unions as a whole were not committed to anything so grandiose as the achievement of Socialism through political action; on the contrary, they often regarded the state with suspicion as being associated with repression. Nevertheless they favoured paternalist legislation to safeguard their members' interests and prompted or sustained the collectivist tendency in a number of ways. For example, one ⸤f the main functions of the large cotton and coal unions was to see that the Factory Acts were effectively enforced in the mines and workshops. To give only one specific instance: at a time when many miners were not in favour of nationalization (even of royalties) and when the experiments in miners' co-operatives had failed, the main union effort went into attempts to get existing working conditions made more bearable through government pressure on employers. This was why, during the 1870s and 1880s, the appointment of a Minister of Mines was continually urged as a means in particular of enforcing safety measures.[33] Union pressure was important, too, in the establishment of the conciliation procedures already referred to. Subsequently, of course, the degree of programmatic political commitment on the part of the unions has increased notably. They have added greater weight to this and similar purposes with their larger numbers – membership is now over 11 million – and their growing significance in an economy increasingly subject to their pressure exercised both through government and particular employers. The fact that collective bargaining has tended to develop on a national scale, the increasing trend (until perhaps very recently) to insist on uniform national wage-rates and conditions, has ensured that the industrial field is more and more unlike the libertarian paradigm of the market economy. Nor would the restoration of so-called 'free collective bargaining' constitute a revival of the competitive ideal because the negotiations would (it is envisaged by the unions) be conducted in the context of a statist, planned society with effective central control of prices other than that of labour. And it is not without relevance that all union successes in raising minimum standards of payment and conditions of work simply increase the fixed costs of industry thereby perhaps worsening the unemployment problem and thus (on certain views at least) inviting more government intervention as a remedy.

33 Barry, op. cit., pp.112–13.

Conditions of living

H. G. Wells stressed in his *Anticipations* that the 'growth of the great cities is the essential phenomenon'; equally the Webbs pointed to the importance of what they called the 'massing of men'.[34] This aggregation of people in towns, a process facilitated by better roads and the coming of the railway, occurred too in parts of the country, especially in the North and the Midlands, that had hitherto been relatively desolate. Something of what happened may be indicated by reference to the change between about 1770 and 1891 in respect of the percentage of the population living in towns of 20,000 inhabitants or more. At the first date this proportion was 13.5 per cent (of which 9.5 per cent related to London); at the second it was 53.6 per cent of a larger overall population (with 14.5 per cent in London): the capital was growing, more so were the other urban centres.[35] And the process continued. By 1961 the overall density of population in Great Britain had gone up to 573 per square mile, 80 per cent of the people lived in towns, and nearly 40 per cent lived in Greater London and the six provincial conurbations.[36]

Quite early on some older townships grew enormously. For instance, the population of Manchester more than trebled between 1773 and 1801 as did that of Leeds in the three subsequent decades. As for the capital, more than a million extra people moved into Greater London in the first forty years of the nineteenth century bringing the number of its inhabitants to 2¼ million; by 1911 it was five million more and comprised something like one-fifth of the entire population of England and Wales.[37] What happened in the metropolis is exemplified by the growth of Battersea. In the early decades of the last century it was a rural area with a population in 1831 of some 5000. During the next fifty years there was a great influx of working people so that by 1881 it had become a suburb of

34 H. G. Wells, *Anticipations of the Reaction of Mechanical and Scientific Progress upon Human Life and Thought* (1901; 2nd edn, London, 1914), p. 33; S. and B. Webb, *The Development of English Local Government, 1689–1835* (London, 1963), p. 70. Cf. J. Ortega y Gasset, *The Revolt of the Masses* (1930; London, 1963), p. 9 on 'the fact of agglomeration'.

35 See the table in E. P. Hennock, 'Finance and Politics in Urban Local Government in England, 1835–1900', *Historical Journal*, vi (1963), p. 212 n. 2 and the sources there cited; and the similar figures in A. Briggs, *Victorian Cities* (1963; Penguin, 1968), pp. 59–60, 86.

36 J. B. Mitchell, 'The Population of Great Britain' in J. B. Mitchell (ed.), *Great Britain: Geographical Essays* (Cambridge, 1962), p. 33.

37 P. Deane and W. A. Cole, *British Economic Growth, 1688–1959: Trends and Structure* (1962; 2nd edn, Cambridge, 1967), p. 8; B. R. Mitchell and P. Deane, *Abstract of British Historical Statistics* (1962; Cambridge, 1971), pp. 19, 24; C. L. Mowat, *Britain between the Wars, 1918–1940* (1955; London, 1968), p. 227. Macaulay's description of the growth of London in the century after the Restoration is justly famous, *The History of England* (London, 1889), i. 170ff.

over 107,000 with another 23,000 being added in the following decade. Wandsworth (of which Battersea is a part) experienced a 200 per cent increase of population between 1861 and 1881.[38] Some of the towns which grew so fast were completely new, such as Middlesbrough and Birkenhead. In 1801 the former consisted of a few farm-houses with a population of about twenty-five. With the coming of the railway, the docks, and the iron industry it grew rapidly and by the end of the century was little short of 100,000. Similarly Birkenhead was a hamlet of fifty inhabitants in 1818 but through the establishment of shipbuilding yards and the docks it, too, expanded very quickly.

But this rapid concentration of people in growing towns – there were parts of Liverpool in 1884 with a density of 1200 persons to the acre – entailed many problems of housing, disease, water supply, drainage, sewage disposal, lighting, poverty, and so on.[39] As well, these urban developments had an unsettling effect on general social stability and public order. Security was bound to seem diminished when masses of people were herded together in these difficult conditions of association without community and when, too, there appeared the new social phenomenon of urban working-class districts in which (in contrast to most rural areas) not one person of wealth, influence, or education lived. In conversation with Lord Liverpool, Chateaubriand praised the stability of British institutions but the Prime Minister replied, 'Qu'y a-t-il de solide avec ces villes énormes?' These enormous towns meant disorder, crime, and the possibility of 'une insurrection sérieuse'; they were (in Tawney's graphic phrase) 'little better than mining camps' in which people had been thrown together 'without traditions or organization'.[40]

This is not to suggest the problems were completely new in themselves or that the bad conditions were entirely the creation of the manufacturing system. The early-modern or eighteenth-century town was hardly a salubrious place as, for instance, Hogarth's paintings and engravings indicate or as Professor Redford's description of the insanitary habits of the early Mancunians shows quite clearly.[41] Rural circumstances as well were invariably deplorable and far from the bucolic idyll often pictured by the romantic imagination faced with

38 C. Wrigley, 'Liberals and the Desire for Working-Class Representatives in Battersea, 1886–1922', in K. D. Brown (ed.), Essays in Anti-Labour History: Responses to the Rise of Labour in Britain (London, 1974), p.126. Living conditions in Battersea are described, ibid. pp.127–8.

39 The reference to Liverpool is from A. Briggs, Victorian Cities, p.18.

40 Vicomte de Chateaubriand, Mémoires d'outre-tombe, ed. Levaillant (Paris, n.d. [1948]), iii.126; R. H. Tawney, The Radical Tradition (1964; Penguin, 1966), p.17. On the increase in crime, cf. the Webbs, op. cit., pp.83–91.

41 A. Redford, The History of Local Government in Manchester (London, 1939–40), vol.i, ch. V.

proliferating urban slums.[42] In addition circumstances were not uniform and might vary substantially from one place to another. Moreover, it is a mistake to suppose that no improvement took place at all until the nineteenth century was well under way: in the end what was done by private or local initiative proved perhaps woefully inadequate but this simply indicates the unprecedented scale of the problems involved not that no response was made at all. And by any measure the creation of the middle-class suburb and the building of such a large number of new towns designed for working-class occupation were themselves major constructive efforts in the attempt to cope with the process of indus-trialization, urban concentration, and population growth. As usual in history, it is a mistake to apply later standards of achievement to an earlier period.[43]

What was undoubtedly quite new was the scale of things and their manifestness. Lower-class misery was hardly an unprecedented pheno-menon; but it was now a bigger one and concentrated in the large towns where, as Halévy said, 'it was exposed to universal gaze and became a public scandal.'[44] Sanitary conditions, for instance, which had long prevailed and been acceptable in the lower density of the countryside were, it was gradually realized, impossible in a crowded urban area, a lesson the trauma of a cholera or typhus epidemic quickly reinforced. As a result the often ghastly state of affairs was more investigated and widely reported than ever before in both official and privately-sponsored inquiries. There can have been few official documents that have had so great an influence as Chadwick's findings in 1842 on the 'Sanitary Condition of the Labouring Population' or the subsequent Royal Commission reports on 'the State of Large Towns and Populous Districts'. Moreover, perhaps for the first time, the possibilities of economic improvement and technical change seemed to suggest that things might be otherwise, might be better than they were or, indeed, ever had been.

To take just one aspect of what happened. As the population grew and concentrated in the towns, people were more and more densely packed into the available living space; though much was done, the building and construction industries of the day could hardly keep pace with the demand for dwellings, and overcrowding and general squalor resulted.

42 See the vivid account in E. Gauldie, *Cruel Habitations: a History of Working-Class Housing, 1780–1918* (London, 1974), Part I, 'Housing in Pre-Industrial and Rural Society'; also the comments on conditions in the Welsh countryside in I. G. Jones, *Health, Wealth and Politics in Victorian Wales* (Swansea, 1979), pp. 10–11.

43 On the frequent contemporary impression of the high level of prosperity in towns, see I. G. Jones, op. cit., p. 12.

44 E. Halévy, *A History of the English People in the Nineteenth Century* (1913–46; 2nd trans. edn, London, 1961), i.281.

Facilities provided on a traditional scale proved inadequate: refuse accumulated; the primitive drainage arrangements could not cope with the human and industrial waste; the water supply was limited, perhaps very severely, and often tainted; smoke was a major pollutant. The smell could be foul and to the outsider quite unbearable, not surprisingly when, for instance, in some parts of Manchester there was – to cite an extreme case – only one public privy to every 215 persons; and during a cholera outbreak at Leeds seventy-five cart-loads of manure were removed from one cul-de-sac.[45] The serious epidemics that occurred from time to time served as a sharp index of unhealthiness affecting all social classes.

There are many contemporary descriptions of this mushrooming and insalubrious state of affairs, not all entirely reliable, many concerned simply to be as critical as possible, concentrating as a result not on the average but on the worst conditions to be observed.[46] Manchester – called by Professor Briggs the 'shock city of the age' – provided the basis of some of the most well-known accounts, such as those of Engels, de Tocqueville, and Kay-Shuttleworth. Let a less familiar instance here stand in their stead, a brief statement of conditions at Merthyr Tydfil shortly after the end of the Napoleonic Wars: 'Nothing can be more irregular, or more offensive to the eye, probably nothing more injurious to the health of the inhabitants, than the arrangement of the streets and houses. Indeed it is scarcely correct to say that there is in the place what can properly merit the name of a street.' For the houses were erected with no regard to plan or proximity to other buildings so that as the population increased the number of dwellings simply spread 'over an immense extent of ground in every possible direction, communicating with each other for the greater part by narrow lanes and avenues, which are generally choked with filth.'[47]

In *Coningsby* (1844) and *Sybil* (1845), Disraeli graphically highlighted the industrial slums of Wodgate and the decay of its rural counterpart, the town of Marney. The urgency of the problems they represented – especially the great urban centres, 'undrained, unpoliced, ungoverned and unschooled' as they largely were in the early days of the century – was indicated by the rising death rates of the time which were often as unhappily manifest in towns that were not heavily industrialized as in

45 Briggs, op. cit., p.146.
46 For critical assessment of, for instance, some of the accounts of Manchester, ibid., pp.102–17; T. S. Ashton, 'The Treatment of Capitalism by Historians', in F. A. Hayek (ed.), *Capitalism and the Historians* (1954; Chicago, 1965), ch.1; and L. Benevolo, *The Origins of Modern Town Planning* (1963; trans., Cambridge, Mass., 1971), pp.21–2, 31.
47 T. Rees, *A Topographical and Historical Description of South Wales* (London, n.d. [1815]), pp.646–7.

those that were. For instance, between 1831 and 1841 the average death rate in major towns went up by 50 per cent; in some places such as Birmingham and Bristol it doubled. And these figures did not begin to decrease decisively until the last quarter of the century. Even then, of course, great problems of pauperism and ill-health remained, despite the general growth of wealth and prosperity, as was revealed by many contemporary inquiries such as those of Booth in London and Rowntree in York.

All these matters invited more or less urgent attention from some kind of public authority; and the manner of their treatment is intimately connected in particular with the development of local government which, as gradually reformed and made more efficient during the course of the last century, acquired an enormously increased control over the activities and resources of citizens. And central government itself, which had naturally also been concerned from the outset, became more and more involved, albeit often reluctantly, in an advisory, regulatory, or substantive capacity and as a source of considerable financial aid. Something is said of these developments and in more detail in the chapter dealing with local government in *A Much-Governed Nation*, volume iii of the present work. Here, therefore, a cursory outline must suffice.

In the first stages, initiatives of various kinds taken by the traditional local bodies or through voluntary effort were important, for instance by securing private legislation to set up an Improvement Commission or local Board of Health. In fact, during the first forty-five years of the nineteenth century, nearly 400 local Improvement Acts were passed imposing limitations on owners of land and capital and conferring sanitary powers on over 200 local authorities.[48] In this way, something was done in such matters as paving, sewerage, and lighting in the particular areas concerned. But it was not enough; nor was it done in all places. In the event, central government had to act either to deal with these social evils itself or to build up, by appropriate legislation coupled with technical and financial help, a system of new authorities in the counties and towns which could tackle them locally. The result was a massive augmentation in one form or another of government supervision and other action. It is sometimes not appreciated how, quite early in this process, considerable powers of investigation and enforcement were acquired by public officials to deal with the health and cognate problems of the growing towns. Chronicling the work of Sir John Simon at Manchester, Dr Lambert observes that by the 1850s there was in that city 'a local authority interfering systematically and on a relatively large and increasing scale with the welfare, the external and domestic conditions of

48 F. Clifford, *A History of Private Bill Legislation* (London, 1885–7), ii. 300.

its citizens.'[49] The powers involved were, it is true, granted in an *ad hoc* way and were invariably merely permissive rather than compulsory. But they could involve placing restrictions on the unhindered use of private property or otherwise curtailing rights of ownership in the public interest. Practical necessity thus drove men who disapproved in principle of government intervention to support extensions of public regulation.

For purposes of illustration one important area of concern – that of housing – must stand as example for many.[50] In this sphere there were numerous attempts to cope with the problem and improve standards. Houses were often built, for instance, by employers as with the Birkenhead Dock Company which put up the first ever working-class flats in 1847 or as with such well-known 'company towns' as Swindon or Port Sunlight. Quite a lot of activity was undertaken for philanthropic reasons by organizations like the Society for Improving the Condition of the Labouring Classes, the Peabody Trust, and the Improved Industrial Dwellings Company. Individuals were also involved in the pursuit of housing improvement, persons such as Angela Burdett-Coutts and Octavia Hill. And W. C. Mearns's *Bitter Cry of Outcast London* (1883) is simply the most well-known of the many demands that something be done about the condition of the 'abject poor'. This was really the nub of the problem. The housing needs of the middle classes had been met by the speculative creation of suburbia. The artisans and 'labour aristocracy' were largely catered for, too; and improvements in their standards of accommodation were also stimulated by the voluntary and philanthropic activity already mentioned as through the experimental construction of 'model' houses and tenements and, later on, through the garden city movement. It was the housing of paupers and of unskilled labourers that constituted the main difficulty. And it was really to deal with this problem that public authority was finally invoked.

The first major legislation here was the two Artizans' and Labourers' Dwellings Acts passed in 1868 and 1875. These gave local authorities power to require necessary work to be done on property condemned by public health officials and even, in the event of default, to buy such property compulsorily and provide for its rebuilding either by philanthropic housing companies or by creating their own housing estates. What could be done in even a short period by the use of such powers is

---

49 R. Lambert, *Sir John Simon, 1816–1904, and English Social Administration* (London, 1963), p. 186.
50 Excellent accounts, only partly marred by a firm collectivist commitment on the part of the authors, are provided by E. Gauldie, *Cruel Habitations* (which has already been cited) and Professor J. N. Tarn's two studies, *Working-Class Housing in 19th-Century Britain* (London, 1971) and the fuller *Five Per Cent Philanthropy: an Account of Housing in Urban Areas between 1840 and 1914* (Cambridge, 1973). For the later period there is M. Bowley, *Housing and the State, 1919–1944* (1945; London, 1947).

shown by the achievements of Joseph Chamberlain's mayoralty at Birmingham between 1873 and 1876.[51] But few local authorities were driven by such an energumen; there were, too, difficulties particularly in respect of financial provision; and it has been argued that these powers actually worsened the housing situation in some respects by concentrating on demolition and failing to provide for a firm and positive policy of housing construction as well. Yet the portents were clear and, after the message was further spelled out by the reports of the Royal Commission on Working-Class Housing which appeared in 1885, further legislation followed. The Consolidating Act of 1890 substantially extended and reformed the scope of public responsibility in this respect though, outside London, most local authorities were even then slow to act on the powers it gave. There was, indeed, still under way a debate about the propriety or efficacy of state intervention in the field of housing construction. In 1903, for instance, James Parsons published a criticism of the LCC which had ten years before first embarked on the building of what we now call 'council houses'. State action, he argued, would not improve building efficiency or design, entailed all the well-known defects of functionarism, and would diminish commercial incentive by cutting off the flow of capital to the private sector and so prevent the building of many homes. On the other hand, a few years later Kirkman Gray replied that social problems must be dealt with by society itself: local authorities should thus act as society's agents to deal with the housing of the poor. Private philanthropy, he said, 'cannot provide a remedy for widespread want which results from broad and general social causes'. Nor ought it to be expected to do so: 'the provision of such remedies is the proper responsibility of the State and should be accepted as such.' For the modern city, he went on in Idealist style, is 'an instrument of the State for realising the highest life of individuals.'[52] Yet though by that time opinion was shifting in favour of local government action, especially at the bottom end of the housing scale, councils were still loath to take up the task though, with some variation over the years, the amount of loans for this purpose sanctioned annually by the Local Government Board continued to increase and on the eve of 1914 totalled over three-quarters of a million pounds.[53] In some ways the main hindrance was one of attitudes and rested on the same sort of issue that had plagued

---

51 See the account in J. L. Garvin and J. Amery, *The Life of Joseph Chamberlain* (London, 1932–69), i.188–200.

52 J. Parsons, *Housing by Voluntary Enterprise* (1903), pp.66–7 and B. K. Gray, *Philanthropy and the State* (1908), pp.x, 68; both cited by Tarn, *Five Per Cent Philanthropy*, pp.143–4. Oddly, Professor Tarn refers to 'Kirkham Gray' – it should surely be 'Kirkman'?

53 Gauldie, op. cit., Appendices 3–5, pp.321–5.

the question of the Poor Law for so long: if those who could not afford an economic rent were subsidized then the housing dole they received placed them perhaps in a more eligible position than the independent artisan and this was widely felt to be unjust as well as socially inexpedient.

A major change in this regard was, however, brought by the Great War. There was not only the lower level of building for five years coupled with the pent-up demand for housing (especially in the context of rent control) but, more importantly, the provision of adequate accommodation was seen as a proper measure of social justice for those who had fought: 'Homes fit for Heroes'. It was expected that government should assume responsibility for their housing as such. The Housing Act of 1919, associated with the name of Lord Addison, embodied this crucial departure of principle. Previous legislation on the subject had been primarily concerned with slum clearance as a matter of public health; now there was envisaged a major extension of government action in the housing sphere as a kind of social service in its own right. Local authorities were given the task of surveying housing needs in their areas and of making and carrying out plans for the provision of the dwellings required. The Treasury was to help financially by giving subsidies so that rents could be fixed at a level those needing the houses could afford. And standards superior to those of the past were envisaged. In the inter-war period, over one million council houses were built under these legislative auspices (and well over twice this number of houses by private builders).[54] Perhaps even this did not deal with the housing problem created by a century of industrial change and by world war.[55] But Professor Bowley has stated that this council house building 'was perhaps the outstanding peace time experiment in state intervention in this country in the provision of a necessity of life, which had formerly been supplied almost exclusively by independent private enterprise.'[56] Of course, the pattern of public intervention has been reinforced since the Second World War. In the twenty years from 1946 to 1965 nearly 4.8 million housing units were built and, in contrast to the inter-war years, council housing predominated providing some 57 per cent of this total (as compared with 28 per cent between the two world wars).[57] Thus, in a century and a half, government has moved from marginal concern through reluctant involvement to very active commitment as voluntary

---

54 Bowley, *Housing and the State*, Appendix II, Table 2, p.271.
55 For some critical comments, see P. Abrams, 'The Failure of Social Reform: 1918–20', *Past and Present* (no.24; April 1963), pp.56–7.
56 Bowley, op. cit., p.vi.
57 See the table in D. Butler and A. Sloman, *British Political Facts 1900–1979*, 5th edn (London, 1980), p.303.

or private effort seemed unable to cope with the problem; and now it provides directly one out of every two houses built as well as being indirectly involved (through tax allowances and the like) in the other also.

To revert finally from this specific example of housing to the general question of the towns and conditions of living in them. Much had been done in this regard through the agency of the local authorities; and the general progress of this 'municipal Socialism' was wittily summed up many years ago by Sidney Webb – an ardent advocate of the tendency – in what must surely be one of his most well-known passages:

> Our unconscious acceptance of this progressive Socialism is a striking testimony to the change which has come over the country of Godwin and Malthus. The 'practical man,' oblivious or contemptuous of any theory of the Social Organism or general principles of social organisation, has been forced by the necessities of the time, into an ever deepening collectivist channel. Socialism, of course, he still rejects and despises. The Individualist Town Councillor will walk along the municipal pavement, lit by municipal gas and cleansed by municipal brooms with municipal water, and seeing by the municipal clock in the municipal market, that he is too early to meet his children coming from the municipal school hard by the county lunatic asylum and municipal hospital, will use the national telegraph system to tell them not to walk through the municipal park but to come by the municipal tramway, to meet him in the municipal reading room, by the municipal art gallery, museum and library, where he intends to consult some of the national publications in order to prepare his next speech in the municipal town-hall, in favour of the nationalization of canals and the increase of the government control over the railway system. 'Socialism, sir,' he will say, 'don't waste the time of a practical man by your fantastic absurdities. Self-help, sir, individual self-help, that's what's made our city what it is.'[58]

INTERVENTION TO PROTECT INDUSTRY

> Great Britain has ... passed out of the age of easy affluence .... [S] he has lost the adventitious advantage of mere priority . . . and the process has been . . . economically disagreeable.
> R. H. TAWNEY, *The British Labor Movement*, 1925, p. 48

It is broadly true to say that, up to the outbreak of the Great War, government intervention in economic and social life was primarily to protect people in their work and in their homes from the untoward effects of industrial change and urban concentration though, of course, there

58 S. Webb, *Socialism in England* (London, 1890), pp. 116–17.

had been other aspects of state regulation as well. For example, government had long taken a special interest in the great chartered corporations like the East India Company; and as the nineteenth century wore on it took steps to adjust the legal framework of a growing commerce, for instance by passing the Companies Acts as a means of limiting the liability of shareholders and preventing or mitigating the consequences of fraud and bankruptcy. There were, too, the attempts to alleviate the effects of free trade on domestic agriculture as through Peel's 'general scheme' to help farmers become more efficient after the repeal of the Corn Laws, an interesting early example of government action to sustain an important part of economic life. As well, the state intervened quite early on to improve conditions of operation in respect of merchant shipping though really this was more similar in nature to the domestic Factory Acts than anything else. But perhaps the most important precedent in this more general regard was the political control of railway development. From the beginning of the modern railway system a great deal of supervision was exercised by many public bodies including Parliament, the Board of Trade, and such special authorities as the Railway Commission set up in 1846. This regulation had various purposes: to prevent excessive amalgamation that might lead to monopoly, waste of capital through unnecessary duplication of lines, or excessive and untoward speculation; to ensure safety by vetting construction plans and through the inspection of track; to prescribe charges and fares; to protect individual property interests; and so forth. To take one particular instance only, the Cheap Trains Act of 1883 compelled companies to offer workmen's fares when required to do so by the Board of Trade and this was specifically for the purpose of relieving housing congestion in town centres by thus encouraging the migration of the working class.[59] In fact, so extensive a degree of communal concern was recognized to exist in the railways that, though the policy was never successfully pressed, the idea of public control or even nationalization did not, to many who considered the matter, seem at all beyond the bounds of propriety. For instance, in 1842 the Political Economy Club – and this was J. S. Mill's own view also – agreed the railways ought to be placed under the jurisdiction of the state.[60] And although acting with some diffidence, two years later Gladstone, as the responsible minister, persuaded Parliament to include in the Railway Act he promoted provision for the state purchase of new lines on certain conditions. Clearly, as Dicey said, the kind of policy involved in this context

59 S. A. Pope, *The Cheap Trains Act* (1906), p.15, cited in A. Briggs, *Victorian Cities* (1963; Penguin, 1968), p.15.
60 M. Blaug, *Ricardian Economics: a Historical Study* (New Haven, Conn., 1958), pp.193–4; J. S. Mill, 'Chapters on Socialism' (1879), *Collected Works*, ed. J. M. Robson *et al.* (London, 1963ff), v.730.

accustomed public opinion to the idea of state management or supervision of industrial and commercial affairs where circumstances seemed to warrant it.[61]

In such varied ways, then, a basis existed on which to establish a further dimension of public action which, as time wore on, seemed to be increasingly invited. It is true that an attitude hostile to state involvement was widespread whether this took the form of actual intervention or merely that of aid. As to the former the common view was, as Lord Lansdowne said in 1854, that 'It will be universally admitted that governments are the worst of cultivators, the worst of manufacturers, the worst of traders'.[62] Hostility even to lesser forms of involvement was symbolized by Goschen's refusal in 1890 to help Baring's banking house avoid insolvency: it was not, he believed, proper to pledge public money to assist a private firm. But in time such reluctance was overcome because it seemed increasingly necessary to help British industry become more efficient than it would be unaided and to shelter it, as a national interest, against the forces that challenged it. Specifically it seemed more and more urgent to protect it against growing foreign competition, and workers and employers alike joined in a growing chorus to demand such help.[63]

British economic development was one of the most remarkable phenomena of the nineteenth century. But the transience of this country's hegemony and the unfavourable consequences of the 'early start' in industrialization were not long in declaring themselves. The great acceleration of economic growth began to slow down and by the end of the century was running at only half the rate of the early decades, about 1.7 per cent per annum as compared with 3.5 per cent. Given the development of other economies, this meant a relative decline which was signalled during the last quarter of the century by the USA and then Germany surpassing Britain in the production of such industrial staples as pig-iron and steel. It was also indicated by the failure of Britain to make any decisive contribution to technology during this period.[64] There were various aspects to this economic rivalry. Contrary to widely held expectation, other countries did not follow Britain's free-trade lead but

61 A. V. Dicey, *Lectures on the Relation between Law & Public Opinion in England during the Nineteenth Century* (1905; 2nd edn, London, 1920), pp.245–8.

62 Parliamentary Papers, 1854 (vol. xxvii), p.245 cited by L. Silberman in his introduction to H. Taylor, *The Statesman* (1836; Cambridge, 1957), p.xix.

63 See the example relating to the demand for state aid by chambers of commerce from the early 1890s in J. Harris, *Unemployment and Politics: a Study in English Social Policy 1886–1914* (Oxford, 1972), p.217 n.1.

64 Perkin, *The Origins of Modern English Society*, pp.410–11; R. C. K. Ensor, *England 1870–1914* (1936; Oxford, 1968), pp.277, 281–2, 501–4.

developed their own resources behind the security of a protective tariff which left the domestic economy here in a vulnerable position once the sheltered foreign industries had achieved a competitive level of activity. Cheap cotton goods from the East threatened our textiles; the coal industry, having worked out many of the more easily exploited seams, had to meet the growing competition of other producers (and ultimately of oil); as a result of technical change hitherto unusable iron ore deposits abroad could be exploited; and our farms were, during the 1870s and after, subjected to the long-delayed effects of the repeal of the Corn Laws, to the competition of a great inflow of agricultural produce from abroad made possible by the increasing availability and cheapness of transport (as by the railway opening up the American heartland), the invention of the refrigerated ship, and the fuller use elsewhere of such innovations as mechanical reaping. The amount of arable land fell rapidly in the quarter of a century before 1914; and this at a time when the population increased by more than half. The country thus became more and more dependent on the export of industrial goods or services simply to sustain the food imports required by its growing number of inhabitants. Yet, as already stated, foreign competition and tariff barriers hindered commercial effort.

The seriousness of the situation, at least in its potential scale, was the subject of much contemporary comment that ranged widely and radically; and there began that 'critical inquest into the state of the British economy' which has been going on ever since. There was (it was suggested) too much investment abroad and too little capital deployed at home to re-equip industry or direct it into new channels away from the old staples; there was not enough long-term research or technical education and the work force was under-trained and inefficiently used so that productivity was low and slow to improve; commercial leadership was said to be inferior because too many of the best brains went into the professions and the public service rather than industry with the result that business management was not good, or not taken seriously, enough. Some of these criticisms may have been to a degree misdirected, exaggerated, or even invalid.[65] But it is undoubtedly the case that, having had an early start, Britain was now being outstripped in many respects by other nations; and paradoxically, and at the peak of her political power, Britain's commercial position had started on a long secular decline, at

65 See discussion of these matters with contemporary reference and citation by T. C. Barker in C. B. Cox and A. E. Dyson (eds), *The Twentieth-Century Mind: History, Ideas and Literature in Britain* (London, 1972), i.53–69; also by G. R. Searle, *The Quest for National Efficiency: a Study in British Politics and Political Thought, 1899–1914* (Oxford, 1971), on both of which I have drawn here.

least as measured by comparison with economic rivals.[66] Kipling's warning call to imperial humility held also the grain of economic truth: it was not only navies and military pomp that could melt away. If the age seems to us to have been one of optimism and progress, people at the time experienced a notable 'mood of doubt'.[67]

Of course, in part the reality was masked by the economic lead which had been achieved and, for instance, by the exploitation of colonial markets and by the value to the country's balance of payments of the so-called 'invisible' items, services rendered to other nations such as banking, insurance, shipping, and the like, and by the interest accruing from large capital holdings overseas. But the competitive pinch was being felt in various ways. Some were politically very sensitive as when surplus foreign capital was invested in British firms which (like shipping) were of great economic and military significance: in at least one such case in the early years of this century the Cabinet itself intervened and granted a subsidy to keep the Cunard line in British hands.[68] And the situation was worsened by the distortions imposed by a war economy between 1914 and 1918, certain innovations notwithstanding: something like 15 per cent of all long-term foreign assets were sold; there were heavy shipping losses of about one-third of the merchant marine; the structure of industry was warped to achieve wartime ends; machinery was run down or not replaced; London lost its complete dominance as a financial centre; export markets and opportunities were lost to foreign competitors and the development of new products delayed; as well, the position of the trade unions was enhanced because of the shortage of labour and this had a substantial effect on the industrial scene.[69] It was not, of course, that British industry did not continue to improve in some respects: but there was no longer the earlier overall pre-eminence and in some areas foreign rivalry hit hard. R. H. Tawney sardonically remarked that 'free competition lost in attractiveness in proportion as it gained in reality.' Of course, he was a reformer and a Socialist. But he was also a renowned historian and his analysis of the changed economic scene, written in 1925, is well worth attention for it succinctly summarized the basis on which increased public control was more and more demanded:

66 Cf. A. Shadwell, *Industrial Efficiency: a Comparative Study of Industrial Life in England, Germany and America* (1905; new edn, London, 1909), pp. ix, 647–8, and ch. xviii *passim*.

67 Cf. H. House, 'The Mood of Doubt', in H. Grisewood *et al.*, *Ideas and Beliefs of the Victorians: an Historic Revaluation of the Victorian Age* (1949; New York, 1966), pp. 71–7.

68 For this and other examples, see J. L. Garvin and J. Amery, *The Life of Joseph Chamberlain* (London, 1932–69), iv. 408–10.

69 Barker, in Cox and Dyson, op. cit., i. 82–6; and on the post-war difficulties, J. Lovell, ibid., ii. 34–40.

Economic progress depends, after all, upon two broad groups of factors – on the one hand, national resources, inherited economic advantages, accumulated momentum; on the other hand, human energy, intelligence, science and organization. If the first are scanty or failing, it becomes more crucial than ever to cultivate the second. Great Britain has for a generation passed out of the age of easy affluence which reached its zenith in the last third of the nineteenth century. With the world-wide adoption of modern industrial technique, she has lost the adventitious advantage of mere priority. She has found her true level, and the process has been as morally salutary as it has been economically disagreeable. But the changed situation imposes a change of policy. She must conserve her natural resources, develop by improved education the capacities of all grades of her workers, cultivate science not only in coping with physical nature but in organizing industry and social institutions, and take every possible step to ensure that production is carried on in an atmosphere of good will and coöperation.

From this diagnosis Tawney himself drew the conclusion that 'a programme of social reconstruction' was vital.[70] This had become, increasingly, a not unusual reaction.

From the point of view of direct government involvement in these problems, whether proposed or actual, three major concepts or phases of policy are relevant here, centring on the ideas of national efficiency, tariff reform, and industrial rationalization.

Pessimism about Britain's future was heightened by the crisis of the Boer War. There were military reverses, evidence of faulty administration, scandals even; there was concern, too (as has already been noted), about the apparent physical degeneration of the racial stock indicated by the poor health of many men who volunteered for the army. As Kipling said, the war was 'no end of a lesson', a real blow to feelings of national superiority, sharpening the alarm that already existed or where latent bringing it to the surface. Perhaps, it was felt, a complete change of purpose was necessary with the coming of the new century and the passing of the old order symbolized by the death of the Queen. An important outcome of this critical maelstrom of event and sentiment was 'the ideology of national efficiency', a miscellaneous and complex series of beliefs, assumptions, and demands calculated to restore the country's confidence. The major elements comprising these views have been

70 R. H. Tawney, *The British Labor Movement* (New Haven, Conn., 1925), pp.22, 48–9. Cf. A. J. Penty, *Post-Industrialism* (London, 1922), pp.119–21.

described by Dr Searle whose account I largely follow here.[71] And the point of relevance in the present context is that many facets of the doctrine intimated the need for some form of government action or supervision as, for instance, in one of the key documents, Arnold White's *Efficiency and Empire* (1901).[72]

One aspect of the matter was a belief in the superiority of certain foreign models of conduct, notably Germany and Japan. The former, in particular, suggested courses of military reorganization and developments in social welfare and educational arrangements that (it was often urged) the British government might follow with great advantage. The felt need for eugenic improvement (revealed by the declining birth-rate and the evidence about physical unfitness) was not diminished by official inquiry and among the less extreme suggestions put forward was the policy of a 'National Minimum' by which government should raise physical standards and educational levels of achievement. Rosebery, the leader of the Liberal Imperialists and the foremost political spokesman of a policy of efficiency, frequently spelled out its requirements in respect of government action to reform education, housing, sanitation, and so on.[73] This sort of policy appealed greatly to the Webbs and other Fabians who joined in demanding the pursuit of imperial greatness through national efficiency.[74] Nor was the administrative dimension neglected, for there were proposals canvassed to create a more efficient Cabinet and departmental organization and the like (and which re-emerged in the later recommendations of the Haldane Committee). Imperial federation, with the world-wide mobilization of the resources of the empire, was seen by many observers as the only way for Britain to maintain its position of parity in an age of international giants and incidentally to deal with particular problems such as settling surplus population, ensuring food supplies, markets, and so on. Industry, too, was to be revived through all these indirect avenues of improvement and, as well, more specifically by the public development of means of transport and communication and by the provision of greatly improved facilities for scientific and technological research which was to be stimulated with government aid.[75] The mood was one which contributed to a number of contemporary changes as varied as the establishment of the Committee

---

71 G. R. Searle, *The Quest for National Efficiency*, ch. III. See also B. Semmel, *Imperialism and Social Reform: English Social-Imperial Thought, 1895–1914* (London, 1960), ch. III.

72 Repr. Brighton, 1973, with an introduction by G. R. Searle.

73 See the passages cited in Semmel, op. cit., pp. 62–3; also ibid., pp. 234–6.

74 As in Sidney Webb's article 'Lord Rosebery's Escape from Houndsditch', *Nineteenth Century and After*, l (1901), pp. 366–86.

75 See e.g. the proposals of Sir John Brunner put forward in 1904, in J. Harris, *Unemployment and Politics*, pp. 217–19.

of Imperial Defence in 1902 and the passage in the same year of the Education Act. Similarly, the inception and carrying through of the scheme for national labour exchanges owed a great deal to the work of the young William Beveridge who was motivated not so much by philanthropic purposes as by a passion for improvement and 'obsessive dislike' of the social and individual waste involved by unemployment: he was confident indeed that the exchanges 'would inaugurate a new era of industrial efficiency'.[76] It was also part of the environment in which the tariff reform campaign took hold: for this, too, was concerned with the defence and improvement of Britain's economic position.

The growing intensity of foreign competition was one of the main factors behind this campaign. Increasingly there were appeals (not perhaps always well-founded) for British industry to be shielded from 'dumping' and from other expressions of the rivalry of firms abroad that often received government subsidies (as to encourage large-scale organization), that were not disadvantaged by restrictive and expensive factory legislation or by active trade unions, and which were protected by a tariff wall. Such practices as these, established in defiance of free-trade principles, could (it was argued) only be met by similar action on the part of the British government. 'Safeguarding', 'reciprocity', 'fair trade', or even a general protective tariff were increasingly suggested as feelings of economic nationalism began to emerge. In 1881 the Fair Trade League was established to campaign against the indiscriminate application of the free-trade principle and to urge its use only in respect of countries that admitted British products on a similar basis. Symbolically, Friedrich List's *National System of Political Economy* was translated into English for the first time in 1885 over forty years after it first appeared. The Royal Commission on the Depression of Trade and Industry (1885–6) still supported free trade but there was a powerfully argued minority report which recommended the 'fair trade' solution to Britain's problems. And, of course, in 1903 Joseph Chamberlain publicly advocated a complete programme of 'tariff reform' or general protection of British industry, arguing that Britain should repudiate its long-standing adherence to the doctrine of general free trade. There were, of course, many factors lying behind this advocacy: political tactics, the desire to cement imperial relations, the creation of an additional source of revenue to finance social reform; but, above all, the need to restore British industry by securing a protected domestic base for improvement. While no immediate success was achieved by Chamberlain's campaign, the economic strains and distortions imposed by the demands of the Great War led to the beginnings of change. In 1915, in a step of major symbolic significance, the so-called McKenna duties were imposed on

76 ibid., p.285.

various 'luxury' imports. Introduced for wartime purposes they never-theless continued after the end of hostilities for protectionist reasons. And various *ad hoc* interventions of a similar kind to deal with post-war difficulties culminated at the time of the major economic crisis in the Import Duties Act of 1932 which led to general protection, a 10 per cent duty being imposed on most manufactured imports. Britain's adherence to the principle of free trade was, after a period of dilution, thus formally brought to an end and replaced by government manipulation of the customs barrier as a means of safeguarding British industry.

And this step was associated indeed with a further process of state intervention through the policy usually called 'rationalization' or 'Mondism', after Alfred Mond (the creator of ICI), one of its major exponents in the 1920s when the terms came into general use. What they entailed was the reorganization of industry on 'scientific' lines to make it more efficient by eliminating waste of labour, time, and materials; reducing costs; amalgamation of units to take advantage of economies of scale; the more effective use of research; and so on.[77] Of course, this could have been done simply at the initiative of the firms concerned and often was. But in many cases government aid and pressure, perhaps of a substantial order, were required. Something of the need involved had emerged during the Great War and the reconstruction period which followed. For instance, the Balfour Committee had urged in 1918 that substantial state assistance to industry would be essential to this end and to enable it to adapt to the conditions of peacetime competition. In this context the government, as well as giving financial aid and providing tariff protection, often actively assisted in the process of industrial reorganization which was, in effect, the price paid by industry for the help of the state. Thus amalgamation was imposed on the railway companies; attempts were made to promote combination and reorganiz-ation in the coal industry and to control its production; overall supervision of electricity supply was prescribed; and a co-ordinated system of road transport was envisaged. In this way it was hoped to establish an efficient array of basic facilities as a foundation for economic improvement. In the same fashion government acted to rationalize other industries to make them more competitive and productive. In the 1930s a programme of reduction in the number of spindles was carried out in the cotton industry; marketing boards were established in respect of certain agricultural products to regulate output and prices; loans were given to shipping and shipbuilding; and so forth.[78] Despite opposition of various

77 A good, brief, contemporary account is L. Urwick, *The Meaning of Rationalisation* (London, 1929).
78 A detailed summary of the process of industrial rationalization in Britain is given in F. E. Lawley, *The Growth of Collective Economy* (London, 1938), i. 403–17.

sorts and from different quarters, these policies were increasingly accepted and demanded as the 1920s and 1930s wore on. Sir Alfred Mond provided a justification of the idea in a famous address on 'The Rationalisation of Industry' in 1927; it was urged by the Liberal *Yellow Book* the following year as a major means to business efficiency; it was a central part of the Mosley Memorandum of 1930; and was taken up by the group of young Tory MPs exemplified by Harold Macmillan and his 'middle way'.[79] Some proponents of these schemes saw them as a means of putting private enterprise on its feet, as a device to avoid nationalization; others saw them as a preliminary to this latter end. Either way, a much greater degree of government involvement was required than would have been acceptable to earlier generations. It was seen, too, as a clear corollary of the policy that the machinery of government itself required reorganization if it was effectively to fulfil the greater role demanded of it.[80]

Taken together, then, these policies of national efficiency, tariff reform, and rationalization, as they emerged over the early decades of this century, invited substantial steps towards a collectivist economy. Their introduction was piecemeal but was none the less cumulatively significant. Moreover they intimated, even if they did not overtly entail, the further notion of the planned economy itself, the idea of government intervention to attempt nothing less than the systematic management of economic life as a whole.

INTERVENTION TO MANAGE THE ECONOMY

Planning is forced upon us . . . not for idealistic reasons, but because the old mechanism . . . is no longer adequate. . . .
H. MACMILLAN, *Reconstruction*, 1933, p.18

Though perhaps little has been achieved in comparison with the anticipation of improvement or even of perfection aroused, the idea of the planned economy has become a commonplace: it is, in economic terms, the apotheosis of collectivism as so far revealed. The emergence of this theme in recent times may be indicated under two headings. The first deals with a series of specific problems that have arisen since 1918 and which have led to augmented government intervention in the economy in addition to that already recounted; the second concerns developments in economic thought and the emergence of the concept of planning itself.

79 Mond's lecture is reprinted in his *Industry and Politics* (London, 1927), pp.210–21; Liberal Industrial Inquiry, *Britain's Industrial Future* (London, 1928), p.128; for Macmillan, see *The Ideological Heritage*, ch.7.
80 e.g. Urwick, op. cit., pp.136ff.

Specific problems

Control of monopolies and cartels

The problem of monopoly had always exercised at least the radical mind. Land in particular had long been a candidate for public ownership or regulation as a means of taking this crucial and naturally limited resource out of the control of a small social group. But there were also industries or services to which the normal process of competition and private enterprise might seem inappropriate, as with the railways and tramways or the supply of gas and water, and these were also regarded as properly subject to municipal or national supervision or even ownership. There remained the trusts and other combinations established for private advantage and, as well, those large-scale industrial and commercial organizations created by or under the aegis of the state itself as part of the way to economic improvement. And here again the question of their control by some public agency was a matter of increasing moment. In fact, the pressures of competition, the effects and cost of technological change, as well as the process of rationalization, alike led to the emergence in some industries of very large units of production and management. In shipping the Cunard and White Star lines merged; a cartel was created in the steel industry, the British Iron and Steel Federation; the joint-stock banks were reduced in number from 104 in 1890 to eighteen in 1924; after the Great War the 120 companies operating the railways were reduced to four large groups; London transport facilities were brought under unified supervision; and so on. Many of these larger units were indeed created by legislation or at least on the active insistence and with the help of government. But once they had come into being, inevitably there were demands that control be exercised over their operations so that their actual or near monopolistic position was not exploited to the public disadvantage in respect, for instance, of the price, quality, or supply of goods and services concerned. Again, it was only government that could take steps to deal with this either by prohibiting, dissolving, or supervising them; taxing them; or by absorbing and administering them itself, a solution that had long been recommended especially, of course, by Socialists.[81] The idea of nationalization began to find favour in all parties as a means to make these large bodies, often supported with public funds, accountable to the community. It was a Conservative government which in 1939 bought out the two large airlines which had been in receipt of public subsidy and amalgamated them in the British Overseas Airways Corporation.

---

81 For an early Socialist discussion of the inevitability of the large industrial and commercial firm and so of the need for state control, see W. Clarke's paper in G. B. Shaw et al., Fabian Essays (1889; Jubilee edn, London, 1950), pp. 83–94.

But of course, a major – perhaps the determining – economic and social factor in stimulating greater public control of economic life was the experience of unemployment especially during the great depression of the 1920s and 1930s.

The maintenance of full employment

During the nineteenth century unemployment was invariably seen in Malthusian terms as a matter of personal worthlessness and over-population; and the standard kind of remedy envisaged, so far as one was thought possible, was, in addition to the usual philanthropy, a mixture of procreative restraint, emigration (as well as the prevention of any excessive foreign influx), and what was called 'home colonization', that is, the settlement of 'unwilling idlers' on unused land. A typical review of various proposals is that of the popular scientific writer Hugo Reid in his *What Should Be Done for the People?* (1848) which urged the state 'to fulfil its task of finding employment at a sufficient rate of wages' for those who are unable to do so for themselves. To this end, for instance, it should provide the capital to settle excess labour on the waste lands.[82] Collective action was envisaged, therefore, at a quite early stage but although there were exceptions – as with the Poor Employment Act of 1817 which systematized the existing practice of making government loans available to assist social and commercial investment in canals, roads, and public buildings – the intervention of the state itself was usually regarded with some diffidence.[83] The Malthusian League, for instance, was hostile not merely because its views were anti-Socialist but also on the ground that all such policies directed attention away from the central problem of family limitation and the moral issues involved; while the economic theory of the day refused to accept the possibility of any imbalance between the supply of and demand for labour – if individuals were out of work it was because they demanded too high wages – and urged as well that the attempt to create employment by public action could only worsen affairs elsewhere. Similarly the official mind at its most stringent, as in the so-called 'Treasury view', held that government spending, whether financed by deficit or taxation, could do little to lessen

82 H. Reid, *What Should Be Done for the People? An Appeal to the Electors of the United Kingdom* (London, 1848), pp.23–4. Various schemes for home and overseas colonization are reviewed in E. E. Barry, *Nationalisation in British Politics: the Historical Background* (London, 1965), pp.32–4, 39, 47–54; and J. Harris, *Unemployment and Politics: a Study in English Social Policy, 1886–1914* (Oxford, 1972), pp.115–44, 187–99.
83 For the 1817 Act, see H. Roseveare, *The Treasury: the Evolution of a British Institution* (London, 1969), pp.224–5.

widespread depression or unemployment.[84] By and large, then, any social and other deficiencies entailed by unemployment were deemed acceptable as the proper consequence of individual inadequacy or idleness or as merely incidental accidents of a general tendency towards growth and prosperity.[85] And so long as such attitudes prevailed then the call for government action on any large scale was obviously likely to be muted.

But by the turn of the nineteenth century voices of concern were increasingly heard and many observers began to suggest that the conventional view provided an inappropriate as well as an unfeeling frame of reference in which to see the problem. The matter was coming to be regarded as one of social and not personal responsibility. There were many reasons for the emergence of the new point of view.

Interestingly, one early factor was the American Civil War: for it was difficult to accept that contemporaneous distress in the cotton manufacturing areas was due to the indolence of those affected when it was obvious the trouble was primarily caused by the famine of raw material resulting from the Federal blockade. So in this case – as in the earlier examples of relief works in the Irish emergency of the 1840s or at the time of the Crimean War[86] – the need was duly and quickly recognized in the Public Works (Manufacturing Districts) Act of 1863 which, to deal with the unemployment created, allowed the Boards of Guardians more easily to undertake sanitary works, paving and road improvements, and the like, and as well granted loans for this purpose. Lord Derby (who had a special interest) said during the Lords' committee stage that, while as a general rule the intervention of government in matters of this kind was not desirable, the Bill before the House was in the circumstances a proper exception.[87] But, of course, an important precedent was created. As time wore on there was, too, an increasing volume of humanitarian, radical, and other criticism of the misery and poverty created by unemployment and a growing belief that a great many contemporary ills could be traced to this source. There were thus the social consequences to be considered not only in respect of the workers directly concerned but, through the loss of income involved, of their dependants and even whole

84 R. Ledbetter, *A History of the Malthusian League, 1877–1927* (Columbus, Ohio, 1976), pp. 15, 105, 109–11, 150–5; Harris, op. cit., pp. 1–2; B. A. Corry, *Money, Saving and Investment in English Economics 1800–1850* (London, 1962), p. 155.

85 For contemporary treatment of the matter in the Hogarthian terms of the good and idle apprentices, see C. Fox, 'The Development of Social Reportage in English Periodical Illustration during the 1840s and Early 1850s', *Past and Present* (no. 74; February 1977), pp. 105–6.

86 For an instance of the latter, see F. W. Hirst, *In the Golden Days* (London, 1947), p. 18.

87 172 Parl. Deb. 3s., 7 July 1863, col. 34. See also J. Lambert, *Modern Legislation as a Chapter in our History* (London, 1865), pp. 13–14; and for a detailed account N. Longmate, *The Hungry Mills* (London, 1978).

communities. This led the matter to be related to the other major issue of poverty and reform of the Poor Law. Hence the activities of the many private agencies seeking to find work for the deserving unemployed, to encourage thrift to tide over periods of difficulty, and so on. As well, many observers wondered whether in an age of manifest progress in so many fields these obvious social deficiencies need any longer be accepted as inevitable aspects of the human condition.[88] Further, the increasing voice of the trade unions was an important element in demanding assuagement of the hardships suffered by those who were out of work. The opening address at the Trades Union Congress in 1879 posed the question whether it was really necessary that 'every few years large multitudes of the people should, through no fault of their own, be reduced to such a destitute condition?'[89] Moreover, at a time when (as already indicated) there was a rising concern about the relative decline of British economic power and the growth of foreign competition, the pursuit of national efficiency could (it was thought by an increasing number of observers) tolerate no such waste of economic resources as that involved in a large amount of unused labour; nor was it possible to be sanguine about the unrest that might ensue. It was gradually being realized, too, as a result of information acquired from trade union records and social inquiries and casework that the problem was not a uniform one and was more diverse or complex than often supposed. For instance, those unemployed were not always the same people; different industries and areas were affected in sundry ways and to a diverse degree; there was a regular seasonal or cyclical variation; dead-end jobs and casual work were often to blame; as, too, was technological change or the long-term decay of a particular industry. Moreover the unemployed themselves fell into many different categories from the highly-skilled to the indolent. A growing literature emerged dealing with the subject, analysing it, and proposing remedies not simply on a moral or personal level but in respect to general industrial organization or commercial circumstances.[90] The problem thus came increasingly to be recognized as a major issue of public policy. William Clarke, the Fabian, urged in 1888 that the '"unemployed" question is the sphinx which will devour us if we cannot answer her riddle'; and, a few years later in 1893, John Burns was quite clear the matter was the definite responsibility of the whole of society, 'the all-absorbing question' which all governments now had to

88 e.g. A. Marshall, *Principles of Economics* (1890; 8th edn, London, 1930), pp.3–4.
89 Cited in Barry, op. cit., p.131.
90 See e.g. the list of items appearing between 1890 and 1905 recorded in J. Burns, *The Unemployed*, Fabian tract no. 47 (1893; London, 1906), p.19. For the development of Beveridge's views, see J. Harris, *William Beveridge: a Biography* (Oxford, 1977), ch.6, esp. pp.117–18.

face.[91] And when, in the following decade, a policy of tariff reform was being urged, its exponents were careful to explain that one of the advantages it would bring was that a high level of employment could be more easily maintained: in 1905 Chamberlain even referred to the prospect of 'full' employment.[92]

The traditional view of the out-of-work question, that unemployment could not be eliminated and that, in any case, only the undeserving or the foolhardy went to the wall, was thus causing more and more misgiving. The result was a growing acceptance of the need for government action either to mitigate the consequences of being without a job or, more radically, to prevent the circumstances that led to this occurrence. And if a certain degree of unemployment would always exist, even be essential to the health of any economic system (for instance, because of technological advance, labour being replaced by machines, or because resources were redeployed as a result of changes in demand) then at least the machinery for reallocating freed or unused labour should be effective and, if not automatic, monitored and where necessary stimulated; and as well, proper aid should be available to those affected during any interim.

Of course, at this stage there was by no means any widely accepted account or theory of unemployment, no real glimpse of a general policy that might largely eliminate or control the problem. But many expedients or palliatives were suggested to cope with its worst aspects. In the 1880s further attempts had been made to deal with pockets of unemployment through public works; and in 1886 Chamberlain (then President of the Local Government Board in the Liberal administration) gave encouragement to such policies by sending a circular to local authorities urging them to make jobs available in this way in times of poor trade. In fact, this approach had little practical effect for various reasons not least the difficulty of raising the necessary funds at short notice. During the 1890s, too, there were a couple of Royal Commissions and two major Parliamentary inquiries on the best way to tackle the matter though no practical consensus emerged from their deliberations and little was achieved.[93] At this time, as well, among the many policies put forward the old idea of a 'labour bureau' in each locality, co-ordinated by a central labour exchange, was revived and began to gain popularity; a number of such registries was set up in different parts of the country under various auspices. In 1902 the Conservative government authorized their establishment in the London boroughs where they had previously been declared *ultra vires* by the district auditor. At the same time it

91 W. Clarke, 'The Basis of Socialism: Industrial', in Shaw *et al.*, *Fabian Essays*, p.67; Burns, op. cit., p.5.
92 C. W. Boyd (ed.), *Mr. Chamberlain's Speeches* (London, 1914), ii.318.
93 Harris, *Unemployment and Politics*, pp.76–9, 90–101, 336.

encouraged the creation of unofficial 'distress committees' to help provide work; and three years later these bodies were given legal status and powers, the larger towns being obliged to set them up with some support from the rates and, subsequently, a Parliamentary grant. In this way Balfour's administration, albeit somewhat half-heartedly, initiated the legislation against unemployment which was extended so considerably during the following decades.[94] Later the Asquith government, as a result in particular of the internal pressure exerted by George and Churchill, took further and major steps to elaborate and extend these devices.[95] An Act of 1909, supported by all parties, authorized the establishment on a country-wide scale of a system of labour exchanges to co-ordinate the placing of workers.[96] Two years later the National Insurance Act, developing a field previously pioneered by some trade unions, provided *inter alia* that workers in major industries where there was marked seasonal fluctuation in employment (about one-sixth of the industrial labour force) should be covered by a compulsory unemployment insurance scheme. Similarly, in pursuit of the policy of spending on public works to counteract fluctuations of trade, a Development Commission and a Road Board were set up in 1910 to channel funds into agriculture and rural industries, fishing, roads, harbours, rivers, and canals, not only to enhance these national resources but with a view to improving employment prospects. In these ways, and to a greater degree than ever before, the attempt was being made to organize the labour market (or at least a certain aspect of it) through government action, if not in accordance with any strategic plan of social reform then in response to the specific demand for an effective national minimum in conditions of employment and for 'the right to work'. It was an opinion very emphatically expressed in the minority Poor Law Report of 1909 that it was administratively possible, if it were sincerely wished to do so, to remedy most of the evils of unemployment; certainly the Webb policy had been to stress the need for a national authority to regulate systematically the supply of labour, enforce minimum earnings, and supervise the Factory Acts and wage boards.[97]

---

94 E. Halévy, *A History of the English People in the Nineteenth Century* (1913–46; 2nd trans. edn, London, 1961), v. 370–1; Harris, *Unemployment and Politics*, pp. 157ff, 208–10. On the action taken, see e.g. the account of what was done in Manchester to relieve the unemployed during the first few years of the century in A. Redford, *The History of Local Government in Manchester* (London, 1939–40), iii. 140–7.

95 Harris, *Unemployment and Politics*, ch. VI.

96 For a review of these developments particularly as they affected the Board of Trade, see Harris, *William Beveridge*, chs. 7–8.

97 B. Webb, *Our Partnership* (London, 1948), p. 480.

Of course, all this was only a form of amelioration; but it was a vital first step. Beveridge himself believed these changes were 'revolutionary' and had a major significance 'in expanding the direct functions of Whitehall.'[98] The state had at least embarked on a policy of insurance against unemployment and was subsequently obliged both to extend its scope (as in 1916 and 1921 by which time the scheme covered almost the entire working class) and to meet the commitment involved during the massive unemployment of the inter-war years. It had clearly been recognized, too, that charitable or local effort could not cope with the problem and that government itself had to do much more than supervise or co-ordinate these piecemeal responses. The effects of unemployment were so widespread and contributed so much to economic inefficiency that they had to be considered a matter of the greatest concern requiring for their treatment a concerted national policy.[99] What was involved or achieved has been well summarized by Sir Ronald Davison (one of the officials concerned) in a book he wrote after retiring from the Civil Service:

> The history of modern unemployment policy really begins before the Great War. This is not so much because of the extent of the pre-war problem, as because there was a fundamental change in the attitude of the community towards its unemployed citizens about the years 1909 to 1911. It was then that the new sense of social responsibility took shape in the creation of a national system of employment exchanges and a limited experiment in compulsory unemployment insurance. The former were to reduce unemployment to the minimum, whatever the state of the labour market; the latter was to compensate the genuine worker for unavoidable interruptions of wage-earning.[100]

No doubt these developments were only pragmatic responses to contemporary problems. Nevertheless, they did involve recognition of the inadequacy of existing machinery and constituted a further step in the enlargement of government control over industry and the creation of institutions to implement this commitment.[101] Beatrice Webb had predicted in 1911 that the administration of unemployment benefit would make possible 'the increased control of the employer and wage-earner by the state.'[102]

---

98 Draft of speech (1960), Beveridge Papers, III 34, in Harris, *William Beveridge*, p.150.
99 On the background to and origins of this change of emphasis, ibid., ch. V.
100 R. C. Davison, *British Unemployment Policy: the Modern Phase since 1930* (London, 1938), p.3. For a recent critical but measured assessment of what was achieved up to the Great War, see Harris, *Unemployment and Politics*, ch. VII.
101 Harris, *Unemployment and Politics*, pp.362–5.
102 Mrs Webb's diary (13 May 1911), in *Our Partnership*, p.475.

After the Great War – during which a Ministry of Labour was created in 1916 – the unemployment problem worsened. To an apparently basic and increasing *malaise* in British industry was added the disruptive effect of the war on the domestic economy and on international trade. At the beginning of 1921, the number out of work in Britain exceeded 2 million and never sank below 1 million until 1940. This represented between 5 and 10 per cent of the total working population. During the 1920s, however, there was relatively little long-term unemployment and what there was was largely concentrated in the coal industry; and it was widely assumed that a general improvement in world trade would soon occur so that any measures taken need only be of a temporary or merely palliative nature. However the government did embark on a limited programme of public works of various kinds. It introduced an industrial transference scheme to ameliorate the uneven geographical distribution of unemployment; it gave subsidies in aid of exports to farmers and to various industries; the de-rating provisions of 1929 were intended to relieve (at Treasury expense) the tax burden of both industry and agriculture; and so forth.[103] But not only did the number out of work increase (in 1931–2 it reached nearly 3 million) as well the proportion of those unemployed for more than a year rose to something like one-quarter of all those without jobs. Moreover, this state of affairs was concentrated in several major industries and in particular parts of the country, the so-called distressed or special areas like South Wales and Tyneside that were especially hard hit. In Wales, in 1937, nearly two out of every five persons had been unemployed for over a year; the previous year in Crook, Co. Durham, 71 per cent of workers had had no job for five years.[104] Contrary to popular view, the picture was not uniformly black however. Some regions continued to increase in prosperity – the Midlands and the South-East, in particular, enjoyed a substantial burst of growth led by the housing, electrical, and motor industries.[105] But because of the ill-favoured areas and the failure of the existing insurance and related schemes to cope with the haphazard impact of the trade depression, demands for state action inevitably intensified, demands that more and more involved the suggestion that government had the responsibility so to regulate the country's economic life as to eliminate these manifest deficiencies in its functioning. It was

---

103 For a concise review, see K. J. Hancock, 'The Reduction of Unemployment as a Problem of Public Policy, 1920–29', *Economic History Review*, xv (1962–3), esp. pp. 328–9 and §§III–IV.
104 J. Lovell in C. B. Cox and A. E. Dyson (eds), *The Twentieth-Century Mind: History, Ideas and Literature in Britain* (London, 1972), ii. 46.
105 P. Addison, *The Road to 1945: British Politics and the Second World War* (London, 1975), p. 26.

very clear – at least to radicals like Beatrice Webb – not only that the prevention of unemployment was likely to be 'a difficult and slow business' but also that it would involve 'far more control of capitalist enterprise' than had hitherto been envisaged. The Macmillan Committee on Finance and Industry urged in 1931, less partially in political terms but by no means less strongly, that the 'endeavour of domestic management should be to promote the stability of output and of employment at a high level'.[106] Remedial measures taken included the extension of the Unemployment Insurance scheme, as by the creation of the Unemployment Assistance Board in 1934 to administer a centralized system of needs payments outside insurance, a clear recognition, it was said, that 'a specialized second line of defence against the social ills of unemployment was going to be a permanent necessity of the modern state.'[107] Steps were also taken to try to help the 'special areas' through two commissioners (who had, however, little real effect); labour migration was further aided; industrial training schemes instituted; grants given for social improvements and in aid of local rates; land settlement schemes were established; trading estates created; loans granted to special undertakings; and the like.[108] What was done constituted a series of *ad hoc* measures: certainly not compatible with Spencerian *laissez faire* or with any consistent collectivist policy either. The former, ruthless as it seemed, leaving people to their doom was unpalatable; the latter was neither widely formulated nor accepted. Yet the creeping pragmatic growth of intervention continued (though the actual effect of government policy was, in fact, probably light compared with that of other factors in assisting the process of recovery).[109]

However, with the coming of the Second World War, unemployment figures naturally fell dramatically, being as low as 84,000 by January 1944. And, rightly or wrongly, the wartime means of control whereby this position was achieved were regarded as a precedent for dealing with the peacetime situation to come. In 1943 the Machinery of Government Committee of the Cabinet discussed post-war responsibility for employment policy and accepted that (in the words of a memorandum submitted by Ernest Bevin) 'the maintenance of full employment will be an integral part of the Government's economic, financial and industrial policy' and that this should be the responsibility of a single department to ensure

106   M. Cole (ed.), *Beatrice Webb's Diaries, 1924–1932* (London, 1956), p.29; Finance & Industry Committee Report 1930–1 (vol. xiii), Cmd. 3897, §282(iii).
107   Davison, op. cit., p.35.
108   All these matters are summarized, ibid. chs. II–VI.
109   For a statement of this apposition, ibid., pp.106–10. See also H. W. Richardson, 'The Basis of Economic Recovery in the Nineteen-Thirties: a Review and a New Interpretation', *Economic History Review*, xv (1962–3), p.361.

effective control.[110] In the previous year Sir William Beveridge had presented his famous report on social insurance and there, as well as in his *Full Employment in a Free Society* (1944), he argued that the avoidance of mass unemployment could be achieved in peacetime. Of course, by this time the perhaps rather different Keynesian policies were becoming widely accepted in official and political circles as showing how the level of employment was not simply a matter of controlling production and organizing the labour market but of manipulating public spending and consumer demand. In the same year the Coalition government accepted the objective of sustaining full employment in a famous White Paper.[111]

When peace came in 1945, therefore, there was a widespread acceptance of the idea that the level of employment could and would, in contrast to pre-war days, be managed or planned by the authorities. And while immediate post-war experience seemed to bear out the possibility of this fulfilment, more recent events have tended to cast a certain doubt on the policies involved.

Problems since 1945

If before the Second World War the major economic issue was the depression as manifested particularly in mass unemployment, then in the decades immediately after the end of hostilities the new problems to emerge were those associated with the balance on external trade and the need to increase industrial output. Lately, of course, the difficulties of inflation have come to the fore and in a previously quite unexpected context associated as they have been with the effects of recession, the re-emergence of substantial unemployment, and the failure of productivity to grow as expected. And just as the pre-war predicament called forth a growing government involvement (which was then temporarily stimulated still further by the impetus of the war years) so these various post-war exigencies have further compounded the process of collectivist development. What follows is the merest sketch of a no doubt partial and impressionistic kind. It is simply intended to highlight some of the modes, and the extent, of government involvement in these affairs.[112]

110 PRO, CAB 87/74, Machinery of Government Committee, meetings of 22 June and 7 October 1943. The citation is from the memorandum submitted to the former meeting, p. 2 §4.

111 For Beveridge's views, see Harris, *William Beveridge*, pp. 428 ff. There is a full account of the genesis of Coalition employment policy in Addison, op. cit., pp. 242–6.

112 There are superbly concise summaries of the post-war situation (on which I have drawn here) by W. Carr and S. Pollard, in Cox and Dyson, op. cit., vol. iii, chs. 1–2. See also Pollard's *The Development of the British Economy, 1914–1967* (1962; 2nd edn, London, 1970), chs. VII–VIII.

The economic effects of the war on Britain were indeed very considerable. Physical resources were destroyed; capital equipment was run down and its distribution directed to wartime purposes; export markets were given up or lost; foreign assets were sold to the detriment of earnings on the invisible account; currency reserves were depleted and external debt piled up, as with the so-called sterling balances; technological opportunities were forgone; and so on. The result by 1945 was a distorted and deteriorated economy which faced a huge deficit on overseas trade that could not easily be eliminated. There was, too, an acute dollar shortage at a time when Britain (like many other countries) depended on the USA for vital supplies of food and raw materials, a shortage exacerbated by the sudden and unexpected end of Lend-Lease. Further, the terms of trade worsened, high overseas defence costs continued, industry needed to be reorganized and revivified, and a sterling crisis supervened. In these circumstances it was simply assumed that government would play a major part in directing the economy, preserving in the peacetime world the role it had sustained during the war: much of the apparatus of supervision was indeed simply taken over or developed from the wartime system of administration. And so government continued to be enmeshed in a mass of detailed management: by direct nationalization in some cases; limiting consumption by rationing and allocation; providing subsidies of various kinds; controlling building and supplies of raw materials; overseeing the movement and use of capital and labour; influencing investment decisions; determining the location of new industrial development; improving the organization and efficiency of firms by stimulating mergers, giving financial aid, imposing training schemes; developing research and science-based industries; restricting imports and the flow of foreign exchange; and the like. Of course, there were alterations of tone and emphasis from time to time as when the emphasis on physical control gave way to more general fiscal manipulation or when a deliberate attempt was made to co-ordinate the various elements of economic development in the National Plan of the mid-1960s. But the general tendency of direction was clear.

Something of the difficulties of these attempts on the part of government to regulate economic life were naturally very apparent. The level of employment was still the ultimate criterion of success, so deep had pre-war experience seared. So, when it seemed necessary, the authorities would apply an appropriate expansionary stimulus which was by then the orthodox remedy for any slackening in the economy. Unfortunately this was rarely without an accompanying untoward effect: home demand was stimulated, thereby producing an increase in imports and causing, too, a diversion to the domestic market of goods that might have gone for export. This led to balance of payments difficulties and consequences deleterious to the stability of the pound. This, in turn, caused government to reduce the expansionary stimulus. This process constituted the so-called stop-go cycle that seemed to characterize both the economy and government policy in the 1960s. Productivity increased in secular terms but never seemed to reach take-off; and the ideal of a planned long-term expansion appeared forever just beyond the grasp. The basic point in the present context is not so much whether this kind of impasse might have been avoided but that it was widely accepted as the responsibility of government alone to take the steps (whatever they might be) that were necessary to deal with it.

Latterly, of course, inflation has become the central focus of concern and again it is pretty generally held that in the last resort only government can effectively tackle it, though there is little agreement as to the possible or desirable means of its doing this or on the extent to which its own policies have led to the prevailing difficulties. Of course, exotic factors, such as the increasing cost of materials from abroad (especially oil), have contributed to the recent rise in price levels. But even allowing for this, much has to be attributed to the actions of governments over the past ten years, if not before, and this in particular relation to policy on employment and industrial relations and to the generally high level of public expenditure.

The significance of the latter as an index of official activity was noted in the first chapter.[113] The point is that public spending is apparently quite irreducible in the sense that it never seems to diminish and only to increase as the extent and cost of services and subsidies provided, especially in the welfare field, are continually augmented; and this continues regardless, it seems, whether there is any real economic growth or not. It used to be thought – as suggested in a famous article published many years ago by Professor Colin Clark – that a practical limit of some 25 per cent of GNP would be found to exist: beyond this, inflation and a fall in the supply of goods would occur.[114] By now this particular point has long been passed; though it may be that, at the higher level now reached, the caveat still applies. The basic mechanism involved is simply that this growing public expenditure has to be financed either by taxation or borrowing. But the former cuts profit margins or incentives, both personal and commercial, while the latter, as well as being (through the financial forms employed) a prime cause of inflation, may also create a scarcity of funds and limit investment possibilities. It cannot be insignificant that the rate of return on industrial capital fell from 14 per cent in 1955 to less than 2 per cent twenty years later, and this at a time

113 See pp. 31–5 above.
114 C. Clark, 'Public Finance and Changes in the Value of Money', *Economic Journal*, xl (1945), pp. 371–89.

when the highest possible development of the 'marketed' sector of the economy was desirable not least because on its buoyancy depends the very success of government policy itself. Here again there is a further point at which government enters the scene either as a source of aid to hard-hit firms or industries (through such devices as investment and development grants or regional aid) or with the intention of taking such 'lame ducks' more directly under the public wing. The irony is that the need for such assistance may be due substantially to these high taxation and borrowing levels in the first place: government policy thus helps make industry inefficient and this incapacity invites more state aid and intervention still.

These are tendencies which have been developing a long time but their force has recently been compounded by developments in the fields of employment and industrial relations and associated financial policy. In the late 1960s unemployment began to rise above the level which had been usual since the war and by early 1972 exceeded one million, an occasion *The Times*, reflecting common opinion, described as 'shocking'.[115] The Heath government, not least because of its industrial relations policy and the need to accommodate the unions as much as possible, moved to counter this rise in the number of workless by bolstering demand through the by then conventional technique of reflationary spending. In other words, it added substantially to the deficit existing in respect of the already high level of public expenditure. Moreover, it did this in such a way as to produce (in the absence of any corresponding production increase) a pronounced inflationary effect. A deficit can be financed in three ways: by the sale of gilt-edged stock to the public; by foreign borrowing; and by the sale of Treasury Bills to the banks. In critical circumstances the first is likely to be limited by public confidence and the need not to deprive industry of funds; the second will obviously offer only limited opportunities; so the third device was largely employed. But the banks regard these Bills as increasing their liquid assets and so as enabling more credit to be created through loans to customers. And if this happens at a rate faster than economic growth (or than can be compensated by the earnings of North Sea oil) there will be an inflationary effect. There was a very substantial one as we all know, rising to well over 20 per cent per annum by the end of the 1970s. As well, given the position and strength of the trade unions, the result of their activities was not more employment but rather effective pressure for higher wages; this, too, nullified the primary purpose of the government's exercise.

A quantitative indication of these matters is given by what is nowadays called the Public Sector Borrowing Requirement, that is, the

115 'A Million Out of Work', *The Times* (21 January 1972), p.13.

extent of the deficit on central and local government account and on that of the nationalized industries. It is a figure which has grown enormously in recent years; and it has been estimated that in 1975–6 a standard rate of income tax of about 65p would have been necessary to cover the current PSBR.[116] Nor is it unimportant that there is an inbuilt exponential factor: being financed by borrowing, a deficit creates debt charges; and the higher it goes the greater the proportion of the extra borrowing which has to be incurred simply to meet these costs – as New York City discovered a while ago.

To meet this sort of dilemma and to cope with the problems of Britain's current economic position, there now seem to be three notionally distinct types of solution on offer. The first, the monetarist analysis, holds that the basic cause of inflation and its consequences is the excessive stock of money and credit in relation to real output. So the policy recommended is obvious: reduce government expenditure and borrowing and keep them under strict control.[117] The second, in the traditional post-war style, wishes to moderate the effects of demand management by ensuring the regulation of wage levels and increases and so necessarily of other prices too. The nub of the matter here, therefore, is an effective income and price control policy. The third, more overtly collectivist in form, looks to the establishment of a tightly managed siege economy behind a barrier of import controls as a means of regulating these domestic matters in planned autarkic fashion. Clearly, only the first envisages less government activity than at present and the reader can judge as well as I the prospects of its political and electoral success. The second might seem to involve merely a diluted version of, or step on the way to, the third. Certainly the idea that economic life should be regulated to some degree or, more than this, substantively planned by government is one that has become increasingly widespread over the years. It is indeed a notion that has a long and varied pedigree in the history of recent economic thought.

Economic thought and the concept of planning

It is invariably difficult to assess the relation between ideas and practice, to determine how far the latter waits on theory or to what extent concepts simply reflect what has already occurred and merely fit more or less congenially into what happens actually to be under way. Do ideas mould events or do various collections of them lie around waiting for the state of affairs to make them relevant as stimulus, explanation, or

---

116 A. Robinson, 'The House of Commons and Public Expenditure', in S. A. Walkland and M. Ryle (eds), *The Commons in the Seventies* (Fontana, 1977), p.265 n.10. See also Table 7, p.157 below.

117 Some aspects of monetarist policy are briefly reviewed on pp.153–63 below.

justification? Fortunately, this question need not be tackled here, though it must always be hovering in the background as an omnipresent methodological worry. At the least, different aspects of economic thought over the past couple of centuries have reflected or played a part in the debate about the proper role of government in economic life. Although the supposed link with different social classes is a typical over-simplification, Marx indicated the apposition or range of economic ideas involved in his famous inaugural address to the Working Men's International Association in September 1864 when he referred to 'the great contest between the blind rule of the supply and demand laws which form the political economy of the middle class, and social production controlled by social foresight, which forms the political economy of the working class.'[118] The specific point to be reviewed in this section is indeed the way in which dominant tendencies in economic thought have changed from those in which a prejudice against the state was by and large manifest to those in which a contrary sentiment prevails.

Classical political economy and the state

There is a most interesting dichotomy of influence and interpretation lingering about the reputation of the classical school, that is, such writers as Smith, Malthus, Ricardo, Senior, Mill, and McCulloch. Their doctrines have invariably, or at least very often, been associated with an extreme *laissez faire* point of view.[119] The reasons for this are fairly obvious. Most of these writers developed their ideas in a reaction against mercantilism with its stress on the vital economic role of public authority; they certainly did champion the market and nagged about the untoward consequences of state intervention; and (perhaps most important of all) certain of the school's apostles, from Bentham to Harriet Martineau, indeed emphasized the crucial importance of the 'let alone' principle often without the prudent reservations sometimes otherwise acknowledged. Yet the general or popular reputation of the classical doctrines as thus established is (as now widely recognized) misleading as to the detailed views of most of their major exponents.[120]

118 K. Marx and F. Engels, *Selected Works* (Moscow, 1951–8), i. 383.
119 Some random instances: Sir A. Gray, *The Development of Economic Doctrine: an Introductory Survey* (1931; London, 1963), p. 176; G. H. Sabine, *A History of Political Theory* (1937; London, 1944), pp. 656ff; J. A. Spender, *The Government of Mankind* (London, 1938), p. 306.
120 Professor A. J. Taylor's *Laissez-faire and State Intervention in Nineteenth-Century Britain* (London, 1972), esp. chs. 3–4 provides a good brief introduction to the debate about this matter and also has an excellent annotated bibliography as a guide to the main contributions to the discussion. The definitive analysis is L. C. Robbins, *The Theory of Economic Policy in English Classical Political Economy* (London, 1952); other excellent treatments are A. W. Coats (ed.), *The Classical Economists and Economic Policy* (London, 1971), and D. P. O'Brien, *The Classical Economists* (1975; Oxford, 1978), esp. ch. 10.

Not only were these economists not a uniform school with a monolithic point of view about the role of the state, they were also in their different ways prepared to accept the case for positive public action where this could be specifically justified. If there was a general presumption against state intervention, particular exceptions were always admitted and the case for them urged. Equally, if the idea of a natural harmony of interests was usually present to their minds they were also very much aware of the real conflicts inherent in economic life and the need to moderate the tensions that might ensue. As F. W. Hirst tartly commented on one occasion, 'Laissez-faire is a principle which the great Reformers applied broadly and rationally, not with the stupid narrowness attributed to them by so many modern critics'.[121] Within a broadly libertarian framework, therefore, important concessions about the need for public action could be found in those very writings which were often or widely supposed to regard it as anathema.

For example, Adam Smith admitted the basic importance of government's responsibility for defence and the need to establish also an adequate system of justice and public order. And, perhaps more significantly, he accepted in addition that the commonwealth had a duty of 'erecting and maintaining' public institutions and works which could not be sustained by the mere pursuit of individual or group interest. By this he meant, for instance, good communications which were so essential to commerce (roads, bridges, harbours, canals, and the like); the protection and regulation of foreign trade companies; and the provision of educational facilities where these were not otherwise available.[122] Malthus, if he strongly disapproved of the Poor Laws, nevertheless believed the state might properly in some circumstances support emigration as a 'slight palliative', prevent the exploitation of child labour, assist in the educational field, and aid large families.[123] McCulloch, writing a generation later and forced to consider the question of intervention more explicitly, held that it was absurd to apply laissez faire principles without regard to the prevailing circumstances. He certainly believed adults should fend for themselves as much as possible but bluntly said that anyone who held to an extreme application of laissez

121 F. W. Hirst, 'Liberalism and Wealth', in Six Oxford Men, Essays in Liberalism (London, 1897), pp. 82–3.
122 A. Smith, An Inquiry into the Nature and Causes of the Wealth of Nations (1776; World's Classics, 1904), ii. 332–4, 350ff. For another typical eighteenth-century view, see my 'Blackstone and the Office of Government', in R. Schnur (ed.), Die Rolle der Juristen bei der Entstehung des Modernen Staates (Berlin, 1983), ch. XX. Cf. R. L. Crouch, 'Laissez-Faire in Nineteenth-Century Britain: Myth or Reality?', The Manchester School, xxxv (1967), pp. 199–215.
123 T. Malthus, An Essay on the Principle of Population (1798; Everyman, 1967), ii. 30–7, 131–2 and n, 212–15, 255.

faire principles was 'fitter for bedlam than for the closet or the Cabinet'. Specifically, he accepted interference in the matter of children's education and conditions of work and thought it proper for the state also to act in respect of the destitute poor, housing and health regulation, the building of canals and railways, the subsidizing of some unprofitable private enterprise, the establishment of employers' liability for mining and factory accidents, and much more.[124] Nassau Senior was equally direct: for if in his earlier days he had envisaged a strictly limited role for government, he later asserted that the only criterion is one of 'expediency' in the service of the community and the general benefit. 'It is the duty of a government', he said, 'to do whatever is conducive to the welfare of the governed. The . . . most fatal of all errors would be the general admission . . . that a government has no right to interfere for any purpose except that of affording protection'. For example, the state might properly deal with the pauper problem and it could also regulate house building if there was a danger to health from bad sanitation.[125] In fact, on almost any question of their day, the classical political economists reflected a far from rigid anti-statist viewpoint. In his masterly survey of these matters, Lord Robbins lists an impressive array of public functions they permitted or advocated; and Professor Blaug has shown how, in respect of the Factory Acts for instance, they recommended state intervention where self-interest was unenlightened, as in the case of children and young persons, even though they were very dubious about the further extension of the principle.[126] Obviously, the belief that government intervention would do harm and prevent optimum prosperity was there in the works of these writers but it was not exclusively there. It was, in the practice, rather a matter whether a solution to any given problem presented itself: if it did and if it required government action, this was accepted more often than not even though, on the whole, economists (like the public at large) felt that government was so often simply powerless to deal with such things or inefficient in attempting to do so: and the relatively primitive administrative machinery of the day has in this regard always to be borne in mind. Basically, perhaps, the whole question of their attitude was one of context or time. Malthus may have adopted in many respects a hard view that poverty

---

124 D. P. O'Brien, *J. R. McCulloch: a Study in Classical Economics* (London, 1970), pp. 285–91; D. Read, *Cobden and Bright: a Victorian Political Partnership* (London, 1967), pp. 3–4; McCulloch to Lord Ashley (28 March 1833), in E. Hodder, *The Life and Work of the Seventh Earl of Shaftesbury K.G.* (London, 1887), i. 157–8.

125 N. Senior, *Industrial Efficiency and Social Economy*, ed. S. L. Levy (London, 1929), ii. 301–3; ibid., vol. ii, Part X 'Government Control and Social Progress', *passim*.

126 Robbins, op. cit., lectures II–III, and the summary review in lecture VI, pp. 188–90; M. Blaug, 'The Classical Economists and the Factory Acts – a Re-Examination', *Quarterly Journal of Economics*, lxxii (1958), esp. p. 223.

was natural and inevitable; but later, after a generation or so of notable economic growth, this rigid unfeeling image would itself seem overly pessimistic.[127] As well, in a sometimes bitter *Methodenstreit*, new types of economic ideas were emerging, notions directly and explicitly hostile to the concept of *laissez faire* itself and to the extreme anti-statist case presented by the likes of Herbert Spencer and the members of the Manchester School, and associated, too (often somewhat unreasonably), with the classical political economists.

New types of economic thought
The formal gravamen of the charge against the classical school was not, at least directly, the inadequacy of its (supposed) view of the extent of legitimate state intervention but rather the abstractness and unreality of the method of analysis employed. It was this, critics held, which led to misleading generalization and inappropriate prescription. Classical political economy was assumed by its proponents to constitute a series of unassailable deductions from ineluctable premises about human nature. It was a science urged in a style that could lead J. A. Hobson to assert that the economic principles which supported a policy of free trade were closely analogous to 'the laws of the physical universe' being based on 'the same irrefutable logic' and understanding.[128] All this gave the argument its strength: a 'method so clear, solutions so simple, carried all before them.'[129] Yet many observers were beginning to see these principles, and thus the programmes taken to be dependent on them, as being unreal: a 'logical artifice', Toynbee says, 'less real than the island of Lilliput'.[130] The case was fallible or inappropriate, the relative reflection, in fact, of a specific set of historical circumstances now passing away. Mill remarked in 1870 that it had begun to dawn on an increasing number of people that some of the 'universal maxims' of classical political economy were 'merely English customs' and, he added sarcastically, it was doubtful whether, 'even as such, they have any claim to the transcendent excellence ascribed to them.' Or, as Tawney put it somewhat later and in his even more pungent and blunt way, the supposed laws of political economy were revealed as 'little more than statements of the nastier habits of Lancashire Cotton Spinners.'[131] From

127 See J. S. Mill, 'The Claims of Labour' (1845), *Collected Works*, ed. J. M. Robson *et al.* (London, 1963ff), iv. 367–8.
128 J. A. Hobson, 'The Logical Foundations of Free Trade', *The New Age* (10 September 1903), p. 585.
129 A. Toynbee, 'Ricardo and the Old Political Economy', in T. S. Ashton (ed.), *Toynbee's Industrial Revolution* (1884; Newton Abbot, 1969), p. 9.
130 ibid., pp. 6–7, 28.
131 J. S. Mill, 'Leslie on the Land Question' (1870), *Collected Works*, v. 672; R. H. Tawney, *The British Labor Movement* (New Haven, Conn., 1925), p. 23. Cf. *Toynbee's Industrial Revolution*, pp. 22–3, 28–9.

the technical point of view, it seemed that in its preoccupation with the perfect functioning of the market system envisaged, conventional theory underestimated the complexity of economic reality and, in particular, the significance of practical and supposedly short-term frictions. It failed properly to take account of such factors as cyclical fluctuation; the growth of large-scale corporations, trusts, and cartels; and the failure of free trade in the face of protection and similar reflections of economic nationalism. Equally its presuppositions were impugned: the rational economic man with effective knowledge as either producer or consumer; free competition between equal units; impersonally determined price levels; the assumption that individual and social interest would coincide; and so on. The models and explanations deployed failed to correspond with or adequately to explain the working of the actual state of economic affairs which was rather the resultant of a host of such forces as custom, habit, and local conditions. It all constituted (in Jevons's phrase) a 'metaphysical incubus' that was best dispensed with.[132] A fresh start was required employing more realistic concepts more closely founded on empirical data. And as, however misleadingly, conventional economics was associated with a *laissez faire* emphasis, so the new, supposedly more concrete, understanding of economic life was explicitly associated with the idea of an active role for the state in dealing with the problems revealed. The Cobden Prize essayist for 1880 asserted, 'We have had too much *laissez-faire*' and went on to prescribe an antidote that would 'insist on and realise the greater function of Government in the modern state. We need a great deal more Paternal Government – that bugbear of the old economists.'[133]

The association between such a collectivist tendency and the new style of economic analysis derived from a number of the intellectual influences that assisted in its establishment. Among these were the German historical school with its stress on the role of corporate authority, the diatribes of critics such as Ruskin, and the paternalist emphasis associated with much of the new economic history of the day (as in the work of Toynbee, Cunningham, and Ashley).[134] Similarly, contemporary studies of the social scene, especially in the context of the great depression, lent force to this tendency. Something of what was entailed by the new economic ideas, including their collectivist overtones, is

---

132 W. S. Jevons, *The State in Relation to Labour* (1882; London, 1887), ch.I, esp. pp.16–17; also *Toynbee's Industrial Revolution*, pp.23–4.
133 A. N. Cumming, *On the Value of Political Economy to Mankind* (Glasgow, 1881), pp.46, 48.
134 B. Semmel, *Imperialism and Social Reform: English Social-Imperial Thought, 1895–1914* (London, 1960), chs. X–XI. On Ruskin's influence in sounding the death-knell of the old political economy, see the striking tribute in *The New Age* (25 January 1900), p.57.

indicated by the writings of Cliffe Leslie. He believed that the principles of economic life, instead of being established *a priori*, should 'be sought in history' and related to the general laws of 'social evolution'. He accepted, too, that in this context 'the authority of the economic theory hitherto dominant with respect to individualism, competition and non-interference' had been 'visibly shaken'. As a result, and in order to meet moral and social obligations, it was necessary to accept that market forces must be controlled by legislation, and the particular interests of capitalists and landowners similarly restricted. The Australian pro-tectionist, David Syme, a friend of Leslie's, equally insisted on the importance of the good of the community as a whole and on its right to be shielded from the unacceptable effects of competition.[135] Again, Toynbee, whose critical attitude to the classical school reflected much of what was passing in the progressive mind of the time, believed an historically based understanding would show that no 'universal for-mula' about the functions of the state could be established and that the 'proper limits of Government interference' were relative to the nature of each particular society and the stage of civilization it had achieved. That is to say, there was no general rule to demand that government should be as limited as possible. Furthermore, if attention were paid to con-temporary problems the need for greater public intervention and collective ownership would be clearly demonstrated.[136] Those observers, Toynbee said,

> who have applied the historical method to political economy and the science of society, have shown an unmistakeable disposition to lay bare the injustice to which the humbler classes of the community have been exposed, and to defend methods and institutions adopted for their protection which have never received scientific defence before.
>
> The fact is, that the more we examine the actual course of affairs, the more we are amazed at the unnecessary suffering that has been inflicted upon the people. . . . For while the modern historical school of economists appear to be only exploring the monuments of the past, they are really shaking the foundations of many of our institutions in the present. The historical method is often deemed conservative, because it traces the gradual and stately growth of our venerable institutions; but it may exercise a precisely opposite influence by

135 T. E. C. Leslie, 'On the Philosophical Method of Political Economy' (1876), in *Essays in Political Economy* (2nd edn, London, 1888), p.175; 'The History and Future of Interest and Profit', ibid., pp.267–8; D. Syme, *Outlines of an Industrial Science* (London, 1876), pp.182–3. There is a valuable and well-documented discussion of the background in G. M. Koot, 'T. E. Cliffe Leslie, Irish Social Reform, and the Origins of the English Historical School of Economics', *History of Political Economy*, vii (1975), pp.312–26.
136 *Toynbee's Industrial Revolution*, pp.31–2, 129.

showing the gross injustice which was blindly perpetrated during this growth. The historical method is supposed to prove that economic changes have been the inevitable outcome of natural laws. It just as often proves them to have been brought about by the self-seeking action of dominant classes.[137]

Towards the end of the last century, then, many economists were explicitly turning their backs on *laissez faire* and accepting that the 'mere conflict of private interests' would never produce a well-ordered economic commonwealth. An increasingly complex industrial society could 'not permanently remain without a systematic organization' so that growing legislative interference was inevitable.[138] The ground was well prepared for the economics of welfare. Alfred Marshall (who as a young man had dallied, albeit somewhat diffidently, with Socialism) wrote in the concluding pages of his influential *Principles* that through the provision of educational facilities, aid and control in sanitary matters, housing, and the like, 'the State seems to be required to contribute generously and even lavishly to that side of the wellbeing of the poorer working class which they cannot easily provide for themselves . . . . Evil may be lessened by a wider understanding of the social possibilities of economic chilvalry.' The 'resources of the rich' may be turned, by the tax-gatherer, 'to high account in the service of the poor, and may remove the worst evils of poverty from the land.' Implicit in Marshall's point of view, therefore, was a not inconsiderable social radicalism requiring for the achievement of its goals the supporting hand of government. And this remains true even though his great influence could not perhaps be firmly invoked in support of the further pursuit of substantive state regulation of the economy itself.[139]

With this array of academic and professional economic authority to sustain the collectivist tide, it was no wonder it simply came to be assumed that government must at least accept responsibility for the condition of the labouring classes and perhaps much more.[140] The wheel

137   ibid., p. 58.

138   J. K. Ingram, 'Political Economy', *Encyclopaedia Britannica*, 9th edn (Edinburgh, 1885), xix. 400–1.

139   A. Marshall, *Principles of Economics* (1890; 8th edn, London, 1930), pp. 718, 719. Cf. his evidence to the Royal Commission on the Aged Poor, in C. L. Mowat, *The Charity Organisation Society, 1869–1913* (London, 1961), p. 124. For the earlier 'tendency to socialism' (Marshall's phrase), see his *Industry and Trade* (1919; 4th edn, London, 1923), p. vii, and R. Harrison, 'Two Early Articles by Alfred Marshall', *Economic Journal*, lxxiii (1963), pp. 422–30. For critical discussion, see R. McWilliams-Tullberg, 'Marshall's "Tendency to Socialism"', *History of Political Economy*, vii (1975), pp. 75–111, esp. p. 105.

140   Cf. A. V. Dicey, *Lectures on the Relation between Law & Public Opinion in England during the Nineteenth Century* (1905; 2nd edn, London, 1920), pp. 447–8 n. 2, and the letter there cited.

had indeed turned full circle as the rueful remarks of a hostile Conservative pamphleteer testified: 'The last decade has witnessed a revolution in our theories of political economy, in our views of the rights of the individual, in our definition of the duties of the State.'[141]

But the most influential tendency in recent economic thought to nurture this inclination of affairs is that associated with the late Lord Keynes.

The Keynesian revolution

It was gradually recognized, and the implications of the recognition increasingly grasped, that government spending was not, as had so often been thought, a negative factor in the economic situation but could itself generate income and spending power and thus be an instrument of economic policy not least to control or eliminate unemployment. And this trend of analysis was especially characteristic of the so-called 'new economics' of J. M. Keynes, the doctrine expounded in the famous tracts *A Treatise on Money* (1930) and *The General Theory of Employment, Interest and Money* (1936). Of course, there was a quite extensive pre-history to such ideas. It had long been appreciated by administrators and politicians that the level of employment could be affected by spending on public works and other capital projects. A large pamphlet literature on this possibility existed even in the early nineteenth century.[142] And, in particular, J. A. Hobson had in the 1880s developed a theory of under-consumption that in many ways closely anticipates the later theories and policies.[143] In fact, glimpses and intimations of Keynesian doctrine can be found in many places, for instance in the writings of Major Douglas and the social credit school and in those of some Guild Socialists.[144] Moreover, at the practical level, the role of the Budget and taxation policy as an instrument of general social reform and regulation was being grasped before the Great War.[145] But it was Keynes and his associates

141 'A Plain Tory', *Tory Democracy and Conservative Policy* (London, 1892), p. 12. For another Tory comment on this change of emphasis, see A. Milner, *Arnold Toynbee: a Reminiscence* (London, 1895), p. 49.

142 B. A. Corry, 'The Theory of the Economic Effects of Government Expenditure in English Classical Political Economy', *Economica*, n.s., xxv (1958), p. 34 and n. 4.

143 Hobson first developed the idea in a book he wrote jointly with A. F. Mummery, *The Physiology of Industry Being an Exposure of Certain Fallacies in Existing Theories of Economics* (London, 1889): see e.g. the summary in the Preface, p. iv. Cf. Hobson's 'The Economic Cause of Unemployment', *Contemporary Review*, lxvii (1895), pp. 744–60, esp. pp. 751, 754, 758.

144 e.g. A. J. Penty, *Guilds, Trade and Agriculture* (London, 1921), pp. 34–6 on the significance, for the level of employment, of expenditure and of any imbalance between investment and consumption.

145 M. Freeden, *The New Liberalism: an Ideology of Social Reform* (Oxford, 1978), pp. 140–5.

who systematized and gave wide political and academic plausibility to these notions. Throughout the 1920s, Keynes and others (in a circle that included Walter Layton, Hubert Henderson, Philip Kerr, and Seebohm Rowntree) hammered away at these views and their practical application. Working in 1926 and 1927 under the chairmanship of D. L. George, their ideas formed the basis of the famous Liberal *Yellow Book* which constituted a sort of new deal proposed for Britain. This, and the other Liberal policy documents, were capped for the 1929 election by a summary of the conclusions dramatically entitled *We Can Conquer Unemployment*. This was possibly the point at which these economic ideas broke into general public view: 'Here, implicitly,' says A. J. P. Taylor, pungently though with a certain over-simplicity,

> was the end of Gladstonian finance and of the classical economics which followed in unbroken line from Adam Smith. Lloyd George's programme repudiated the system of *laissez faire* and balanced budgets, under which Great Britain had once grown great and was now, it appeared, stagnating. Instead there were to be great public works . . . paid for by a deliberate deficit.[146]

Unused capital and the unemployed would be set to work to generate a prosperity which would ultimately absorb the cost involved. Keynes's ideas were also apparent in the proceedings of the Committee on Finance and Industry which sat from 1929–31. Although a member of the Committee, he gave evidence to it; and his cross-examination of Sir Richard Hopkins, a senior Treasury official, is regarded as a symbolic confrontation of new and orthodox economic views. Nor, of course, was Keynesian influence confined to any one part of the political spectrum: in addition to the Liberal context already mentioned, Mosley in the Labour Party and Macmillan among the Conservatives were early exponents of Keynesian-inspired policies.[147] At the same time, not all party stalwarts were thus convinced: in the Labour Party, to take but one instance, Aneurin Bevan had grave doubts and thought such policies could be no substitute for a full programme of Socialist reform; while on the other side many Conservatives and Liberals repudiated the financial unorthodoxy and degree of state management involved.[148] Keynes himself expounded the doctrine and its implications widely in a series of articles in *The Times* in 1937 on how to avoid a slump.[149]

146 A. J. P. Taylor, *English History 1914–1945* (1965; Penguin, 1970), pp. 338–9. Cf. volume ii, *The Ideological Heritage*, ch. 5.

147 On Mosley's economic ideas, see the summary in T. A. Smith, *The Politics of the Corporate Economy* (Oxford, 1979), pp. 28–31. For Macmillan, see pp. 147–8 below and volume ii, *The Ideological Heritage*, ch. 7.

148 M. Foot, *Aneurin Bevan: a Biography* (London, 1962–73), ii. 56.

149 J. M. Keynes, 'How to Avoid a Slump', *The Times* (12–14 January 1937).

The concepts involved in Keynesian economics are, of course, quite complex and technical though (in what might be called 'vulgar' form) basically simple. They are based on criticism of the idea that there is, in the private enterprise system, an effective and automatic mechanism of adjustment that comes into play to produce an optimum use of resources. Specifically they rest (so far as the present context is concerned) on the notions of 'deficit spending' and 'demand deficiency'. The orthodox doctrine of public finance involved belief in the neutrality or ineffectiveness of public spending and in maintaining, so far as possible, a balanced budget. It was held that the state could not in the long run increase the level of demand and so of employment. Churchill said in his 1929 budget speech that it was 'orthodox Treasury dogma, steadfastly held, that whatever might be the political or social advantages, very little additional employment can, in fact, and as a general rule, be created by State borrowing and expenditure.'[150] Equally firmly believed was the idea that income, through taxes and other revenue, must match expenditure on government services of various kinds. This, it was thought, was the principle of all good housekeeping, public or private. If there was a slump and government income fell, it followed that it was necessary for government to cut expenditure to achieve financial equilibrium. Thus in the 1931 general election, at the height of just such a crisis, the appeals of each party called for a balanced budget.[151] Keynes argued that this was quite the wrong thing to do if the object was to achieve a revival of the economy, the goal then mainly in view. The suggestion was that if there is a slump, and so a substantial amount of unused resources, it is because not enough things are being bought (i.e. there is a deficiency in aggregate demand). This process would show itself especially in the industries that were producing heavy capital goods of which it is possible more easily to defer the replacement. For example, if the demand for ships or industrial machinery fell, if such investment declined because of some crisis of business confidence, real or imagined, then the industries producing these goods would lay off labour and draw on stocks of material instead of buying more. The unemployed workers would then have less to spend on consumption and so help to depress the commodity and service industries. Following from this, too, ancillary trades supplying the things used in building ships or machinery would be hard-hit and themselves lay off workers and cut back stocks with comparable results. This is the so-called 'multiplier effect', the original falling off in the demand for heavy

150 Cited in D. Winch, *Economics and Policy: a Historical Study* (London, 1969), p.109.
151 F. W. S. Craig (ed.), *British General Election Manifestos, 1918–1966* (Chichester, 1970), pp.64, 66, 72, 73, 74. Cf. the discussion of conventional opinion in R. Lekachman, *The Age of Keynes: a Biographical Study* (1966; Penguin, 1969), pp.36–9.

capital goods (investment) being reproduced like ripples in a pond till the results are widespread and disastrous. To Keynes the implication was clear: government could not allow these crucial decisions to remain entirely in private hands; it had to act to prevent these consequences spreading; and to try to reverse them. And it should do this by remedying the original deficiency in demand by stimulating fresh consumption and more importantly by creating pump-priming investment to fill the gap. It should lower interest rates and taxes, give subsidies, undertake public works, or otherwise increase its own spending. Even completely wasteful employment will, he said, have the result of increasing useful output and labour. The Treasury could (he wrote in a famous passage) even fill old bottles with banknotes, bury them deep in disused mine shafts, pile town rubbish on top and, on the principle of *laissez faire*, leave it to private enterprise to dig the notes up again. Of course, it would be more sensible to build houses but if this reasonable course is closed for some reason then the other will in the end serve the purpose concerned just as well.[152] So government should thus stimulate activity and do this even if it means incurring a deficit on its budget: that is, it should act contrary to the canons of orthodox public finance. In this way it would create or raise incomes and so stimulate consumption and investment. This would, through the multiplier effect and despite some leakage, thereby help to sustain employment and economic activity at a higher level. Another aspect of the general theory was that if the distribution of income was more equal than it had been in the past then the economic situation would be eased. This was because there was, among lower income groups, less possibility of saving and a greater propensity to consume. Demand could, therefore, be increased by a redistribution of income (through taxation) and economic buoyancy thereby the more sustained. Similarly, if completely different circumstances prevailed and demand was excessive rather than deficient, then government should aim for a surplus of revenue over expenditure and thus help to relieve shortages and control inflation. This corollary, which did not at the time seem relevant, may have become so since: but it has hardly been observed in the practice.

In these ways then, Keynes urged that, without changing the basic characteristics of a capitalist or private enterprise system, it was possible for government to manage the economic life of a country to prevent waste of resources, especially labour resources, and to avoid extremes of boom and depression. Of course, as Keynes himself recognized, the 'central controls necessary to ensure full employment will . . . involve a large extension of the traditional functions of government.' But even so,

152 J. M. Keynes, *The General Theory of Employment, Interest and Money* (1936; London, 1942), p. 129.

this need not involve a great degree of socialization and it has to be accepted not least because it is the price which must be paid to sustain the remaining, still substantial, field for the exercise of private initiative and responsibility.[153] This regulatory doctrine became accepted by all three major political parties in this country and was the basis of the policy of full employment endorsed by the wartime Coalition government and for long by subsequent administrations. Indeed, the expectation that government should in peacetime supervise the economy of the country might be dated from the publication of the Full Employment White Paper in 1944 which was thus, in Lord Robbins's words, 'a turning-point in the history of domestic policy.'[154] In this way, the idea of government control of the general level of economic activity became the norm though in practice, of course, the matter was complicated by the problems of foreign trade and the external balance, inflation, and the like. Yet a hundred years ago – even fifty years ago – it would have been quite unthinkable that in peacetime (or even in war) a government should unbalance the budget and incur a deficit as part of its normal policy. That this kind of management is nowadays a commonplace – or perhaps, more accurately, has been until recently generally accepted – is in a notable way due to the influence of Keynesian thought. At the same time, it must, in conclusion, be noted that there has of late been a growing volume of criticism of this sort of policy as both productive of inflation and other evils and irrelevant to contemporary problems. It might be, for instance, that a substantial part of the unemployment experienced in recent years has been due not to a Keynesian deficiency of demand but to other factors: an enormous increase in the bargaining power of the unions which has forced up wages and by thus increasing labour costs reduced the possibility of employment; or a structural deficiency in British industry deriving from insufficient capital investment and research or too little development of plant embodying new technology. If this is indeed the case, then a very drastic revision of views and policies is vital. Keynes himself seems to have been aware of the problems of inflation that might arise when collective bargaining and full employment were combined; though he rather put the question to one side as a political difficulty to be met *ambulando*.[155] In fact, of course, the solution long attempted was a combination of price and wage controls ('incomes policy') coupled with an effort, largely ineffective, to limit the bargaining power of trade unions. However, recent events have driven the general point about Keynesian policy very firmly home. As the then Prime Minister told the Labour Party Conference in September 1976:

153 ibid., pp. 378–80.
154 Lord Robbins, *Autobiography of an Economist* (London, 1971), p. 188.
155 See the letters in D. E. Moggridge, *Keynes* (Fontana, 1976), p. 130.

The cosy world we were told would go on forever, where full employment would be guaranteed by a stroke of the Chancellor's pen, . . . is gone. . . . We used to think that you could spend your way out of a recession and increase employment by cutting taxes and boosting Government spending. I tell you in all candour that that option no longer exists, and that in so far as it ever did exist, it only worked . . . by injecting a bigger dose of inflation into the economy followed by a higher level of unemployment as the next step.[156]

But there is a further dimension still to be explored. For it is really but a short way from the notion of demand management to the idea of economic planning as such. Perhaps Keynes himself – given his belief in 'moderate' regulation of a reformed capitalism – would not contemplate this development with equanimity; but it is feasible to urge that, in order to make a high-demand economy work, something more than macro-economic manipulation is required and that it is necessary to take detailed powers of control over wages and prices and thus introduce a further notable increment of collectivist intervention.[157] There is indeed a continuum or progression to be recognized in this context ranging from *ad hoc* regulation of market deficiencies through fiscal management and the mixed economy to full-scale collectivist organization based on a considerable degree of public ownership and substantive economic planning.

The idea of economic planning

There are four basic aspects to the development of the idea of economic planning in Britain. First, a need had to be felt for the conscious and systematic control of economic resources to secure an effective rationalization of industry, achieve greater competitiveness, ensure a high level of properly directed investment and technical development, and not least prevent unemployment and its untoward social consequences. This need was increasingly felt as the century wore on and may be said to have reached an initial peak in the economic crisis of the inter-war years. Secondly, an intellectual case had to be made in behalf of the idea of planning coupled with its effective propagation. During the same period its appeal was widely regarded in all parties and not necessarily most strongly on the left of the political spectrum. Thirdly, an effective technique of controlling the economy had to be available. In Britain some variant of Keynesian macro-economic regulation was increasingly deemed suitable in this regard because it could (or so it seemed) attain the high and increasing level of productive activity required without at the

156 *Report of the Seventy-Fifth Annual Conference of the Labour Party, Blackpool, 1976* (London, 1977), p.188.
157 For Keynes's belief, see Moggridge, op. cit., pp.44–5, 161–3.

same time either undermining the system of private ownership and enterprise or going over to some sort of social and political totalitarianism: though, of course, in certain quarters neither possibility was necessarily eschewed. Finally, experience of central planning and control was required; and this was provided above all by acquaintance with two extensive periods of wartime administration at home and by observation of what other countries were getting up to abroad, whether the activities of Gosplan in Soviet Russia or of the New Deal in the USA. Naturally, the actual story is rather more complex than this schematic outline might imply; but something of its course will be suggested in the remainder of this section. And it is important to remember that, in Britain at least, any fuller meaning of the concept of economic planning, so far as peacetime is concerned, relates only to the period since 1945; some would have it not even then, and this despite Lord Robbins's assertion over forty years ago that planning was already the 'grand panacea' of the age.[158] One sees what he meant: yet at that stage the notion was surely rather more abstract or tentative than he allows. A better perspective is that suggested in 1947 by Lord Franks and Sir Hubert Henderson who regarded the concept as a fresh idea requiring new expertise and means and as having only recently become popular.[159] But that there were earlier intimations is undoubted.

Not without a certain paradox perhaps, the idea of controlled industrial and commercial development may be discerned as implicit in the private enterprise system itself. However much an entrepreneur might be opposed to state planning of the economy, his own business operations depended for success on carefully supervised management. It is true the object was private profit, but to this end skill and experience were applied to develop production with maximum economy and efficiency. As de Ruggiero remarked, 'Modern industry . . . is the child of rationalism'.[160] And when we enter the age of the cartel or multinational, the activities of which may dwarf those of entire countries, then it is not wholly absurd to transfer the vision of large-scale organization to a community as a whole. And, in this country at least, the notion of a plan (though it was not always called this) has long existed in various spheres or aspects of public life. With notable justification it has been said that the age of mercantilism constituted 'England's first planned economy'.[161]

158 L. Robbins, *Economic Planning and International Order* (1937; London, 1938), p. 3.
159 Sir O. Franks, *Central Planning and Control in War and Peace* (London, 1947), pp. 7, 15; Sir H. Henderson, *The Uses and Abuses of Economic Planning* (Cambridge, 1947), p. 5. Cf. A. Budd, *The Politics of Economic Planning* (Fontana, 1978), p. 13.
160 G. de Ruggiero, *The History of European Liberalism*, trans. R. G. Collingwood (1927; Beacon Press, 1959), p. 97.
161 E. Lipson, *A Planned Economy or Free Enterprise: the Lessons of History* (London, 1944), ch. II.

More specifically, what is a commercial treaty but a kind of plan for the development or control of particular economic activities? The use of a tariff or a policy of protection (increasingly urged from the beginning of this century) is to be seen in a similar light. It is, said one observer, the 'most obvious instrument of national planning in the sphere of international business'.[162] Again, the notion of town planning (in itself quite an old idea) acquires a new vogue as the only rational response, first to the urban blight created by years of haphazard growth, and then to the modern traffic problem arising in particular from the development of the internal combustion engine.[163] This constituted such an important aspect of the involvement of government in moulding the life of the community that it may be regarded as a major immediate precedent to the more general idea and so worth some specific attention.

Private landlords and speculators, wanting to enhance the long-term value of their estates, had themselves often planned residential developments very carefully.[164] And as far back as the 1870s, the Housing Acts had begun to envisage the preparation of reconstruction schemes for whole areas of insanitary property existing in the large urban centres. From 1909 onwards, specific legislation on town planning appeared on the statute-book; a literature on the subject emerged (one of the first representatives of the genre, B. Meakin's *Model Factories and Villages*, came out in 1905); and local authorities were submitting schemes for planned urban development to the Local Government Board: thus a newspaper report of 1912 recorded Birmingham's submission of its first town-planning scheme for approval.[165] This was the era, too, in which notions of planned suburbs, model houses and villages, and the garden city movement acquired a notable impetus and popularity. There had been some quite early examples of this sort of development in Britain as with J. S. Buckingham's scheme for a model city (1849) and that at Saltaire (1852). Bedford Park dates from 1875–8, and then come the major and most well-known instances: Bournville (1879), Port Sunlight (1888), New Earswick (1902), Letchworth (1903), Hampstead Garden

162 L. Robbins, *Economic Planning and International Order*, p.14.
163 See e.g. W. Ashworth, *The Genesis of Modern British Town Planning: a Study in Economic and Social History of the Nineteenth and Twentieth Centuries* (London, 1954); and L. Benevolo, *The Origins of Modern Town Planning* (1963; trans. Cambridge, Mass., 1971).
164 T. Sharp, *Town Planning* (1940; Penguin, 1945), pp.14–16; F. Choay, *The Modern City: Planning in the 19th Century* (New York, 1969), pp.12–14, 24; Perkin, *The Origins of Modern English Society*, pp.77–8.
165 *Daily News* (3 January 1912), cited in the *OED sub* 'town planning'.

Suburb (1907), and Welwyn (1920).[166] The development of the large council estate at Wythenshawe near Manchester took place after 1921 and was an important example of such post-war schemes.[167] Herbert Morrison lived in one of these garden cities, Letchworth, during the Great War while working on the land as a conscientious objector and later he proposed, as a major item of Labour policy, the establishment outside London of new towns on similar lines.[168] Thus was established one link with the future. And it was all a stimulus to the wider application of the notion of planning by government itself as a means of dealing with urban blight and similar housing and environmental problems. There were basically two sorts of response. One was that improvement must start from scratch and create ideal communities of a new kind. In this tradition are the Utopias of Owen and Fourier and the later visionary pictures of that ilk painted by H. G. Wells as in his *Anticipations* (1901), *A Modern Utopia* (1905), and in many other publications. The other was the series of attempts to treat particular defects in existing urban life through sanitary improvement, building controls, traffic regulation, and so forth. It is, of course, rather on these latter lines that (the new towns apart) actual urban planning has developed in this country.

Nevertheless the idea of regulated development on a broad scale was definitely in the air by the beginning of this century. Partly it was associated with the mood of pessimism about Britain's economic and military future that seemed to set in towards the end of the Victorian age and to receive confirmation in the reverses of the Boer War. Some observers were led to believe, as with Lord Milner, that the national decline would not be effectively treated through piecemeal reform but required complete reorganization according to some clearly formulated plan.[169] In May 1912, in a series of articles in the *Daily Mail* (the leading halfpenny newspaper of the time), H. G. Wells wrote that what Britain needed was 'nothing less than a national plan of social development' in which issues that had previously been treated *ad hoc* – labour unrest, employment and working conditions, national health, water supply,

166 For the garden city movement, see E. Howard, *Tomorrow: a Peaceful Path to Social Reform* (London, 1898) reissued as *Garden Cities of Tomorrow* (1902; London, 1974); also G. Darley, *Villages of Vision* (London, 1975). There is an excellent summary of these developments in J. N. Tarn, *Five Per Cent Philanthropy: an Account of Housing in Urban Areas between 1840 and 1914* (Cambridge, 1973), ch. 9.

167 See A. Redford, *The History of Local Government in Manchester* (London, 1939–40), vol. iii, ch. xli.

168 B. Donoughue and G. W. Jones, *Herbert Morrison: Portrait of a Politician* (London, 1973), pp. 41 ff, 48 n., 86, 89–90.

169 G. R. Searle, *The Quest for National Efficiency: a Study in British Politics and Political Thought, 1899–1914* (Oxford, 1971), p. 60.

education, towns – were embodied in an imaginative coherent whole.[170] This radical approach was urged, too, by the idiosyncratic Patrick Geddes.[171] Yet it was undoubtedly the wartime embodiment of the concept that provided the final or major stimulus. The plan of campaign had long been a crucial example of the attempt at rational control of human affairs, but (as indicated in the previous chapter) the military requirements of modern times extended filaments of claim and regulation throughout society.

It was thus the Great War itself and its aftermath that really familiarized people with the idea of planned action on a large scale to achieve given communal goals, either victory or 'reconstruction' afterwards. To produce enough shells, to provide food despite the submarine campaign, or to cope with the adaptation of industry to wartime conditions, required the careful consideration of all the problems involved and rational dispositions made in advance to meet them. In fact the preparations for war made by the Committee of Imperial Defence before 1914, including the famous War Book, probably constituted the largest planning exercise ever undertaken by a government agency up to that time (work subsequently continued during the inter-war period by the Joint Planning Committee of the CID). So that if Socialists had not by then developed the concept of planning, the military bureaucrats certainly had. Then the Coalition government manifesto for the 1918 general election spoke of 'plans' which had been prepared by public authorities to improve the condition of the people.[172] A Ministry of Reconstruction had been set up in 1917 to produce these post-war schemes and its many committees and working parties dealt with a wide range of issues in this context including health, agriculture, electricity, the future of industry and transport, as well as the machinery of government itself. This array of work also provided early instances of how the best-laid plans can misfire: for example, the demobilization scheme which was worked out led to riot and mutiny and had to be speedily altered, hardly a happy augury for the idea of rational control of more complex matters still. But the very activity involved in planning for

170 H. G. Wells, *Experiment in Autobiography: Discoveries and Conclusions of a Very Ordinary Brain (Since 1866)* (London, 1934), ii. 663–5.
171 On Geddes, see P. Kitchin, *A Most Unsettling Person: an Introduction to the Ideas and Life of Patrick Geddes* (London, 1975); and P. Boardman, *The Worlds of Patrick Geddes . . .* (London, 1978). Lewis Mumford's *The Culture of Cities* (1938) is perhaps the most well-known treatment of these themes by a disciple of Geddes. Cf. Mumford's 'Patrick Geddes, Victor Branford, and Applied Sociology in England . . .', in H. E. Barnes (ed.), *An Introduction to the History of Sociology* (1948; abridged edn, Chicago, 1969), ch. XVI.
172 F. W. S. Craig, *British General Election Manifestos 1918–1966* (Chichester, 1970), pp. 2–3.

reconstruction (even if some of the schemes were produced merely as window-dressing to allay possible discontent) nevertheless implied the continuation in principle of the system of wartime government supervision and of the attempt to bring public affairs into some kind of rational order.[173] Again (as already noted) trade difficulties in the post-war period led to proposals for the 'protection' and 'rationalization' of industry which, if it were to be done, involved intervention by government more extensive and systematic than ever before in time of peace. Likewise the idea of nationalization, first premeditated over half a century earlier, emerged strongly at this time and for similar reasons as in the new Labour Party constitution of 1918. It was clearly taken to imply the conscious pursuit of 'social justice and economic freedom' through such communal control.[174] This was spelled out very clearly, too, in the new policy statement *Labour and the New Social Order* (1918) which had largely been drafted by Sidney Webb. This document was premissed on the assumption that social rebuilding after the war would require 'a deliberately thought out, systematic, and comprehensive plan' and that an increase in production could only be based on this 'indispensable marshalling of the nation's resources'. The new order would be founded 'not on the competitive struggle for the means of bare life, but on a deliberately planned co-operation in production and distribution'.[175] If some important aspects of these schemes were relatively unexplored, clearly the notion of a crucial regulation of capitalism was present so that it is hardly correct to say that the idea of planning was unknown to the Socialist vocabulary before the problem of mass unemployment emerged and prior to the impact of the Soviet five year plan of 1928.[176] At the same time it is true that planning is not always, during this period, raised as a matter central to the aims of the Labour Party.[177] For this there were good reasons. Planning might seem to entail the direction of labour and the control of wages which many people in the trade unions regarded as unacceptable. A plan was seen, too, as a merely exotic or Communist

---

173 Cf. A. J. P. Taylor, *English History 1914–1945* (1965; Penguin, 1970), p.132.

174 See the 1918 Labour Party manifesto, in Craig, op. cit., pp.5–6.

175 Labour Party, *Labour and the New Social Order: a Report on Reconstruction* (London, 1918), pp.4, 5.

176 As asserted by e.g. F. Bealey (ed.), *The Social and Political Thought of the British Labour Party* (London, 1970), introduction, p.27; C. A. R. Crosland, *The Future of Socialism* (London, 1956), p.86. There is an admirable and well-documented rebuttal of this misconception in A. Oldfield; 'The Labour Party and Planning – 1934, or 1918?', *Bulletin of the Society for the Study of Labour History* (no.25; Autumn 1972), pp.41–55.

177 e.g. 'F. W.', *The Labour Party: What It is; What It Wants; How It Means to Get It* (London, n.d. [c. 1920?]) does not mention the idea at all.

nostrum and so as undesirable; or as the reflection of a kind of unpractical intellectualism. And, of course, the free-trade tradition in the Labour movement was a very strong one. Nevertheless, as in other parties, the germ was stirring.

Once more, a most obvious example of these tendencies during the inter-war years was housing and town planning. After 1918 there was (as noted in an earlier section of this chapter) a great burst of house building creating on a large scale the ugly rash of council house estates and blocks of flats so familiar in and around our towns. Not only did these developments in themselves involve government activity on an unprecedented scale at both central and local level (through, for instance, the use of substantial compulsory powers and the disbursement of considerable subsidies), they also drew attention to the problem of regulating this growth in an overall manner especially in those places where land was likely to be scarce. Some local authorities acquired supervisory powers by private Act of Parliament and this was especially important where co-operation between different councils was necessary. There was also general legislation. For instance, the 1929 Local Government Act provided for supervision by joint committees of local authorities; a Town and Country Planning Act of 1932 empowered some local councils to adopt and enforce planning schemes; in 1935 there was a statute to restrict ribbon development. Yet most of the powers given were optional, while procedure was slow and could involve heavy compensation payments.[178] The overall result was that by 1939 there had been relatively little progress in the town-planning field though what had been done intimated important possibilities.

But the prospect of another surge of housing development after 1945 redirected attention to town planning which some people at least saw as the real test of the political system: 'plan we must – not for the sake of our physical environment only, but to save and fulfil democracy itself.'[179] In 1940 the Barlow Commission (set up three years previously to consider the distribution of the industrial population) had recommended planned action on a national scale to deal with the problems of industrial location and growth (including residential development) especially as these affected the growing imbalance between the relatively thriving south-eastern parts of the country and the hard-hit areas elsewhere. In this context the Coalition government had accepted, as early as 1941, the need for a rational plan and a central planning authority as part of the policy essential to meet the problems of town and country reconstruc-

178 For an example of the difficulties, see the Manchester plan discussed by Redford, op. cit., iii. 305–7.
179 T. Sharp, *Town Planning*, p.116.

tion.[180] The Uthwatt and Scott Committees (both of which reported in 1942) recommended that to ensure the best post-war use of land in town and country for this purpose there should be a permanent system of planning by a central authority. The outcome of all this was the creation in 1943 of the Ministry of Town and Country Planning on the basis of an interim department set up the previous year to combine the functions of the then Commissioners of Works and existing planning powers. Various pieces of legislation followed dealing with, for instance, ribbon development, and granting interim authority for the period of post-war reconstruction especially in 'blitzed' and 'blighted' areas. A beginning was made with the proposed 'new towns' as part of a policy of 'planned decentralization from congested urban areas' – a New Towns Act became law in 1946. And many places had instituted their own schemes for post-war reconstruction, the most famous of which was Professor Abercrombie's County of London Plan (1943). These developments in environmental control may be said to have culminated in the Town and Country Planning Act of 1947 by which considerable compulsory power was given to public agencies and substantial activity envisaged. A recent, perhaps sceptical, commentator summarized these wartime and post-war schemes as resting on 'the revolutionary idea' that

> in future all physical change would only take place with the agreement of a new army of 'enlightened' planners. The great areas of our cities requiring reconstruction after the blitz would be designated 'comprehensive development areas'. Every inch of the country would be covered by 'Development Plans', apportioning each area to its own suitable 'use' or 'zone'. Industry would be decentralized. New towns would be created. Slums would be cleared, urban motorways built. And, perhaps above all, by the nationalization of all development values through the so-called 'Development Levy', the process of change for the public good would be entirely freed from the distortions of the private interest.

All was now set for the realization of the vision.[181]

It was indeed all rather like H. G. Wells plus Le Corbusier. And there was a further impetus in the 1960s with the proliferation of more comprehensive development plans intended to go beyond the previous

180 See Lord Reith's statement as Minister of Works and Buildings, 119 H. C. Deb. 5s., 17 July 1941, cols. 849–54. An interdepartmental committee examined the scheme for such an authority: see J. M. Lee, *Reviewing the Machinery of Government, 1942–1952; an Essay on the Anderson Committee and its Successors* (n.p. [London], 1977), p.21, referring to PRO, CAB 87/20.

181 C. Booker, 'Physical Planning: Another Illusion Shattered', *National Westminster Bank Quarterly Review* (February 1977), pp. 58–9.

aim of simply rebuilding war-damaged areas and coping with the problems of reconstruction. The object was rather to create new city centres and the like in place of the old and merely existing. This was the era of the Buchanan Report on traffic, the idea of a motorway box round London, plans for rebuilding Covent Garden and Piccadilly Circus, the explosion in public housing activity including the development of tower blocks, the large new town at Milton Keynes, and so on right up to the Community Land Act (1975) which increased the planning powers of local authorities by taking all development land into public ownership. Though this legislation has since been repealed, substantial powers remain and have even been added to by, for instance, the creation of Urban Development Corporations.[182]

Of course, town and country planning is a particular problem, though it is also potentially of very wide scope indeed, touching on such matters as public health and sanitary reform, the distribution of industry and the 'special areas' (or whatever is the current term for the decaying parts of the country), traffic problems and road development, housing, the preservation of farm land, conservation of the environment, and so on. And with this expanding margin of scope, town and country planning, although specific in origin, does tend thus to lead to a rather different idea, that is, the notion of a substantive order imposed by government not merely on the land and its use but on the economy, indeed on the life of the community, as a whole. It is this more extensive notion which only begins to gather strength after the great slump, really perhaps only with the Second World War and its aftermath.

The general effect of the great depression of the 1930s in this respect was considerable: it ended the long era of free trade and gave rise to a protective tariff and a system of import quotas; schemes for reorganizing and subsidizing the production and marketing of many agricultural products; the rationalization – either voluntary or compulsory – of industries that were ailing or under intense competitive pressure; a policy for the location of industry as a help to the distressed areas; and the development of social aid as with unemployment insurance and assistance schemes and the opening of training centres. It led to the final abandonment of the gold standard and so to complete acceptance of the idea of a currency managed by government, for example through the exchange equalization fund; it produced government policies for programmes of public works, cheap money, guaranteeing interest on the cost of important construction, supervision of investment policy, and the creation of effective demand. From these circumstances emerged the idea of overall economic planning, though even so its implications were not

182 For details, see *KCA* (1981), p. 30683A.

always fully worked out in any detail.[183]

In 1931 the Labour Party election manifesto urged that the very survival of our civilization depended on a plan and committed the party to 'the definite planning of industry and trade so as to produce the highest standard of life for the Nation.'[184] In the same year the TUC placed on record its view that 'only by comprehensive planning of our economic development and regulated trading can the needs of the present day be met'.[185] In the same year the organization called Political and Economic Planning was founded. PEP was an association of civil servants, businessmen, professional people, and academics and arose out of a fusion of previously separate groups which had been studying economic and social problems. One of these, for instance, had arisen around the *Week-End Review* which had just published an article by Max Nicholson on 'A National Plan for Great Britain' envisaging, among other things, a smaller Cabinet for purposes of more effective central direction, a planning council for each industry, and the specific co-ordination of transport, fuel, and power.[186] Like the Fabians before them, PEP wanted to influence Establishment thinking through the presentation of well-prepared reports, and during the 1930s such documents were produced on a number of subjects including the basic industries, housing, and the social services. The direct influence exerted at the time was probably slight; nevertheless high-level opinion was thus being prepared for the changes of the next decade.[187] 1932 saw a report issued by the TUC Economic Committee on the public control and regulation of industry and trade.[188] A good example of the advanced radical thought of the day was G. D. H. Cole's articles outlining Socialist policy in the *New Clarion* magazine in which the attempt was made to provide a complete programme for Socialism and which included the policy of the conscious planning of the whole economy together with the public ownership of land, industries, and major services. Similarly, H. Dalton wrote a few years later of the spread of the idea of planning in Socialist and non-Socialist circles alike, not least as a result of the experience of the Great War and of the example provided by the 'Soviet experiment'.[189]

183 Cf. Wells's comments, *Experiment in Autobiography*, i.262–4.
184 Craig, op. cit., pp.69–70.
185 *TUC Report* (1931), p.406.
186 P. Addison, *The Road to 1945: British Politics and the Second World War* (London, 1975), pp.38–9.
187 ibid., p.39.
188 *TUC Report* (1932), pp.206–19.
189 G. D. H. Cole, 'An Outline of Social Policy', *New Clarion* (18 June–17 September 1932), esp. 'A Socialist Economic Plan', ibid. (2 July 1932), p.77; H. Dalton, *Practical Socialism for Britain* (1935; London, 1936), Part V, esp. pp.246–9.

Despite contemporary difficulties in the Soviet Union, the Russian example (though not, as sometimes supposed, the origin of the idea of economic planning) was indeed not without influence and was quickly taken up by many people, on the left in particular.[190] One factor here, at least so far as effect on the politically committed and on intellectual circles was concerned, was undoubtedly the conference held in London in 1931 which, while primarily centred on the history of science and technology, also presented, through these Russian papers, an optimistic picture of scientifically planned growth in the Soviet economy.[191] As well, a number of prominent publicists – such as Shaw, Wells, Lady Astor, and the Webbs – visited Russia and were impressed with what they saw. On returning from such a tour in 1933, Herbert Morrison assimilated the idea of planning by asserting – somewhat dubiously in fact – that it was not 'peculiarly Russian or Bolshevik' but had always been 'the essence of the Socialist idea'.[192] Dalton and his 'kindergarten' were also profoundly influenced by the example of Soviet planning.[193] Nor did such impressions falter with the years: for instance, Harold Laski's later works are typically replete with fulsome reference to the inspiring nature of the Russian precedent in undermining faith in unplanned *laissez faire*.[194] E. H. Carr wrote (after the Second World War) that the economic impact of the Soviet Union on the rest of the world could 'be summed up in the single word "planning"'. If, he went on, we are all planners now, 'this is largely the result . . . of the impact of Soviet practice and . . . achievement'.[195]

In the context created by this sort of spirit, the Labour programme of 1934 entitled *For Socialism and Peace* said the party policy of economic reorganization would be one of 'full and rapid Socialist planning, under central direction' and on the basis of extensive public ownership.[196]

190 e.g. M. Dobb, *Russia Today and Tomorrow* (London, 1930), ch. V; Cole and Dalton, loc. cit. The reception of the first five year plan is documented in S. and B. Webb, *Soviet Communism: a New Civilisation* (1935; 2nd edn, London, 1937), 602–3 n. 1.

191 *Science at the Crossroads: Papers Presented to the International Congress of the History of Science and Technology, 1931* (1931; London, 1971), esp. p. 5, and e.g. on the crucial problems of electrification, pp. 115ff.

192 *Daily Herald* (26 September 1933), in Bealey, op. cit., p. 27. Cf. B. Donoughue and G. W. Jones, *Herbert Morrison: Portrait of a Politician*, pp. 254–5. See also Barbara Wootton's *Plan or No Plan* (London, 1934) which favourably regards the Russian system and suggests its adoption in Britain, chs. II, IV and V §§x–xiii.

193 Dalton, loc. cit.; Addison, op. cit., p. 49.

194 e.g. H. J. Laski, *Trade Unions in the New Society* (London, 1950), p. 29.

195 E. H. Carr, *The Soviet Impact on the Western World* (London, 1947), p. 20.

196 Labour Party, *For Socialism and Peace: the Labour Party's Programme of Action* (London, 1934), pp. 5, 14–15. For discussion of this document, cf. Oldfield, art. cit., pp. 41–6. A series of earlier party pamphlets had discussed detailed aspects of the planning proposals, e.g. *The Land and the National Planning of Agriculture* (London, 1932) and *The National Planning of Transport* (London, 1934).

Three years later Attlee, by then party leader, announced (in the statement of ideas and programmes he then published) that he believed it to be impossible 'to contend against the tendencies which are making more necessary every day a planned society'.[197] Nor was the appeal of this sort of solution confined to the Labour Party. The Liberals had produced a series of programmes such as the famous *Yellow Book* on Britain's industrial future (1928). Sir Arthur Salter had made a sweeping call for democratic planning and government intervention in business in his *Recovery: the Second Effort* (1932). He also popularized these themes. In a broadcast talk given in December 1934 under the title 'Planned Socialization and World Trade' he envisaged both the considerable extension of nationalization 'to bring more than half the country's economic life under public ownership and management' and, as well, growing state control of the remaining private sphere.[198] The cognate views of the expert administrator were represented by Sir Josiah Stamp who in 1934 wrote that:

> State control of industry is imperative . . . . You have only to take the cotton industry to see the difficulties of reliance on individualism . . . . We have got to realise that the State is going to be continually invoked in view of what is happening in Lancashire and Yorkshire, in coal and shipping. Nothing but a planned regimentation of trade, as in Russia, will get us out of our dilemma.[199]

And the Conservatives – most importantly in political practice because they dominated the National government of the day – moved in the same direction despite substantial antipathy to this tendency within their ranks. It was they who sponsored the inter-war protectionism, the housing and town planning legislation, and the inquiries on industrial distribution already mentioned. And many among them advocated sweeping and planned government control of industry to ensure its reorganization and economic survival in an increasingly competitive world. The object was to create a reformed and efficient private enterprise system, one based, it might be urged, simply on an extension of the best principles of commercial management. Harold Macmillan was especially active in this way. His *Reconstruction* (1933) put 'the case for planning' as did *The Middle Way* (1938): 'Planning is forced upon us . . . not for idealistic reasons, but because the old mechanism which served us when markets were expanding naturally and spontaneously is no

---

197 C. R. Attlee, *The Labour Party in Perspective – and Twelve Years Later* (1937; London, 1949), p.198.
198 Salter's talk was reprinted in *The Listener* (12 December 1934), pp.978–9.
199 *Daily Herald* (11 September 1934), in F. E. Lawley, *The Growth of Collective Economy* (London, 1938), i.3 n.1.

longer adequate when the tendency is in the opposite direction.'[200] An all-party volume, of which Macmillan was one of the major sponsors, recommended in 1935 a 'plan for Britain' which envisaged *inter alia* control over the location of industry and the creation of an efficient planning body at the centre to act as a sort of economic general staff.[201] All this had some effect though it is probably true to say that the idea of planning was never fully domesticated in the Conservative Party until the notion was accepted, formally at least, in the early and mid-1940s as with the 'Four Years Plan' which was part of the Conservative programme for the 1945 election.[202] Even so, a turnover article in *The Times* could say in 1935 that 'many of us consider . . . advocates of *laissez-faire* to be themselves the most dangerous people in the country – more dangerous than Socialists or Fascists.'[203]

By the 1930s, then, the slogan of planning had already become diffused to an important extent over the British political scene. But it did mean rather different things to different groups of people and in respect of the degree of collectivism it implied. It might to some entail state control over the whole of production and foreign trade with the object of providing, through this substantive order, for the needs of the whole community. In the more widespread and limited sense, it involved the reorganization and rationalization of particular industries under public auspices and with some form of state assistance: subsidies, a tariff, compulsory amalgamation, the compensated destruction or replacement of machinery and other capital equipment, price support through marketing boards, manipulation of investment, special treatment for the distressed areas, negotiation of international trade agreements, and the like. And it was frequently recognized that, properly, some new agency of central control was desirable to promote and supervise the regulation of the country's resources for industry, housing, recreation, and so on.

It was the Second World War which drew together the hitherto disparate strands of tendency; as it was the basic economic difficulties afterwards which ensured the subsequent continuation of the same ethos. A libertarian-inclined Conservative Party pamphlet published some years later well summed up this development (which it did not find wholly congenial). During the war, it said, the

> State became an almost insatiable consumer of labour and material resources. It reduced, by prohibitions, by rationing, and by penal taxation, both the volume and the variety of private consumption; it

---

200 H. Macmillan, *Reconstruction: a Plea for a National Policy* (London, 1933), p. 18.
201 *The Next Five Years: an Essay in Political Agreement* (London, 1935), esp. chs. I–II.
202 Craig, op. cit., p. 89.
203 W. Gavin, 'The Marketing Boards: Benefit or Menace? . . .', *The Times* (22 July 1935), p. 13.

altered the structure and size of whole industries, by decree, by manipulation of raw material supplies and by direction of labour. It exercised almost unlimited powers of requisition and conscription, and acquired the attributes of a monopolist on an unprecedented scale. It became the sole arbiter of the volume and direction of investment, borrowing itself for current expenditure far in excess of its current revenue, while sustaining for most of the war a huge balance-of-payments deficit which was none the less real for being concealed by Lease-Lend.

Then, recalling the crucial economic and social bane of pre-war days, the pamphlet continued:

From this apparent ability of the State to abolish unemployment at will and to induce an immense increase in production of those things which were needed, many people concluded that post-war reconstruction and national prosperity in peace-time could be achieved by the State with equal efficiency. The war ended in a burst of enthusiasm for 'Planning', which became almost a cult;. . . .[204]

Something of this sentiment was revealed in the Report of the Reconstruction Committee of the Royal Institute of British Architects which in September 1942 came out strongly

in favour of the setting up of a National Planning Authority with power to co-ordinate the proposals of the various Government Departments concerned with planning, having under it: (1) a National Planning Committee of experts to draw up a national plan; and (2) a Development Commission responsible for ensuring its smooth working; providing local authorities and public utility companies with the necessary credits; and carrying out those portions lying outside the scope of private enterprise or local authorities.

In addition elaborate regional and local machinery was envisaged; and so was the use of compulsion if the necessary degree of voluntary co-operation was not forthcoming on the part of the interests and bodies concerned.[205] And, of course, all the main political parties committed themselves to some form of planning during the reconstruction period. In 1942, for instance, a Labour Party report on *The Old World and the New Society* stated, 'The basis of our democracy must be planned production for community use . . . . A planned society must replace the old competitive system . . . . We have learned in the war that the anarchy of

204 E. Powell and A. Maude (eds), *Change is our Ally*, CPC no. 133 (London, 1954), pp. 25–6.
205 See the account in *KCA* (1940–3), p. 5372A.

private competition must give way to ordered planning under national control'. In the same year, the annual conference, in a resolution entitled 'A Planned Economic Democracy', stated there must be no return 'to an unplanned competitive society, which inevitably produces economic insecurity, industrial inefficiency and social inequality.'[206] The Conservatives were hardly less forward with the Prime Minister's commitment in 1943 to a four year plan and their acceptance of a full employment policy.[207]

Not only, then, did the period of hostilities result in an extremely high degree of control of available resources for war purposes, it also intimated the path for the future. Of course, there were disagreements but they were largely those of emphasis. The main difference of stress was perhaps revealed in the lectures given in 1947 by Sir Oliver Franks and Sir Hubert Henderson. The former had wartime experience of central planning and control at the Ministry of Supply and, although he recognized that there were substantial differences between the war years and peacetime circumstances, he firmly believed that the problems of the latter could be tackled by drawing on the lessons of wartime control and, too, by learning from its deficiencies especially those revealed by excessively large and rigid organizations. On this basis he accepted the inevitability and desirability of a radical expansion of the function of government in the economic field and thus a continuing revolution in many traditional or established attitudes. Henderson, on the other hand, goes only part of the way thus indicated and is sceptical of the more grandiose and detailed schemes of control. Planning is no 'magic talisman' by which all our economic difficulties might be 'charmed away'. He is moreover very clear about the dangers of trying to extrapolate on the basis of wartime experience: the objects of planning in peace are rarely so clear and simple; there is not the same unity of communal will and purpose; it is not possible so easily to ignore objects of policy necessarily neglected in wartime (at least to some degree) such as the international balance. But despite such reservations he is sure that 'planned arrangements of various sorts' may provide considerable help in solving the country's economic difficulties.[208]

In the years since 1945 fashions and possibilities in these matters have changed from time to time depending on the apparent success or failure

---

206 Both passages in A. Budd, *The Politics of Economic Planning*, pp. 60–1.

207 For the four year plan, see *KCA* (1940–3), p. 5676A. On Conservative acceptance of planning during the war and the immediate post-war period, see *The Ideological Heritage*, ch. 7.

208 O. Franks, *Central Planning and Control in War and Peace*, esp. pp. 17–24; H. Henderson, *The Uses and Abuses of Economic Planning*, passim.

of the various experiments and expedients.[209] Immediately after the war, close regulation was continued with detailed targets for output, manpower distribution, and the like; but the disadvantages of this style of control appeared fairly quickly and for a range of reasons, from union dislike of the interference with free collective bargaining to the electoral liability involved in perpetuating a system of control associated with unpleasant wartime hardship. In any case, it seemed that the economic and political objectives in view might be achieved just as well through a policy of demand management operating to a flexible long-term plan. This, in turn, instead of leading to steady growth of the kind sought, bogged down in the stop-go cycles described earlier. From this state of affairs emerged a fresh attempt at appropriate regulation through a copy of the French system of 'indicative' planning combined with an incomes policy. On this basis, co-ordination and consultation with industry rather than its control simply was the order of the day and new machinery, notably the National Economic Development Council, was established to achieve this. With the crusading return to office in 1964 of a Labour government dedicated to scientific management, the previous order was replaced by the attempt at a National Plan involving an intendedly co-ordinated industrial development outlined and controlled in some detail by the Department of Economic Affairs. The failure of this scheme and the demise of that office led to a loss of credibility in some circles in the idea of national planning as such and there was talk of 'Selsdon man' and a reversion to market policies. In the outcome, what supervened was a kind of crude Keynesianism pushed to extremes and which contributed greatly to the march of inflation and the subsequent crisis. The response to this was another attempt to plan the so-called 'Industrial Strategy' as a flexible framework for major economic decisions. What this meant in practice was a renewed emphasis on public ownership plus an attempt to regenerate industry through the National Enterprise Board and a series of planning agreements together, of course, with the control of incomes as a means to diminish inflationary pressure. Who knows what the future holds, what will come next? All that can reasonably be assumed is that (unless the Thatcher government's deliberate libertarian break for the social-market economy is successful) some form of planning will subsequently again be attempted. For, rightly or wrongly and despite the many planning disasters that have occurred hitherto, it is widely accepted nowadays as a basic necessity of economic life that the government of the day should try substantively to regulate its

209 A brief, up-to-date account is provided by Budd, op. cit. See also T. A. Smith, *The Politics of the Corporate Economy* (London, 1979), Part II. A closer look is taken at the development of the machinery of economic control in *A Much-Governed Nation*.

activity to a greater or lesser degree.[210] This means it must, in the public interest, control the currency, external trade, the level and form of production, wages, prices, and conditions of work and living – planning indeed not only the economic aspect of affairs but social life as a whole. Consider, as exemplification of this view, the recent remarks of the Director of the Centre for Environmental Studies:

> It is no longer possible to insulate economic from physical planning, or the private from the public sector, whether at regional scale . . . or at town scale. . . . The more we learn about human settlements, the clearer it becomes that their development can only be understood, and urban policies can only be formulated, if both are conceived as integral parts of the development and policies of the whole society in which we live.[211]

Nor is the deliberate egalitarian purpose disavowed or the intention completely to reject in any event the cash-nexus of the market as a basis of judgement.[212]

Perhaps, by way of summary, it may be said that the intervention of government nowadays occurs in a number of different but related ways.[213] First of all, it intervenes to protect people in respect of their conditions of work, their rights as customers, as citizens with an interest in their environment of living and recreation, as shareholders, and so on, all in the pursuit of order and social justice. Secondly, government is a customer for a vast array of industrial goods and services. It absorbs over half the GNP and so touches most aspects of commercial life and production. Thirdly, its agencies provide a substantial number of services: ports and telecommunications; the infrastructure and operating facilities of transport services; safeguarding services to do with health, police, and fire protection; provision of education, and labour services from job centres to ACAS. Then, as an industrialist, government manages crucial and very large enterprises such as electricity, gas, railways, canals, airways, and others. As well, it deals in the foreign relations of industry, treaties, trading agreements, tariffs, and the like. Then, formally, it has (as we have seen) the responsibility for managing in some way and to some degree the nation's currency and economic resources as a whole instead of entrusting these matters to the play of

---

210 For well-documented examples of failure, see P. Hall, *Great Planning Disasters* (London, 1980).

211 D. Donnison, 'Ideas for Town Planners', *Three Banks Review* (December 1972), pp. 9, 11.

212 ibid., pp. 12–13. See also Donnison, 'Liberty, Equality, Fraternity', ibid. (December 1970), pp. 3–23.

213 Cf. J. Davies, 'Industry and Government', ibid. (June 1967), pp. 16–17.

impersonal economic forces; and it does so often by the formulation of precise objectives to be achieved over a given period. In this role, it fosters one form of industrial effort or one area rather than another as with its encouragement of microelectronic technology.[214] It rewards and directs success, enterprise, research, and investment; tries to sustain a level of employment consistent with other objects and deals in a range of ancillary matters concerning redundancy, sickness, redeployment, and the like; it moulds housing and education policies with the production of resources as well as social objectives in view. And monetary policy is the servant of all this. Government no longer merely consults those concerned in economic life; it tries not simply to be their partner but their supervisor: a new mercantilism in the making indeed, that has not unjustly been described as 'the corporate state'.[215]

Herbert Spencer, who was, of course, hypersensitive about all such tendencies, published an essay in 1902 in which he deplored the development of regimentation and of what he called the 'militant society'. In this brief analysis, he wrote that 'System, regulation, uniformity, compulsion – these words are being made familiar in discussions on social questions. Everywhere has arisen an unquestioned assumption that all things should be arranged after a definite plan.'[216] This was really hardly the case at the time when he wrote, though he was correct to discern that the proclivity would gain ground; and it is perhaps a token of his prescience that he saw it so clearly and so early. It is surely true now. This is the mark of the progress or the decline – it depends how it is regarded – that we have achieved since. Or, at least, it has been true until recently. For in the past few years there have emerged afresh economic doctrines intended to restore the state to what are seen as its true economic functions by rolling back the extent of its substantive intervention in the details of economic life so that it may concentrate on its real, more limited but still vital, tasks.

The monetarist counter-revolution

The dominant Keynesianism of the 1950s and 1960s has increasingly (though, of course, by no means universally) come under attack. This was not simply because the doctrine seemed to be the basis of a continuing collectivist tendency, but rather because economic experience

---

214 For this example, see J. Haslam, 'An Appraisal of Microelectronic Technology', *National Westminster Bank Quarterly Review* (May 1979), pp. 55–64.
215 e.g. by J. T. Winkler, 'The Coming Corporatism', in R. Skidelsky (ed.), *The End of the Keynesian Era: Essays on the Disintegration of Keynesian Political Economy* (London, 1977), ch. 10.
216 H. Spencer, *Facts and Comments* (London, 1902), p. 134.

had revealed a new dimension of difficulties to which the orthodox analysis apparently offered no solution and which, indeed, the programmes it entailed, and especially its 'monetary incontinence', seemed likely to exacerbate. Specifically the belief that government could manage economic affairs and secure the efficient allocation of resources, full employment, and fair rewards by the manipulation of demand or other means of 'fine-tuning' and do this better than the unregulated (and, therefore, unstable) free market was much less credible when pursuing the sort of fiscal policies involved led simply to inflationary recession ('stagflation' or 'slumpflation' in the journalistic jargon). It seemed to result, that is, in little or no growth (above all in the crucial private sector) accompanied by increasing unemployment deriving from structural faults in the economy (national and international) coupled with union resistance to adaptation and a more or less rapid rise in the price level arising notably because of the extent of public sector spending. As one interested commentator put it, 'change is in the air. Just as the classical system of economic management was thought to have failed in 1929–33, so . . . the theory of the nicely-managed growth economy died in the 1970s.'[217]

In this context an alternative theory or analysis began to make headway. Sometimes it is called 'supply-side economics' because it stresses not the manipulation of demand by government but instead the stimulation of production, that is, the supply of goods and services, through incentives to trade provided without substantive intervention. This is why it is also referred to as 'the market approach' because it repudiates first-order state control of the competitive process. More usually, and popularly, it is simply described (in a kind of synecdoche) as 'monetarism'; and this is a not wholly inappropriate name because a renewed stress on the quantity theory of money is an important foundation, if by no means the whole, of the doctrine. In some quarters this new (or perhaps, more accurately, refurbished) approach seems set fair to become a new orthodoxy. More explicitly than Keynesianism perhaps, it is (in its major expositions) part of a coherently worked-out political theory for, while its supporters would claim that the economic analysis is logically rigorous and empirically valid in its own right, the technical argument is explicitly set within or associated with a complete picture of the nature of society as a whole and of the proper role and office of government within it. In these terms monetarism constitutes a libertarian reaction against the accumulated collectivism of the age. Of

---

217 A. Walters, *Economists and the British Economy*, IEA Occasional Paper no. 54 (London, 1978), p. 31. M. Friedman discusses a series of specific deficiencies in Keynesian analysis and prescription in *The Counter-Revolution in Monetary Theory*, IEA Occasional Paper no. 33 (1970; London, 1978), §III.

course, there are quite wide variations within this economic school (if such it is).[218] Some exponents of the doctrine stress that one key lesson to be learned from the failure of Keynesianism and its theory of economic management is that there are no inexorable monetary principles either that can provide a basis for the prediction of short-term consequences and so of infallible policy.[219] And while very specific prescriptions are often urged, there are again differences of emphasis in the style of policies invoked as with the debate whether the money supply should be cut quickly, as a sort of shock treatment to achieve immediate financial and psychological impact, or instead reduced more gradually so as to create an environment in which there is more certainty of expectation and stability of decision.[220]

The intellectual origins of the new monetarism are varied. Much is owed to classical political economy, of course, and especially to Adam Smith; to Irving Fisher with whom exposition of the modern quantity theory is most associated; to Ludwig von Mises and the group of Austrian economists who followed him; and to the so-called Chicago School. As with the Keynesianism which these ideas seek to criticize and replace, the matter is often extremely technical in terms of the theoretical economic analysis involved. I shall not attempt to scale these professional heights but shall content myself with a bare (and no doubt unsatisfactory) summary of its main aspects in the general version presented by Professor M. Friedman, often, even usually, regarded as the leading world exponent of monetarist economics and an authority whose ideas are said to have been of some influence on the policy and attitude of the Conservative administration which took office in 1979.

There is a basic libertarian stress on the primacy of individuality which is believed to be optimized in a society where political power is dispersed and the economic structure of which rests on a free competitive market.[221] This system of voluntary exchange must operate within a legal framework of non-discriminatory rules sustained as umpire by a limited government which is itself bound by those rules. The market and the economic freedom it represents is not only a necessary condition of political freedom but also the automatic regulator of economic activity. It does, of course, presuppose the maintenance of law and order, the enforceability of contracts, a well-defined array of property rights, and a

218 e.g. N. P. Barry, 'Austrian Economists on Money and Society', *National Westminster Bank Quarterly Review* (May 1981), p.20.
219 Friedman, *The Counter-Revolution in Monetary Theory*, pp.26–8.
220 M. Friedman, *From Galbraith to Economic Freedom*, IEA Occasional Paper no. 49 (1977; London, 1978), pp.44–51.
221 On these general political themes, see M. Friedman, *Capitalism and Freedom* (Chicago, 1962), introduction and chs.I–II; M. and R. Friedman, *Free to Choose: a Personal Statement* (Penguin, 1980).

stable currency; and government's task in these respects is vital and should be its central concern.[222] Its attention should not, therefore, be improperly diverted to other matters unrelated to this focal role as referee. At the same time certain public works and institutions that could not efficiently be provided by the market mechanism must be undertaken. This is also true of a number of paternalistic responsibilities that cannot be avoided in respect of those who cannot look to their own interests, such as the mentally deficient or children. In each case there is no formula to give a precise indication where government involvement should stop; though caution is needed because there is always the danger of excessive growth in any such functions assumed.[223] One thing is quite clear and specific, however: substantive government intervention in the economy is itself to be eschewed. The state must not undertake 'any functions that can be performed through the market, both because this substitutes coercion for voluntary co-operation in the area in question and because, by giving government an increased role, it threatens freedom in other areas.'[224] It is, in any case, less likely to provide the goods consumers want and at acceptable prices. The regulation and the expenditure this entails are invariably disincentives to the initiative and innovation necessary to progress. The increased level of taxation required, like inflation, promotes immediate consumption rather than saving and investment; the capital stock deteriorates from want of the latter; the technology is in consequence deficient; the old industrial cities will become run down; the workforce will be less productive; and the rate of growth will be low. Also government will tend to create money and credit at faster rates than products and services are forthcoming and inflation necessarily follows as does the decline in real income.

Such a catalogue of deficiencies is, indeed, like a description of the present troubles brought about by a period of misguided collectivism. (Certain of the relevant economic variables are indicated for the last decade in Table 7.) The problem is to overcome inflation, to stimulate production through improved incentives and opportunities, and to restore the market mechanisms. Several policies are jointly urged to this end.[225]

222 Professor Hayek, however, believes that sound money can only be achieved by depoliticizing the currency, allowing bank money and foreign currency to circulate thus depriving government of its control in this matter. In such circumstances, the argument runs, competition and self-interest will ensure that only sound money will survive.

223 M. and R. Friedman, *Free to Choose*, pp. 47–54; M. Friedman, *Capitalism and Freedom*, p. 34.

224 M. Friedman, *Capitalism and Freedom*, p. 39. For 'The Tyranny of Controls' and their disadvantages in international trade and the domestic economy, see *Free to Choose*, ch. 2.

225 Friedman's summary of what is involved is in *From Galbraith to Economic Freedom*, pp. 46–56, on which the following account is largely based.

Table 7 Certain economic variables, 1970–80

Year	Industrial production (1975 = 100)	GNP (£b)	Retail prices (1970 = 100)	Purchasing power of the £ (1970 = 100)	Money supply (M3) (£m)	PSBR (£m)	Real personal disposable income per head (1975 prices) £	Unemployment (m)
1970	99.6	44.1	100.0	100.0	17,666	– 4	1147	0.56
1975	100.0	94.7	184.4	54.0	37,595	10,484	1318	0.87
1980	105.0	191.4	360.7	27.5	69,574	12,373	1512	1.66

Source: Lloyds Bank, The British Economy in Figures (1981).

First, there must be a substantial cut in government expenditure, not least to improve incentives to work, save, and invest through reduction of the burden of taxation and by making more money available to the job-creating private sector. This reduction must be general, across the board, for selective cuts will only arouse in each case sectional resistance, the so-called 'cries from the cornucopia'; though 'uncontrollable' social and pensions programmes, subsidies, and the like must obviously be a prime target. And the reduction must be a real one – as much as the equivalent of 10 per cent of the national income in three years or so. Anything less (as with merely slowing down the rate of growth in public spending) will not be sufficient to have the desired effect. The goal is a balanced budget at the lower level of expenditure compatible with the kind of limited government in prospect.

Secondly, there must be a reorganization and simplification of the tax system which at present encourages wasteful consumption. Long-term incentives must be introduced to encourage saving and investment as by bigger tax write-offs, a reduction in capital gains tax, and in income and profits taxes. Special allowances and marginal rates of tax must be reduced or eliminated so that the necessary revenue can be raised at lower rates. And the system must be index-linked so that government does not (as at present) gain from inflation.

The budget and government spending must thus be adjusted. This is in order that it should be feasible to hold down the rate of growth in the quantity of money, control of the money supply being the third point of policy. Long-term inflation is 'always and everywhere a monetary phenomenon that arises from a more rapid expansion in the quantity of money than in total output' though there is no exact or mechanical linkage.[226] Monetary restraint is a crucial weapon, therefore, though by itself it can never be enough to achieve the goal in view (no single element of policy can be uniquely effective and extrinsic factors may be vital). This monetary point is really little more than a reassertion of that basic illustration of the laws of supply and demand, the quantity theory of money: that is (crudely) that the price level reflects the size of the money supply. For instance, the great depression of the 1930s was (on this analysis) due basically to a substantial fall in the quantity of money and its velocity of circulation.[227] It follows that the great inflation of the present day is due to a substantial monetary growth and can only be dealt with by an appropriate monetary correction. The measures used can vary depending on the sources of the excess growth in the money supply and the nature of the financial and other institutions concerned.

226 M. Friedman, *Monetary Correction*, IEA Occasional Paper no. 41 (1974; London, 1978), p.10; and cf. *Free to Choose*, pp.299, 309.
227 Friedman, *The Counter-Revolution in Monetary Theory*, pp.15–17.

'For example, if monetary growth has reflected the financing of government expenditures by the printing press, it can be ended by (a) reducing government spending; (b) raising taxes; (c) financing the deficit in the government budget by borrowing from the public rather than by creating money.'[228] But the curing of inflation involves unpleasant side-effects such as a phase of economic slow-down and increasing unemployment. The former may be 'fairly protracted' and the latter 'relatively high' so that a firm political will is needed to tackle the problem.[229] At the same time steps may be taken to ease these consequences as by the use of 'escalator clauses' in levying taxes and in public and private contracts tying them to changes in the price level. Index-linking of this kind (as in threshold agreements used in many wage settlements) helps mitigate for those involved the hardships imposed by an inflation that cannot be accurately forecast; they will also help facilitate the disinflationary consequences of a fall in the money supply.[230]

Fourthly, there should be rapid denationalization on a wide scale. This could be done by auctioning off the assets to the highest bidder but, in view of likely Labour threats of renationalization without compensation, this course is probably not practicable. More feasible would be the transfer of the assets of publicly-owned industries to a mutual fund in which every person would have a share: after all this is simply giving the industries to the people or nation at large which is supposed to own them. 'And if the trade unions object, then give the nationalised industries to the unions.'[231]

Then there should be a gradual but radical reorganizing of welfare services in order to introduce a crucial element of choice, to restore some competition in the provision, to facilitate transfer from the government to the private sector, and to reduce the size and influence of the bureaucracy at present involved. This could be pursued in various ways as by a system of vouchers or cash payments coupled with a charge for previously 'free' or subsidized services such as education, housing, medical aid, and so on. A negative (or reverse) income tax might also be used with the great advantage that it makes across-the-board provision possible thus simplifying the whole business as well as concentrating aid where it is really needed, on the low-income groups. Finally, it is necessary to reduce or abolish production-retarding regulations that consume capital but create no wealth. 'The urgent need today is to eliminate restrictions, not to add to them.'[232]

228 Friedman, *Monetary Correction*, p. 12.
229 ibid., pp. 9, 15–18.
230 ibid., pp. 9–10 and §§II–VII; M. and R. Friedman, *Free to Choose*, pp. 323–7.
231 Friedman, *From Galbraith to Economic Freedom*, p. 53.
232 M. and R. Friedman, *Free to Choose*, p. 94.

Obviously the thrust of all this will be notably to reduce the government's role in the economy in important respects though its task in other matters remains vital. So far as the question of unemployment is concerned, for instance, the argument is that it simply is not a matter of macro-economic demand deficiency, it is micro-economic and structural. People are out of work rather because they lack marketable skills than that there is a shortage of jobs as such. Government has a role in helping to train work-seekers without inflating the whole economy and to improve vocational and geographical mobility. This may involve such matters as the sale of council houses, the elimination of rent control, and the introduction of new forms of lease such as the 'short-hold'. In this context, too, government must move to limit or end trade union privileges which inhibit the necessary economic flexibility, as by bringing union-imposed working arrangements within the scope of the monopoly and restrictive practices legislation thus placing the workers' organizations alongside those of business itself. Similarly the 'employment protection' measures should be removed from new jobs created by private enterprise. Government also has the responsibility for dealing with 'spill overs' or 'neighbourhood effects', such matters as noise, pollution, congestion, and so forth. It must also seek to improve the free flow of international trade and of movements of capital and labour. Any tendency to monopoly needs to be dealt with though not by bureaucratic regulation; rather it should be treated by removing the incidental controls that sustain it, such as those on prices, tariffs, quotas, and other regulations.

In sum, even though it must above all avoid substantive economic intervention, there remains a considerable role for government in a free society:

> A government which maintained law and order, defined property rights, served as a means whereby we could modify property rights and other rules of the economic game, adjudicated disputes about the interpretation of the rules, enforced contracts, promoted competition, provided a monetary framework, engaged in activities to counter technical monopolies and to overcome neighbourhood effects widely regarded as sufficiently important to justify government intervention, and which supplemented private charity and the private family in protecting the irresponsible, whether madman or child – such a government would clearly have important functions to perform. The consistent liberal is not an anarchist.
>
> Yet it is also true that such a government would have clearly limited functions and would refrain from a host of activities that are now undertaken . . . .[233]

233 M. Friedman, *Capitalism and Freedom*, p. 34.

Thus, 'What we urgently need, for both economic stability and growth, is a reduction of government intervention'.[234]

What is sought above all, then, is not recovery in the old Keynesian style but a radical adaptation of industrial structure and attitudes in an attempt to face the realities of economic life in the 1980s. This is the task the Thatcher administration set itself; and inevitably the question is asked how the policy has fared in the context of the deliberately chosen purpose. Of course, any judgement is likely to be *ex parte* but a brief opinion may be hazarded.[235] What is readily apparent is a double failure: to acquire a sufficient stringency early enough in its term of office; and to maintain even that momentum which was achieved. There is, too, the danger that for electoral purposes the government may be so far persuaded from its course as to indulge in a hypocritical bout of Keynesian-type reflation of the economy, a U-turn which would be as meretricious and dishonest as it would be ineffective, not to say disastrous. On monetarist terms the kind of knowledge necessary accurately to fine-tune the economy in this way is simply not available; moreover the likely result would be little effect on unemployment, coupled with increases in wages, prices, and interest rates: an outcome the electorate would be likely to penalize in any case.[236]

When the Thatcher administration was formed it had (or worked out) a monetary and fiscal plan, the so-called 'medium-term financial strategy', together with policies designed to reduce market distortion. The broad thrust of the line of advance rested on various points of policy of the kind already outlined.[237] The long-term objective was, of course, to improve the operation of the market and extend the scope for competition in both public and private sectors.

> Progress to date includes large reductions in the penal higher rates of personal tax, the abolition of controls on foreign exchange, dividends, incomes and prices, some limited disposal of public sector assets . . ., some toughening of merger restrictions, and the law limiting union picketing activities. There is also a more critical attitude to industrial aid, exemplified by the lower profile of the National Enterprise Board . . . .

At the same time increased aid has been given to the British Steel Corporation and British Leyland; uneconomic coal pits are to be maintained and coal subsidized against imports; moreover 'there is little

234 ibid., p. 38.
235 Useful assessments from different politico-economic stances are P. Minford and D. Peel, 'Is the Government's Economic Strategy on Course?', *Lloyd's Bank Review* (April 1981), esp. pp. 11–18; and Sir A. Cairncross, 'Two Years without Cheers', *Three Banks Review* (March 1981), pp. 3–16.
236 Cf. Minford and Peel, art. cit., p. 13.
237 ibid., pp. 13–15.

else in the pipeline, except vague suggestions'. Consequently, it 'is hard to resist the conclusion that the government has . . . lost its momentum on market issues.'[238] It has also seemingly lost way in respect of the issues affecting the unemployment problem such as dealing with the effects of union monopoly power, the tax and social security structure, and the distortions in the housing market (as with restrictions on rent and on council house transfers).[239]

Many economists regard the government's policies as having failed, as untimely, or too narrowly conceived. It would be generally accepted, I suppose, that a sort of essentialist Keynesianism is no longer possible (if it ever was); but nor (it would be urged by most British economists) is a simplistic monetarism. Some synthesis is necessary, perhaps. As Professor Peston recently put it, it may well be that 'the lessons of the monetarist experiment have been learned by everybody concerned, namely, that fiscal, monetary, and wages policy have to be rationally combined if real progress is to be made.'[240]

But progress towards what? The basic economic point is, of course, that Britain (and other western industrial countries also) faces not merely a cyclic depression, like, say, that of the 1930s, but something much more fundamental: the need for profound change in its established industrial pattern. This is perhaps a prospect of transformation as great as that involved in the old Industrial Revolution itself. In this sense things have come full circle from the point at which this account of our economic and social affairs started. The symptoms of the crisis are clear. There is increasing decline in large and basic industries which have become unwieldy and inefficient such as steel, textiles, shipbuilding, and car production. This is the result partly of domestic factors as with failure to invest in improved machinery and to develop new technology, bad management, restrictive practices and uncompetitively high wages (and so costs) deriving from the power of vested trade union interests. It is also the consequence of exotic factors such as rising energy and raw material costs and the fierce competition from low-wage but rapidly industrializing less developed countries. But whatever the precise causes, in any case, the real question is whether the British economy can show sufficient flexibility to secure the necessary adaptation. A further and, in the present context, most relevant issue is what role government can or should play in this process of economic rejuvenation.

238 ibid., pp.14–15.
239 ibid., pp.15–17.
240 M. Peston, 'The Integration of Monetary, Fiscal and Incomes Policy', *Lloyd's Bank Review* (July 1981), p.13. The need for a wages policy is urged, from a Keynesian point of view, by N. Kaldor and J. Trevithick, 'A Keynesian Perspective on Money', ibid. (January 1981), pp. 18–19.

What might be involved in the structural change is fairly clear: a switch to profitable products; investment in new and different machinery; rationalization of the labour force as by eliminating overmanning or its reduction as by, for instance, early retirement; retraining for workers who lose jobs; changing the emphasis of the educational system to an appropriate vocational and technical emphasis. Innovation is crucial as by moving to market products others cannot yet make or make well and cheaply: special steels, perhaps, or ships for specialized purposes; certain high quality textiles; electronics and microprocessing; service industries. Nor should there be any subsidizing of those ventures, whether new or established, that lose money. Moreover it is essential to realize that restructuring is not a once-for-all change however radical, but a *continual* process of adaptation. The economy must be always flexible – which rather suggests that the rigidities of collectivist control and manipulation might best be avoided: to that extent the libertarian attitude to the economic role of the state might seem more appropriate. There is, too, a longer-term ray of hope in respect of Third World competition. The less developed countries have often emerged as strong economic rivals because they have combined modern technology with low wage costs and a compliant labour force. Yet as they prosper, not only will they seek to buy more from advanced countries like Britain but, at the same time, their own wage levels will rise towards that of the industrialized world thus undermining their competitive advantage.

SOCIAL CONDITIONS AND INFLUENCES

If there is one feature in the national life of the last sixty years on which Englishmen may justly pride themselves it is the amelioration of the social condition of the workers . . . . It is Social Reform which has made the Queen's reign memorable and glorious.
G. W. E. RUSSELL, *Collections and Recollections*, series 1, 1903,
p. 199

It is often difficult, if not impossible, to distinguish between the economic and the social and, in truth, a good part at least of the affairs to be reviewed now might easily have found its home elsewhere in this long chapter. Nevertheless, what is to be examined here is, if something of a miscellany, not thereby without significance. Two specific matters will be looked at in respect of their effect on or reflection of the development of collectivism: growing data about social conditions, and improved communications. Then, government involvement in the spread of educational facilities and the development of police forces will be sketched as two examples among many of the ways in which public authorities were drawn into the treatment of social need.

Growing data about social conditions

An obvious point – and one related both to the impetus of political change and the development of opinion favourable to it – is that there was a growing accumulation of factual data about social and economic conditions which seemed to demand attention and remedy. Indeed Professor MacDonagh has suggested that 'the exposure of the actual state of things in particular fields was in the long run probably the most fruitful source of reform in nineteenth-century England.'[241] J. S. Mill observed at the time that the contemporary 'increase of sympathy for the poor' was due at least in part to growing detailed knowledge of their distress made public by a range of official and private inquiry. It was not that the poverty and deprivation were new but rather that their scale and nature were being more effectively documented.[242] For instance, the cholera epidemic of 1831–2 revealed to those involved at the Privy Council Office the vast extent of misery that prevailed and led to the feeling that too little was being done to alleviate it.[243] Later, in 1883, Goschen similarly suggested that the main factor in the development of state interference was the awakening of the public conscience, and that the main reason for this in any particular case was the revelation 'in striking colours' of 'facts previously unknown or ignored' which stirred the public and aroused emotion to demand 'the application of immediate and direct remedies.'[244] Of course, the revelation of the extent of suffering, waste, and disease that existed did not necessarily invite intervention by the state: the circumstances might, for example, rather be seen simply as a greater opportunity for the exercise of personal philanthropy and Christian charity. This was certainly the reaction of Spencer and those who thought like him as well as of a much wider and perhaps more orthodox range of opinion. Yet it was realized, relatively quickly by some, that evangelism, desirable as it was, cleared out no sewers, and that philanthropic aid, though useful, was too limited in scope to make a real impact on the enormous problems faced. All the data being collected, all the experience acquired, intimated that the basic issues were social rather than individual in origin and so wide and so deep that they needed communal treatment. They pointed, as Beatrice Webb said later, to the 'irrelevance' of merely private charity.[245]

241   O. MacDonagh, *Early Victorian Government, 1830–1870* (London, 1977), p.6.

242   J. S. Mill, 'The Claims of Labour' (1845), in *Collected Works*, ed. J. M. Robson *et al.* (London, 1963 ff), iv.371. Cf. Macaulay's comments in *The History of England* (1849–61; London, 1889), i.202, 205, 208.

243   See the citations in R. J. Morris, *Cholera 1832: the Social Response to an Epidemic* (London, 1976), p.197.

244   G. J. Goschen, . . . *Laissez-faire and Government Interference* (London, 1883), pp.6–7.

245   B. Webb, *My Apprenticeship* (Penguin, 1938), ii.298.

A good example of the way in which public action was seen to be the corollary of what inquiry revealed is the contribution of Viscount Howick (later Earl Grey) to the Commons' debate on the factory question in 1844. Having urged that government was responsible not merely for the protection but also for the welfare of the people, he went on to argue that this required more than was currently being achieved. It was especially the case, he said, when the state of the manufacturing districts was borne in mind; and he spoke of the impact of examinations of their condition:

> When we look at the dense masses of population that are there collected, or rather heaped together, without any adequate provision either for their moral or physical well-being; when we learn, as by recent inquiries we have learnt (I must say for one, to my astonishment and dismay) – when we learn what abuses prevail, and how much misery exists amongst the thousands of human beings crowded together in the busy seats of our commercial and manufacturing industry; when we consider this state of things, surely we must feel that we have trusted too much in a case where it does not apply, to the maxim that men should be left to take care of their own interests . . . .

He added that it would have been much better had government interfered earlier to deal with the causes of this unfortunate and unacceptable situation.[246]

The inquiries in question here were both official and private; and obviously the former themselves constituted a kind of public intervention. They included the numerous investigations conducted by Parliamentary select committees and by royal commissions as well as the reports and returns completed by departments and their officers, and later by such cognate bodies as departmental committees, advisory councils, and working parties. The amount of information and comment thus accumulated was enormous and on a great variety of subjects from accidents in coal mines to the wages of agricultural labourers, from the condition of the handloom weavers to the health of large towns.[247] And all this information greatly influenced the creation and development of opinion not least because much of it was reported in the quality press.[248] With that unerring instinct of his, Wellington always distrusted Blue

---

246 74 Parl. Deb. 3s., 3 May 1844, cols. 638–50: the passage cited is at col. 647.
247 Something of the nature and extent of these inquiries is indicated in the volumes of P. and G. Ford, *Select List of British Parliamentary Papers, 1833–1899* (Oxford, 1953) and *A Breviate of Parliamentary Papers, 1900–1954* (3 vols, Oxford, 1951–61); C. J. Hanser, *Guide to Decision: the Royal Commission* (Totowa, N.J., 1965), esp. Appendix 2. See also the lists and other references in J. E. Pemberton, *British Official Publications* (1971; 2nd edn, Oxford, 1973), chs. 6, 11.
248 Cf. H. J. Laski, *Democracy in Crisis* (1933; London, 1934), pp. 99–100.

books: he knew they would undermine Cabinet control of policy by creating external pressures to do this or that.[249] Of course, it is necessary to adopt a proper caution in the present assessment or use of many of the data thus presented. Some observers recognized at the time the way in which official documents could mislead, as J. R. McCulloch believed that Sadler's Factory Report contained 'false statements, and exaggerated and fallacious representations'. Equally historians have later found reason to be diffident about accepting the array of fact and opinion in the Blue books at their face value.[250] Yet their impact is clear and undoubted; and one detailed example discussed in an earlier chapter illustrates the way in which such materials invited government intervention.[251]

Then, in addition to these official investigations, there were also many private inquiries of different types. There was the work of the various statistical societies both in London and in a number of provincial centres.[252] There were also the published accounts of personal observation of the industrial or social scenes and their problems, including the numerous examinations of the condition of the working classes of which Engels' is just the most well-known (and not the most reliable). There were, too, the more extensive or systematic surveys like those of Henry Mayhew, Charles Booth, and Seebohm Rowntree as well as the extensive material obtained in the course of case-work by such bodies as the Charity Organization Society. All this constituted a vast and continually growing literature, the broad effect of which was to provide much disconcerting information, especially about the condition of the un-skilled labourers in the towns, to the effect that, as Rowntree urged, 'No civilisation can be sound or stable which has at its base this mass of stunted human life.'[253] Campbell-Bannerman, for one, read Rowntree's book on poverty in York and was much impressed and disturbed, subsequently using the material in his speeches.[254] Morley was equally moved by this study and recommended it to Churchill who publicly pronounced its revelations to be terrible and shocking. He wrote of 'the

249 P. Guedalla, The Duke (1931; London, 1940), p. 334.
250 McCulloch's opinion is reported in E. J. Evans, Social Policy 1830–1914: Individualism, Collectivism and the Origins of the Welfare State (London, 1978), pp. 46–7 citing Edinburgh Review, lxi (1835), pp. 463–4. See also the papers in F. A. Hayek (ed.), Capitalism and the Historians (1954; Chicago, 1965), esp. intro. and chs. 1, 5.
251 For the impact of the facts revealed by the medical examination of military recruits, see pp. 68–9 above.
252 On which see M. J. Cullen, The Statistical Movement in Early Victorian Britain: the Foundations of Empirical Social Research (Hassocks, 1975), esp. Part II.
253 Cited in C. B. Cox and A. E. Dyson (eds), The Twentieth-Century Mind: History, Ideas and Literature in Britain (London, 1972), i.21. For other contemporary inquiries, see R. C. K. Ensor, England 1870–1914 (1936; Oxford, 1968), p. 513 n. 4.
254 J. Wilson, CB: a Life of Sir Henry Campbell-Bannerman (London, 1973), p. 391.

duty of a man to man' and of 'the doctrine that honest effort in a wealthy community should involve certain minimum rights', asserting, too, that the mere existence of 'this festering life at home' makes 'world-wide power a mockery' and 'defaces the image of God upon earth'. As he put it elsewhere in another comment on Rowntree's survey, 'For my own part, I see little glory in an Empire which can rule the waves and is unable to flush its sewers'.[255]

The impact of the work of Charles Booth may be taken as another example here. In the 1880s and 1890s he had organized inquiries in the East End of London and had found that a third of the families investigated were living at or below bare subsistence level.[256] And although he was strongly individualist in temper and prejudice, Booth emerged from his prolonged study of the London poor with proposals that were hardly compatible with these views. His remedy was for the state to take charge to remove the entire class of underprivileged persons (like those living in poverty on casual earnings) from the daily struggle for existence. And the degree of collectivism Booth was thus prepared to accept is indicated by the fact that he believed something like 3 million people came into this category over the country as a whole.[257] The logic of Booth's opinion lay in the assumption that, by extending in this respect what he called 'Socialism', the cause of 'Individualism' would be sustained elsewhere, though he recognized indeed how far the former had already proceeded. So a major lesson he learned from his work was this:

> Our Individualism fails because our Socialism is incomplete. In taking charge of the lives of the incapable, State Socialism finds its proper work, and by doing it completely, would relieve us of a serious danger. The Individualist system breaks down as things are, and is invaded on every side by Socialistic innovations, but its hardy doctrines would have a far better chance in a society purged of those who cannot stand alone. Thorough interference on the part of the State with the lives of a small fraction of the population would tend to make it possible, ultimately, to dispense with any Socialistic interference in the lives of all the rest.[258]

On Booth's memorial tablet in the crypt of St Paul's Cathedral is the inscription, 'Through his long life he had at heart the welfare of his

255 R. S. Churchill *et al., Winston S. Churchill* (London, 1966 ff), ii. 30–2.
256 A series of exemplary extracts from Booth's *The Life and Labour of the People of London* (17 vols, London, 1902–3) is easily accessible in e.g. A. Fried and R. M. Elman (eds), *Charles Booth's London . . .* (London, 1969) or E. R. Pike, *Human Documents of the Age of the Forsytes* (1969; Newton Abbot, 1972), pp. 67–135.
257 See the passage cited in Webb, *My Apprenticeship*, ii. 301–2.
258 C. Booth, *Poverty*, i. 167, cited ibid., ii. 302.

fellow citizens, and believing that exact knowledge of realities is the foundation of all reform, he dedicated himself to the examination of the social, industrial, and religious condition of the people of London'.[259] And this work (like that of Rowntree) was of substantial influence. For instance, it was cited by Herbert Samuel in his study of Liberal doctrine and policy in those passages where he specifically rebutted Spencer's anti-statism and where he was urging the need for the problems of poverty and other vital matters of social reform to be tackled by public authority.[260] Nor is it a coincidence that within a few years two of those who had been associated with Booth's investigations were to be centrally involved in the creation and implementation of major early experiments in social control. These were Sir Hubert Llewellyn Smith who between 1906–10 helped institute and organize the national network of labour exchanges and between 1911–14 the system of compulsory unemployment insurance; and Ernest Aves who took a leading part in the establishment and administration of the Trade Boards set up under the Act of 1909.[261] Summarizing the impact of Booth's work, with which she too was involved, Beatrice Webb said it added fresh impetus to the general adoption in Britain of what Fourier some years before had called 'guaranteeism', that is, the policy of securing to each individual a national minimum of conditions in respect of his life and work. This, she said 'may, or may not, be Socialism, but it is assuredly a decisive denial of the economic individualism of the 'eighties.'[262]

And such views spread all the more as means of communication of all kinds were improved.

Improved communications

In the first part of the nineteenth century any manifest evil or abuse might not necessarily be widely known outside the particular area concerned or group of persons immediately involved. Hence there was a vital role to be played in the process of change whether by voluntary or government action by the gathering and dissemination of current news or other knowledge. What might be called the political public was affected by Parliamentary debate or by the kind of official report or private inquiry already referred to, either directly or as reported in the press or as discussed in the quality reviews. But the wider body of the community could not be so closely affected in a similar way until it was more literate

259 Cited in Pike, op. cit., p. 67.
260 H. Samuel, *Liberalism: an Attempt to State the Principles and Proposals of Contemporary Liberalism in England* (London, 1902), pp. 9–10 and nn, p. 18 and n. 1.
261 B. Webb, *My Apprenticeship*, ii. 302–4.
262 ibid., ii. 304.

and until the means of a more effective dissemination of information was established. Nor of course did this wider opinion necessarily matter so much politically until the franchise was extended.

It seems likely that even during the eighteenth century there had been a notable increase in the number of people who could read (even if they could not write), one indication of which is the fact that by the early nineteenth century the handbill and poster had become major means of spreading information, regulation, and warning.[263] Certainly, by the mid-nineteenth century popular reading matter was of quite considerable amount, making clear that it is a myth to suppose that the working classes were completely illiterate before the Act of 1870 began to alter the formal educational position. At who else, for example, did Edward Lloyd aim his 'penny dreadfuls'? Even before 1870 a considerable proportion of the nation's children would have received some kind of education such that it is thought, for instance, that as early as the 1840s possibly as many as three-quarters of the working population as a whole had some reading ability.[264] They would want appropriate journalistic pabulum. The removal in the decade after 1853 of various taxes (on advertisements, newspapers, and paper) which had inhibited the expansion of the popular press was also important in this regard: one result, for instance, was that by 1860 *Reynolds' Weekly*, which circulated widely in the manufacturing districts, printed as many as 350,000 copies.[265] Increasing educational provision simply intensified a process already well under way: when the halfpenny *Daily Mail* appeared in 1896 it built up within three years to a circulation of over half a million.[266] Similarly libraries were flourishing, cheaper books and magazines were becoming more widely available, and so forth. In 1870 Munby noted (as though it was yet something of an exception) that one of the milkwomen he knew could read; yet it was estimated shortly after the third Reform Act (1884) that out of the new national electorate of over 2 million less than 40,000 were illiterate; and by the early years of the present century, Lady Bell found in Middlesbrough that a notable proportion of a sample of households whose men were

263 On this early literary explosion, see J. H. Plumb, 'Political Man', in J. L. Clifford (ed.), *Man Versus Society in Eighteenth-Century Britain: Six Points of View* (Cambridge, 1968), pp. 10–11; J. Viner, 'Man's Economic Status', ibid., p. 31. For the use of the handbill and poster, see e.g. R. J. Morris, *Cholera 1832*, p. 115.

264 R. K. Webb, 'Working Class Readers in Early Victorian England', *English Historical Review*, lxv (1950), p. 349. On the extent of the educational provision, see pp. 185–7 below.

265 E. L. Woodward, *The Age of Reform 1815–1870* (1938; 2nd edn, Oxford, 1971), p. 632 n. 2.

266 E. Halévy, *A History of the English People in the Nineteenth Century* (1913–46; 2nd trans. edn, London, 1961), v. 9; Ensor, *England 1870–1914*, pp. 310ff, 532–6.

employed in her husband's factory either read a newspaper or novels, a quarter of them with some taste.[267]

This growing readership had two aspects relevant here. First, it did, however baldly or badly, disseminate more widely than before some knowledge of political and social problems and the possibility of their treatment or remedy by government action. Thus the entire country was being reduced to the dimension of a single constituency. Secondly, the press, in not wanting to present anything likely to be distasteful to its growing body of readers, reflected mass feelings and demands, for its circulation (and its advertising revenue) depended on this: as the famous editor H. W. Massingham once admitted, the modern newspaper is primarily an organ of business supplying the wares it thinks its customers want and changing them whenever a new demand arises. An outstanding reflection of this was the frank remark of Lord Northcliffe who said, during the Boer War, that if he believed two-thirds of England was pro-Boer he would change the policy of the *Daily Mail* like a shot to conform with this trend.[268] The rise of the *Daily Mirror* illustrates the same point. It had been a right-wing paper for women but was transformed by Cecil King and Guy Bartholomew into 'a left-wing *vox populi*' agitating against the figures and forces of the radical demonology from Colonel Blimp to the Old School Tie.[269]

> No doubt but ye are the People – your throne is above the King's.
> Whoso speaks in your presence must say acceptable things:
> Bowing the head in worship, bending the knee in fear –
> Bringing the word well smoothen – such as a King should hear.[270]

The press thus tended to go with the growing collectivist tide and aid its flow. Legislative intervention, which once would have been condemned, was either passed by in silence or positively advocated; *laissez faire* was treated as an exploded doctrine; the movement towards intervention was accepted and the contributions of its advocates given prominence.[271] J. S.

267 D. Hudson, *Munby: Man of Two Worlds. The Life and Diaries of Arthur J. Munby 1828–1910* (1972; Abacus, 1974), p.280; Ensor, op. cit., p.147; Lady Bell, *At the Works: a Study of a Manufacturing Town* (London, 1907), p.162.

268 H. W. Massingham, 'The Press and the People' (1924), in H. J. Massingham (ed.), *H.W.M.: a Selection from the Writings of H. W. Massingham* (London, 1925), pp.131–2.

269 P. Addison, *The Road to 1945: British Politics and the Second World War* (London, 1975), pp.143, 152.

270 R. Kipling, 'The Islanders' (1902), ll.1–4, in *Rudyard Kipling's Verse: Inclusive Edition, 1885–1926* (London, 1927), p. 298.

271 Cf. H. Spencer, *The Man Versus the State* (1884; Penguin, 1969), p.98.

Mill early and percipiently summarized the matter when he wrote, in his clear and direct way, in the essay on 'Civilization':

> A...powerful...instrument of combination...has but lately become universally accessible – the newspaper. The newspaper carries home the voice of the many to every individual among them; by the newspaper each learns that others are feeling as he feels, and that if he is ready, he will find them also prepared to act upon what they feel. The newspaper is the telegraph which carries the signal throughout the country, and the flag around which it rallies. Hundreds of newspapers speaking in the same voice at once, and the rapidity of communication afforded by improved means of locomotion, were what enabled the whole country to combine in that simultaneous energetic demonstration of determined will which carried the Reform Act. Both these facilities are on the increase, everyone may see how rapidly; and they will enable the people on all decisive occasions to form a collective will, and render that collective will irresistible.[272]

Discussion in the press was even more important in many respects than debate in Parliament; its editors became the new rulers of the political world, playing a role, as Halévy said, like that of the demagogue in the republics of antiquity.[273] Even as early as 1806, Wellington had advised his brother to look for journalistic allies. 'It appears', he wrote, 'that the Newspapers have at last made such progress in guiding what is called publick opinion in this Country, that no Man who looks to publick station can attain his objects, without a connection with & assistance from some of the Editors.' Trollopians will recall here the influence exerted on Barsetshire and even national affairs by 'the daily Jupiter'.[274]

Later developments – the spread of education, the coming of wireless and television as well as the cinema (all of which themselves have been the occasion for greater direct involvement by government) – have continued to mould and augment the force of popular opinion and to help create greater social homogeneity. This 'New Behemoth' (as Professor Mowat called it), when allied with the growing electorate, induced uniformity of response and, as well, united demand for the safeguarding of collective interests.[275] It came to constitute a vital link between public men and voters, providing information, ventilating issues, concentrating attention, and helping to create a climate of opinion

272 J. S. Mill, 'Civilization' (1836), Collected Works, xviii.125.
273 T. Carlyle, 'The French Revolution' (1837), in Works (People's edn, 1871–4), iii.24 and 'Latter-Day Pamphlets' (1850), ibid., xx.188–90; Halévy, op. cit., i.169.
274 Guedalla, The Duke, pp.129–30. For Trollope, see e.g. The Warden (1854; Everyman, 1975), ch. VII, esp. pp.100–2.
275 C. L. Mowat, Britain between the Wars, 1918–1940 (1955; London, 1968), p.240.

which, in the circumstances, would invariably be favourable to the collectivist tendency.

Thus the media, in fostering a wider and quicker – though not necessarily deeper – appreciation of current affairs, certainly produce a more intensive reaction to public issues. In modern circumstances, this will often constitute a swiftly expressed dissatisfaction coupled with a demand for appropriate response: as the recent report of the Commission on the Constitution observed, 'Thus government, however reluctant it may be at the outset, may be compelled to extend its sphere of activity.'[276] I do not possess a television set myself and rarely have the opportunity to view – and what I have seen makes me think the general programme standard is pretty appalling – but I can well understand that today TV is a vital part of the political scene and can affect the whole basis of British democracy. Viscount Eccles put the point well when he observed that for millions of families it adds a new dimension of experience for they now live on two levels: the direct ambit of their circumscribed daily life and the notionally limitless panorama presented on the television screen. Inevitably the two dimensions are compared and just as ineluctably this is likely to lead to the wish for changes in the former.[277] To see *Cathy Come Home* is for most people probably to believe (however illogically) that government should do something about the housing problem presented. Moreover, television seems to be much the most effective means by which politicians can communicate with the electorate and conduct that political auction which has been so marked a feature of modern democracy and so conducive to the growth of government responsibilities.

As well, the fundamental changes taking place in the physical means of communication have had a similar effect in sustaining the collectivist tendency, not least (but not only) because government and its agencies have been involved in one degree or another, often very closely, with the development of roads, railways, and the air.

The history of the development of modern means of transport is a most fascinating subject, one the byways of which it is difficult to resist. Unfortunately it is necessary here to concentrate on the broad outlines of the matter and on aspects of its political and social impact. The significance of what occurred rests on what H. G. Wells called the destruction of time and space, a great surge of mobility. It is probably hard nowadays to grasp the difficulties in the way of travel that, despite many improvements, existed in this country before the mid-nineteenth

---

276 The Constitution, R. Com. Rep., 1972–3 (vol. xi), Cmnd. 5460, p. 80 §246. A good recent instance of the role of national publicity in leading to government action is described in R. Kimber *et al.*, 'The Deposit of Poisonous Waste Act 1972: a Case of Government by Reaction?', *Public Law*, xix (1974), pp. 198–219.
277 Viscount Eccles, *Politics and the Quality of Life*, CPC no. 471 (London, 1970), p. 14.

century. Facilities were often slight and the cost considerable. The result was a high degree of geographical fixity: most people lived their whole lives in the environs of the place where they were born, as is readily apparent if one examines the parish and episcopal records for any area for the seventeenth and eighteenth centuries. Transport was based, as it had been for millennia, on the horse and the boat; and it could take as long to travel from London to the provinces as in Roman times. Evidence of all kinds bears witness to the bad state of the roads, for instance, and the impediment to travel this necessarily created. In 1729 a West Country road near Bath was so bad that a coachman could not guarantee to make a journey on it of only sixty-four miles in less than four days.[278] A fast post-chaise could, it is true, go from London to Edinburgh in the same time; but the stage-coach took nearly three times as long and a goods wagon as much as three weeks.[279] The impediment to commerce and social connexions alike may be imagined.

Gradually at first, and then quickly, changes came. Roads were improved, often through the agency of a turnpike trust; river navigation received attention and, in the latter half of the eighteenth century, a considerable system of deadwater canals was built. The speed of travel increased. In 1830 the Edinburgh mail coach took just under two days; two years before, Cobden travelled in the Peveril of the Peak coach from London to Manchester in the 'marvellously short space of twenty hours'.[280] But by then the railway had come. This was the really great step forward, a transport revolution indeed.[281] Rail or tram-roads had long existed, of course; the crucial change was the invention of an effective steam locomotive. The first steam-hauled public railways in the world opened in Britain in 1825 for the carriage of freight and five years later for passengers. During the first thirty years of railway development, over 7000 miles of track were built and most of the trunk lines were complete; it was possible to travel between major cities in Britain not in days but in a few hours, and relatively cheaply too. The line mileage then grew quickly and more than doubled by the 1870s. As early as 1851 the railways were carrying some 80 million passengers a year; fifty years

---

278 Lady Irwin to Lord Carlisle (27 October 1729), Historical Manuscripts Commission, XV, Appendix 6, p. 61, in H. Perkin, *The Age of the Railway* (1970; Newton Abbot, 1971), p. 17.

279 Cf. Scott's reference to the three weeks taken by the 'Northern Diligence' to travel from Edinburgh to London in the mid-eighteenth century, *Waverley* (1814; Everyman, 1937), p. 408.

280 J. Morley, *The Life of Richard Cobden* (London, 1881), i.15. Cf. A. Redford, *The History of Local Government in Manchester* (London, 1939–40), ii.9 n.2.

281 Cf. G. Alderman, 'The Victorian Transport Revolution', *Historical Journal*, xiv (1971), p. 635.

later, the total had risen to over 1100 million.[282] There followed the development of the electric tramcar and the internal combustion engine, the automobile being quickly transformed from a rich man's toy to a means of day-to-day transport. Something of the proportion of the changes entailed by these inventions is indicated by the fact that in 1904 there were 8400 private cars, while shortly before the Second World War the number registered was almost 2 million; but by 1977 the number was almost 14 million. During the same period the total of public transport vehicles – buses, coaches, and taxis – rose from 5300 to 112,000; while in the fifty years from 1922 the total of goods vehicles went up from 150,000 to some 1¾ million.[283] The kind of rapid and extensive growth involved may be indicated by a single small example, that of the development of bus services in one part of Cheshire. In 1911 the Crosville company had two vehicles and carried 80,000 passengers; by 1941, in the reduced operating circumstances of wartime, there were nevertheless 1101 buses and 100 million passengers.[284]

The point at issue in all this is the way in which these changes in means of transport had a bearing on the growth of government intervention. There was indeed a multiplicity of effects. The pulse of things quickened: 'railways', said Carlyle in a delightfully expressive phrase, 'have set all the Towns of Britain a-dancing.'[285] The centuries-old immobility of population was altered in a relatively few years; people as well as goods could move at a speed and on a scale hitherto unimagined. It was the railway, too, that made possible the creation of the great towns and factories with all that this implied in respect of public control to deal with the problems thus unleashed. The psychological effect was considerable. There was a transformation of ideas of space and time. As the pulse of things quickened and complex interchange intensified, established attitudes were called in question. The change wrought even by the humble bicycle is sufficiently exemplary. Despite the still poor and dusty roads, it opened liberating and even adventurous prospects for a wide range of persons. H. G. Wells told of this in a charming tale, *The Wheels of Chance* (1896), a symbolic chronicle of how the hero, a draper's

282 B. R. Mitchell and P. Deane, *Abstract of British Historical Statistics* (Cambridge, 1962), pp. 225–6.

283 K. B. Smellie, *A History of Local Government* (1946; 4th edn, London, 1969), p. 61; *Whitaker's Almanack* (1979), p. 1184.

284 J. M. Lee, *Social Leaders and Public Persons: a Study of County Government in Cheshire since 1888* (Oxford, 1963), p. 88.

285 T. Carlyle, 'Latter-Day Pamphlets' (1850), in *Works*, xx. 226. See, too, the passages from H. Booth, *An Account of the Liverpool and Manchester Railway* (1830; London, 1969), pp. 89–90, in H. Perkin, *The Age of the Railway*, p. 92; also H. Spencer, *First Principles* (1862; 6th edn, London, 1945), pp. 410–11, and *Essays* (revised edn, London, 1891), i. 56–8.

assistant, finds that the new surroundings to which his safety bicycle leads 'strip off the habitual servile from him'.[286] A *fortiori* this may be true of the motor-car as even G. K. Chesterton (normally so diffident about or hostile to modern technology) recognized.[287]

Not least these changes have helped produce a more homogeneous society and encouraged higher levels of political expectation. Pressures have been created for improved and more uniform social treatment and opportunity. It was, for instance, the railways that for the first time brought national politicians face to face with supporters (and opponents) outside their own constituencies. At the opening of the Liverpool and Manchester railway in 1830,

> the crowds craned forward calling out 'Which is the duke?', so little did they know the appearance of the prime minister. In the 1860s Gladstone was beginning that stumping of the country, making speeches at mass meetings of middle-class reformers and working-class 'Lib-Labs', which was to make him 'the people's William'. The railways contributed an important element to the politics of mass democracy.[288]

Politics became, as it were, a continuous Midlothian campaign for the attention and support of a wider political public which had to be sustained and pandered to if its votes were to be won. There were, indeed, scale economies in many public activities. Movements like the trade unions or pressure groups like the Anti-Corn Law League could organize on a nation-wide basis. For instance, the speakers of the latter were able swiftly to move from one centre to another; and Cobden deliberately used the penny post to keep the constituencies informed by sending out packets of tracts and so on.[289] Equally, of course, political tension could be mitigated in so far as control could be exercised more effectively: the telegraph (a service operated by the state) passed information and instructions more swiftly and it was easier than ever before to move troops and police.

In a nice passage Goschen indicated another aspect of what was implicit in the transport revolution:

286 H. G. Wells, *The Wheels of Chance* (1896; Wayfarer's Library, n.d.), p. 138. Cf. the comments in Wells's *Experiment in Autobiography* (London, 1934), ii. 543. The 'new dimension' thus brought to British social life has been recently reviewed in D. Rubinstein, 'Cycling in the 1890s', *Victorian Studies*, xxi (1977–8), pp. 47–71.

287 G. K. Chesterton, *The Outline of Sanity* (London, 1926), IV. 4, 'The Free Man and the Ford Car', esp. pp. 174, 179–80.

288 H. Perkin, *The Age of the Railway*, pp. 116–17.

289 J. Bright and J. E. T. Rogers (eds), *Speeches on Questions of Public Policy* (London, 1878), p. 37.

As society becomes more complex, more crowded, as conflicting interests jostle each other more and more, so will the cry for more regulation become louder from day to day. Till some years ago the street traffic in the metropolis regulated itself. The rules of the road were held to suffice. The stream of vehicles passed to and fro under the very wide application of 'laissez-faire' and 'laissez-passer'. But when blocks became more frequent, collisions more numerous, street accidents more and more a common occurrence, the cry arose for the police. Society in the shape of two policemen stationed itself in all the important thoroughfares. Coachmen were stopped, drivers directed, foot-passengers assisted, refuges constructed. Freedom of passage ceased. The principle of individual liberty yielded to organised control.

He goes on, too, to generalize the theme:

Similarly on the highways of our industrial traffic, and in the movements of society along its various tracks, it would appear that collisions became so frequent, and accidents so numerous, complications, crowding, and disputes so intolerable, that the police of the State are summoned at every turn. Regulations unnecessary and odious in a simpler state of civilisation not only became acceptable, but were loudly demanded.[290]

There was indeed a multiplicity of ways in which government became directly involved. Letter-carrying and related services mushroomed, thus increasing enormously the work of the Post Office which also, in time, took over telegraph and telephone business as well as supervising wireless matters. And from the beginning, government was concerned with the highway improvements. This was obviously the case where work was done for military or political reasons, as with Marshal Wade's roads in the Highlands after the Forty-five or the creation of a swifter link with Ireland after the Union in 1801: between 1815 and 1830 the Holyhead Road Commission spent £750,000 on improvements and was, said the Webbs, 'virtually a central Government Department'.[291] The turnpike trusts and the canal companies needed statutory authority for their establishment as did the railways. In respect of the last, too, their operation was subject to a range of regulation respecting fares, safety, timetables, and a host of other details. Again the coming of the motor vehicle not simply required substantial road building and improvement in respect of so many things from drainage to lighting, but control in

290 G. J. Goschen, . . . Laissez-Faire and Government Interference (London, 1883), pp.14–15.
291 S. and B. Webb, The Development of English Local Government, 1689–1835 (London, 1963), pp.157–8.

many other respects such as traffic discipline, compulsory insurance, safety, and, latterly, pollution, congestion, and other social costs – not to mention government interest in the revenue to be obtained from taxation. The cost and effort involved in a trunk road or motorway building programme is obvious.[292]

In this fashion, then, the authorities have, over the years, been drawn more and more into the regulation and development of transport and its ancillary facilities because of their impact on the public interest both directly and because their efficient operation was vital to the proper working of the economic and commercial system. Piecemeal regulation has led, it seems ineluctably, to widespread control and even ownership and to a state policy supposed to envisage the nature and needs of transport as a whole, with this itself seen merely as part of the process of even wider social planning. London transport is a familiar paradigm case: from *ad hoc* attempts to deal with the traffic problems of the metropolis there emerged, in due time, the LPTB and, more recently, the overall responsibilities of the Greater London Council.[293] Implicit in early municipal tinkering with the carriageway and in the man with the red flag lay the Ministry of Transport, the state ownership of British Leyland, road fund licences, and all the other paraphernalia of growing government concern.

The treatment of social needs

The increasing mass of information about social deficiencies, needs, and problems and its swifter communication to a growing political public engendered a variety of pressures for improvement; and in the end this meant increased government activity at both central and local level in pursuit of minimum national standards and the creation of greater personal opportunities for all. Obviously it is not possible here to show how this has happened with the whole range of protective and social services. But the gradually increasing involvement of government may be illustrated by reference to two such areas of provision: police, and primary and secondary education. The former was the largest focus of local expenditure during the last century, necessarily so when the crucial problem of government was to secure a basis of public order at a time of rapid economic change and deep social disturbance. The latter is currently by far the most expensive service offered by local government

292 One recent general study is P. M. Townroe (ed.), *Social and Political Consequences of the Motor Car* (Newton Abbot, 1974).

293 A recent survey of the various bodies and problems involved is M. F. Collins and T. M. Pharoah, *Transport Organization in a Great City: the Case of London* (London, 1975); see also T. C. Barker and M. Robbins, *A History of London Transport: Passenger Travel and the Development of the Metropolis* (London, 1963–75).

today. So, in their different ways, both are key instances of the extension of state functions to meet growing social needs.

Police

The maintenance of order, the protection of life and property, that is, policing in the restricted or narrow sense, has always been seen as a fundamental function of government though one which exists in the crucial borderland fringing individual liberty and public need. And in Britain a major responsibility in this regard had always belonged to local officers of various sorts. But one consequence of the 'massing of men' was a great increase in crime which aroused considerable concern. For instance, between 1770 and 1829 there were no less than seven Parliamentary inquiries into the policing of the metropolis alone where, of course, the problem seemed especially acute.[294] A constabulary had been established in Ireland but in Britain itself, apart from the watchman, unpaid parish constable, or similar local functionary, there were only the yeomanry or the army to depend on. This military arrangment was usually adequate enough to maintain order in the event of riot or insurrection but it was an extreme resort and much damage might be done before it was invoked as the Gordon riots showed.[295] But the establishment of what now seems the obvious alternative, an effective domestic police based on preventive principles, was often strongly resisted on the ground that it would constitute a body of spies, oppressive like the French *gendarmerie*, and hardly to be reconciled with 'that perfect freedom of action and exemption from interference which are the great privileges and blessings of society in this country.'[296] Something of the extreme passion aroused by the proposal is witnessed by a famous passage from the pen of the eccentric John William Ward, 1st Earl of Dudley, who wrote in 1811: 'They have an admirable police at Paris, but they pay for it dear enough. I had rather half a dozen people's throats should be cut in Ratcliffe Highway every three or four years than be subject to domiciliary visits, spies, and all the rest of Fouché's contrivances.' Yet (as Ward went on to say) it might be possible to avoid that extreme by devising some plan 'that would unite protection with liberty.'[297] Something had to be done, as was indeed increasingly

294 H. Finer, 'The Police and Public Safety', in H. J. Laski *et al.*, *A Century of Municipal Progress, 1835–1935* (London, 1935), p.275.

295 For one recent review of these matters, see S. H. Palmer, 'Calling Out the Troops: the Military, the Law, and Public Order in England, 1650–1850', *Journal of the Society for Army Historical Research*, lvi (1978), pp.198–214.

296 Report from the Select Committee on the Police of the Metropolis (1822), p.11, in E. Halévy, *A History of the English People in the Nineteenth Century*, ii.287.

297 S. H. Romilly, *Letters to Ivy from the first Earl of Dudley* (London, 1905), letter of 27 December 1811, pp.146–7.

obvious, to deal with the growing and varied array of lesser crimes.

In London an attempt had been made to tackle this problem by attaching police officers to the courts of the stipendiary magistrates as with the famous 'runners' – 'the dashing heroes of the Bow Street Office' as Scott called them – and the police patrols that developed later on this basis. In 1792 this kind of arrangement was extended in some degree to the whole metropolitan area.[298] There were also various private 'securicors': for instance, the West India merchants had in 1778 set up a river or 'marine' police to stop the pilfering of cargoes in the Port of London. Numerous suggestions had been made from time to time how it would be possible to deal more effectively with these questions on a wider scale, as with the abortive measure of 1785 which was intended to create a police force for the capital as a whole. Ten years later the Benthamite magistrate, Patrick Colquhoun – who, with John Harriott, had been involved in the earlier creation of the dockside and river patrols – brought out his *Treatise on the Police of the Metropolis* urging the need for a special force under unified control in London itself and which might, as well, be in various ways a focus for police activity throughout the country. 'Let it', wrote Colquhoun,

> once become the duty of one body of men to charge themselves with the execution of the Laws for the prevention of crimes, and the detection of offences – let them be armed with proper and apposite powers for that purpose, and the state of Society will speedily become ameliorated and improved; a greater degree of security will be extended to the peaceful subject, and the blessings of civil liberty will be enlarged.[299]

Opponents of the idea were not so sure, especially about the last point. But Peel (persuaded not by any Benthamite theory but rather by his experience in Ireland where he had been impressed by the work of the peace preservation corps set up in 1814) had become convinced of the need for an adequate police in the capital. He was chairman of a Parliamentary committee which recommended this and he said, too, on becoming Home Secretary in 1822 that he intended to achieve the goal in view.[300] In this he had the powerful support of the Duke of Wellington who was influenced by the fear that the loyalty of the Guards might not

298 Parts of the statute are reprinted in E. N. Williams (ed.), *The Eighteenth-Century Constitution, 1688–1815: Documents and Commentary* (Cambridge, 1960), pp.297–9. Scott's phrase is to be found in *Waverley*, p.64.

299 P. Colquhoun, *A Treatise on the Police of the Metropolis*, 7th edn (London, 1806), p.562. For the earlier venture, see Colquhoun's *A Treatise on the Commerce and Police of the River Thames . . .* (London, 1800).

300 Halévy, op. cit., ii.108–9; O. MacDonagh, *Early Victorian Government 1830–1870* (London, 1977), pp.168–9.

always be relied on; so it was better, by a system of civil police, to prevent the sort of circumstances that required the use of the military from arising in the first place.[301] A force of 'new police' was thus created for the metropolis in 1829 and placed directly under the control of the Home Department, an arrangement regarded by such opponents as Toulmin Smith as an example of irresponsible centralization.[302] Despite the criticism, a City of London force was also set up ten years later. The success of the new police owed everything to the preventive system on which it was based and to the ethos created by the first two commissioners.[303] The statute itself and the debates during its passage brought out succinctly the essentials of an efficient police service: a sufficient number of fit and competent officers; an adequate scope of authority and area of operation of individual forces as well as effective arrangements for co-operation between them; unity of command; the availability of resources sufficient for these ends; and responsibility to a proper public body or official. If the development of police forces was the outcome of intensified urbanization, their emergence also dictated the achievement of efficiency in the respects mentioned and thus the involvement, aid, and stimulus of central government.

Given the criteria indicated, provision outside London was hardly satisfactory. Attempts had been made to deal with a growing range of police problems in various ways. In some places private 'prosecution societies' had been formed to ensure the proper enforcement of the law. Voluntary police unions had sometimes been established to secure co-operation and a wider area of action for the traditional authorities. And improvement or police commissions had been set up by private Act in many towns to achieve, among much else, a higher standard of watch and ward through a paid force of watchmen. Yet this was hardly effective enough to deal with Wodgate and its inhabitants especially in times of general unrest as during the Chartist period; and it did not touch at all the rural areas where there were often patches or periods of agrarian disturbance. Further, after the practical abandonment of punishment by transportation in 1840, there was concern about the presence in Britain of so many more criminals and undesirables than before. And slowly, therefore, the new model police system was extended (or imposed)

301 P. Guedalla, *The Duke*, pp. 315–16.
302 See e.g. 'Further Centralization of the Police', *The Parliamentary Remembrancer*, vi (1863), pp. 69–72.
303 It is a fascinating story admirably told in a series of works by Charles Reith, e.g. *British Police and the Democratic Ideal* (London, 1943) and *A New Study of Police History* (London, 1956): the key was the principle of developing individual initiative and a sense of responsibility on the basis of the methods used by Sir John Moore to train his light infantry regiments.

throughout the country often against the stiff resistance, or despite the apathy, of the existing authorities.[304]

In 1835 each of the reformed municipal corporations was required to set up a watch committee to supervise an adequate body of day and night police. But there was opposition on all sorts of grounds not least the expense; and even if the project were embarked on there was difficulty in recruiting suitable men and knowing how to organize them efficiently. All this was especially true where a town was small; and, in practice, what was done often left a great deal to be desired: twenty years after the Act, thirteen corporate towns had still not used the police powers it granted. Following the report of a Royal Commission, an Act of 1839 attempted to deal with police in the county areas. A major problem was, of course, the parochial basis of the rural arrangements which were thereby fragmented and to this extent prevented efficient police work. But, although this measure gave the justices increased powers, these were permissive only and their effective adoption was by no means general. Inquiry later showed that by 1853 only twenty-two counties (and parts of seven others) – that is, less than half of them – had used the new powers granted in 1839 to establish a 'rural police', and that the rest largely remained, as before, dependent on 'Alfred's tithingmen', the parish constables. Moreover, there was invariably no link or co-operation between the different constabularies.

By the mid-century, then, an organized police of some sort existed in a good many if not all of the municipalities and in certain rural areas but not in others. However, these forces often numbered no more than a handful of men; arrangements for joint action were scrappy or non-existent; and corruption, drunkenness, and the like were, in fact, quite common. There followed, in due course, the Police Act of 1856 which was intended to remedy this situation in both counties and boroughs. It made the establishment of a force compulsory and added the incentive of an increased Home Office grant subject to satisfactory inspection. A similar Act concerning Scotland was passed the following year. Toulmin Smith, on behalf of the Anti-Centralization Union which opposed these measures, argued that the 25 per cent grant, subject to central supervision, was a 'naked bribe' acceptance of which could only lead to servile subjection to the proposed Inspectors of Constabulary: three irresponsible and London-based 'Military Dictators' he called them.[305]

---

304 It used generally to be assumed that, in the end, change came outside London because the efficiency of the Metropolitan Police coupled with the mobility provided by the railways drove criminals into the relatively less well policed areas. But doubt has been thrown on this 'migration thesis' by e.g. J. Hart, 'Reform of the Borough Police, 1835–1856', *English Historical Review*, lxx (1955), pp. 411–27.

305 J. T. Smith, *Government and its Measures* (London, 1857), pp. 5–6 and note*.

Nevertheless, by 1857 there were 239 forces in England and Wales.[306] But many, being based on the traditional localities, were still too small or inefficient as the visits of inspection clearly revealed; and so pressure for further reorganization continued and intensified. Consequently in 1888 the Local Government Act imposed mergers on certain police authorities and insisted on higher population minima for others. It also created a new county police authority, the justices being replaced by a standing joint committee composed of equal numbers of JPs and county councillors. Later developments have largely been concerned to improve the existing array of county and borough forces in a similar way so as to achieve a higher degree of technical operation. Thus smaller forces have been eliminated and amalgamations enforced on the local authorities to increase the size and resources of the police area and so the efficiency of the forces concerned. This was the work of various measures including the Police Acts of 1919, 1946, and 1964 and the reorganization carried out under the authority they granted. The results of this process can be seen in the fact that between 1900 and 1977 the number of forces in England, Wales, and Scotland fell from 243 to 51.[307] And there is a not insubstantial weight of opinion in favour of taking the further step to a national police. Certainly, although (except in the metropolitan district) direct operation by the central government is avoided and the various forces are administered under the formal aegis of local police authorities (consisting of local councillors and, in England and Wales, magistrates), the supervisory power of the Secretary of State has nevertheless become considerable. This is because large subsidies are given to the local bodies to cover a substantial part of their police costs and, as well, the minister has, since 1964, been answerable to Parliament for the actions of provincial police as well as that of the capital. Recently, too, the Home Office Inspectorate of Constabulary has been strengthened; a rigorous control is exercised over the appointment of chief officers; and many important policy decisions are taken by committees of civil servants and senior police officers with the local authorities either excluded or only lightly represented.[308] Moreover, over the past few decades, the development of co-operation between forces has been encouraged in the eight police regions, and since the Second World War there have been established regional crime and traffic squads, forensic laboratories, and so on. This is entirely justifiable on grounds of economy and efficiency

306 J. P. Martin and G. Wilson, *The Police: a Study in Manpower* (London, 1969), p. 12.
307 D. Butler and A. Sloman, *British Political Facts 1900–1979*, 5th edn (London, 1980), p. 292; *KCA* (1965–6), p. 21426A. In Scotland, the reduction in the same period has been from 64 to 20 forces. In Ireland, of course, there was a single constabulary as there now is in N. Ireland.
308 T. Judge, 'Halting the Trend Towards a National Police Force', *Municipal Review*, xlvi (1975–6), p. 105.

but, coupled with the undoubted decline of local authority control, points inexorably towards further centralization based on regional police forces. This tendency is, too, likely to be reinforced if the recent great increase in crimes of violence and offences against property continues.[309]

The wheel is in process of completing a revolution, therefore. A medieval, even Saxon, basis of watching which continued right up to the last century proved incapable of coping with the consequences of major industrial and social change. It was necessary to create a more adequate machinery of police. At first, the localities acted for themselves; then central government intervened to stimulate and then to make universal and compulsory the establishment of effective forces. Finally, we are perhaps on the verge of a national police organization under similar aegis. Three-quarters of a century ago Maitland wrote: 'Look at the police force, that most powerful engine of government.'[310] We should do well to heed his advice and his implied warning at one of the most significant consequences of collectivist development.

Education

Education is intrinsically important in the present context. Sidney Webb rightly referred to 'our system of national education' as 'that tremendous development of Collectivism'.[311] When government was originally faced with the problem of educational need it adopted a very diffident attitude, revealing a great reluctance to become involved. But it was none the less drawn in and now, of course, we may be facing or anticipating (with horror or satisfaction depending on our point of view) the creation of a government-controlled monopoly of schools entirely financed from public funds and unified in terms of social purpose and educational organization.

There was a whole range of pressures and factors indicating the need to educate the people. One was religious: in a Protestant country especially, it was thought, everyone should be able to read the Bible and similar morally-improving books; and an understanding of the wonder of God's works in history and nature was not only appropriate as a form of worship but also practically useful. Dissenters, in particular, had always stressed the importance of education as their flourishing academies showed. Nor, often in response to the Nonconformist effort,

---

309 Known crimes of violence against the person in England and Wales rose from 4800 in 1949 to nearly 63,000 in 1974; offences against property rose from 92,000 to 493,000 during the same period: see Sir R. Mark, *Policing a Perplexed Society* (London, 1977), pp. 76–7.

310 F. W. Maitland, *The Constitutional History of England*, p. 415.

311 S. Webb, *Labour in the Longest Reign, 1837–1897*, Fabian tract no. 75 (London, 1897), p. 61.

were Anglicans unaware of the significance of educational provision. Similarly a simple humanitarian impulse urged that human beings should not grow up merely as unlettered savages as with (to take an instance that has just fallen to hand) the East Riding will of 1780 which provided that shares held in a local canal company should be used for the maintenance of a schoolmaster to teach the village children to read and write.[312] As well, education might (in the prevailing Malthusian terms) help provide that element of moral restraint which alone could mitigate the pressure of population. Equally, sheer expediency was hardly absent from consideration: unless the masses in the manufacturing districts received a sound education based on proper ethical principles, there might be unrest and disorder, even revolution.[313] Likewise, the industrial changes increasingly demanded an educated work force; and, in time, there was the fear that economically (and militarily) the country might be overtaken by foreign rivals if the full potential of ability in the community were not developed. Further, it was clear that with more and more people getting the vote, untoward consequences might follow if the electorate remained ignorant and unsophisticated. It was this kind of concern that underlay much of the disquiet surrounding the Acts of 1867 and 1884 which substantially extended the franchise. The consequence was the view that, as put in Lowe's famous remark, it will be absolutely necessary to 'prevail on our future masters to learn their letters'.[314] There were, too, various grounds, appealing to the intellectual fashions of the day, for thinking that educational facilities were vital. To the utilitarian, for instance, it was crucial if the greatest happiness was to be achieved that men should be trained to be as alert as possible in the perception and pursuit of their interests. It was for this reason that Bentham had in 1797 sketched out a programme of popular education; and both he and James Mill believed that this was the key to the formation of character: hence their experiment with J. S. Mill's upbringing and training.[315] Similarly educational reform ranked high in the priorities of many philosophical idealists as with Green and his circle.[316] Many of the classical economists, too, thought that government intervention in the educational sphere might be justified for a number of reasons. Adam Smith was a little

312 C. Towse, *A Garton Estate History, 1537–1800* (n.p. [Cardiff], 1980), p.20.
313 See e.g. the speeches of Sir James Graham in 1843, in Halévy, op. cit., iv.64 n.2.
314 188 H. C. Deb. 3s., 15 July 1867, col.1549. The whole speech is an excellent example of the realistic response of a critic to a change of which he strongly disapproves.
315 e.g. E. Halévy, *The Growth of Philosophic Radicalism* (1901; trans., rev. edn, London, 1949), pp.282–91.
316 M. Richter, *The Politics of Conscience: T. H. Green and his Age* (London, 1964), pp. 350–62 describes Green's practical involvement with educational reform; but the fullest account is now P. Gordon and J. White, *Philosophers as Educational Reformers. The Influence of Idealism on British Educational Thought and Practice* (London, 1979).

ambivalent on the matter but was clear nevertheless that the public could, with advantage, aid and stimulate the education necessary to the common people, for instance by the establishment of parish or district schools. McCulloch held the same view and J. S. Mill, although acutely aware of the problems involved, conceded that government action in the case of education was desirable because it was obvious that the uneducated could not properly judge matters of cultivation, while the principles of the market could not apply.[317] Or, fundamentally, the provision of educational facilities could simply be seen as a basic human need or right. In his essay on 'Chartism' (1839), Carlyle spoke of this as an 'eternal duty' of government: 'Who would suppose that Education were a thing which had to be advocated on the ground of local expediency, or indeed on any ground? As if it stood not on the basis of everlasting duty, as a prime necessity of man. It is a thing that should need no advocating'. And he went on to draw the conclusion that, 'To impart the gift of thinking to those who cannot think . . . : this, one would imagine, was the first function a government had to set about discharging.' Hence the need, above all, for an effective Minister of Education.[318] There was, then, as the nineteenth century wore on an increasing volume of support, albeit of diverse origin, in favour of extending or improving educational facilities though this did not necessarily, at least at first, involve or invite the intervention of government.

In fact, there was, even at the beginning of the nineteenth century, a miscellany of schools of different kinds, and the opportunities of instruction available were perhaps greater than is often popularly supposed: though to say this is not, of course, to suggest that these facilities were adequate, let alone good, or that more than a small minority of children was affected.[319] In lowland Scotland, where they have invariably ordered these matters better, there had been a system of parish elementary schools for over a hundred years. It was neither free nor compulsory; but the opportunity was there to be grasped, at some sacrifice, by all but the very poor, as the examples of James Mill and Carlyle show. There was nothing of quite this kind in England and

317 Smith, *An Inquiry into the Nature and Causes of the Wealth of Nations* (1776; World's Classics, 1904), ii.419–21; D. P. O'Brien, *J. R. McCulloch: a Study in Classical Economics* (London, 1970), pp. 345–7; J. S. Mill, 'Principles of Political Economy' (1848), *Collected Works*, iii.947–50.

318 Carlyle, 'Chartism' (1839), in *Works*, xi.175; 'The New Downing Street' (1850), ibid., xx.126.

319 For a convenient summary, see J. Lawson and H. Silver, *A Social History of Education in England* (London, 1973), chs. VII–VIII. T. H. Green gives a succinct historical survey of educational development up to his time in 'Two Lectures on the Elementary School System of England' (1878), *Works*, ed. R. L. Nettleship (London, 1885–8), iii.413–55. Green had, of course, been an assistant commissioner to the Royal Commission on Education appointed in 1864, ibid., vol.iii, pp.xlv ff.

Wales though various types of school did exist there. There were the old-established grammar schools; endowed schools begun by religious or other foundations; charity schools set up by the Society for Promoting Christian Knowledge and similar bodies or by groups of philanthropic citizens; parish schools run under the aegis of the local clergyman (like that described by Trollope in *Framley Parsonage*);[320] the so-called 'dame schools' (often perhaps merely child-minding establishments); and the 'ragged' and industrial schools which had been founded in some places to give pauper children or those whose parents had been imprisoned a rudimentary education and teach them a trade. In the same way, the early Factory Acts were ostensibly concerned as much with moral and other education as anything else. In addition there were, after 1780, the Sunday schools at which some elementary secular as well as religious teaching was undertaken and some of which extended their activities into the week. And in 1796 the Quaker, Joseph Lancaster, began the first of the monitorial establishments that later went by his name and that of Andrew Bell (their dual rationale being cheapness as well as the formation of character). Robert Owen had introduced infant schools in his factory communities. Mechanics institutes, having begun in the mid-eighteenth century, flourished after the 1820s: by 1850 there were over 600 of them. To give a particular example, at the end of the Napoleonic Wars, Swansea, with a population of some 8000 and probably a not untypical place in this respect, had a 'Free School' dating from the late seventeenth century and (according to one account) 'rivalled the zeal of the rest of the kingdom in providing for the education of the poor by the establishment of Lancasterian and other schools' which (it was said) could not 'fail to be eminently beneficial in their effects on the morals of the rising generation among the lower orders'.[321]

Something of the effort involved may be indicated by reference to the religious schools. The Church of England was perhaps best placed to react to the growing educational need though it was often slow to do so. Yet in order to match the influence and activities of the Dissenters, particularly in the towns, it did begin to redeploy its resources and this included spending more money on schools and training establishments, the so-called 'Normal' schools. And in the outcome its educational effort was for various reasons greater than anything accomplished by the Nonconformists.[322] The National Society for Promoting the Education

320 A. Trollope, *Framley Parsonage* (1861; Everyman, 1973), pp. 10–11. For the role of the mid-nineteenth-century parson in the education of the people, see G. K. Clark, *Churchmen and the Condition of England, 1832–1885: a Study in the Development of Social Ideas and Practice from the Old Régime to the Modern State* (London, 1973), ch. 4.
321 T. Rees, *A Topographical and Historical Description of South Wales* (London, n.d. [1815]), p. 724.
322 G. K. Clark, *The Making of Victorian England* (1962; London, 1965), p. 175.

of the Poor in the Principles of the Established Church, which did not, in fact, embrace the whole range of Church educational activities, was set up in 1811 (three years after the British and Foreign School Society which, while formally undenominational, had substantial Nonconformist support); and, within a quarter of a century, it had founded 6000–7000 day schools alone with half a million children in them. By 1867 about 1½ million children were in Church day schools and nearly 150,000 in some 4000 night schools.[323] From his vantage point in the Ecclesiastical Commission, A. J. Munby noted in 1860 that 'Every where churches, schools, parsonages are building' in the clerical effort 'to keep pace with the growth of the nation'.[324] And to leaf through the enumerators' returns of a mid-nineteenth century census is to be struck by how often the description 'scholar' is applied to children in by no means well-to-do households. It has been estimated, too, that even in the 1830s about 60 per cent of Lancashire children went to school.[325] Of course, standards varied and were often low; attendance was irregular and not free. But clearly more of the younger generation of those days were receiving some kind of formal education than might have been supposed. In a way, therefore, the further problem of the last part of the nineteenth century was not so much to create a literate or reading public as such but to fill gaps, ensure more uniformity, and level up the degree of attainment.[326]

In this context, the development of education is paradigmatic. It is the story of how a range of voluntary effort proved, in the end, unable to cope with the problem faced and how, in default, state intervention seemed increasingly necessary. But this was embarked on rather reluctantly and developed at first slowly and with caution because of the

323 H. J. Burgess, *Enterprise in Education: the Story of the Work of the Established Church in the Education of the People prior to 1870* (London, 1958), pp. 207–8, 210.
324 Hudson, *Munby: Man of Two Worlds*, p. 57.
325 Woodward, *The Age of Reform 1815–1870*, p. 478 n. 2.
326 It should be noted that the question of the quality of educational provision in the early and mid-nineteenth century is a matter of acute controversy among historians of the matter as indicated, for instance, by H. Silver's review of E. G. West's *Education and the Industrial Revolution* (London, 1975) in *TLS* (7 November 1975), p. 1340. Professor Silver represents the traditional radical view about educational inadequacies while Professor West's position is a revision of this at one time established picture. Much of the writing about the development of education (as reflected in Silver's work, for instance) seems to be infused with a tone of carping or grudging condescension, stern wonderment that our ancestors so lacked good sense and intentions as not to have created a national system of comprehensive schools at least by 1870. This manner tends to mean that what was done is, in its description, invariably belittled in some way. Perhaps naïvely I attribute this to a sort of a-historical radicalism on the part of these commentators. How much better they would have done than such fumbling predecessors as Lowe, Sandon, and Lingen! But it may well be that I misjudge these contemporaries who are perhaps in any case not so much historians as crusading sociologists.

cost entailed and because public involvement seemed improper in so important a matter concerning parental choice and religious and moral influence. Joseph Priestley had summed up the conventional view when he wrote that education, though crucial, was one of 'those things in which the civil magistrate has no right to interfere'. For such intervention was incompatible with 'the proper design of education', 'the great ends of civil societies', the natural rights of parents, and 'the true principles of the English government'.[327] Many of Priestley's fellow Dissenters agreed and firmly repudiated the idea that public money should be used to support schools for fear this might compromise their independence and the opportunities for religious teaching in their own style; and, as well, because they felt that if the state entered the field most help would go to the established Church, and they were not anxious for the rates and taxes they paid to be used to sustain Anglicanism. Yet such a concern was also shared in other circles; for instance, J. S. Mill's anxiety about the untoward effects of establishing a system of education which was wholly or largely in the hands of the state equally reflected this worry and was widely known.[328]

It was because of this kind of diffidence that general proposals to introduce a national system of schools (like those put forward by Whitbread in 1807, Brougham in 1820, and Roebuck in 1831) failed to find sufficient support. Yet the principle of compulsory education was embodied in the early Factory Acts like that of 1833 which provided for two hours' instruction each day (albeit defectively because no funds were provided for the purpose). Moreover, in the same year, in a step that marked the beginnings of state support, the government made a grant in aid of education for the first time: under the aegis of the Privy Council, £20,000 was provided to the two voluntary societies 'for the erection of school houses for the education of the poorer classes in Great Britain.'[329] The following year the Poor Law Amendment Act imposed on the elected Boards of Guardians some responsibility for educating pauper children.[330] After 1839 there was a Privy Council Committee on Education to co-ordinate and oversee the use of public funds so committed but, given the religious difficulties and pressures, its role did not become so considerable as had been anticipated though a body of

327 J. Priestley, *An Essay on the First Principles of Government*, 2nd edn (1771), pp. 76–99, in J. A. Passmore (ed.), *Priestley's Writings on Philosophy, Science and Politics* (New York, 1965), pp. 305–13.
328 J. S. Mill, 'On Liberty' (1859), *Collected Works*, xviii. 301–4. Nor was this sort of disquiet unreflected in twentieth-century libertarian comment: see e.g. H. Cox, *Economic Liberty* (London, 1920), pp. 181–3.
329 Cited F. Smith, 'The Nation's Schools' in H. J. Laski *et al.*, *A Century of Municipal Progress, 1835–1935* (London, 1935), p. 222.
330 Halévy, *A History of the English People in the Nineteenth Century*, iii. 113–14, 125.

inspectors was created as a sort of 'missionaries of education' and in fact the department quite rapidly became one of the largest offices of its day.[331] In 1847 the Committee took the initiative in starting a scheme to improve the skill and qualifications of teachers. This was an important step because it was the first occasion that government had been effectively involved other than in aiding the building of schools. There had also been set up a small department of science and arts in the Board of Trade which *inter alia* gave grants and bounties to teachers. It was joined to the Privy Council Committee in 1856 as a Department of Education, and the holder of the office of Vice-President of the Privy Council Committee became, in effect, minister of education. The grants paid by the state to schools which accepted inspection had risen to £541,000 by 1856 and to £836,920 three years later. This increase was an important factor in extending central supervision and stimulating a rise in standards because the committee issued minutes explaining the conditions on which support from these funds would be given and, in due course, a system of regular inspection grew up. In 1860 the rules were ordered into a proper educational code: as, willy-nilly, more money was spent (and Treasury concern grew) it became increasingly necessary to exercise more supervision over its use.[332] In this way, Britain had governmental inspection of schools and a public code of education before any teaching institutions were created at public expense and before there was any specific local organization for educational purposes. It is a very good example of the experimental and empirical not to say rather haphazard way in which many important changes have been introduced in this country.[333]

The crucial point in the end was, indeed, cost: it became impossible for the religious and other voluntary societies to provide, from their own funds, schools and related facilities (such as training colleges for teachers) adequate to meet the growing need. For instance, in 1852 an unofficial inquiry was held into the educational state of two wards in Manchester that included prosperous as well as poor families and were reasonably representative of the town as a whole. A house-to-house investigation showed that nearly half of the children had never been to day school; and of those who had been sent, fewer than one-fifth had

---

331 G. Sutherland, *Elementary Education in the Nineteenth Century* (Historical Association, no. G76; London, 1971), pp.19–20 (but cf. p.26); R. Johnson, 'Administrators in Education before 1870: Patronage, Social Position and Role', in G. Sutherland (ed.), *Studies in the Growth of Nineteenth-Century Government* (London, 1972), p.111.

332 For Treasury resistance to this growth of expenditure, see H. Roseveare, *The Treasury: the Evolution of a British Institution* (London, 1969), p.226.

333 See J. Redlich and F. W. Hirst, *The History of Local Government in England*, ed. B. Keith-Lucas (1958; 2nd edn, London, 1971), pp.190–1.

attended for more than five years, and only one-thirtieth for eight years: the majority had been for less than three years. Some of the children had only attended evening classes or Sunday schools; and of over 12,000 children who should have been to school, nearly one-third had received no formal instruction at all.[334] Pressure groups had emerged (for instance, the Central Society for Education and the National Public School Association) to campaign for various solutions to the problem. A Royal Commission was appointed in 1858 to inquire into the state of popular education and three years later it recommended elected boards of education in the counties and larger boroughs with the duty of examining standards in existing schools; if found satisfactory, a grant would be made from the rates to the school managers, the so-called 'payment by results' system. But the government of the day did not act fully on the suggestion for fear of denominational squabbles. However during the 1860s, for various reasons, the Nonconformists reversed their previous opposition to state aid and formed the National Education League (1869) to demand a universal system of public education which should, if undenominational, be free and compulsory. In addition, Anglicans had also come to recognize that specific claims would have to be foregone if the pressing educational problems were to be met effectively. Reliance on voluntary action and the degree of state aid hitherto available would not be enough. Professional opinion was represented, for instance, by Matthew Arnold who had been an inspector of schools since 1851 and who was by no means afraid of government action. A group of MPs led by the Tory, Sir John Pakington, was pressing for a state-aided system of elementary schools. Moreover the electoral reform Act of 1867 appeared to make some basic educational initiative essential and urgent; there was also the matter of training the labour force to help meet international competition.

The outcome was W. E. Forster's Education Act of 1870, one of the major measures of Gladstone's administration, by which government assumed some responsibility for national education, though the purpose was not so much to supersede as to complement existing facilities. It provided that if an area was without elementary schools (that is, if the existing voluntary system was proving inadequate) then school boards elected by the ratepayers were to be set up to build and maintain schools out of the rates (which were to be levied by the councils). From then on growth continued albeit not in a uniform way. One of the problems was how to ensure attendance; and in 1880 after ten years of school provision

334 'Report upon the Statistical Inquiry Instituted by the Executive Committee of the National Public School Association in St. Michael's and St. John's Wards, Manchester, November–December 1852' (dated 25th January 1853), in Redford, *The History of Local Government in Manchester*, iii.148.

it was possible to make education compulsory between the ages of five and ten, while in 1891 it was made what is called 'free', the parents of children attending school no longer having to pay fees, the cost being defrayed from the rates and general taxation. The effect on the remaining illiteracy seems to have been considerable. By 1895 there were 2½ million children attending the (largely Anglican) voluntary schools and nearly 2 million at the Board Schools.[335] Equally the administrative chains tightened. The number of H.M. Inspectors of Education doubled in the decade after 1870 (rising from 62 to 131) and the number of 'examiners' in the central office increased from 13 to 30.[336] But the Act of 1870 provided only for elementary education and, though some school boards did establish 'Higher Grade' schools, these catered only for a minority and were in any case of doubtful legality. More advanced facilities had to be sustained in other ways. In Manchester, for instance, the School of Art came under the financially exiguous care of the Public Free Libraries Committee; and secondary education was provided only by the endowed schools administered by the Charity Commissioners and, locally, by the corporation's Charitable Trusts Committee. Nor was there any real provision for further financial support than already existed. Co-operation between the council and the school board was sometimes arranged only with difficulty even over such a simple matter as playgrounds.[337] When belatedly the Technical Instruction Acts were passed in 1889 and 1891 to establish schools to give directly vocational teaching useful to industry and commerce, the local authorities and not the school boards were made responsible. Similarly in 1889 Mundella introduced experimentally in Wales a system of secondary schools operating under the new county councils. After 1870 there was, therefore, a system of multiple control which inevitably created problems of co-operation and co-ordination which were further exacerbated by religious differences. Although, as a unifying measure, a central Board of Education had been created in 1899 as a result of the recommendations of the Bryce Commission, it was still the case that, as the Court of Appeal declared in the Cockerton judgment of 1901, a school board had no power to provide out of the rates education beyond elementary level.[338]

335 Halévy, op. cit., v.145, 165. For one contemporary reaction, see A. C. Doyle, 'The Naval Treaty', in *Sherlock Holmes . . .: the Complete Short Stories* (1928; London, 1937), p.515. Shavians will recall, however, that Henry Straker gave the credit for the progress of the clever artisan not to the Board-school but to the polytechnic, *Man and Superman* (1901–3; Penguin, 1946), p.93.

336 Sutherland (ed.), *Studies in the Growth of Nineteenth-Century Government*, pp. 266–8.

337 Redford, op. cit., iii.150–3.

338 *R. v. Cockerton* [1901], 1 KB, 726.

The 1902 Act introduced by Balfour's government dealt with this situation. In educational terms the constructive importance of this Conservative measure was immense. It abolished the 2500 or more school boards and made 238 local authorities – the county and county borough councils (plus a few boroughs and UDCs which continued to be responsible for the elementary provision in their area) – the sole 'local education authorities' for elementary and, significantly, other levels and forms of instruction including teacher training. The Act also ended the distinction between the rate-maintained and voluntary schools. In this way the arrangements were completely reorganized, a national system created for the first time, and secondary and technical education recognized as a state responsibility. The real significance of the measure was put by Sidney Webb as follows: 'for the first time the Bill definitely includes *as a public function* education as education – not primary education only, or technical education only, but anything and everything that is education from the kindergarten to the University.'[339] Certainly, as one result, the number of children in secondary education doubled in five years and then rose even more rapidly: for instance, the number of scholarships to secondary schools increased nearly tenfold between 1900 and 1912.[340] Another result was, of course, to create further elements of government provision and control: a larger body of school inspectors, free meals, the establishment of special schools, medical inspections of schoolchildren, and many others; and, of course, a general increase in expenditure which had to be properly monitored.[341] Nor did these developments occur without resistance from those who objected to the compulsory principle involved.[342]

Other legislation followed, the most important items being the Fisher Act of 1918 and the Butler Act of 1944. The former envisaged, again, quite extensive developments increasing the powers of local education authorities and the Board, augmenting by some 50 per cent the latter's financial aid, removing exceptions to compulsory schooling up to the age of fourteen years (before 1914, 40 per cent of children left before that age), and much else, comprehending a complete system of education from nursery school to evening class.[343] Yet many of the Act's proposals came

339 From an article in the *Daily Mail* (17 October 1902), in J. L. Garvin and J. Amery, *The Life of Joseph Chamberlain* (London, 1932–69), iv. 510 (italics in text cited).

340 Halévy, op. cit., v. 205; D. S. L. Cardwell, *The Organisation of Science in England: a Retrospect* (London, 1957), p. 161.

341 Halévy, op. cit., vi. 82, 84; and for these developments in Manchester, see Redford, op. cit., iii. 158ff. The number of 'examiners' was thirty in 1880; between 1900 and 1912 seventy-nine new posts were created: see Sutherland, op. cit., p. 268.

342 See e.g. Sir R. K. Wilson, *The First and Last Fight for the Voluntary Principle in Education (1846–1858)*, (London, n.d. [1916]).

343 Mowat, op. cit., p. 208.

to nothing as a result of the very high cost of the changes in view and of the problems of the 1920s and the spirit of economy then engendered. For instance, in between the wars many classes remained very large – over fifty – despite efforts to reduce their size.[344] The Hadow Report of 1926 on 'The Education of the Adolescent' recommended the break at eleven or twelve years of age and the provision thereafter of different types of 'post-primary' school. But progress in this reorganization varied from place to place, while the raising of the school-leaving age to fifteen was to have taken place in September 1939. However despite all the difficulties and setbacks, opportunities for secondary education increased. The number of grammar-type schools in England and Wales rose from 1205 to 1307 in the eleven years after 1920; in the same period the number of junior technical schools rose from 84 to 177. The number of free places was expanded at the same time from 34.2 to 42.7 per cent and the chance of gaining such a place improved from 1 in 40 in 1914 to 1 in 13 in 1929.[345] As well, an increasing array of special educational facilities was provided.

The Second World War stimulated thought about educational needs and problems, and the Education Act of 1944 was the outcome.[346] It raised the status of the central authority to a ministry and thus symbolically fastened on government a changed responsibility: from superintendence to control. It also envisaged, of course, an extension or improvement of facilities and thus greater expense (and regulation, therefore) in order to achieve more equality of educational opportunity for all. This has been the theme, too, of subsequent action as with the extensive and costly reorganization on comprehensive lines undertaken in recent years both on local initiative and by ministry directive.[347] To all this there need only be added a reference to the way in which the whole system of higher education has been created by, and thus made dependent on, local or central government funds. So far, for instance, as the universities are concerned, they first received a Parliamentary grant in 1889 from which the present system of financing has sprung and which

344 Cf. A. J. P. Taylor, *English History 1914–1945* (1965; Penguin, 1970), pp.241 and n.1, 386.
345 Mowat, op. cit., p.207.
346 See the description of this process and its problems (not the least of which was the continuing matter of the Church schools and religious instruction), in Lord Butler, *The Art of the Possible* (London, 1971), chs. 5, 6. For a sketch of later phases of this matter as concerning religious interests, see the comments of Lord Boyle in the *TLS* (19 September 1975), p.1045, reviewing S. Koss, *Nonconformity in Modern British Politics* (London, 1975).
347 See Lawson and Silver, op. cit., ch. XI, esp. the section on 'Secondary Education and Sociologists' which outlines the development and implementation of the comprehensive idea; on which see also D. Rubinstein and B. Simon, *The Evolution of the Comprehensive School, 1926–1966* (London, 1969).

has brought with it an increasing degree of regulation not to say control: we all now jump cravenly to the UGC whip.

At all levels of education, then, from nursery school to post-graduate institute, government is now omnipresent and its funds essential. Over a period of a century and a half we have moved from a diffident and tentative public involvement to, in effect, a tendency and intention to establish a very substantial control indeed. Other social services have reflected this pattern: there have been different speeds and intensity of development but the direction has been basically the same. Voluntary action has proved insufficient and has been supplemented by minimal government financial help which has notably increased; this has brought with it the need for supervision; and so the progression has continued to the point that, in the late 1970s, an official review of the British educational system noted that 'Most expenditure on education comes from public funds' representing in total some 6 per cent of the Gross National Product.[348]

348 *Education in Britain*, Central Office of Information Reference Pamphlet no. 7 (1955; 9th edn, London, 1979), p.1.

4

POLITICAL MATTERS

The idea of the State is one which is little grasped in England.
SIR E. BARKER, 'The "Rule of Law"', *Political Quarterly*,
May 1914, p.139

SIR ERNEST BARKER'S dictum, cited as epigraph to this chapter, echoed a famous comment made decades before by Matthew Arnold.[1] Each was deploring the phenomenon observed, and wished to see public authority play a greater role in society as an aid to the development not only of humane conditions of life and work but also the moral and cultural fulfilment of the people. To the extent that government in Britain did not, in their view, undertake this burden (whether from lack of purpose or absence of administrative means) then to that degree it failed in its duty as a state. This was, of course, simply to observe correctly the traditional dominance of libertarian tendencies in British life, though it was also to underestimate the collectivist proclivities already long afoot. But as it happens these latter inclinations, much intensified since Arnold and even Barker wrote, have led precisely to what they deemed to be lacking: a British State. In the process of its emergence (as chronicled in this volume) certain political occasions and constitutional ideas have been of no little account as the present chapter will indicate.

PARLIAMENTARY SOVEREIGNTY AND LEGISLATIVE CHANGE

The sovereignty of Parliament is (from a legal point of view) the
dominant characteristic of our political institutions.
A. V. DICEY, *Introduction to the Study of the Law of the
Constitution*, 1885, 10th edn, 1964, p.39

One point of crucial significance is that in Britain there is a high degree of concentration of legal power coupled with an absence of formal restraint on the use of that power. The basic concept is one of Parliamentary sovereignty which is to say that, from the constitutional

1 See p.29 above.

point of view, there is no question that cannot be determined by the Queen in Parliament through the usual process of legislation. There are no 'reserved' subjects beyond Parliament's competence and no special procedures for matters of high constitutional concern; there is no complete separation of powers; there are none of the hindrances usually embodied in a written constitution. Nor are there any of the restrictions which apply in a federal system: the supremacy of the basic constitutional document; a division of functions between national and regional authorities; or the existence of a judicial tribunal which may invalidate legislation as unconstitutional, for our courts do not challenge any law properly passed by Parliament. The result is a characteristic of the British system of government that has often been noted by commentators, its 'evasive fluidity' or flexibility, for it is, in principle, relatively easy to mould or adapt.[2] It follows that there is no legal or constitutional impediment to the use of this sovereign power for collectivist purposes. It is indeed this understanding that lies behind Dicey's no doubt pejorative remark that Parliamentary sovereignty is 'an instrument well adapted for the establishment of democratic despotism.'[3] Naturally it is necessary to distinguish in this matter between the concept itself on the one hand and the political and other forces that have set it to work in a collectivist direction on the other.

This doctrine of the sovereignty of Parliament has in modern times been commonly received. Yet it derives from ancient roots and may properly be seen in affinity with such earlier ideas as the Roman Law 'imperium' and the related papal claim to 'plenitudo potestatis'; it is curiously linked, too, with theories about absolute monarchy and the divine right of kings. Just as the notion of a power which could (in Bodin's well-known phrase) give orders to all and receive none from them shifted from emperor to pope to king, so it could be assumed by an assembly. In 1565 Sir Thomas Smith had written that the 'most high and absolute power of the realme of Englande, consisteth in the Parliament' and he listed the formidable extent of the jurisdiction claimed in its behalf. In this he was followed by Lord Chief Justice Coke who said that the High Court of Parliament had a jurisdiction for making laws 'so transcendent and absolute, as it cannot be confined either for causes or persons within any bounds.'[4] Perhaps these legal authorities did not

2 The phrase cited is from H. Craik, 'The Cabinet Secretariat', *The Nineteenth Century and After*, xci (1922), p.915.
3 A. V. Dicey, *Lectures on the Relation between Law & Public Opinion in England during the Nineteenth Century* (1905; 2nd edn, London, 1920), p.306. And cf. Laski's comments, in *A Grammar of Politics* (1925; 5th edn, London, 1948), p.303.
4 J. Bodin, *The Six Bookes of a Commonweale* (1606; Cambridge, Mass., 1962), pp.[161]–[162]; T. Smith, *De Republica Anglorum: a Discourse on the Commonwealth of England* (1583; Cambridge, 1906), pp.48–9; E. Coke, 4 *Inst.* 36.

really mean to assert a sovereignty so untrammelled as their dicta imply. Yet the attributes they had in view might not unwarrantably be applied to a body which, in due course, raised armies, deposed and executed a king, and in other ways entirely changed the political structure of the realm. Nor, after the Restoration, was Parliament's claim to legal supremacy abated. Did it not replace one monarch by another and settle the Crown by legislation?

At least since the sixteenth century, then, the legislature has invariably been regarded as 'the very essence of all government' in this kingdom, 'the *supream power* of the Common-wealth'.[5] To be sure, the idea of natural or fundamental law might imply restraint on the exercise of this power, limitations on its use which should not be ignored or transgressed. Nevertheless it is, in this general perspective, a matter for no surprise that in the middle of the eighteenth century Sir William Blackstone, in his great survey of English law, employed the by then traditional language and attributed to the legislature a

> sovereign and uncontrolable authority in making . . . laws, concerning matters of all possible denominations . . . : this being the place where that absolute despotic power, which must in all governments reside somewhere, is entrusted by the constitution of these kingdoms . . . . It can, in short, do every thing that is not naturally impossible; and therefore some have not scrupled to call its power, by a figure rather too bold, the omnipotence of parliament.[6]

At about the same time the Swiss jurist, Jean Louis Delolme, similarly wrote that the 'basis of the English constitution, the capital principle on which all others depend, is, that the legislative power belongs to parliament alone'. And he went on to explain the nature of its authority in this way: 'As its bare will can give being to the laws, so its bare will can also annihilate them; and, if I may be permitted the expression, the legislative power can change the constitution, as God created the light.'[7] He observed further, in a famous footnote, that 'it is a fundamental principle with the English lawyers, that parliament can do every thing, *except* making a woman a man, or a man a woman.'[8] De Tocqueville in

5 R. Hooker, *Of the Laws of Ecclesiastical Polity* (published 1593–1662), VIII. vi. 11, in *Works*, 7th edn (Oxford, 1888), iii. 408; J. Locke, *Two Treatises of Government* (1690), ed. Laslett (Cambridge, 1960), II. xi. 134, pp. 373–4.

6 W. Blackstone, *Commentaries on the Laws of England* (1765–9; 6th edn, Dublin, 1775), i. 160–1. Cf. ibid., i. 47–9, 51, 90.

7 J. L. Delolme, *The Constitution of England* (1771; new edn, London, 1822), pp. 51, 186–7.

8 ibid., p. 112n (italics in original). The point arises in a discussion of legal fictions: Delolme referred to the ingenuity of the old Roman lawyers who, in this way, had in certain kinds of action called a daughter a son.

his day also commented on the prevalence of the doctrine of Parliamentary omnipotence; and he expressed this epigrammatically in the observation that, because Parliament could mould political arrangements as it wished, the constitution could be said not to exist at all.[9]

This doctrine indeed was to prove a major theme of nineteenth-century commentary as well. If it was not entirely unchallenged it was widely reflected: in the jurisprudential speculations of such legal theorists as John Austin; and in the constitutional commentaries like that of Walter Bagehot. The latter, for all the stress he gave to the role of the Cabinet, concluded that 'we are ruled by the House of Commons'.[10] So when in 1885 Dicey published his *Law of the Constitution*, the position of Parliament as 'an absolutely sovereign legislature' was well established. It was normally seen as having unlimited lawmaking powers; and no person or agency had the right to set aside or override any statute it had passed.[11] This conventional view was well summarized by the Duke of Devonshire in 1893 during a debate on the Government of Ireland Bill:

> In the United Kingdom, Parliament is supreme not only in its legislative but in its Executive functions. Parliament makes and unmakes our Ministries; it revises their actions. Ministries may make peace and war, but they do so at pain of instant dismissal by Parliament from Office, and in affairs of internal administration the power of Parliament is equally direct. It can dismiss a Ministry if it is too extravagant, or too economical; it can dismiss a Ministry because its government is too stringent or too lax. It does actually and practically, in every way, directly govern England, Scotland, and Ireland.[12]

This extreme doctrine of Parliamentary supremacy has, of course, latterly been subjected to considerable and forceful criticism mainly on the ground that, while there may be no formal constitutional limits to its authority, in practice the power of the legislature depended on the extent to which its writ would actually be obeyed; and it was in fact becoming

9   A. de Tocqueville, *Democracy in America* (1835–40; Fontana, 1968), i.122.
10 J. Austin, *The Province of Jurisprudence Determined . . .* (1832), ed. Hart (London, 1968), pp.193–4; W. Bagehot, *The English Constitution* (1867; Fontana, 1966), p.155. For one challenge to the doctrine, see Disraeli's 'Vindication of the English Constitution' (1835), in W. Hutcheon (ed.), *Whigs and Whiggism: Political Writings by Benjamin Disraeli* (London, 1913), pp.148–9.
11 A. V. Dicey, *Introduction to the Study of the Law of the Constitution* (1885; 10th edn, London, 1964), pp.39–40 and, generally, ch.I 'The Nature of Parliamentary Sovereignty'; also 8th edn, London, 1920, introduction, pp.xviii–xix.
12 17 Parl. Deb. 4s., 5 September 1893, cols.33–4. S. Low cited most of this passage in his *The Governance of England* (1904; London, 1922), pp.57–8. He stated that he himself disagreed with the 'extreme theory of parliamentary omnipotence' here exemplified but acknowledged that it was still current, ibid., pp.56–7.

more and more restricted by electoral and other political forces. In effect, it was conditional in its use and was indeed actually wielded by external agencies – the Cabinet, departments and other executive offices, the parties, and a range of groups of political importance. This is certainly true to a very great extent. Nevertheless it is Parliamentary authority itself which these other bodies work through and seek to influence. So (subject only to the effects of membership of the EEC which indeed raises another crucial perspective) the principle is still true today that 'as a proposition of the law' it is Parliament that 'has the right to make or unmake any law whatever':

> No Act of Parliament can be held *ultra vires* on any ground of contravention of generally accepted principles of morality or of law.... [No] court can declare invalid the provisions of an Act of Parliament on any ground. There is no such doctrine as the unconstitutionality of legislation by Parliament.[13]

As just implied, however, the extent to which and the way in which this legal power is or has been actually exercised will depend upon political and other circumstances: hence Dicey's prudent distinction between 'legal' and 'political' sovereignty.[14] But it follows that, given the appropriate practical conditions, 'the omnipotence of Parliament' in Britain could be used to accomplish even basic changes by ordinary enactment and thus be 'directed by bold reformers towards the removal of all actual or apparent abuses'.[15] The 8th Duke of Argyll, discussing the unwritten constitution, commented on its 'wholly unprotected nature'. Every part of it, he wrote,

> is at the mercy of ordinary legislation. The process which passes a road act, or delegates to some parochial authority the power of making sewers, is the same process exactly which is competent to subvert the Monarchy, to break up the constitution of Parliament, to confer arbitrary powers upon local majorities, and to prostrate all personal liberties under the feet of the village tyrant.[16]

Or as a more recent and not less committed participant urged with special reference to the possibility of increased intervention:

13 Professor E. C. S. Wade's Introduction (1959) to Dicey, *Law of the Constitution*, pp. xxxiv–xxxv, liii, lxxix.
14 Dicey, op. cit., pp. 71 ff. Cf. F. W. Maitland, *The Constitutional History of England* (1908; Cambridge, 1974), p. 339; and, for earlier controversy on these matters, H. T. Dickinson, 'The Eighteenth-Century Debate on the Sovereignty of Parliament', *Trans. R. Hist. S.*, 5s., xxiii (1976), pp. 189–210.
15 Dicey, *Law & Public Opinion*, p. 305.
16 G. D. Campbell, Eighth Duke of Argyll, *The New British Constitution and its Master-Builders* (Edinburgh, 1888), p. 3.

The absence of a written constitution gives British politics a flexibility enjoyed by few nations. No courts can construe the power of the British Parliament. It interprets its own authority, and from it there is no appeal. This gives it a revolutionary quality, and enables us to entertain the hope of bringing about social transformations, without the agony and prolonged crises experienced by less fortunate nations. The British constitution, with its adult suffrage, exposes all rights and privileges, properties and powers, to the popular will. The only checks are those that arise from a sense of justice and social propriety. Thus, in the Parliament of 1945–50, a large section of the economic apparatus was transferred from private to public ownership .... [The] transfer was made smoothly, peacefully and with political decorum.[17]

This, then, is the point. The hallowed legal and constitutional doctrine of the sovereignty of Parliament meant that there was to hand a means of securing radical change by legislation that could not be effectively challenged in the courts or in any other formal way and which was thus available for purposes of substantial reform. Given the conditions of nineteenth-century politics, before the development of the modern party machine and its discipline, this power could be, and was, often set in motion by individual MPs or peers, or groups of them, or indirectly by influential and active associations outside Parliament, especially as official business then claimed much less time. A considerable number of social reforms was achieved by invoking the power of the state in this way. And then, of course, once the control of party was firmly established, this legislative sovereignty was used more frequently, steadily, and consistently. Nor were the collectivist possibilities of this state of affairs unremarked by libertarians. For instance, Toulmin Smith was quite clear that a body of unlimited power, however representative and whatever the suffrage by which it was elected, 'is merely organized oligarchism; centralization in its most dangerous and irresponsible form'.[18]

These last remarks point to a further political dimension: for once Parliament, or rather its increasingly dominant chamber, the House of Commons, became a democratically representative body, then its legal authority could and would be used ever more widely to pursue the goal of social justice which, in various ways, appeals to a mass electorate, and to this end, therefore, to extend still further the intervention of the state in the life of the nation.

---

17 A. Bevan, *In Place of Fear* (London, 1952), p.100.
18 J. Toulmin Smith, *The Metropolis and its Municipal Administration* (London, 1852), p.25.

THE EXTENSION OF THE FRANCHISE AND ITS EFFECT

... more and more the people throng
The chairs and thrones of civil power.
TENNYSON, *In Memoriam*, 1850, XXI.15–16

G. K. Chesterton once wrote that, above all, modernism reflected 'the apotheosis of the insignificant'. 'This tide of importance of small things', he continued, 'is flowing ... steadily around us upon every side today'. It is true he was writing about the literary tendency to describe the apparently trivial in some detail as a means of stressing its real consequence. Yet 'this turbulent democracy of things' (as he also called the phenomenon) does indeed have a political aspect.[19] The enormous multiplication of individuals in themselves normally of little or no account (except, of course, to themselves) helped create or release political pressures of the most substantial moment, the recognition of which was one of the major facts of recent constitutional history. Parliamentary sovereignty was set to work in a collectivist direction not least because of the movement towards universal suffrage, the political acknowledgement of the mass of the individually insignificant. Lord Ashley wrote in that *annus mirabilis* 1848 that, 'All things are tending to a change. We are entering on a new political dispensation; and many of us probably will outlive the integrity of our aristocratical institutions.' Men are talking, he went on, they know not why and they do not reflect how, of '*this* slight concession and *that*; of an "enlargement of the franchise," and other vagaries.'[20] Three decades later (and on the eve of the third Reform Bill) Lord Acton wrote to Mary Gladstone that, 'We are forced, in equity, to share the government with the working class'. Interestingly the considerations on which this view was based were, Acton believed, 'made supreme by the awakening of political economy.' For Adam Smith and the other theorists of the classical school had urged not only freedom of contract between capital and labour but, as well, that labour was the main (or even the only) source of wealth. If this is true, Acton went on, it was difficult to resist the conclusion that the class on which national prosperity thus depended 'ought to control the wealth it supplies, that is, ought to govern instead of the useless unproductive class, and that the class which earns the increment ought to enjoy it.'[21] Implicit, therefore, in the general attitudes of the day were the policies of extending the franchise and redistributing the national wealth. And it

19 G. K. Chesterton, *Robert Browning* (1903; London, 1919), pp.164–6.
20 Diary (13 April 1848) in E. Hodder, *The Life and Work of the Seventh Earl of Shaftesbury, K.G.* (London, 1887), p.393 (italics in original).
21 Lord Acton, *Letters ... to Mary ... Gladstone* (London, 1904), pp.91–2 (letter of 24 April 1881).

might seem reasonable to suppose that the power of the vote, once thus extended, would be used precisely to achieve the latter goal through mastery of the state.

Two questions arise at this point about the submission of our politics to the arbitrament of popular election. First, what was the series of changes that occurred in respect of the local and Parliamentary franchises after 1818?; and, secondly, what was their specific effect? The latter, in particular, is a matter of some moment in the present tale.

The process of extension

The local franchise

Developments in respect of the right to vote in local government elections are perhaps less well-known than those which altered the Parliamentary franchise. Yet they had a certain priority and were hardly less important in practical terms especially in the earlier phases of collectivist development when the impact of local bodies on the life and pocket of the citizen was greater. It is a fascinating and complex story that has been superbly told by Professor Keith-Lucas on whose account I largely rely for the following brief summary.[22]

Before the nineteenth century a good many local agencies were (what was known as) 'close' or 'select', that is, they were oligarchies of the 'principal inhabitants' who continually renewed their hold on office by a process of co-optation. This was particularly true of the chartered municipal corporations and the benches of magistrates which administered county business though at the parish level affairs were invariably more 'open'. Sometimes there was a mixture of *ex officio* and elective membership: this was often the case, for instance, with turnpike trusts or improvement commissions. Though exceptions were slowly admitted, basically the local government franchise was founded on the principle that only those who contributed to the funds used by a local body should have a vote in the choice of its elected members. Given all this, two types of franchise prevailed until the very end of the last century. First there was a system of plural voting by which those who paid more rates had more votes. This scheme was introduced for the parish and a number of its many committees in 1818 and after; in 1834 for elections to the Boards of Guardians which administered the Poor Law; and in 1848 for the local Boards of Health. Secondly, a vote was given in other cases to every resident ratepaying householder as in the Municipal Corporations Act of 1835 and for county council elections after 1888.

22 B. Keith-Lucas, *The English Local Government Franchise: a Short History* (Oxford, 1952) in which appendix A, pp. 226–36, summarizes the provisions of the thirty-eight major statutes affecting this franchise up to 1949.

One interesting experiment, introduced for School Board elections in 1870, was the use of the cumulative vote, a system in which (as in traditional multi-member Parliamentary constituencies) an elector had as many votes as there were places to be filled and which he could distribute among the candidates as he wished: as he could give all his votes to one candidate only it was regarded as a safeguard for the interests of religious minorities. Single or widowed women occupiers had (by a custom judicially upheld in 1739) enjoyed voting rights in some local elections and even held parish office; and this practice was confirmed by early nineteenth-century legislation. Readers of Charles Dickens' *Sketches by Boz* (1836) will recall how the great beadle election depended on decoying the female vote, in particular that of the old woman who made muffins, a canvassing affair depicted in Cruikshank's amusing illustration. Nor were women excluded from elections that were later introduced. A franchise like the one already existing was granted in respect of local Boards of Health, for instance, and for some of the later Improvement Commissions; after 1869 women had the vote in municipal elections on the same conditions as men though in 1872 the courts held that this did not apply to married women, a disqualification removed ten years later. In 1870 they were given the vote in School Board elections. Manxwomen enjoyed the local franchise and female persons were admitted to vote for Scottish town councils in 1881.[23] By the Local Government Acts of 1882 and 1888, qualified women might vote in county and county borough elections. Any restrictions in respect of marriage and candidature were later removed as by the Acts of 1894, 1907, and the post-war statutes.[24] Clearly this long process of recognition of the right of women to take part in politics at local level was an important factor or precedent in pressing for the Parliamentary franchise.[25] Nor was local practice without a similar effect in other respects as well. For one thing the secret ballot had been in use in parochial elections since Hobhouse's Act of 1831. For another, something like a householder suffrage was already in process of development by mid-century. The traditional ratepayer franchise excluded the lower classes, either because it was the practice to leave the poorer dwellings off the rate-book or because the rates were paid by the landlord (often specifically to disfranchise the tenant). But this situation was potentially transformed by the practice of 'compounding' which was considerably extended after 1850. This was the arrangement by which, even though the landlord or

23 For the Manx case, see M. A. Butler and J. M. Templeton, *The Isle of Man and the First Votes for Women* (n.p. [Sheffield], n.d. [1980]), pp. 6, 9–10, 15.

24 B. Keith-Lucas and P. G. Richards, *A History of Local Government in the Twentieth Century* (London, 1978), pp. 18–19.

25 Cf. the case put in W. E. H. Lecky, *Democracy and Liberty* (1896; London, 1899), ii. 543.

owner paid the rates, the tenant was regarded in principle as a ratepayer on the assumption that he paid a rent containing an element to cover local taxes. This led in many areas to a notable increase in the number of smaller tenants who were enfranchised: in some places the local electorate was more than doubled.[26] Then there were, of course, further extensions of the local franchise in various ways: by the reduction of the residence requirement, as in 1869, and by the establishment of elected county councils in the 1880s. By the beginning of the new century, there was a basically uniform system resting on the ratepayer franchise and which was formally standardized in 1918. The next major change did not come until after the Second World War when the hitherto unique foundation of a claim to a vote in local elections – occupation of land or buildings – was supplemented by another: residence in the area concerned. The general effect of this step was to assimilate the Parliamentary and local franchises. The property qualification for election was abolished (except for the City of London) in 1969 but re-introduced in 1971 together with a new qualification based on place of work. In terms of merely democratic advance, the local franchise obviously in some respects ran ahead of the Parliamentary changes while in others it lagged behind: it was both stimulus and anomaly.

There is no general run of published figures of the numbers of local voters before 1920. The continuing growth of the electorate over the last century and a half or so can only be indicated, therefore, by reference to particular cases where data have survived. In Swansea, for instance, the number of electors was 747 in 1839, 3470 in 1866, 6414 in 1870, and by 1890 had risen notably to 16,169.[27] Professor Keith-Lucas has published similar information in respect of two municipal boroughs as in Table 8.

The Parliamentary franchise

Perhaps it is most appropriate here simply to indicate at the outset the nature and extent of the main legislative changes involved and then briefly to say something about the manner of this process, all as a preliminary to consideration of its impact (in conjunction with the parallel changes in the local sphere) on the development of collectivism.

The principal phases or aspects of the growth of the Parliamentary electorate are summarized in Table 9 which is largely reproduced from

26 On the Small Tenements Rating Act (13 & 14 Vict. c. 99), see Keith-Lucas, *The English Local Government Franchise*, pp. 68–71, 230. One reason for the development of compounding was that it produced a higher rate yield: 'so, as an incident to a financial expedient, the municipal franchise grew rapidly wider', ibid., p. 71.

27 G. Roberts, *The Municipal Development of the Borough of Swansea to 1900* (Swansea, 1940), p. 46.

Table 8   *The number of municipal voters in Maidstone and Ipswich, 1831–1950*[28]

Year	No. of voters in Maidstone	Population of Maidstone	No. of voters in Ipswich	Population of Ipswich
1835	850[29]	15,387	1,212	20,201*
1861	2,097	23,016	3,879	37,950
1891	5,145	32,145	10,681	57,360
1911	6,146	35,475	14,871	73,932
1921	14,827	37,216	31,641	79,371
1931	19,798	42,280	42,394	87,502
1948	36,638	53,060	73,967	103,400

*1831 census

Strathearn Gordon's *Our Parliament* though additions have been made to take account of changes introduced since 1948.[30]

Seen overall (and as implied in the table) the whole process certainly looks like the gradual development of mass democracy. And so it was. After remaining virtually unaltered for several centuries, the right to vote in Parliamentary elections was then radically transformed over a relatively short period. Not without difficulty of course: as Sidney Webb said, from one point of view English political history from the 1830s on was 'the record of the reluctant enfranchisement of one class after another, by mere force of the tendencies of the age.'[31] Yet this sort of generalization, although not wholly inaccurate, may mislead so far as understanding of the individual steps in the legislative series is concerned. Care is needed, in particular, in assessing the significance of the earlier statutes: as Maitland warned in another context we must avoid

28 Based on Keith-Lucas, op. cit., Appendix B, pp. 237–42.
29 839 after the Municipal Corporations Act, 1835.
30 S. Gordon, *Our Parliament* (1945; 6th edn, London, 1964), pp. 50–1; data after 1966 from D. Butler and A. Sloman, *British Political Facts 1900–1979*, 5th edn (London, 1980), p. 209; *Annual Abstract of Statistics*, No. 110 (1973), Tables 7 and 9. It should be noted, however, that the earlier electoral figures in this table can only be approximations: estimates vary substantially and allowance has to be made for defective or duplicate registration. For alternative reckonings, see C. Cook and B. Keith, *British Historical Facts 1830–1900* (London, 1975), pp. 115–17; F. W. S. Craig (ed.), *British Parliamentary Election Results 1832–1885* (London, 1977), Table 3, p. 623, and the companion volume for the period 1885–1918 (London, 1974), Table 4, pp. 582–3.
31 S. Webb, 'The Basis of Socialism: Historic' in G. B. Shaw *et al.*, *Fabian Essays* (1889; Jubilee edn, London, 1950), p. 36.

Table 9   Principal changes in the electorate, 1831–1970

Date	Title of amending Act	Main classes of population added	Electoral qualifications		Remarks	Statistics to show the effect of these changes*				
						Date	Total electorate	Population aged 20 years and over	Electorate as percentage of population over 20 years	
1831			Counties – 40s. freeholders Boroughs – a medley of narrow and unequal franchises							
1832	Representation of the People Act, 1832, 2 & 3 Will. 4 c. 45 (known as the 'First Reform Act')	Small land-owners, tenant farmers, and shopkeepers	Counties { 40s. freeholders £10 copyholders £10 leaseholders £50 tenants at will Boroughs { £10 house-holders		Similar Acts which were passed for Scotland and Ireland in 1832 differed in detail from the English Act	Before (1831) After (1832)	509,391 720,784	10,207,000 10,207,000	5.0 7.1	
1867	Representation of the People Act, 1867 30 & 31 Vict. c. 102 (sometimes called the 'Second Reform Act')	Smaller agricultural owners and tenants; artisans and many town labourers	Counties { 40s. freeholders £5 copyholders £5 leaseholders £12 tenants at will Boroughs { All occupiers of dwelling houses rated to poor rates, lodgers occupying £10 lodgings		Reform Bills were introduced in the Commons in 1852, 1854, 1859, 1860, and 1866. Similar Acts which were passed for Scotland and Ireland in 1868 differed in detail from the English Act	Before (1864) After (1868)	1,130,372 2,231,030	13,051,816 13,625,658	9.0 16.4	
1884	Representation of the People Act, 1884 48 & 49 Vict. c. 3 (sometimes called the 'Third	Agricultural and other labourers in country	Counties and Boroughs { A uniform householder and lodger franchise in effect giving a vote to every man over 21 who		The Ballot Act was passed in 1872. No woman could yet vote	Before (1883) After (1886)	2,955,190 4,965,618	16,426,233 17,394,014	18.0 28.5	

Year	Act	Counties and Boroughs	Description	Effect		Electorate	Population	%
1918	7 & 8 Geo. 5 c. 64 and Parliament (Qualification of Women) Act, 1918 8 & 9 Geo. 5 c. 47	Counties and Boroughs	tion by abolition of property qualification in counties. Qualification now either six months' residence or occupation of £10 business premises. *Women* Enfranchised at 30 and over	graduates and holders of the business premises qualification was restricted to two votes, including one for residence	After (1921)	19,984,037	26,846,785	74.0
1928	Representation of the People (Equal Franchise) Act, 1928 18 & 19 Geo. 5. c. 12	Women 21–30	Women enfranchised at 21. In effect every man or woman of 21 and upwards thereafter entitled to vote	Male and female adult suffrage achieved	Before (1927) After (1931)	21,895,347 29,175,608	29,654,721 30,096,135	74.0 96.9
1948	Representation of the People Act, 1948 11 & 12 Geo. 6 c. 65 (Consolidated in 1949)		University constituencies and all plural voting abolished	'One man (or woman) one vote'	After (1951)	34,915,112	(Dec. 1950) 36,078,000	96.7
1969	Representation of the People Act, 1969 17 & 18 Eliz. 2 c. 15	Men and women 18–21	Every person over 18 entitled to vote	Reduction of voting age to 18	Before (1966) After (1970)	35,964,684 39,342,013	36,947,000 (est. no. over 18 in 1971) 39,857,200 (est.)	97.3 98.7

*These figures refer to Great Britain and Ireland until the separation of Eire: thereafter to Great Britain and Northern Ireland only.

The available statistics of population upon which the diagrams at the end of this table are based relate to persons aged 20 years and over and not to those aged over 21. When the relevant allowance is made it will be seen that complete adult suffrage for both sexes has been achieved within a century.

being prejudiced by what was at the time future history.[32] An impressive array of recent scholarship has reinforced this point very firmly.[33] It should be remembered, for instance, that the electoral impact of the Reform Acts of 1832 was very limited and created, too, 'an extraordinary jumble of qualifications'.[34] It is true the electorate was increased by some 50 per cent, that 'rotten' and some 'pocket' boroughs were abolished and seats redistributed to places elsewhere, including the new manufacturing towns, and that the legislation proved a perhaps crucial precedent, establishing the principle of change in a form of property and an area of public policy long held sacrosanct and untouchable.[35] Yet the effect was in important respects also retrograde or neutral: the traditional county franchise was diluted by the addition of votes in some ways more easily subject to influence, and the role of the great landowners was in effect hardly diminished; the introduction of the uniform borough qualifi-cation eliminated some of the constituencies where 'potwalloper' or similar 'ancient right' franchises had hitherto enabled a popular voice to prevail; the matter of redistribution was settled not without reference to Whig calculations of electoral advantage; the enfranchisement of the new urban areas was intended rather to sustain the political integrity of the counties (which otherwise the growing towns would have dominated electorally) than to extend a democratic principle (which was why so many county members were in favour of reform); and the rotten boroughs were abolished, again, not merely because of what they were but as a means of eliminating a rival source of political corruption. Robert Lowe summarized the matter thus: 'The main principle of the reform of 1832 was not the reduction of the franchise. In some boroughs [it] was raised. The principle was, to take electoral power out of the hands of corporations.'[36] And, in fact, in most respects the traditional forces of

---

32 F. W. Maitland, *The Constitutional History of England* (1908; Cambridge, 1974), p. 325.

33 There is an admirable brief summary of this research by a major contributor, H. J. Hanham, in *The Reformed Electoral System in Great Britain, 1832–1914* (London, 1969). See also the firmly realistic assessment of N. McCord, 'Some Limitations of the Age of Reform' in H. Hearder and H. R. Loyn (eds), *British Government and Administration* (Cardiff, 1974), esp. pp. 192–4; and, of course, D. C. Moore's monumental *The Politics of Deference: a Study of the Mid-Nineteenth Century English Political System* (Hassocks, 1976). For an earlier expression of the view that it was practical political considerations and not general principle which led to the early Whig reforms, see P. A. Gibbons, *Ideas of Political Representation in Parliament, 1651–1832* (Oxford, 1914), pp. 46–7.

34 Hanham, op. cit., pp. 33–5 citing A. Paul, *The History of Reform*, 3rd edn (1884), pp. 172–4.

35 Cf. J. S. Mill, 'Coleridge' (1840), *Collected Works*, ed. J. M. Robson et al. (London, 1963 ff), x.153; and 'The Claims of Labour' (1845), ibid., iv. 369–70.

36 R. Lowe, *Speeches and Letters on Reform*, 2nd edn (London, 1867), p. 12.

political influence remained in being as before; nor were they usually subject, in any case, to the test of actual electoral contest. And all this is hardly surprising when, as Professor Moore definitively argues, the first Reform Act (like its successor) was in essence an attempt 'to perpetuate the roles and status of the traditional élites' and the conventional structure of deference that sustained them.[37] It was widely remarked at the time that the first House of Commons elected after 1832 was very like its unreformed predecessors: it was still largely dominated by country gentlemen and members of the aristocracy; often indeed the newly enfranchised industrial areas continued for a long time to return Tory or aristocratic members.[38] Trollope portrays an election in the 1850s as a bout between candidates nominated by rival patrons representing the aristocracy and the monied oligarchy: democracy, he notes, would have very little to say to it on one side or the other.[39] Although the property qualification for MPs was modified in 1838 and abolished twenty years later – with the odd effect that a man could be qualified to sit but too poor to vote – it was not until some time had elapsed that any great change occurred in the composition of the House of Commons, until perhaps members of the rising middle and professional classes were sufficiently endowed financially to forsake their business pursuits for the leisured occupation of politics. Dr Kitson Clark, in a beautifully articulated analysis of the continuities that persisted amid the political change, makes it quite clear that, in respect of electoral practices, the first half of the nineteenth century was, in many ways, still like its predecessor.[40]

The same sort of considerations may also be applied to the Reform Acts of 1867 and 1868. They were hardly innovatory to any startling degree being simply a recognition in the national context of what had for some time been under way in the municipal field.[41] Nor was the redistributive effect so great or so clear as has sometimes been suggested.[42] Again, the immediate context of the legislation was tactical party struggle and interest rather than the pursuit of democratic principle, the intention being once more to maintain the integrity of the

37 Moore, op. cit., pp. 15, 430–1.
38 E. Halévy, *A History of the English People in the Nineteenth Century* (1913–46; 2nd trans. edn, London, 1961), iii.63; McCord, loc. cit., p. 194.
39 Trollope, *Framley Parsonage* (1861; Everyman, 1973), pp. 357–8; *Dr Thorne* (1858; Everyman, 1967), p. 1.
40 G. K. Clark, 'The Electorate and the Repeal of the Corn Laws', *Trans.R.Hist.S.*, 5s., i (1951), pp. 109–26.
41 Cf. Disraeli's comment, in W. F. Monypenny and G. E. Buckle, *The Life of Benjamin Disraeli* (1910–20; rev. edn, London, 1929), ii.290.
42 For a corrective, see G. K. Clark, *The Making of Victorian England* (1962; London, 1968), pp. 54–8, 230.

county electorate and so the 'traditional social nexus', specifically the position of the Tory squirearchy.[43]

On the other hand, the extension of the secret ballot to Parliamentary elections in 1872 (whatever the political intentions behind the change) can hardly be underestimated as a contribution to making the power of the wider vote effective, although corruption was not thereby eliminated – the general election of 1880 was the most costly ever.[44] Standing in January 1874 as Conservative candidate in his father's borough of Woodstock, Lord Randolph Churchill wrote, 'You see, with the ballot one can tell nothing – one can only trust to promises, and I have no doubt a good many will be broken'.[45] Eviction in rural areas, after a vote regarded by a landlord as untoward, became less easy.[46]

By the third quarter of the century things had certainly changed and (as we shall see) the prospect was regarded by some people with considerable concern. Even so, as Professor Hanham put it, 'the electoral system still had about it a very old-fashioned air'.[47] The electorate was still a quite small proportion of the adult population, perhaps 17 or 18 per cent; despite the development of industry and the large towns, rural Britain still returned the vast majority of MPs with the result that many densely populated areas were under-represented; distinct voting qualifications persisted as between counties and boroughs; and so on. It was not until the series of reforms proposed by Gladstone's second government which, after some political manoeuvring and log-rolling, were placed on the statute book by agreement between 1883 and 1885, that anything like a uniform system of Parliamentary representation prevailed over the whole country. By this legislative package, expenses and other election aids were limited; a more or less common franchise was established by extending the householder and lodger vote to the counties; and a major redistributive step was taken, after some party bargaining, by the creation of single-member constituencies of, in theory if not in practice, uniform

43   See e.g. D. C. Moore, *The Politics of Deference*, p. 399–400, and the 'Epilogue' esp. pp. 430–1. Cf. R. Blake, *Disraeli* (London, 1966), p. 759.

44   Hanham, *The Reformed Electoral System*, p. 24; J. E. Gorst, 'Elections of the Future', *Fortnightly Review*, n.s., xxxiv (1883), pp. 690–2, in H. J. Hanham, *The Nineteenth-Century Constitution 1815–1914* (Cambridge, 1969), pp. 291–3.

45   W. S. Churchill, *Lord Randolph Churchill* (1906; London [1951]), p. 55. Contrast the picture of farmer retainers of the late 1850s voting whichever way their landlord wished, in F. W. Hirst, *In the Golden Days* (London, 1947), pp. 52–3.

46   For examples of such evictions and the effect of the Ballot Act, see N. Masterman, *The Forerunner: the Dilemmas of Tom Ellis 1859–1899* (Llandybie, 1972), pp. 23–5. Trollopians will contrast the position and attitude of the two Dukes of Omnium as indicated in *The Eustace Diamonds* (1873; Panther, 1973), p. 409, and *The Prime Minister* (1876; London, 1974), i. 194–5.

47   Hanham, *The Reformed Electoral System*, p. 24.

size.[48] Thus the traditional basis of representation, the diverse forms of local community with their varied blocs and networks, gave way in principle to a new artificial division created especially for the purpose, consisting of a more or less average number of electors and not necessarily having any other unity or character of its own.[49] This change implied the future dominance of the great urban areas and of mere numbers. Moreover, for the first time specifically working-class constituencies came into being making possible, in due course, the development of a Labour Party.

After this it only remained to give a Parliamentary vote to women, a matter, in effect, of extending once more to the national political field what had in various forms long existed in a local context.[50] This step might have been taken earlier than it was and may perhaps have been delayed by the bad impression created by the activity of the suffragettes. If so, this was not the first or last time that so-called radical agitation will have impeded reform. The innovation came, in the end, in 1918 basically because of changes in women's status in general, for instance during the war; and numerically it was the most significant of all the electoral reforms. Completed a decade later, it was thus that universal manhood suffrage on a minimal residential qualification came to prevail, tinkered about with since, eliminating anything anomalous to the rule of 'one man' (or, I suppose, 'one person'), 'one vote', and, in conformity with our curious not to say absurd contemporary concept of maturity, reducing the age of political adulthood to eighteen. Presumably the process can hardly go further unless it be to grant extra votes to the young and the impoverished on the ground that they alone have an uncorrupted vision of the common weal.

The impact of extension

Of course, it would be wrong to suppose that, even before the development of a mass franchise, political influence could not be exerted by those who had no vote if they were sufficiently determined.[51] But it

48 For a recent account of this last development, its rationale, and the party compromises involved, see M. Steed, 'The Evolution of the British Electoral System', in S. E. Finer (ed.), *Adversary Politics and Electoral Reform* (London, 1975), pp. 40–2; also J. Roper, *The Development of the Single Member Constituency Electoral System in the Anglo-American Democracies* (unpublished Ph.D. thesis, University of Kent at Canterbury, 1980).

49 Cf. Maitland, op. cit., p. 363.

50 Cf. the comment in M. Oakeshott, *Rationalism in Politics and Other Essays* (London, 1962), p. 124. Manxwomen had been given the right to vote in elections to the House of Keys in 1881; see Butler and Templeton, op. cit., pp. 1, 13, 15.

51 See e.g. the account of Oldham radicalism in J. Foster, *Class Struggle and the Industrial Revolution: Early Industrial Capitalism in Three English Towns* (London, 1974), *passim*.

was undoubtedly the case that the various increments of electoral reform (whether the effect was intended or not) released a spirit of democracy that recast every part of the ancient English state.[52] In his fascinating biography of Wellington, Philip Guedalla summarized the transition that occurred (albeit with a certain degree of anachronism) in reference to the Duke's own baffled response:

> This was not politics as he had learnt them. For politics according to the rules were a genteel affair in which residents in Mayfair governed England by the simple process of making speeches to one another in Westminster. That was the old *terrain*, on which he could manoeuvre with fair proficiency. But now the ground was unfamiliar; Westminster had ceased to be the sole battlefield of politics, and operations were in progress all over England; strange, unauthorised belligerents had elbowed the recognised players into corners; and where once the game of politics had turned upon the evolutions of competing groups, it now depended on the incalculable appetites of crowds.

And, of course, the Duke 'was never at his best with crowds' whether they cheered or hooted him. He 'had no taste for them' and had devoted the best years of his life 'to obstructing their desires.' Like so many others of his generation and class, he 'had learnt a deep distaste for democracy'.[53]

Certainly, there had been a traditional fear that democracy must mean arbitrary government. The classics and those who followed them had invariably believed in Polybian fashion that a preponderance of the populace must degenerate into the rule of the mob and so in turn invite tyranny. Hobbes suspected (in Aristotelian vein) that it must be dominated by mere demagoguery.[54] A not untypical Enlightenment opinion is that of the irascible Josiah Tucker, an eighteenth-century Dean of Gloucester. Experience will almost universally tell us, he believed, that 'when a multitude are invested with the power of governing, they prove the very worst of governors.' They are 'rash', 'precipitate', 'giddy and inconstant', and 'ever the dupes of designing men'. Besides, he adds, 'a democratic government is despotic in its very nature' and this 'because it supposes itself to be the only fountain of power, from which there can be no appeal.'[55] In this long-existent vein, the cumulative extension of the

52 Cf. J. Redlich, *The Procedure of the House of Commons: a Study of its History and Present Form* (1905; trans., London, 1908), vol. i, p. xxx.

53 P. Guedalla, *The Duke* (1931; London, 1940), p. 357.

54 For the classical view, see e.g. Aristotle, *Politics*, 1292[a]; Polybius, *The Histories*, vi. 9; Hobbes, *The Elements of Law Natural & Politic*, ed. Tönnies (1889; Cambridge, 1928), p. 94 §5.

55 J. Tucker, *Four Letters on Important National Subjects* (1783), p. 98, in H. T. Dickinson, *Liberty and Property: Political Ideology in Eighteenth-Century Britain* (1977; London, 1979), p. 275.

right to vote was, during the nineteenth century, often felt to be unlikely or undesirable, deplored, or at least regarded with concern. In the 1850s the prospect of a further advance of the franchise aroused a flurry of anxiety in the periodical press.[56] Further, it is only necessary to read Carlyle's essay 'Shooting Niagara: and After?'or the introduction to the 1872 edition of Bagehot's *The English Constitution* to realize the intensity of the fears and even the hatred that the second Reform Act evoked. Lord Derby, although calling it a 'great experiment', nevertheless described it as 'a leap in the dark' (referring to the famous *Punch* cartoon and symbolically echoing perhaps Hobbes's remark about the approach of death); while the poet, Coventry Patmore, saw 1867 as marking a Tory betrayal,

> The year of the great crime,
> When the false English nobles, and their Jew,
> By God demented, slew
> The trust they stood twice pledged to keep from wrong.[57]

A variety of motives and reasons was at work in this sort of reaction. One was the belief that, as Toulmin Smith argued, in a really free country representation could never be a matter of numbers merely but rested properly on the different interests or communities of which the realm consisted. Lord Lytton (who in his younger days had supported the 1832 Reform Bill) referred slightingly to what he called 'Koom-Posh-erie', government by the ignorant merely because they were the most numerous.[58] This was, too, the sort of concern expressed, at a quite different level, by J. S. Mill in his consideration of the possible consequences of popular democracy. As in his essays 'On Liberty' (1859) and 'Representative Government' (1861) he anticipated a tendency to control and uniformity, and tried to indicate ways in which nevertheless individuality, culture, and expertise might be protected against mass tyranny and mediocrity. And if Kipling ridiculed the consequences of demagoguery working on ignorance in his story of the village that voted

56 See e.g. 'Representative Reform', *Edinburgh Review*, xcvi (1852), esp. pp. 460–9; 'Reform', *Quarterly Review*, cv (1859), pp. 261, 274. For the unlikelihood of the development of a mass franchise, see J. S. Mill, 'De Tocqueville on Democracy in America [II]' (1840), in *Collected Works*, xviii. 166. I owe these references to a paper on 'Party and Democracy in Nineteenth-Century Britain' by my colleague Dr J. Roper.

57 Derby's remarks are at 189 Parl. Deb. 3s., 6 August 1867, col. 952; Patmore's verse is cited in Monypenny and Buckle, op. cit., ii. 293. There is a brief review of some typical reactions to the 1867 Act in R. T. McKenzie and A. Silver, *Angels in Marble: Working-Class Conservatives in Urban England* (London, 1968), pp. 3–8.

58 For Smith's view, see *Parliamentary Remembrancer*, ii (1859), pp. 2–3; *English Gilds* (EETS, o.s., no. 40; 1870; London, 1963), introduction, pp. xxi–xxiii. Lord Lytton's remarks are in *The Coming Race . . .* (1871; World's Classics, 1928), pp. 52–3, 74, 106.

the earth was flat, more recent and extreme critics still have gone much beyond this and spoken of a 'vertical invasion of the barbarians', of 'hyperdemocracy' inducing necessarily a kind of 'total politicalism', 'the absorption of everything and of the entire man by politics'. In harsh and bitter language this is to acknowledge the inevitable extension of the public sphere and the role of the state as a consequence of the rise of democracy and the mass man.[59]

This possibility was indeed discerned from the outset in terms both of the inevitability of cumulative increments of social reform and, beyond this, of the likelihood of an attack on the institution of private property as such, each through the extension of government action. In the *Chapters on Socialism*, which he wrote specifically to draw out the implications of the changes in the franchise, J. S. Mill said that the Act of 1867,

> admitted within what is called the pale of the Constitution so large a body of those who live on weekly wages, that as soon and as often as these shall choose to act together as a class, and exert for any common object the whole of the electoral power which our present institutions give them, they will exercise, though not a complete ascendancy, a very great influence on legislation.

This would, he surmised, ultimately place at risk the 'whole field of social institutions' not excluding existing property arrangements.[60]

At the least there would be a slow but substantial growth in the amount of legislation directed to tackling the social problems of the day and this especially as distress of various kinds was what led to much of the popular support for Parliamentary reform which had, therefore, to be justified by results.[61] Even in this limited fashion, electoral change was the death-warrant of *laissez faire*.[62] G. J. Goschen, for instance, who had himself supported the Act of 1867, recognized that the lower classes would use their electoral influence to lessen the stringency with which the dominant anti-statist doctrine was applied. 'Compulsory legislation', he wrote, 'is less repelling to the lower than to the middle and upper classes.

59　Kipling's story, written in 1913, appeared in *A Diversity of Creatures* (London, 1917). The other phrases cited are in J. Ortega y Gasset, *The Revolt of the Masses* (1930; 2nd edn, London, 1963), pp. 14, 40; and *History as a System and Other Essays Toward a Philosophy of History* (1941; Norton, 1962), p. 71. Cf. M. Oakeshott, 'The Masses in Representative Democracy' in A. Hunold (ed.), *Freedom and Serfdom* (Dordrecht, 1961), pp. 151–70.

60　J. S. Mill, 'Chapters on Socialism' (1879), *Collected Works*, v. 706–8, 711.

61　A. Briggs, 'The Background of the Parliamentary Reform Movement in Three English Cities (1830–2)', *Cambridge Historical Journal*, x (1950–2), pp. 315–16.

62　The phrase is J. A. Williamson's: see his *The Evolution of England: a Commentary on the Facts* (1931; 2nd edn, Oxford, 1944), p. 430.

Government interference and protection have more attraction for those who find their class surrounded by evils and troubles' from which they can scarcely otherwise perceive a way out.[63] He later opposed further extension of the franchise precisely because he believed it would result in more compulsory philanthropy and greater regulation of trade.[64] On the other hand many politicians accepted this, of course. For example, in a speech he made in 1867, specifically to welcome new voters to the constitution, Viscount Sandon told the Stone Constitutional Association how vital it was to tackle the problems of the great cities in which so much of the new electorate lived. Statesmen, he said, 'can find no greater and no more important work' than to make these places 'more healthy and more decent' for people to live in.[65] In fact, quite soon after the passage of the second Reform Act, Conservative literature begins to stress how much the party has done for the working man and the trade unionist; a frequent feature of its leaflets is a list of the reforming legislation for which Tories have been responsible. This becomes, indeed, a recurring theme in Conservative propaganda.[66] Joseph Chamberlain represented a forceful recognition of this tendency, declaring that the 'primary object' of a democratic legislature was 'to carry out the decisions at which the nation has arrived'.[67] In a speech made during the campaign for the 'unauthorized programme', he specifically repudiated *laissez faire* and justified intervention in the context of the recently extended franchise. Having listed many of the social evils of the time, he went on:

> It is not enough to treat these as the inevitable incidents of the struggle for existence – the natural concomitants of our complex civilization . . . . Because State Socialism may cover very injurious and very unwise theories, that is no reason at all why we should refuse to recognise the fact that Government is only the organisation of the whole people for the benefit of all its members, and that the community . . . ought to . . . provide for all its members benefits which it is impossible for individuals to provide by their solitary and separate efforts . . . . It is only the community acting as a whole that can possibly deal with evils so deep-seated . . . . When Government represented only the authority of

63 G. J. Goschen, 'The Leap in the Dark' and 'The New Electors: or Probable Effects of the Reform Bill on the Strength of Parties', *St. Pauls*, i (1867–8), pp. 8–22, 148–62. The citation in the text is at p. 160.

64 235 Parl. Deb. 3s., 29 June 1877, cols. 557–68, esp. cols. 562–6.

65 *Staffordshire Advertiser* (27 July 1867), in P. Smith, *Disraelian Conservatism and Social Reform* (London, 1967), p. 104.

66 Cf. McKenzie and Silver, op. cit., pp. 42 ff on Conservative appeals to the working class after 1867. See also volume ii, *The Ideological Heritage*, ch. 7.

67 J. L. Garvin and J. Amery, *The Life of Joseph Chamberlain* (London, 1932–69), i. 377.

the Crown or the views of a particular class, I can understand that it was the first duty of men who valued their freedom to restrict its authority and to limit its expenditure. But all that is changed. Now Government is the organised expression of the wishes and the wants of the people, and under these circumstances let us cease to regard it with suspicion . . . . Now it is our business to extend its functions, and to see in what way its operations can be usefully enlarged.[68]

Of course, his own activity as a reforming mayor of Birmingham and the content of his proposed policy showed the collectivist line of advance he had in mind. As to his later political incarnation in the Unionist Party, some remarks he made in a letter written in 1907 are relevant (if a little odd or unhistorical in some respects):

The Conservative wing of our Party has become almost entirely democratic. There are very few remaining who belong to the old reactionary Tories. On the other hand, there are still a great many who are indifferent to progress and think they have done enough if they can maintain the existing system of things in what they consider the best of all possible worlds. They will be driven forward by the force of events. You cannot have a Franchise as wide as ours without the representatives being compelled to adopt change as the order of political being.[69]

So much is clear. The centre of political gravity was shifting from Parliament to the platform; mass organizations had to be developed to sustain and direct outside opinion; and, given the frequently artificial nature of the new constituencies, broad national appeals became more usual and important. And, of course, all the reforms undertaken had to be paid for so there was necessarily higher taxation of the more wealthy and thus a degree of income redistribution. It all involved (in Kipling's phrase) 'Robbing selected Peter to pay for collective Paul'.[70] J. A. Froude wrote, after the changes of the mid-1880s, that those who had acquired the vote 'will use it to bring about what they consider to be a more equitable distribution of the good things of this world.' 'I do not', he added, 'see how it can be otherwise'.[71] Libertarian critics quickly fastened on this. For instance, Herbert Spencer, who in his younger days had favoured a degree of electoral reform in order to undermine the political dominance of the landed classes, was later convinced that the mass franchise could only

---

68 C. W. Boyd (ed.), *Mr. Chamberlain's Speeches* (London, 1914), i.163–4. Cf. ibid., i.165–6.
69 Cited in Garvin and Amery, op. cit., vi.917.
70 Cited in C. Carrington, *Rudyard Kipling: his Life and Work* (1955; Penguin, 1970), p.475.
71 J. A. Froude, *Liberty and Property* (London, n.d. [1888]), p.23.

lead to over-legislation, the growth of bureaucracy, and the decline of real liberty. The 'employed classes' can appreciate, he believed, 'nothing but material boons' such as

> better homes, shorter hours, higher wages, more regular work. Hence they are in favour of those who vote for restricting time in mines, for forcing employers to contribute to men's insurance funds, for dictating railway-fares and freights, for abolishing the so-called sweating system. It seems to them quite right that education, wholly paid for by rates, should be State-regulated; that the State should give technical instruction; that quarries should be inspected and regulated; that there should be sanitary registration of hotels. The powers which local governments now have to supply gas, water, and electric light, they think may fitly be extended to making tramways, buying and working adjacent canals, building houses for artizans and labourers, lending money for the purchase of freeholds, and otherwise adding to conveniences and giving employment. While all this implies a wide-spread officialism, ever growing in power, it implies augmented burdens upon all who have means: constituting an indirect redistribution of property.[72]

Of course, it was precisely this consequence of electoral reform that commended it to other sorts of radical. Sidney Webb, for instance, told the Royal Commission on Labour in 1892 that if the vote were given to a tramway conductor he would not be forever content to use it to influence matters of a traditional political kind.

> He will realise that the forces which keep him at work for 16 hours a day for 3s. a day are not the forces of hostile kings, or nobles, or priests; but whatever forces they are he will, it seems to me, seek so far as possible, to control them by his vote. That is to say, he will more and more seek to convert his political democracy into what one may roughly term an industrial democracy, so that he may obtain some kind of control over the conditions under which he lives.[73]

Individualism, as Webb put it elsewhere, cannot survive the advent of the masses to political power. Or, as John Burns agreed, working people

---

72 H. Spencer, *An Autobiography* (London, 1904), ii. 367–9. See also ibid., i. 221, ii. 55–6; Spencer's letters to J. S. Mill, in D. Duncan, *The Life and Letters of Herbert Spencer* (London, 1908), pp. 93, 94–5; and his *Principles of Sociology* (London, 1876–96), ii. 593.

73 Labour, R. Com., Minutes of Evidence, 4th Report, 1893–4 (vol. xxxix), C. 7063-I, q. 3935.

now possessed through elective institutions the power 'to embody in law their economic and material desires.'[74]

What many feared, too, was that a wider franchise giving the vote to those who were themselves property-less would entail not merely measures of social reform and so some redistribution of wealth but an attack upon the institution of private property itself. This was really the nub of the matter and was grasped right at the outset of the reform movement as the speeches of Peel and Wellington during the debates of 1831 make quite clear.[75] But perhaps the paradigmatic response is that of Macaulay in his Commons' speech in 1842 on Duncombe's motion about the People's Charter. 'The essence of the Charter', Macaulay said, in giving his reasons for opposition, 'is universal suffrage'. He went on:

> If you withhold that, it matters not very much what else you grant. If you grant that, it matters not at all what else you withhold. If you grant that the country is lost . . . . My firm conviction is that, in our country, universal suffrage is incompatible, not with this or that form of government, but with all forms of government, and with everything for the sake of which forms of government exist; that it is incompatible with property, and that it is consequently incompatible with civilisation . . . . If it be admitted that on the institution of property the well-being of society depends, it follows surely that it would be madness to give supreme power in the state to a class which would not be likely to respect that institution . . . .

The Charter, he continued, would give working men 'absolute and irresistible power'. They will become a majority impossible to resist and in 'every constituent body capital will be placed at the feet of labour; knowledge will be borne down by ignorance; and is it possible to doubt what the result must be? . . . What could follow but one vast spoliation?' He envisaged indeed, as an almost inevitable consequence of further electoral reform, a deepening state of social chaos in which the best that could be expected was the restoration of order by 'a strong military despotism'.[76] An equally famous example of concern on this truly

---

74 S. Webb, 'The Basis of Socialism: Historic', in G. B. Shaw *et al.*, *Fabian Essays* (1889; Jubilee edn, London, 1950), p. 56; J. Burns, *The Unemployed*, Fabian tract no. 47 (1893; London, 1906), p. 18. For similar radical or Socialist opinion, see e.g. T. S. Ashton (ed.), *Toynbee's Industrial Revolution* (1884; Newton Abbot, 1969), pp. 137, 149, 179; S. Olivier, 'The Basis of Socialism: Moral', in *Fabian Essays* (edn cit.), p. 116; H. Bland, 'The Outlook', ibid., pp. 190, 199; S. Webb, *The Difficulties of Individualism*, Fabian tract no. 69 (1896; London, 1906), pp. 6, 14–15; R. H. Tawney, *The Agrarian Problem in the Sixteenth Century* (1912; New York, n.d.), p. 341.

75 See the speeches in R. J. White (ed.), *The Conservative Tradition* (1950; 2nd edn, London, 1964), pp. 151–6.

76 Macaulay, *The Miscellaneous Writings and Speeches* (London, 1889), pp. 625–6, 629.

crucial point was Robert Lowe's rejection of reform in 1867: 'Once give the [working] men votes, and the machinery is ready to launch those votes in one compact mass upon the institutions and property of this country.'[77] Clearly, then, it was anticipated that the extension of the suffrage would set government power to work in this very radical way.

There was indeed a simple inter-relationship between the growth of state intervention and extensions of the franchise. Once the process of voting reform was under way, politicians quickly realized that in order to win office and keep themselves there they had to appeal to the growing electorate, to indulge in what has lately been called 'market politics' or 'the welfare auction'. They had to cadge votes, to sway popular emotions, and to concede interests on an ever larger scale. At the same time as (in response to this tendency and to other factors) government intervention increased, then the demand grew that the expanding state, because it did so much, should be made still more representative and responsible. The process was, therefore, self-feeding in this regard. As well, the extension of popular election entailed the possibility of a mass turnover of seats on an unprecedented scale; governments began to get large majorities and so to be more stable. This enabled them to be more consistently active at a time when the tactical situation seemed to require this. The development of labour representation, in time through a specific Labour Party, assisted this same tendency. It was a portent of the future and no coincidence that the Labour Representation League was formed in 1869 and, in the following year, fought its first election to get a working man into Parliament. Sixteen years later, on the eve of a further increment of franchise reform, there were ten such representatives in the Commons and the TUC had revived the idea of a separate Labour Party.[78]

No doubt much that was useful was achieved through this process of electoral competition. But in some respects the 'art of momentarily pleasing the people' could, as Auberon Herbert saw it, seem 'not very noble'.[79] At the worst, the policy auction could be little different from bribery. Lord Bramwell is reported to have remarked, 'A candidate used to gain a seat by paying £5 to each elector; the practice was said to be illegal, it certainly was expensive. A candidate now gains a seat by promising the electors part of their neighbours' property; the practice is said to be legal, it certainly is expensive.'[80] A party could only obtain an

77 R. Lowe, *Speeches and Letters on Reform*, 2nd edn (London, 1867), pp. 54–5. Cf. ibid., pp. 76–7. This little book is probably the most able and concise presentation of the anti-reform case that emerged from the contemporary debates. See, too, the account of the position adopted by Robert Cecil and others in the 1860s in R. B. McDowell, *British Conservatism 1832–1914* (London, 1959), pp. 76–80.

78 M. Beer, *A History of British Socialism* (1919; London, 1953), ii. 223–4.

79 A. Herbert, *A Politician in Trouble About his Soul* (London, 1884), pp. 204–5.

80 Cited in R. H. Murray, *Studies in the English Social and Political Thinkers of the Nineteenth Century* (Cambridge, 1929), ii. 372.

effective majority through the offer of some benefit, and this had to be extracted from the pockets of the wealthy.[81] Perhaps the sort of appeal involved is typified in a particularly crude and blatant form of electoral bribery by George's offer of '9d. for 4d.' during the campaign over the National Insurance Bill in 1911.

Of course, it is not the case that this sort of pressures arising from electoral reform was alone the occasion for collectivist development, aspects of which were already under way before the main extensions of the franchise took place. Nor must it be supposed that so-called working-class interest was necessarily united or moved only in one direction. It seems, for instance, that many of the poorer voters were very hostile to sanitary improvement because of its cost, while others objected for all sorts of reasons to such reforms as the supervision of child labour or the introduction of old-age pensions.[82] It by no means follows that because a political democracy is established a particular type of policy or legislation will necessarily follow in all cases.[83] There is no naturalistic law involved in this. Yet it is undoubtedly true that, as the British experience found out, the kind of collectivist measures that before the mid-nineteenth century were concessions afterwards increasingly appeared in the guise of political necessities. As Cobbett said in 1825 (with a rash of capitals): if the working people are not yet 'A GREAT INTEREST' then by and by they will become one.[84] Perhaps the general effect of all these electoral changes might be summed up by a passage from George Meredith's novel *Beauchamp's Career* first published in 1875:

> . . . the people are the Power to come. Oppressed, unprotected, abandoned; left to the ebb and flow of the tides of the market, now taken on to work, now cast off to starve, committed to the shifting laws of demand and supply, slaves of Capital – the whited name for old accursed Mammon: . . . they are . . . the power . . . . What if, when they have learnt to use their majority, sick of deceptions and the endless pulling of interests, they raise ONE representative to force the current of action with an authority as little fictitious as their preponderance of numbers ? . . . Ask . . . why they should not have comfort for pay as well as the big round . . . '*belly-class*!'[85]

81 Cf. the bitter comments of 'A Plain Tory', in *Tory Democracy and Conservative Policy* (London, 1892), p. 4.

82 For the case of sanitary reform, see Keith-Lucas, *The English Local Government Franchise*, pp. 70, 225.

83 Cf. A. V. Dicey, *Lectures on the Relation between Law & Public Opinion in England during the Nineteenth Century* (1905; 2nd edn, London, 1920), pp. 55–61.

84 W. Cobbett, *Rural Rides* (1830; Everyman, 1966), i.296.

85 G. Meredith, *Beauchamp's Career* (1875; London, 1914), pp. 325–6 (capitals and italics in original). Cf. Kipling's lines cited at p. 170 above.

This was the power to be exerted in future through the ballot box; and the 'ONE representative' was not a despot in the old style but an active representative government in the new. There would be no revolution in Britain, at least not a violent one based on irresistible if evanescent enthusiasm, but rather, through the process of electoral democracy, what the acute French observer, Frédéric Bastiat, called 'a slow social cataclysm, changing all the conditions of life and of society'. For (as Dicey said) the English constitution is a machine which for good or evil gives effect more immediately than any other polity to the opinion of the governing class, now a wide electorate.[86].

Thus the power of Parliamentary sovereignty was set to work in the aftermath of successive extensions of the franchise. But there was a further inherent motive force involved in the sense that, once any administrative change was begun, it tended to develop a thrust of its own.

INCREMENTALISM; OR, ADMINISTRATIVE MOMENTUM

Momentum .... 4b ... in popular use applied to the effect of inertia in the continuance of motion after the impulse has ceased; ....
OED, i.1834

Nineteenth-century observers often commented on the phenomenon that R. Lambert has called the 'self-expanding administrative process' and recognized that it underlay much of the growth of government activity which occurred.[87] A great deal of state intervention began in a piecemeal and diffident, even reluctant, fashion. Many or even most of the influential people in society were formally committed to a belief in *laissez faire* and self-help, in freedom of contract and free trade; and though they might admit the virtues of local self-government, equally they hardly wished to encourage a great deal of activity on its part and were certainly hostile to the growth of centralized power either of regular government offices or extra-departmental agencies. Yet the pressure of circumstances led to sporadic neglect of these principles, public action being recognized as necessary in what were regarded as special cases or conditions, as with the protection of children working in mines and factories or the

86 F. Bastiat, *Cobden et la ligue* (1845), in Sir Louis Mallet's introduction to F. W. Chesson (ed.), *The Political Writings of Richard Cobden* (1867; 4th edn, London, 1903), vol. i, p. xxxi; Dicey to J. Bryce (14 August 1898) in R. S. Rait (ed.), *Memorials of A. V. Dicey* ... (London, 1925), pp.148–9.
87 The concept appears in Sir John Simon's annual report for 1850 as City of London Medical Officer: see R. Lambert, *Sir John Simon, 1816–1904, and English Social Administration* (London, 1963), pp.168–9. On the self-generating administrative tendencies involved, cf. ibid., pp.224–5, 236–7, 437, 456–7, 460 n.95.

prevention of epidemic disease. And this proved in practice to be the genesis of much more than was originally intended, for the device of regulative supervision seemed often to generate its own momentum and to constitute a self-sustaining tendency.[88] Moreover it became a kind of habit, an automatic official response to difficulties of all kinds. So that by the end of the century Sidney Webb, noting the inadvertent nature of collectivist growth, observed the antithesis between attitudes still held in principle and actual practice. Each minister of state, he said, 'protests against Socialism' – that is, government control – 'in the abstract, but every decision that he gives in his own department leans more and more away from the Individualist side.'[89]

The fact of this inherent and cumulative process of government growth, and that it took place almost despite generally prevailing opinions or prejudices has, then, long been recognized and is often, above all, associated with the work of such officials as Chadwick, Simon, and Kay. And latterly there has been some interesting controversy among historians about the manner of this process and the factors which occasioned it, in particular about the part played by Benthamite and similar ideas as compared with practical administrative necessity. One of the principals in this debate, Professor O. MacDonagh, has suggested a plausible account of how these developments may be seen to have occurred, 'a description, in convenient general terms, of a very powerful impulse or tendency, always immanent in the middle quarters of the nineteenth century, and extraordinarily often, though by no means invariably, realized in substance.'[90] Naturally not every specific increment of administrative regulation and authority will, in its appearance and detail, correspond with the outline described because a varying array of factors is involved in each case. Nevertheless the scheme of analysis is undoubtedly the most appropriate so far suggested and has often been exemplified in particular contexts.[91]

88 H. Spencer, *The Man Versus the State* (1884; Penguin, 1969), pp. 92–4.

89 S. Webb, *The Difficulties of Individualism*, Fabian tract no. 69 (1896; London, 1906), p. 18.

90 O. MacDonagh, 'The Nineteenth-Century Revolution in Government: a Reappraisal', *Historical Journal*, i (1958), pp. 52–67: the citation in the text is at p. 61.

91 See e.g. other examples of Professor MacDonagh's own work: 'Emigration and the State, 1835–55: an Essay in Administrative History', *Trans.R.Hist.S.*, 5s, v (1955), pp. 133–59; 'Delegated Legislation and Administrative Discretions in the 1850's; a Particular Study', *Victorian Studies*, ii (1958–9), pp. 29–44; *A Pattern of Government Growth: the Passenger Acts and their Enforcement, 1800–1860* (London, 1961); 'Coal Mines Regulation: the First Decade, 1842–1852', in R. Robson (ed.), *Ideas and Institutions of Victorian Britain* (London, 1967), ch. 3. See also U. Henriques, 'Jeremy Bentham and the Machinery of Social Reform', in H. Hearder and H. R. Loyn (eds), *British Government and Administration* (Cardiff, 1974), esp. p. 173 and n. 13. On the question of coal mines regulation, cf. the view of A. Heeson, 'The Coal Mines Act of 1842, Social Reform, and Social Control', *Historical Journal*, xxiv (1981), pp. 69–88. See also the papers cited below at p. 256 n. 66.

Five stages to the process of incremental administrative growth are distinguished. First of all there was commonly the public exposure of a social evil or problem: a mine or railway accident that might have been avoided, a government or similar report about insanitary housing conditions, about the bad social and economic effects of illiteracy, or something of that kind. The nature and impact of information of this sort has already been mentioned in the preceding chapter. Then there was a demand that the preventable or intolerable circumstances thus revealed be dealt with. Legislation was proposed to cope with these exigencies; the interests concerned would oppose it; and the outcome was some compromise involving perhaps a weakening of the statutory restrictions originally envisaged. But a precedent for action had been established and a responsibility assumed. An example is the railway accident which occurred at Sonning on the Great Western line on Christmas Eve 1841 in which eight third-class passengers were killed and seventeen injured. This event and the public reaction to it contributed to the movement for the reform of third-class railway travel and so to Gladstone's 1844 Act.[92] The second stage ensued with the realization that existing legislation was ineffective, perhaps almost wholly so, was perhaps little more than 'an amateur expression of good intentions'. The obvious remedy was to appoint enforcement officers especially charged with carrying the existing statutes into effect. The initial work of such an inspectorate would quickly reveal the deficiencies of the law and so lead, thirdly, to the demand for more substantial powers as also for the need for adequate central authority to make the work of these agents uniform, to support it against opposition, and to supervise the collection of evidence and further proposals for reform. That experienced public servant, Lord Stamp, noted this tendency in a perceptive comment made in 1924 to the effect that with every activity the government assumed had also come 'the experience that laws without administrative agents are vain, and thence the gamut of inspectors and expert preventers or encouragers or checkers. These, in turn, form their accumulation of expert experience and knowledge, and throw up the subject matter of new legislation.'[93]

92 For this and other similar occurrences and the way subsequent safety developments were initiated, see H. Perkin, The Age of the Railway (1970; Newton Abbot, 1971), pp. 108–10; L. T. C. Rolt, Red for Danger: a History of Railway Accidents and Railway Safety (1955; Pan, 1978), p. 38. On the question of supervision as opposed to control and on the role of legislation, see ibid., pp. 17–19, 40–3, 104, 164–5, 192–3.

93 Sir Josiah Stamp, 'Recent Tendencies Towards the Devolution of Legislative Functions to the Administration', Public Administration, ii (1924), p. 25. On the crucial importance of the inspectorates as a dynamic of administrative change, see also Henriques, loc. cit., pp. 175–8; Clark, The Making of Victorian England, p. 281 and his An Expanding Society, Britain 1830–1900 (Cambridge, 1967), pp. 138–9.

Fourthly, further experience would show that occasional Parliamentary legislation would never be enough to deal with the matters at issue, that what was needed was a continuing process of regulation in the light of growing and changing experience. So that, finally, the executive officers would demand and receive a discretionary initiative to deal with the complex problems arising in practice. In addition, they would branch out into other fields of action: making systematic and experimental investigations, keeping in touch with relevant technical development and foreign experience. They would sometimes even acquire responsibilities quite outside their normal field of operation as when the factory inspectorate was given the job of carrying out emergency public health measures in the industrial districts during an epidemic.[94] Inherent in this whole process there was a strong and cumulative trend towards a much more dynamic role for government than had usually been envisaged. Sceptics like Herbert Spencer saw it quite differently, of course, as a sad process in which the failure of a legislative scheme led to its amendment, further trials, fresh plans, more failures, and yet more schemes for action without it being grasped that it was the regulative enterprise itself which was inappropriate, necessarily defective, bound to result in rigidity of social organization, and thus either domestic collapse or destruction from without.[95] But at the least such libertarian criticism was an acknowledgement that the development was indeed well under way, that (as Professor MacDonagh has it) 'a new sort of state was being born.'[96]

In abstract outline this is the story of the 'interior momentum' behind many of the reforms of the last century especially of the period 1825–75.[97] Thus it describes the process of factory reform and emigration control; educational change emerged after this fashion as described earlier; and it has been conclusively shown that in varied ways the same kind of development took place in the field of public health. For instance, the process of intervention in respect of vaccination had an 'inherent dynamism' of its own. R. J. Lambert, who has studied the matter in detail, reports that 'Each time a private investigation followed by medical pressure and a private Bill induced an otherwise uninformed and indifferent Government to interfere. The failure of each step, proved and publicized by expert report, paved the way for yet another extension

94 N. McCord, 'Some Limitations of the Age of Reform', in Hearder and Loyn, op. cit., pp. 200–1.

95 H. Spencer, *Social Statics* (1851; Farnborough, 1970), pp. 10–12; *The Principles of Sociology* (London, 1895–1902), ii. 257, 261–2; *The Study of Sociology* (1873; Ann Arbor, Mich., 1961), pp. 145ff.

96 O. MacDonagh, 'The Nineteenth-Century Revolution in Government: a Reappraisal', loc. cit., p. 61.

97 Cf. the various case studies in MacDonagh's *Early Victorian Government 1830–1870* (London, 1977); the phrase cited is from p. 61.

of interference.'[98] Similarly the genesis and development of the legislation governing explosives, passed between 1860 and 1875, conforms in
close detail to the MacDonagh model.[99] Moreover the need for this
supervision was recognized by the official primarily concerned to be
necessary in the public interest even though he believed that in principle
all state interference in industrial life was 'absolutely contrary' to the
basic tenets of 'economical science'.[100] The control and prevention of
food adulteration developed after the same pattern.[101] Equally,
MacDonagh's model covers quite closely the development of charity
reform and supervision.[102] But perhaps one of the best examples of the
kind of incrementalism here under review is provided by the work of the
Local Government Act Office of the Home Department between 1858
and 1871.[103] There had been strong resistance to any central control over
local authorities in respect of public health duties as witnessed by the
reform of the General Board of Health in 1854 after Chadwick's
resignation. And the Local Government Act of 1858 was premeditated on
the basis of preventing any further growth of centralized supervision.
Moreover most of the officials in the newly established Local Government Act Office were themselves dedicated to sustaining local autonomy.
However, despite this firm intention, the superintending responsibilities
of the Office continued to increase and one of the main reasons for this
was simply the pressure of demand for advice and help from the localities
themselves. The local boards of health and the sanitary and nuisance
authorities very often had no experience or knowledge of the technical
problems concerned – sanitary science was in its infancy, of course – or
even of the elements of law and procedure involved, and were also
appalled by the cost of the schemes their duties seemed to require. Almost
inevitably many of them turned to the more experienced inspectors in the
central department as a major source of assistance in dealing with these

98 R. J. Lambert, 'A Victorian National Health Service: State Vaccination, 1855–71',
    Historical Journal, v (1962), pp. 3, 17. An early study of factory legislation in cognate
    terms is M. W. Thomas, 'The Origins of Administrative Centralisation', *Current
    Legal Problems* (1950), pp. 214–35.
99 J. H. Pellew, 'The Home Office and the Explosives Act of 1875', *Victorian Studies*,
    xviii (1974–5), pp. 175–94, esp. p. 176.
100 ibid., p. 193.
101 See the account in H. Perkin, *The Origins of Modern English Society 1780–1880*
    (1969; London, 1972), pp. 440–2.
102 D. Owen, *English Philanthropy, 1660–1960* (London, 1965), p. 208 n. 110.
103 For this brief account, I draw on R. M. Gutchen, 'Local Improvements and
    Centralization in Nineteenth-Century England', *Historical Journal*, iv (1961),
    pp. 85–96; and esp. R. Lambert, 'Central and Local Relations in Mid-Victorian
    England: the Local Government Act Office, 1858–71', *Victorian Studies*, vi
    (1962–3), pp. 121–50.

difficult matters. Dr Lambert sums up by saying that the growth of the LGAO is

> a prime instance of that force which occasioned so much state expansion – the self-sustaining and self-generating impulse of administration itself . . . . It found itself unable to follow the dictates of constitutional theory and abdicate its duties . . . . Administrative expediency proved a dynamic and self-educative impulse in the L.G.A.O. as much as in the Medical Department of the Privy Council and elsewhere in central government.[104]

Nor, therefore, was this development the outcome of personal idiosyncrasy or theoretical influence so much as an unintended growth.

Yet in some respects it can be seen to have been inevitable. For if a body of able and sedulous men is put in charge of a branch of the public service, it is (as one commentator has observed) 'certain that they will magnify their office, take a disproportionate view of its claims, and incessantly strive to increase its functions and its staff.'[105] Though it is not necessary to take this implied hostile stance, the point is clear: those involved in the machinery of administrative control will themselves demand and often secure its extension. Goschen had remarked the point in the 1880s when he wrote that the 'successful performance of a certain set of duties by a public department inspires its administrators with the natural desire to extend their sphere of acknowledged usefulness.' 'The more', he adds, 'the public puts upon civil servants, the more will civil servants offer to do for the public.'[106] And during the last century or so this process has intensified not least as the administrative organization was itself made more efficient by various reforms and changes. There might be legitimate and widespread objection to the extension of the powers of government officers who are part of a corrupt and inefficient set of arrangements. But once administration and its personnel are improved this objection can no longer stand in its pure form. So the reform of the Civil Service – for instance, by the adoption of open competition as a means of recruitment – could not but produce in time government offices staffed by men of talent, purpose, and initiative whose career this was, and who would naturally wish to extend their range of functions and make them more effective not least in duty to the community they served. And because their professional integrity was increasingly accepted so, therefore, were the claims to greater authority.

---

104 Lambert, art. cit., pp.149–50.
105 Ramsay Muir, 'The Machinery of Government', in Lord Robert Cecil et al., Essays in Liberalism (London, 1922), p.123.
106 G. J. Goschen, . . . Laissez-Faire and Government Interference (London, 1883), pp.16–17.

It has been well noted that it was the devotion to its functions of a reformed public service that 'has been in a large degree responsible for the development of the positive state.'[107]

Critics of collectivism saw, indeed, that the larger the machinery of bureaucratic control is permitted to grow, the more difficult it becomes to reorganize let alone reduce it. Hence the often fervent opposition to what Toulmin Smith called 'presumptuous *empiricism*' in administrative growth. An office established to perform a specific function acquires an interest in the maintenance of its own structure, an interest which continues even when the need for the function has passed away. As Spencer bitterly observed, the community as a whole becomes habituated to the existence of these offices and their growth:

> In proportion as public agencies occupy a larger space in daily experience, there comes a greater tendency to think of public control as everywhere needful, and a less ability to think of activities as otherwise controlled. At the same time the sentiments, adjusted by habit to the regulative machinery, become enlisted on its behalf, and adverse to the thought of a vacancy to be made by its absence.[108]

Those affected by and subject to state control might thus demand its extension or more effective enforcement: as the 'good' manufacturer might quickly develop an interest in seeing that government inspectors effectively imposed the standards required by legislation on all his competitors. Similarly the professions concerned with the problems of the day, especially the engineers, would be anxious to use their expertise to tackle difficulties in drainage, sanitation, ventilation, and so on. In these and similar ways, then, the extent of interventionist legislation already on the statute book contributed greatly to the moral and intellectual atmosphere in which collectivist ideas would flourish and abound.[109]

Nor has this sort of impetus diminished. Many policies adopted by modern government deal with enormously complex matters and a long time often elapses between the original decision and the completion of the task. Once such a major scheme is initiated it develops a momentum that is maintained or even increased over a lengthy period. Decisions taken to build a motorway network, to introduce a new weapons system, or to reform secondary schooling on comprehensive lines are obviously

107 H. J. Laski, *Democracy in Crisis* (London, 1933), p.99. On the process of Civil Service reform, see *A Much-Governed Nation*, ch. 4.
108 J. T. Smith, *Government by Commissions Illegal and Pernicious* (London, 1849), p.367 (italics in original); H. Spencer, *The Principles of Sociology*, ii.255–6.
109 Cf. A. V. Dicey, *Lectures on the Relation between Law & Public Opinion in England during the Nineteenth Century* (1905; 2nd edn, London, 1920), pp.301–2.

matters of this sort with ramifying consequences and a prolonged process of implementation. They are, moreover, the sort of decisions which it is difficult to alter once taken.[110] And those familiar with Parkinson's Laws will recognize them as simply a series of latter-day reflections on this long-standing process of inherent and incremental administrative growth.

CHANGING ATTITUDES TOWARDS GOVERNMENT

. . . a tone of political feeling which has so completely passed away that it is
somewhat difficult to realise the power which it once possessed . . . .
W.E.H. LECKY, Democracy and Liberty, new edn, 1899, i.7

In a most stimulating essay Professor Norman Baker has argued that in the early 1780s 'a significant change in public attitudes' occurred in respect of 'the expectations entertained of government and the willingness to increase its powers'.[111] Prior to this period and once the Protestant succession was secure, men of political substance and influence were broadly satisfied with the prevailing order and felt that the functions of government could properly be limited to the maintenance of peace and stability at home, defence, diplomacy, the collection of the revenue, and the like: and even in what was thus required, the effective administration was often conducted at a local level. Government was not expected to involve itself in any direct way 'in the provocation or supervision of industrial or technical change', a situation in noticeable contrast with that of contemporary France. Nor, of course, was there to hand appropriate administrative machinery for close centralized control even if it had been desired to exercise it. In general Britain's affairs seemed to be adequately sustained in peace and war with things as they were; on the whole ministers were not anxious to reduce, by reform, opportunities for patronage, while the opposition prevented its substantial increase; the independents dominated the system of local government and would thus resist any increase in central power, not only because of its cost but also because it could only be attained at the expense of their provincial authority.[112] Traditionally British government was supposed to be limited, checked, and balanced through the ancient constitution of the

---

110 See e.g. J. K. Galbraith, *The New Industrial State* (London, 1967), p.13; and T. A. Smith, *Anti-Politics: Consensus, Reform and Protest in Britain* (London, 1972), pp.38–9.

111 N. Baker, 'Changing Attitudes Towards Government in Eighteenth-Century Britain', in A. Whiteman *et al.*, *Statesmen, Scholars and Merchants* (Oxford, 1973), p.202.

112 ibid., pp.202–7.

realm, and any possibility of 'arbitrary' power was jealously watched.[113] Similarly, proposals for reform, like those of the 1760s, always had these conventional reservations in mind. Burke, for instance, exemplified this syndrome of attitudes both generally and in his assessment of the need for domestic political change: where undertaken, its object should be to restore the balance of prescriptive institutions and not to increase the power of the executive.[114] Nor was there, at this stage, any 'administrative momentum', any innate bureaucratic drive to expansion. Even in domestic terms, difficulties of communication simply reinforced a general laxness in compliance to orders; the system of recruitment, appointment, and promotion based on patronage and nomination and stressing connexion and self-service rather than efficiency – that is, the 'very nature of government employment' – dictated 'the slow pace of its machinery' and the performance of government employees. In such circumstances, there could be no Civil Service at all in the modern sense, no sustained bureaucratic drive or ambition.[115] Nor was there really any reason why, to a contemporary, there should have appeared to be any serious deficiencies in British arrangements:

> . . . the facts must be faced that in the period 1715–75 Britain won her wars, avoided major social unrest, expanded her colonial acquisitions, and enjoyed general prosperity, by the standards of pre-industrial society. This was achieved without the assumption of sweeping new powers . . . . Government fulfilled much of that which was expected of it, and thus no major impetus was created for a change in attitude towards or within government.

But, Professor Baker goes on, a change was imminent: and it was the War of American Independence which marked 'a decisive turning-point in both the performance of government and attitudes towards it.' It was widely felt the war should have been won; the defeat was expensive and the tax burden involved onerous, trade was lost, and there were other economic difficulties emerging: high food prices, a substantial level of

---

113 See e.g. J. T. Boulton, 'Arbitrary Power: an Eighteenth-Century Obsession', *Studies in Burke and His Time*, ix (1967–8), pp.905–26. Also J. G. A. Pocock, *The Ancient Constitution and the Feudal Law* (Cambridge, 1957), esp. ch.ix; and his *Politics, Language and Time* (London, 1972), chs.4, 6.

114 Burke's concern with the avoidance of 'arbitrary power' is clearly revealed by his part in the Hastings impeachment: see my 'Burke and State Necessity: the Case of Warren Hastings', in R. Schnur (ed.), *Staatsräson* (Berlin, 1975), pp.549–67.

115 Baker, loc. cit., pp.208–11; H. Parris, *Constitutional Bureaucracy: the Development of British Central Administration Since the Eighteenth Century* (London, 1969), pp.21–8.

unemployment, a rise in bankruptcies, and the like. As a result, the whole structure of government was called into question.[116]

In these circumstances there began to be heard criticism of administrative practices and procedures hitherto accepted complacently and almost uncritically. The short-lived Rockingham ministry took steps to reduce the role of influence and patronage and thus to initiate a change in attitudes to public employment with a stress on 'service' rather than 'place'. The 'economical reform' movement with which Burke was associated was part of this tendency. As Prime Minister, Shelburne too was committed to administrative reform: the Treasury was reorganized, accounting procedures were regularized, sinecures and fees reduced, a new career structure initiated, and a control of departmental papers implemented. All these changes, says Professor Baker, pointed towards 'a new conception of service in which responsibility and honesty were given pride of place within a more institutional framework . . . . The established traditions of government service had been challenged'. In more cases than before, government began to rely on the professional skill of experts; specialization of work in departments was emphasized; more attempts were made to acquire proper information and statistics as a basis for decision. The Treasury began to emerge as the department crucial to central control of both administrative efficiency and financial accountability. And these improvements in the machinery of government were a necessary step in a processs by which Parliament would recognize the possibility of increasing executive power and responsibility. 'Without the changes that began to make both government as a whole and individual government officials more accountable, more responsible, honest, and accessible, it is highly unlikely that Parliament would gradually have come to grant more powers to government and accept its expanding role in society.' There is no doubt, then, that the 'standards by which government was judged for much of the eighteenth century changed after 1782. What had been acceptable earlier was no longer tolerable'.[117]

To this has to be added the effect of changes in crucial constitutional relationships. As the principle is established that the king must govern by the advice of ministers approved by the House of Commons, Parliament is more easily prepared to entrust the Crown with a greater range of powers. In the seventeenth century the Commons wanted to keep ministers out of the House (as indicated by an abortive clause in the Act of Settlement); during the next century this view gradually changed. The

116   Baker, loc. cit., pp. 211–12. Cf. H. Roseveare, *The Treasury: the Evolution of a British Institution* (London, 1969), p. 99; G. E. Aylmer, 'From Office-Holding to Civil Service: the Genesis of Modern Bureaucracy', *Trans. R. Hist. S.*, xxx (1980), pp. 103–4.

117   Baker, loc. cit., pp. 214–19. Cf. Roseveare, op. cit., pp. 118–29.

House got used to having ministers before it; it could support and criticize them as individuals or as a group; it saw them as the leaders of a party with a base in the country rather than as representatives of the monarch simply.[118] That is to say, Parliament came to accept ministers as being constitutionally responsible and, given this, was more prepared to grant them powers than would otherwise have been the case. Legislation increasingly became the business of the ministry rather than the private member and became, too, more systematic and continuous.[119]

And, of course, these tendencies of change in both institutions and attitudes towards them continued during the following period with the Crimean War constituting the same kind of climacteric or symbol as the American Revolutionary War in the previous century.[120] Thus ministries become more responsible to an increasingly representative Parliament; the Civil Service is reformed and becomes more efficient; the contemporary problems create pressures demanding action; and the more highly organized parties coming into existence become the political engines to set this machine acceptably in motion. The result is that people now look to government for a much greater intensity and range of intervention than before: and so 'the inexorable pressures' to collectivism mount as popular demand increases.[121]

A *Times* editorial of 1873 noticed the change of attitudes which was occurring and described it as 'the greatest wonder' of the day. Two or three decades before, it said, 'Government management' was 'synonymous with waste, miscarriage, extravagance, and every other incident of commercial failure' and the 'spending Departments of the State were pointed at as frightful examples of maladministration'. But the 'change which has now come over the spirit of the age is almost incredible' due at least in part to the 'growing conviction that "the State" ought to do more for the people than it does', and that 'Government work is better done than any other work'.[122] L. T. Hobhouse wrote in 1897 that when the basis of government was thus changed, becoming more efficient and responsible to the people as a whole, the opinion of 'the consistent democrat' was substantially modified. He was no longer in permanent opposition to government but instead saw in it 'a machine which he may hope to control in the interest of the public' so that the old *laissez faire*

---

118 Cf. F. W. Maitland, *The Constitutional History of England* (1908; Cambridge, 1974), p. 396.

119 O. MacDonagh, *Early Victorian Government 1830–1870* (London, 1977), pp. 5–6.

120 There is a superb account of the administrative and political consequences of the Crimean conflict in O. Anderson, *A Liberal State at War: English Politics and Economics during the Crimean War* (London, 1967).

121 The Constitution, R. Com. Rep., 1972–3 (vol. xi), Cmnd. 5460, p. 79 §244. Cf. ibid., p. 80 §246.

122 *The Times* (27 March 1873), p. 9.

view was becoming quite untenable.[123] In a similar vein Alfred Marshall noted after the Great War that, as the power of the people 'to govern the Government that governed them' slowly increased, it became possible to entrust to public authority many tasks 'which would have been grossly mismanaged' in the first half of the nineteenth century and which 'would have been hot-beds of corruption in the eighteenth'. As a result 'a certain new tendency to a widening of the appropriate functions of Government gradually set in.'[124] Thus, during the course of a century or so, were beliefs about government and its role completely transformed.

Nor were the changes in social structure without their effect in this regard. What H. G. Wells called the 'deliquescence' of the old social order created a diverse social welter from which emerged various views of government.

The political dominance of the landed aristocracy and gentry declined though very slowly and important positions of authority and influence were long retained, not to mention a formal power of legislative veto. But these privileges were gradually undermined by legal and executive action and by the loss of any special position of wealth. The introduction of open competition in the public service (in place of appointment by patronage and nomination) was another step in this direction though for long mitigated by the dominance of the public school and Oxbridge in the educational system. The abolition of purchase in the army symbolized a similar step, though again the most senior ranks – at least until quite recently perhaps – continued to be a monopoly of the upper or gentry classes.[125] The extension of the franchise was crucial. In due time and together with the introduction of the ballot and redistribution it brought an end, for instance, to the system of patronage boroughs. Similarly there was a sea change in local administration as when the nominated bench of justices was formally replaced by elected councils as the main organ of county government. The character of the House of Lords was equally altered: old families were swamped by new creations many of them representative of industry and trade. By 1923 there were

123 L. T. Hobhouse, 'The Ethical Basis of Collectivism', *International Journal of Ethics*, viii (1897–8), p. 143.

124 A. Marshall, *Industry and Trade* (1919; 4th edn, London, 1923), pp. 42–3. Cf. the earlier comments of G. J. Goschen, . . . *Laissez-Faire and Government Interference* (London, 1883), pp. 19–20; and H. Samuel, *Liberalism* (London, 1902), pp. 23–5.

125 See e.g. C. B. Otley, 'The Social Origins of British Army Officers', *Sociological Review*, xviii (1970), pp. 213–39; and the fuller account in his *The Origins and Recruitment of the British Army Elite, 1870–1959* (PhD, University of Hull, 1965); also P. E. Razzell, 'Social Origins of Officers in the Indian and British Home Army: 1758–1962', *British Journal of Sociology*, xiv (1963), pp. 248–60. On the symbolic and practical role in this context of the Crimean experience, see Anderson, op. cit., pp. 102–4, 107, 111, 128.

708 lay peers of whom 420 had been created since Victoria came to the throne and of this latter number 176 had been created since 1910.[126] A single comparison may symbolize the nature of this social alteration in a crucial political respect. The Whig reform Cabinet of 1830 had thirteen members of whom nine were peers while, of the remaining four, one held an Irish peerage, one was heir to a peerage, and one was a baronet; there was only one untitled commoner among them and he became a peer himself five years later.[127] Compare with this the make-up of a modern government in which there may be two or three peers of convenience and a member of the old-style landed gentry is an increasingly rare creature.[128] What has happened in the interval is thus clearly signalled. It was a process affected, of course, partly by the relative decline of agriculture but above all by progressive taxation of income, in particular by the estate and similar duties on inheritance. A latter-day Tory comment on Harcourt's increase in the death duties in the early 1890s is apt: this was 'a tax which was to become the means of gradually depriving the landed gentry of the resources of progress and service. It was a slower, more painless extinction than the guillotine or the lamp-post' – but extinction it was.[129] All this meant the parallel decline, or better the dilution, of the aristocratic attitude to the role of government. The essence of this was paternalist protection, the fulfilment of the duties of privilege and status: it was such sentiments that underlay a good deal of the early reformism as embodied in administrative acts and the making of the law. With the disappearance of the old hierarchical society this attitude diminished and, although it continued (as will be seen in the volume on *The Ideological Heritage*) in some attenuated form in Tory sentiments of *noblesse oblige*, the obligations it traditionally entailed were not, in fact, widely assumed by the new aristocracy of industry and finance which often rather abdicated them deliberately.

Of course, the early capitalist entrepreneur necessarily often adopted this protective role: Robert Owen is perhaps the paradigmatic example. Such an employer often lived in a large house near his factory and as such, and because he was a magistrate, dominated paternalistically the affairs of the neighbourhood. But in time he or his successor moved away to live in more salubrious surroundings, the part being taken perhaps by a manager without the same interests, ties, or sense of personal responsibility; and often he was replaced as employer by the relative

126 C. L. Mowat, *Britain Between the Wars, 1918–1940* (1955; London, 1968), p.204.
127 The members of this administration are listed in E. L. Woodward, *The Age of Reform, 1815–1870* (1938; rev. edn, Oxford, 1958), p.635. See also ibid., p.76.
128 I exclude here, of course, those successful radical politicians like R. H. S. Crossman, A. Bevan, and J. Callaghan who have in their prosperity taken to the land.
129 J. Biggs-Davison, *George Wyndham: a Study in Toryism* (London, 1951), p.69.

anonymity of a company so that the problems of living and working were taken up, if at all, by public authority which was increasingly seen as saviour or guardian in this respect. As well, if the earlier feeling of businessmen was one that urged the removal of government interference in economic life, this attitude changed (as has been seen) when powerful competitive forces emerged and government aid was needed. In addition the growing professional classes had been more quickly won to collectivist views. The experts and specialists necessary to an increasingly complex industrial society – accountants, engineers, architects, managers and administrators, and so on – had no necessary association with the attitudes or vested interests of either land or capital. Naturally these will often have been assumed but there was also a concept of professional dedication, of functional efficiency, of wanting to see problems dealt with competently. And such feelings will have merged easily with the cognate notions of public service and the communal interest.

An important political reflection of these mutations is the process so fascinatingly described by Professor J. M. Lee by which traditional 'social leaders' were replaced in positions of power by 'public persons'.[130] The former were those who enjoyed social standing and prestige based on family or wealth and this was the foundation of their political role and influence. The latter – Trollope's Phineas Finn is an excellent symbol of the type – were those who, with little or no wealth or social connexion, acquired status by entering public life and achieving success there as politicians or administrators. And the contrast is harshly (but not unjustly) reflected in a recent judgement that 'Baldwin was born rich and gave away much of his fortune anonymously to the nation, whereas Lloyd George was born in poverty and grew rich on politics'.[131] Of course, these public persons found in time that their power base was either expertise or popular support achieved by election: it entailed dealing actively with the problems of the day and continually being seen to be so engaged. Their position depended on and their attitudes reflected the need to extend political intervention.

Over and above all this is the emergence of the so-called working class and its attitude to government.[132] Of course, it is not a coherent group

130 J. M. Lee, *Social Leaders and Public Persons: a Study of County Government in Cheshire since 1888* (Oxford, 1963), *passim*. The process is seen as part of a longer and wider change concerning the need for technical competence or professionalism in government, ibid., p.6. Cf. C. Hollis, *Can Parliament Survive?* (London, 1949), pp.29–31 on a similar theme.

131 C. Carrington, *Rudyard Kipling: his Life and Work* (1955; Penguin, 1970), p.563.

132 The word 'class' was used to denote important social groupings at least as early as the mid-seventeenth century but was increasingly so employed, with overtones of

and has no single articulate view of politics but one sees what is meant by the phrase. The lower orders, moved away from their traditional 'country' or proliferated in the new towns, were thus brought together in mere multitudes which, though they developed their own social patterns of behaviour, had in the conventional sense little or no feeling of association or community. There was in these agglomerations no personal dependence on squire, parson, or master: such old relationships were (in Arnold Toynbee's phrase) 'shattered by the power-loom and the steam-engine'. For instance, when 'huge factories were established there could no longer be a close tie between the master and his men; the workman hated his employer, and the employer looked on his workmen simply as hands.' Most acutely, Sir Walter Scott had commented earlier on this loosening of social ties also attributing it to the same cause.[133] The railway, above all, enabled working people to move and, as J. S. Mill said in 1848, to 'change their patrons and employers as easily as their coats'; there was no old-fashioned sense of social dependence on their part any more. Yet they were in a new sort of formative subjection in being brought together in large numbers 'to work socially under the same roof'.[134] They were increasingly able to read newspapers and political tracts; Nonconformists and other radicals were suffered to go among them and to appeal to their faculties and feelings in opposition to established creeds and beliefs; equally they were encouraged to seek a share in government through the acquisition of the franchise and by the 1880s many of them had it; there were, too, their own unions and other organizations. At first in alliance with the reforming middle classes, there was common cause against the aristocracy, the gentry, and the traditional society they represented; then, in time, there was the revolt of the unskilled working groups against the aristocracy of labour and the employers. Quite simply what J. S. Mill called 'the progress of the mass of the people in mental cultivation' and the growing political importance of mere numbers was bound to bring in its train demands for legislative

---

antagonism implied, from the last years of the following century. See OED and the new Supplement (1972), sub 'class' §§2, 9 with illustrative citations; also A. Briggs, 'The Language of "Class" in Early Nineteenth-Century England', in A. Briggs and J. Saville (eds), Essays in Labour History (1960; London, 1967), p. 43. At the same time, electoral politics in the mid-nineteenth century is best seen in terms of 'blocs', 'groups', or 'networks' rather than 'classes': see D. C. Moore, The Politics of Deference: a Study of the Mid-Nineteenth Century English Political System (Hassocks, Sussex, 1976), 'Prologue', esp. p. 5; also ibid., p. 414.

133   T. S. Ashton (ed.), Toynbee's Industrial Revolution (Newton Abbot, 1969), p. 148; Sir W. Scott to Viscount Montagu (2 January 1820) in H. J. C. Grierson (ed.), The Letters of Sir Walter Scott 1819–1821 (London, 1934), pp. 103–4.

134   J. S. Mill, 'Principles of Political Economy' (1848), Collected Works, ed. J. M. Robson et al. (London, 1963ff), iii. 762.

intervention.[135] This pressure would be brought to bear either through established parties – which in their different ways were anxious enough to palliate the new political Moloch – or through their own representatives. In the general election of 1906 some fifty Labour Party and Labour Group MPs were elected, most of them of working-class origin. Balfour (who had until the previous year been Prime Minister) wrote to the King's private secretary:

> We have here to do with something much more important than the swing of the pendulum or all the squabbles about Free Trade and Fiscal Reform. We are face to face (no doubt in a milder form) with the Socialistic difficulties which loom so large on the Continent. Unless I am greatly mistaken the election of 1906 inaugurates a new era.

As he wrote, too, in another contemporary letter 'the organized labour party is a novel – and disquieting – factor in Parliamentary life.'[136] Balfour's use of the epithet 'Socialistic' is, however, misleading. Few of these Labour MPs could be so described and those Labour candidates who had stood for election openly under this label were all defeated. Yet the social basis of the new group is clear; as were the potential demands implied in its success, in respect of labour legislation and trade union reform for instance, as well as increased welfare provision. Where the state is not repudiated as an instrument of the ruling class and thereby suspect, it is regarded as the essential means of reform either to help co-operative ventures or to achieve change by substantive interference. It is an attitude which, if in some ways similar to that of the rural labourer who looked to the squire for aid and protection when times were hard, is none the less transformed in scale and scope: it sees the state as cornucopia.

135 ibid., iii. 764.
136 A. Balfour to Lord Knollys (17 January 1906), in Sir Sidney Lee, *King Edward VII: a Biography* (London, 1925–27), ii. 449; Balfour to Lord St. Aldwyn (26 January 1906), in Lady Victoria Hicks Beach, *Life of Sir Michael Hicks Beach* (London, 1932), ii. 224.

5

SCIENCE AND SCIENTISM

. . . Science reaches forth her arms
To feel from world to world, and charms
Her secret from the latest moon . . . .
TENNYSON, *In Memoriam*, 1850, XXI. 18–20

THE DEVELOPMENT of the natural sciences was associated with the growth of collectivism in two main ways. There was its contribution to the formation of general attitudes in particular in respect of scientific method; and there was, more specifically, the way in which scientific discovery provided a practical basis for or invited changes in particular aspects of government policy. Something will be said about each. In addition some of the many forms of naturalistic belief will also be briefly reviewed as they bore on the question of public interest and collective action to achieve it.

SCIENTISM AND THE SPIRIT OF THE AGE

Were we required to characterise this age of ours by any single epithet, we should be tempted to call it, not an Heroical, Devotional, Philosophical, or Moral Age, but, above all others, the Mechanical Age . . . . We may trace this tendency in all the great manifestations of our time; . . . .
T. CARLYLE, 'Signs of the Times', 1829, in *The Works*, 1871–4,
vii. 233, 236

We have lately been reminded in most salutary fashion that intellectual historians are particularly prone to 'zeitgeistitis', a complaint obviously to be avoided.[1] But though it may be difficult (or questionable even) to try to describe a climate of opinion, this does not mean that all aspects of such an atmosphere need be obscure. It is quite clear, for instance, that increasingly during the course of the nineteenth century many observers held to a sense of ineluctable progress based on growing scientific knowledge both pure and applied, past and present successes heralding enormous potential for future advance. Indeed from Bacon onwards the

---

1 I find this amusing neologism (if such it is) in S. Collini, 'Political Theory and the "Science of Society" in Victorian Britain', *Historical Journal*, xxiii (1980), p. 225.

belief in the possibility of a great renewal of learning premeditated on this sort of basis had become more and more buoyant. Nor was it merely laymen who were thus impressed. In 1802 Humphry Davy, in a lecture before the Royal Institution, had (in very Baconian terms) contrasted human beings who were ignorant of scientific processes (and thus at the mercy of nature and the elements) with the civilized man who is

> informed by science and the arts, and in control of powers which may be almost called creative; which have enabled him to modify and change the beings surrounding him, and by his experiments to interrogate nature with power, not simply as a scholar, passive and only seeking to understand her operations, but rather as a master, active with his own instruments.[2]

The optimism of the scientists themselves was invariably boundless; and it infected much of the laity. In many minds indeed the possibilities of science replaced the slowly waning certainties of religion. Evolution and the life force were taking the central role in history previously held by the concepts of Christian eschatology. Natural science became increasingly one of the dominating spiritual forces of the time, the key to solve as well all the practical problems of life: it was, as Chesterton wrote, 'in the air of all that Victorian world'.[3]

An instance or two will illustrate the sort of sentiments involved. Thus, in that year of scientific wonders 1859, A. J. Munby confided to his journal the belief that 'the splendid supremacy of physical science' was an intellectual power of dominating force. Four decades later the same theme was repeated by the naturalist, psychologist, and philosopher, James Ward, who wrote that so far as knowledge extends 'all is law, and law ultimately and most clearly to be formulated in terms of matter and motion.'[4] J. S. Mill, surely a major intellectual influence in nineteenth-century Britain, had envisaged in his *Logic* a programme for the development of a 'general Science of Society' based on the view that 'the collective series of social phenomena, in other words the course of history, is subject to general laws, which philosophy may possibly detect'.[5] And, at least in his younger days, Sidgwick (and his friends) had

2 *Collected Works of Humphry Davy* (1839), ii. 311–26, in E. L. Woodward, *The Age of Reform 1815–1870* (1938; Oxford, 1958), p.545.

3 G. K. Chesterton, *Autobiography* (1936; London, 1937), p.105. Cf. H. Spencer, 'On Education' (1861), in *Essays on Education and Kindred Subjects* (Everyman, 1966), pp.42–3.

4 D. Hudson, *Munby: Man of Two Worlds. The Life and Diaries of Arthur J. Munby 1828–1910* (1972; Abacus, 1974), p.28. Cf. ibid., p.64; J. Ward, *Naturalism and Agnosticism* (1899; 2nd edn, London, 1903), i.20.

5 J. S. Mill, 'A System of Logic', *Collected Works*, ed. J. M. Robson *et al.* (London, 1963 ff), viii.906, 931.

accepted with enthusiasm Mill's view that there could be 'a complete revision of human relations, political, moral, and economic, in the light of science'.[6]

'Scientism' is a convenient word to describe all these many and varied forms of belief resting on the notion that the only effective method of thinking and analysis is that deriving from, or deemed characteristic of, the inquiries of modern natural science and technology. (The word 'positivism' might be, and perhaps more often is, used instead; but I wish here to reserve that term to describe the specific form of scientism associated with Auguste Comte and his school.) What is involved is the assumption that real or genuine knowledge is only possible on the basis of matter of fact carefully observed, catalogued, or categorized in some way and, if possible, measured, quantified, and subsumed under a law or functional generality. What is not thus scientifically grounded is nescience: either merely subjective or, if it pretends to the status of knowledge and does not constitute part of logic or mathematics, no more than false or vain philosophy, speculative metaphysics to be cast into the flames. The implication of this position is that scientific method (as variously conceived) is the only means to ensure effective understanding of any aspect of human or natural experience and that genuine knowledge of man and society can only be acquired in the same way that a mastery of nature is achieved.[7]

Now it is quite obvious that scientism has no necessary affinity at all with collectivist political thought and policy. One has only to think of the ideas of Herbert Spencer to recognize this. He surely believed that knowledge of humanity could be obtained only by the exploration and application of scientific concepts; and yet he was among the most extreme libertarians of his age.[8] Indeed there is no ineluctable connexion at all between scientism and any set of social and political ideas. If the truth be told, the naturalistic paraphernalia are simply the fashionable means employed, as in Spencer's own case, to elaborate and sustain a political prejudice already conceived on other grounds. I do not at all mean by this that any deliberate deceit or conscious hypocrisy is involved: it is just that the use of scientific categories is taken as the mark of sound and progressive thought so that ideas – or prejudices – are often naturally cast in this acceptable and persuasive form. Yet it is quite clear that the scientistic attitude, increasingly influential as it was, was in fact very often associated with, or could be made to bear, political and social

6 Cited in A. and E. M. S[idgwick], *Henry Sidgwick: a Memoir* (London, 1906), pp. 39–40.
7 On the scientistic nature of much of the social speculation of the time, see R. N. Soffer, 'The Revolution in English Social Thought, 1880–1914', *American Historical Review*, lxxv (1969–70), pp. 1938–64.
8 For Spencer, see *The Ideological Heritage*, ch. 3.

implications of a strongly collectivist kind; and it is this aspect of the matter which must be indicated here.

For one thing science is in many ways a co-operative enterprise in solving puzzles. And the impact of its success had certain implications in this respect. One was that all questions came to be looked at in this light, as problems solutions to which could be achieved by the application of this something called scientific method. Any kind of difficulty might be overcome by appropriate resourcefulness in its use. For instance, in the journal *Nature* there appeared in 1870 an editorial entitled 'Scientific Administration'. Its author was probably Norman Lockyer, the spokesman of a group of scientists convinced of the social utility of their craft and of the need of state aid to develop it. The article declared that the word 'science' implies 'simply the employment of means adequate to the attainment of a desired end' whether this goal were the establishment of a political constitution, the organization of an army or navy, the spread of learning, the repression of crime, or whatever. The same technique was involved in all such spheres as in chemical experiment.[9] Of course, the notion of science implied is rather old-fashionedly Baconian but the sentiment is clear: that political and administrative matters can be dealt with as problems in the application of scientific method. It is the intention of those concerned (said the editorial introduction to the new journal of the Social Science Association in 1865) to work for the establishment of 'definite laws of the human mind' in its relation to such aspects of the external environment as 'law, education, political economy, and health, laws which will in due course be as accurate and useful as those of experimental sciences such as chemistry or physiology'.[10] In this way Chadwick, for instance, referred to the new Poor Law as 'the first piece of legislation based upon scientific or economical principles' and said the measure had been prepared by 'laborious inductions from a large mass of facts specially examined'. And he recommended the wider and continuing use of this technique in future legislative preparation.[11] A latter-day reflection of the same sentiment is the remark of F. E. Lawley that the 'application of science to industry . . . calls for nothing less than a corresponding use of the scientific method in developing social control and conscious organisation of the economic

9 *Nature*, ii (1870), p.449. For discussion, see G. Haines, 'German Influence upon Scientific Instruction in England, 1867–1887', *Victorian Studies*, i (1957–8), p.221.
10 *Journal of Social Science*, i (1865–6), pp.1–2.
11 E. Chadwick, Foreword to Bentham's *Observations on the Poor Bill* (written 1797, first published 1838), in Bentham's *Works*, ed. Bowring (1838–43; New York, 1962), viii. 440. But cf. the comment on Chadwick's methods in R. Lambert, *Sir John Simon, 1816–1904, and English Social Administration* (London, 1963), p.609 n.34; and the opinions of T. H. Huxley, in Soffer, art. cit., p.1947.

system'.[12] Similarly, Sir William Beveridge, following T. H. Huxley in his vision of a science of society, urged that social inquiry based on 'observation and experiment, comparison and classification' would not merely transform academic studies but also (through the discovery of social laws) man's ability to control his human environment.[13] Of course, the key questions had to be discerned and the scientific method applied to their solution. This was the role of the new administrative élite or technocracy – an idea common enough from St-Simon to the Webbs, and after. And this points to another aspect of the general scientific impact which Carlyle indicated when discussing the 'Genius of Mechanism' in his essay on 'The Signs of the Times' (1829). He noted how the result of the emergence of this spirit was a loss of faith in individual endeavour and the growth of a feeling that before anything effective can be done a collective organization must be created to deal with it.[14]

In the context of this sort of ethos, therefore, if there is a political or social difficulty the necessary response is clear: enquire what are the facts of the situation; determine a rationally conceived rule to cover it (politically, that is, pass a law to regulate it), and then enforce it. It is obvious (in these terms) that resistance could only be the outcome of either grievance, irrationality, or vested interest, and should, therefore, be firmly overridden. The collectivist implication is manifest and a substantial role for state action invited.

THE SCIENTIFIC BASIS OF POLICY

Science . . . is essential to the commonwealth – not only in its simple
application to details of health, of industrial processes, of the arts of war
and peace, but also as the guide of policy, the arbiter of principles that
are to govern action.
C. M. DOUGLAS, 'Science and Administration', in J. E. Hand (ed.),
Science in Public Affairs, 1906, pp. 220–1

Economic and social progress depended, it was increasingly felt, on the specific application of scientific knowledge; and government involvement in this process was increasingly important. In a similar way, once a scientific advance was made there was growing pressure for government to act on this knowledge and use it as a basis for legislative regulation. One entire volume, published in 1906, was devoted to expounding 'a plea for the application to public affairs of science, *i.e.* of systematic and ordered knowledge' and explored the possibilities in respect of such fields as physical health and development, the improvement of town

---

12 F. E. Lawley, *The Growth of Collective Economy* (London, 1938), i.27.
13 W. H. Beveridge, 'Economics as a Liberal Education', *Economica*, i (1921), pp.2–19; the phrase in the text is at p.7.
14 T. Carlyle, *Works* (People's edn, 1871–4), vii.234–6.

conditions, education, the application of technology to industry, and so forth.[15] Moreover an in-built momentum was generated by technical advance that was difficult if not impossible to resist. R. R. W. Lingen (who was a very economy-minded Permanent Secretary to the Treasury during the third quarter of the last century) was once faced with a demand from Sir John Simon for another vaccination inspector and minuted, 'I do not know who is to check the assertions of experts when the government has once undertaken a class of duties which none but such persons understand.'[16]

Public involvement in scientific work tended in practice to be limited to those areas which might be expected to show an immediate return. Given the hitherto restricted experience of laboratory research this was not altogether surprising. Interest in the problems of navigation was, of course, one factor in state concern with astronomical studies; and, for reasons ranging from military need to the exploitation of resources, the sciences of geology and cartography received public help as with the geological survey undertaken in 1832 and the production of Ordnance maps which had commenced three or so decades earlier. On the other hand research into chemistry and physics depended in the first half of the nineteenth century largely on private endowments. Somewhat surprisingly this was true even in respect of the agricultural uses of this work. Indeed many important theoretical developments and their application proceeded at this stage with no state help at all.[17] But there were forces and persons at work to counter this tendency. 'The intellectual significance and practical corollaries of the new discoveries were gradually understood. The ever-increasing number of learned societies in every branch of science, the development of popular lectures, and the cumulative results of research changed public opinion'.[18] The development of railways and similar feats of engineering made people familiar with applied science and aware of its significance. And gradually government was drawn in.

The field of public health and preventive medicine provides one of the best examples of what was involved. The real need for proper sanitation was not made clear, for instance, until the discovery of the microbe showed the link between dirt, smell, and fever: as late as 1850 taste was

15 J. E. Hand (ed.), *Science in Public Affairs* (London, 1906); the sentence cited is at p. 1.

16 PRO, T1 18,953, Simon to Clerk (19 May 1871), Lingen minute of 1 June in R. J. Lambert, 'A Victorian National Health Service: State Vaccination, 1855-71', *Historical Journal*, v (1962), p.16.

17 See the summary of these matters in E. L. Woodward, *The Age of Reform 1815-1870* (1938; Oxford, 1958), pp. 546-9. On the importance of large-scale public maps, see J. B. Harley and C. W. Phillips, *The Historian's Guide to Ordnance Survey Maps* (London, 1964), p.18.

18 Woodward, op. cit., p.550.

still used by inspectors as a test for purity of water. But once a more exact method was known demands for more effective public action were built on this basis. Sir John Simon was one of those administrators who, like Chadwick, was preoccupied with the need for the national government to legislate according to the precepts of science. After the establishment in 1854 of a Medical Council with a committee for scientific inquiries (both to examine cholera), Simon envisaged a single health authority 'working to keep legislation to the level of contemporary science'.[19] Dr Lambert wrote (in his study of Simon and his work) that

> Not only did Simon try to apply newly-ascertained laws of medical science, as in the vaccination system, the law regarding infections and in action against milk- or water-borne contagions, but he deliberately manipulated administration to discover those laws. Starting with the socio-epidemiological investigations of 1859–65, government began to establish an exact scientific basis for its own subsequent legislative and executive actions. And thereafter, through Simon's insight, government directly and continuously promoted abstract research, making the experimental method and the systematic verification of facts the long-term foundation of administrative activity.[20]

It is clear that medical work and experience has, in fact, often conditioned doctors to recognize the need for government action and provision in the sphere of personal and public health and to see state regulation at both central and local level as the only effective means of limiting or eradicating disease.[21] For instance, in 1909 the Chief Medical Inspector at the Local Government Board wrote as follows:

> With wider and more exact knowledge of hygiene, it is being increasingly realized that the whole range of the physical, mental, and to a large extent of the moral life of mankind may be brought within the range of preventive medicine; and that as medical knowledge grows the number of diseases that can be regarded as preventable will increase, and public administration will extend beyond its present limits.[22]

19 R. Lambert, *Sir John Simon, 1816–1904, and English Social Administration* (London, 1963), pp.198, 236.
20 ibid., p.609.
21 For a most comprehensive survey, see J. L. Brand, *Doctors and the State: the British Medical Profession and Government Action in Public Health, 1870–1912* (Baltimore, Md, 1965): for a summary of the factors involved, see esp. ch. XII.
22 A. Newsholme, 'Some Conditions of Social Efficiency in Relation to Local Public Expenditure', *Public Health*, xxii (1909), pp.403–14, in G. R. Searle, *The Quest for National Efficiency: a Study in British Politics and Political Thought, 1899–1914* (Oxford, 1971), p.64.

It was pretty clear that in the national interest government could not afford to ignore any medical advances of this kind.

A good specific example in the public health field is provided by the activity of the state in respect of smallpox vaccination as a major form of preventive medicine.[23] This was the first free medical service unconnected with the Poor Law to be provided on a national scale; moreover after 1853 it was compulsorily applied to each child. The Oriental practice of inoculating against smallpox seems to have been introduced into England in the early eighteenth century by, among others, Lady Mary Wortley Montagu, and the practice of variolation was subsequently not uncommon especially after 1760: in some places it became universal and even compulsion was not unknown.[24] Edward Jenner, the Gloucestershire physician, introduced the different procedure of vaccination with cowpox in the 1790s and, despite a division of opinion about the safety and efficacy of the procedures involved (it now seems that it was by a happy accident that these proved effective), the first formal state action was taken in 1808 when Parliament was induced to set up a National Vaccine Establishment to provide free vaccination at its London stations and to distribute vaccine-lymph to other vaccinators. Further state involvement followed over ensuing decades and (as already mentioned) in 1853 vaccination was made compulsory. But in practice conformity to the law was less than universal and it was Sir John Simon's use of a wide range of scientific data and experience that subsequently led to more effective action which naturally entailed further legislation (in 1861, 1867, and 1871) providing for an extension of state facilities (including the provision of grants) and the mandatory appointment of officials wielding a wide discretionary power to compel enforcement. Developments in this field emerged quite clearly from the pressure of those with medical knowledge and expertise.[25] The nub of the moral and constitutional issues involved was revealed in the Parliamentary debate of 1872 about the legal enforcement of vaccination and the continual imposition of penalties for refusal to comply. Lyon Playfair, at the time

23 The following details are taken mainly from R. J. Lambert, 'A Victorian National Health Service: State Vaccination, 1855–71', loc. cit., pp. 1–18; R. M. MacLeod, 'Law, Medicine and Public Opinion: the Resistance to Compulsory Health Legislation 1870–1907', *Public Law*, xii (1967), pp. 107–28, 189–211; and P. Razzell, *Edward Jenner's Cowpox Vaccine: the History of a Medical Myth* (Firle, Sussex, 1977).

24 P. E. Razzell, 'Population Change in Eighteenth-Century England: a Reappraisal' (1965), in M. Drake (ed.), *Population in Industrialization* (1969; London, 1973), ch. 7, esp. pp. 134–41. On the origins of smallpox inoculation in Britain, see correspondence in the *TLS* (27 May, 17 June 1977), pp. 653, 733. Boswell records an instance in the Hebrides in the early 1770s, *The Journal of a Tour to the Hebrides with Samuel Johnson, LL.D.* (1785; Everyman, 1931), p. 183.

25 Lambert, art. cit., esp. p. 16.

perhaps the most influential MP with scientific knowledge, demolished an attempt to amend the Bill before the House saying that 'individual disbelief in a remedy which science and experience had confirmed beyond all reasonable doubt was no justification for relieving the conscience of that individual at the expense of society.'[26]

There was indeed a kind of general pattern implicit in this particular example. First there exists a social problem, in this case the major scourge of smallpox. A prophylactic treatment is discovered by scientific research. Then government intervenes to make that treatment in turn available, compulsory, and more effective. Clearly more and more intervention and powers of coercion are involved.

Nor was sanitary administration the only field of public health in which scientific work moulded or led to government action. Another excellent example of this process is provided by the introduction and administration of the Alkali Acts from 1863 onwards. These measures were intended to control the fumes emitted from the chimneys of chemical factories especially in the north of England and in Scotland and they constituted the first nationally applied scientific policy for the regulation of an industry, a policy only made possible by previous scientific discovery. It should not be supposed, of course, that nothing at all had been done by public agencies before 1863. A local court leet or improvement commission in its concern with the abatement of nuisances had often been used to take action to control smoke, fumes, and the like. For instance, in 1828 the Hundred Court Leet at Salford dealt with 'noisome and noxious fumes and vapours' emitted by a sal-ammoniac factory at Ancoats; and an improvement commission-was created for Rochdale in 1853 with, among other responsibilities, the task of preventing the untoward discharge of smoke and steam.[27] Of course, whether such action was really effective is another matter; but equally standards vary with the times and depended really on preliminary

26 Cited in MacLeod, art. cit., p.121. This paper reviews, *passim*, the debate about compulsion and individual freedom as it relates to medical ideas and practice. On this issue, see also E. J. Bristow, *The Defence of Liberty and Property in Britain, 1880–1914* (unpublished PhD thesis, Yale University, 1970), ch.2, esp. pp.69ff; also his *Vice and Vigilance: Purity Movements in Britain since 1700* (Dublin, 1977). Two recent studies, J. R. Walkowitz, *Prostitution and Victorian Society: Women, Class, and the State* (Cambridge, 1980), and P. McHugh, *Prostitution and Victorian Social Reform* (London, 1980) discuss the controversy over the Contagious Diseases Acts and indicate *inter alia* the role of medical factors.

27 A. Redford, *The History of Local Government in Manchester* (London, 1939–40), i.42; Rochdale Improvement Act (1853), §cxxii, in E. J. Evans, *Social Policy, 1830–1914: Individualism, Collectivism and the Origins of the Welfare State* (London, 1978), p.82. For the traditional legal position on these 'nusances', see W. Blackstone, *Commentaries on the Laws of England* (1765–9; 6th edn, Dublin, 1775), ii.402–3; iii.122, 217–18; iv.167–75.

scientific breakthrough. The problem was that the Victorian chemical industry which produced sodium carbonate – so vital in the production of glass, soap, and textiles – also vented tons of corrosive hydrogen chloride gas into the atmosphere.[28] It was hoped that very high chimneys would help disperse the fumes but they did not do so. The articulate local public which was affected (and which included some influential property owners) complained and a House of Lords select committee held an inquiry. It emerged from the evidence that recent technical advances now made possible a higher degree than before of condensation of the offending gas (thus producing hydrochloric acid, an important incentive to control because this was of increasing commercial use and value). The result was the passage in 1863 of an Alkali Act to achieve this end with a small inspectorate of qualified scientists to ensure enforcement. The effect was immediate and the amount of acid escaping into the air was quickly brought well within the safety limit: a clear example, this, of administrative change and state intervention being practically initiated by applied scientific development. Nor will it be any surprise – in the context of what has already been said about the process of administrative momentum – that the work of the inspectorate itself revealed problems and possibilities that led in due time to an extension of its powers and the range of its control over other kinds of manufacturing, to consider indeed some of the public health aspects of atmospheric pollution generally and not simply the one cause originally in view. The Royal Commission on Noxious Vapours wrote in its report in 1878 that 'when the law is impotent, it is within the legitimate province of the State to apply other means for reducing these evils to a minimum, and with that object to enforce the adoption of processes as effectual to the best in use, or at least by a system of inspection to render such enforcement possible hereafter'.[29] Industry and science created the nuisance in the first place and thus gave rise to the need for public intervention. In turn this could only be effective if it went hand in hand with scientific possibility and technical advance.

In sum, therefore, scientific knowledge could aid or even produce pressure for government action by seeming to give this pressure intellectual justification and provide practical means of implementation. Equally, of course, scientific inventions could create problems but these, too, often led to inquiry and inspection. The development of nitroglycerine and other explosive substances is a case in point.[30] So also is the more recent growth of the motor car or the exploitation of nuclear technology and microelectronics under government aegis.

28　This account is based on R. M. MacLeod, 'The Alkali Acts Administration, 1863–84: the Emergence of the Civil Scientist', *Victorian Studies*, ix (1965–6), pp. 85–112.
29　Noxious Vapours, R.Com.Rep., 1878 (vol.xliv), C.2159, cited ibid., p.112.
30　See above p.225 and the reference given in n.99.

FORMS OF NATURALISTIC BELIEF

I am a social scientist by profession and I begin by the assumption, common to the civilization of Europe since the eighteenth century, that the methods of science must be used if our studies are to throw light upon social behaviour . . . .

E. F. M. DURBIN, *The Politics of Democratic Socialism*, 1940, p. 27

One area of intellectual concern that was affected by the scientific spirit and which has already been reviewed was classical political economy, for undoubtedly among its aims was to discover the general laws governing certain social phenomena and to this degree it was modelled on the natural sciences.[31] But there were other bodies of doctrine that were similarly affected and these contributed though not exclusively to a collectivist stress. Four were particularly important: utilitarianism, Comteian positivism, social evolutionism in various forms, and psychology.

Utilitarianism

Utilitarianism is the name given to the themes expounded by such writers as Jeremy Bentham, James Mill, and their followers including, of course, the latter's son, John Stuart Mill. For many years during the last century this doctrine, though never unchallenged, bid fair to be master of the intellectual field: 'it was the philosophy in office, so to speak.'[32] Although not the first or most systematic thinker to expound the notions concerned, Bentham is usually regarded as the founder of the school in this country. He held that traditional guides of conduct such as custom, Christianity, and the common law were no longer adequate and might well be positively misleading or otherwise harmful. He felt, therefore, the need for a fresh psychological and ethical standard appropriate to the new age which was unfolding. This criterion was the principle of utility, that is, the concept that in all activity the object is and should be the maximization of individual and social happiness. As a contemporary of Bentham's had it,

> What is the worth of any thing,
> But for the happiness 'twill bring?[33]

---

31 Cf. L. Robbins, 'First Principles', in *TLS* (1 August 1975), p. 870.

32 G. K. Chesterton, *The Victorian Age in Literature* (1913; rev. edn, London, 1920), p. 38. For a recent comment, sceptical of this supposed dominance, see S. Collini, 'Political Theory and the "Science of Society" in Victorian Britain', *Historical Journal*, xxiii (1980), p. 205.

33 R. O. Cambridge, 'Learning: a Dialogue Between Dick and Ned', in *The Works* (London, 1803), p. 10.

In the wider context the goal was, in Francis Hutcheson's famous phrase, the greatest happiness of the greatest number. The concept was a commonplace of the age. However, in the way in which Bentham himself formulated it, an objective and scientific mode of exploring human relationships was supposed to be involved, one that would have, too, the intention of limiting undesirable social conflict and of ensuring peaceful and stable advance.

Now Bentham had a long life (from 1745 until 1832) and wrote a great deal in radically changing circumstances. The existence of variations of viewpoint in his many works is hardly surprising, therefore. *A fortiori* the whole school was never really a unity and its house had many mansions. Consequently, as with the classical political economists, it is difficult to generalize without caveat or careful reservation about the role of the state in either general utilitarian or specifically Benthamite writings.[34] In truth, the doctrine is ambivalent in this regard and can be made (or can be seen) to bear both *laissez faire* and interventionist implications. Halévy's classic analysis in *The Growth of Philosophic Radicalism* is premeditated precisely on the observation in utilitarianism of a dichotomy between a stress on natural or on artificial means of ensuring a social harmony of interests.

First of all, then, it is necessary to recognize that a libertarian emphasis is often to be discerned in utilitarian ideas. There is in the doctrine a kind of sociological atomism which sees society as a collection of free and separate individuals each looking after his own affairs. On these nominalist terms, society exists, too, only in and through these individuals and for their sake. Consequently, utilitarianism was frequently associated with the notion of the free competitive market in which order and regulation were achieved not so much by government action as by the emergence of a natural harmony of interests among competing individuals. On this view the greatest happiness was most expeditiously to be attained by government's standing aside, leaving people to pursue their own concerns which, after all, they know best. Intervention would only cause 'disutility' or 'pain', through taxation for example, and would as well do positive harm by inhibiting initiative and otherwise impeding the possibilities of progress. Bentham himself argues, at least in his earlier economic writings, that action by government cannot raise the quantity of wealth produced but only divert or redistribute it: 'Every statesman who thinks by regulation to encrease the sum of trade, is the child whose eye is bigger than his belly.'[35] With his

---

34 Cf. T. W. Hutchison, 'Bentham as an Economist', *Economic Journal*, lxvi (1956), pp. 301–2; W. H. Coates, 'Benthamism, Laissez Faire and Collectivism', *Journal of the History of Ideas*, xi (1950), pp. 357–63.

35 W. Stark (ed.), *Jeremy Bentham's Economic Writings* (London, 1952–4), i. 201, 234, 252.

usual facility for sloganizing, Bentham summarized this view in lapidary form calling it the 'let-alone' or 'stand-out-of-my-sunshine' principle (the latter referring of course to Diogenes' curt response to Alexander the Great's offer of help). Or, as he said later in *The Institute of Political Economy* (1801–4), 'nothing ought to be done or attempted by government for the purpose of causing an augmentation in the national mass of wealth . . . without some special reason. *Be quiet* ought on those occasions to be the motto, or watchword, of government'.[36] And, in detailed discussion, he went very far in the direction of limiting the 'agenda' appropriate to the political authorities.

There is no doubt, then, that an emphasis on limited government is present in utilitarian writing, but (as already noted) it is not uniquely there or even always dominant. Dicey saw this clearly enough when he recognized the 'despotic' or 'authoritative' element latent in utilitarianism and suggested the importance of its impact on the growth of collectivism; while Halévy brusquely stated that the doctrine of utility was not, in origin or in essence, 'a philosophy of liberty'.[37] How did this other emphasis emerge? And how is it connected with the spirit of scientism?

The basic premiss was that, while each person wished to maximize his happiness, he could be mistaken as to the best way of doing this in respect either of the specific ends involved or the means proposed. Overcoming this sort of difficulties meant adding to the agenda of government: people might thereby be better educated to make more effective choices or, equally, tutorially inclined into more appropriate paths. That is, by means of political or other manipulation, a form of human relationships might be established in which both individuals and society could more effectively achieve optimum happiness than if they were left to their own unaided devices. That the 'uncoerced and unenlightened propensities and powers of individuals are not adequate to the end without the controul and guidance of the legislator is a matter of fact of which the evidence of history, the nature of man, and the existence of political society are so many proofs.'[38] And what makes the enterprise scientistic is the manner in which it was conceived and expounded. Bentham cast himself in the role of great legislator for this purpose (he was always in spirit something of an 'enlightened despot') and tried to

36 Bentham, 'A Manual of Political Economy' (1793–5), in J. Bowring (ed.), *The Works of Jeremy Bentham* (1838–43; New York, 1962), iii.33–5; Stark, *Jeremy Bentham's Economic Writings*, ii.333 (italics in original).

37 A. V. Dicey, *Lectures on the Relation between Law & Public Opinion in England during the Nineteenth Century* (1905; 2nd edn, London, 1920), pp.302, 310; E. Halévy, *The Growth of Philosophic Radicalism* (1901; trans. 1928; new edn, London, 1934), p.84, and cf. ibid., p.432.

38 Stark, op. cit., iii.311.

show, often in the greatest detail, the kind of political, social, and economic arrangements that would be conducive to the end in view. He wanted to explain how the many defects of the existing system of law and administration could be remedied and put on a more rational basis to achieve the general object of all government, 'the total happiness of the community'.[39]

During his undergraduate days Bentham had acquired an interest in the natural sciences; and his ambition was to do for law and moral philosophy (in effect for what we should call the social sciences) what the 'new philosophy' had since the seventeenth century done for the understanding of nature. That is to say, he wanted in principle to reduce all the disparate phenomena of the human world to simple generalizations or laws involving only a few basic concepts or axioms (which would be the equivalent of such ideas as gravity, mass, and force) and which, ideally, should be measurable and capable of being expressed in quantified form. He specifically said he wanted to be the Newton of the moral world:

> The present work as well as any other work of mine that has been or will be published on the subject of legislation or any other branch of moral science is an attempt to extend the experimental method of reasoning from the physical branch to the moral. What Bacon was to the physical world, Helvetius was to the moral. The moral world has therefore had its Bacon, but its Newton is yet to come.[40]

The attitude is rather like that traditionally attributed to Descartes and to Hobbes. And it is no accident that the modern revival of interest in Hobbesian ideas is associated with the utilitarians or that the first, and so far only, complete edition of his works was brought out under the aegis of Sir William Molesworth, a disciple of the school. Carlyle at least gave the attitude the lie direct: 'When *will* there arise a man who will do for the science of Mind what Newton did for that of Matter – establish its fundamental laws on the firm basis of induction – and discard for ever those absurd theories that so many dreamers have devised? I believe this is a foolish question, for its answer is – never.'[41]

The key Benthamite insight was psychological, the axiom that the only knowable motivation, common to all mankind, was the pursuit of pleasure and avoidance of pain, that is, the maximization of utility. The empire of these forces could never be abjured and was the one

---

39 Bentham, *A Fragment on Government and an Introduction to the Principles of Morals and Legislation* (1776, 1789), ed. Harrison (Oxford, 1948), p.281.

40 Cited in C. W. Everett, *The Education of Jeremy Bentham* (New York, 1931), p.36.

41 Cited in D. A. Wilson, *The Life of Carlyle* (London, 1923–34), i.117 (italics in original).

fundamental cause of all human action. And the manner of people's responses to various stimuli could be quantified in terms of the felicific or hedonistic calculus.[42] What was involved here was, first of all, a description or classification of all the different kinds of pain and pleasure as the primary data of analysis. For instance, in his *Introduction to the Principles of Morals and Legislation* Bentham described fourteen different kinds of 'simple' pleasure and twelve kinds of pain. Each was further subdivided and capable of combination in various ways.[43] As well, each of the different pleasures and pains might have a value attached to it which could be roughly measured and which depended on various 'dimensions' such as intensity, duration, purity, nearness or remoteness, sensibility, and so on.[44] Of course, Bentham did not believe that the kind of calculation involved could necessarily be very exact; but it could be accurate enough for practical purposes. He was observing and emphasizing that we all tend to make estimates of this kind in everything we consciously do – 'who is there', he asks, 'that does not calculate' in this way ? – and that it would be a great individual and social step forward if this process were recognized for the basic psychological fact it is and made as considered and precise as possible.[45] In particular, given that everyone is so moved by pains and pleasures then, if sensitivity is known, it should be possible by using amounts or lots of these sanctions to condition people to act in an improved way in their own interest and in pursuit of the general welfare. Of course, motive becomes unimportant as compared with the consequences of actions; and it has to be supposed for purposes of the hedonistic calculation that all pains and pleasures are qualitatively equal. But all this Bentham is prepared to accept in order to achieve a conceptual instrument of pragmatic value; though this also involved him and his followers in much criticism summed up in Tawney's phrase about 'the melancholy mathematical creed' of utilitarianism or, more pungently, in Carlyle's description of it as 'the Pig

42 The best short discussion is still W. C. Mitchell, 'Bentham's Felicific Calculus', *Political Science Quarterly*, xxxiii (1918) in B. Parekh (ed.), *Jeremy Bentham: Ten Critical Essays* (London, 1974), ch. 9. For the modern pedigree of the idea of an ethics cast in mathematical form, see L. T. Bredvold, 'The Invention of the Ethical Calculus', in R. F. Jones *et al.*, *The Seventeenth Century: Studies in the History of English Thought and Literature from Bacon to Pope* (1951; London, 1965), pp. 165–80.

43 op. cit., ch. V. Cf. *A Table of the Springs of Action* (1815), in Bowring, *Works of Jeremy Bentham*, i. 195–219.

44 *Introduction to the Principles of Morals and Legislation*, ch. IV; 'Value of a Pain or Pleasure' (1778), Bentham MSS, Box 27, 29–30, in B. Parekh (ed.), *Bentham's Political Thought* (London, 1973), ch. 7, esp. pp. 114ff.

45 The phrase cited comes from the 'Introduction to the Principles of Morals and Legislation', in *The Works*, ed. Bowring, i. 90–1.

Philosophy' seeing man as no more than 'a dead Iron-Balance for weighing Pains and Pleasures on'.[46]

Now the point of all this in the present context is simply that the criterion of utility and the mode of felicific analysis associated with it could be used not only to criticize and evaluate existing institutions but also as the foundation for a complete and intendedly scientific system of laws and arrangements within the framework of which the greatest happiness could be attained. This took the form in effect of a kind of rationalist blueprint of the perfectly organized society described in its fullest detail in Bentham's vast but uncompleted *Constitutional Code* and which reflected a notable collectivist emphasis.[47] This tendency to approve state intervention may be discerned in two particular respects.

The first is the need Bentham discerned for political interference to eliminate from existing society the influence of what he called 'sinister interests'. By this phrase he meant the existing arrangements of the law, the Church, the corporations, local customs, aristocratic privilege, the monarchy: that is, all those institutions with a vested concern in the established state of affairs and which could be expected to stand in the way of rational reform on scientific principles. As Dicey said, the principle of utility was thus 'big with revolution; it involved the abolition of every office or institution which could not be defended on the ground of calculable benefit to the public; it struck at the root of all the abuses' which then abounded.[48] Bentham was finally confirmed in his belief that the existing institutions of government were corrupt by his failure to secure adequate official support for the introduction of the 'Panopticon', a type of prison building he had designed based on the rational application of utilitarian principles. The problem he faced, therefore, was to describe an alternative political system in which those who controlled power could be prevented from making bad (that is, irrational or merely selfish) use of it. He was thus led to advocate a form of representative government in which the executive and legislature reflected the interests of the majority of the people (and not any partial or

---

46   R. H. Tawney, *The Acquisitive Society* (1921; London, 1943), p.17; T. Carlyle, 'Latter-Day Pamphlets' (1850), in *Works* (People's edn, 1871–4), xx.268–70; 'Sartor Resartus' (1831), ibid., i.152. Cf. his 'On Heroes, Hero-Worship and the Heroic in History' (1840), ibid., xiii.69.

47   The fullest text is reprinted in vol.ix of Bowring's *The Works*. A summary of the proposals is given in T. P. Peardon, 'Bentham's Ideal Republic' (1951), in Parekh (ed.), *Jeremy Bentham*, ch.6. Cf. the comments of J. B. Brebner, 'Laissez-Faire and State Intervention in Nineteenth-Century Britain', *Journal of Economic History*, suppl.viii (1948), pp.59ff.

48   Dicey, *Law & Public Opinion*, p.305. Cf. Bentham's own recognition of the radical implications of the utility principle in his discussion of a remark of Wedderburn's, *Introduction to the Principles of Morals and Legislation*, pp.128–9 n.

sinister interest). The greatest happiness of the greatest number could only be achieved by this 'duty-and-interest-junction-prescribing principle'. Bentham consequently urged such reforms as universal suffrage, annual Parliaments, the ballot, the abolition of the House of Lords, a reorganized magistracy, removal of political abuses and legal anomalies, and so on, doctrine which became the core of radical politics at Westminster and which is most succinctly stated, albeit with some interesting reservations, in James Mill's *Essay on Government* (1820).[49]

The point here, then, is that Bentham was concerned to describe a rational, indeed scientific, system of political organization to replace the traditional arrangements haphazardly provided by history and custom and which were breaking down. They were ineffective and proving incapable of dealing with contemporary problems; there thus existed, unnecessarily, a state of chronic insecurity that was a danger to the maintenance and improvement of civilized life. Intervention was necessary to restore coherence to political relationships.[50]

The second Benthamite line of thought which had collectivist implications concerned the feeling that there was need for a certain interference (by the representative government that should be established) in other, non-political, areas of communal life to achieve scientifically the goal of the greatest happiness of the greatest number. As already indicated it was assumed that men did not always see the path of true interest clearly and might, therefore, have to be authoritatively inclined into the correct course of action or, at least, helped in the pursuit of their goals. Once government had been made representative it ceased to be the suspect sinister interest it would otherwise be and might be used for this purpose. And there were a number of spheres in which Bentham was thus prepared to see it act through responsible ministers and their expert and authoritative agents. One was to achieve proper sanitary and other working conditions in factories; another to protect those who, like children, could not really be considered free persons capable of making a rational contract; yet another was the maintenance of a proper level of public health including such things as the provision of hospitals and of a supply of pure water. He naturally paid considerable attention as well to education by means of which correct ideas might be associated in

---

49 For Mill's reservations about the extent of the suffrage and the political role of property, see *Essay on Government*, ed. Barker (Cambridge, 1937), pp. 45ff, 71–2. On the latter, see also the interesting letter Mill wrote in 1832 to Henry Brougham, in A. Bain, *James Mill: a Biography* (1882; Farnborough, 1970), pp. 364–5; also ibid., pp. 349–50. For discussion, see D. C. Moore, *The Politics of Deference: a Study of the Mid-Nineteenth Century English Political System* (Hassocks, Sussex, 1976), 'Epilogue: the Interpretational Problem', pp. 420ff.

50 Cf. D. J. Manning, *The Mind of Jeremy Bentham* (London, 1968), p. 6.

children's minds.[51] Clearly R. H. Tawney's judgement that Benthamism 'touched only the surface of social institutions' may be most misleading.[52] This is doubly the case as Bentham seems to have reversed his earlier view about government interference in respect of the level of economic activity saying now that if there are unemployed factors of production then it may add to the national wealth by increasing the supply of money so that unused resources or those not fully employed are taken up and set to work.[53] By 1801 he was prepared to write, not wholly accurately, that he had never had, 'nor ever shall have, any horror . . . of the hand of government.'[54] He was prepared, too, to envisage on this basis government control of the Bank of England and of the issue of paper money, of speculation and some aspects of the banking system, and of a substantial part of the insurance business.[55] Government might likewise have a positive role in matters affecting property and income. One guiding idea here was what he called the 'inequality-minimizing principle' which, given the economic structure of the time, could clearly involve a considerable redistribution of wealth.

Bentham's argument was that to achieve the greatest happiness of the greatest number it was not enough that happiness should be maximized for a small group of people in society for this might be outweighed by a vaster sum of misery among the majority. Happiness had, therefore, to be spread more evenly. And, as happiness depended on a feeling of 'security', or freedom from pain and inconvenience, it was vitally related to the possession of wealth and property of various kinds which had, therefore, to be distributed in the optimum way for the purpose in view. Money thus became the measure of the nature of things, the standard for calculating quantities of pain and pleasure.[56] Bentham was well aware nevertheless that a given amount of wealth would be of varying value in the production of happiness for different individuals depending on the goods and money they already possessed. A person who has a large fortune will not receive so much extra utility from the receipt of a further small amount as will someone who has relatively little (Bentham was stating in effect what later came to be known as the law of diminishing marginal utility). He concluded that the nearer the distribution of wealth approached equality (thus, in later language, equalizing marginal utility) the greater would be the total sum of happiness. Bentham seems to have thought indeed in terms of a broadly egalitarian property-owning de-

---

51   Cf. Peardon, loc. cit., pp. 130–1; also J. Viner, 'Bentham and J. S. Mill: the Utilitarian Background', *American Economic Review*, xxxix (1949), pp. 370–1.
52   Tawney, *The Acquisitive Society*, p. 18.
53   Stark, op. cit., i. 270–1; ii. 313.
54   ibid., iii. 257–8.
55   Hutchison, art. cit., p. 302.
56   See the ms. cited in Parekh, *Bentham's Political Thought*, pp. 118–23.

mocracy. This could not involve a strictly maintained equality, of course, as such a state of affairs would entail the continual threat of redistribution and confiscation and would thus cause stagnation and inhibit economic advance. But even the poorest could be guaranteed by government action 'a sufficiency of the principal subsistence for man, *i.e.* corn.'[57] And this point of view, when applied to early nineteenth-century Britain, could clearly mean a radical alteration of the circumstances then obtaining, a change that could only be brought about by government action, for instance to abolish primogeniture in the inheritance of property.[58] Other schemes Bentham suggested to minimize inequality included the stimulation of small savings by a system of 'Frugality Banks', the institution of a system of low-value government annuities, and state aid for the unemployed.[59]

Similarly Bentham's disciple, James Mill, asserted that the object of state action was to achieve the greatest possible happiness of society by ensuring the best distribution of scarce resources: this meant securing to each person the largest feasible quantity of the produce of his labour, potentially a very radical principle indeed.[60] He also thought it proper to this end for government to tax very heavily the unearned increment of development value of land.[61] And certainly many other followers of Bentham, such as Edwin Chadwick, Southwood Smith, and T. Perronet Thompson, were also exponents of the idea of government intervention to achieve various types of social reform. When introducing in 1833 his proposal for a national system of education, Roebuck, one of the Parliamentary radicals, was quite frank about the effect the proposed step would have on the traditional libertarian point of view. Freedom, as absence of restraint simply, was (he said) 'not a good thing'. The real freedom of which people were robbed by existing laws consisted in genuine opportunity of improvement.[62] The radical *Westminster Review* was equally blunt: 'we advocate, both for England and Ireland, the necessity of a national provision for the moral and industrial training of the young. In the old we cannot hope for much improvement. But the new generation springing up might be modelled to our will'.[63] Given this spirit it has been accurately observed, 'What were the Fabians but latter-day Benthamites?'[64]

57 Stark, op. cit., iii. 482.
58 See e.g. Bowring, *The Works of Jeremy Bentham*, i. 305, 313, 358; iii. 229–30; ix. 17–18.
59 ibid., viii. 408 ff; iii. 105–53; i. 314 ff; iii. 72 ff.
60 J. Mill, *Essay on Government*, pp. 4–5.
61 J. Mill, *Elements of Political Economy* (London, 1821), pp. 201–3.
62 20 Parl. Deb. 3s., 30 July 1833, esp. col. 154.
63 Anon., 'Fallacies on Poor Laws', *Westminster Review*, xxvi (1836–7), p. 377.
64 Brebner, art. cit., p. 66.

It should be noted at this point that there has over the past quarter-century been a most interesting and fruitful academic controversy about the impact of Benthamite ideas. In 1958 Professor MacDonagh published an important reappraisal of what he called 'the nineteenth-century revolution in government' and in which he stressed the significance, in the development of government intervention, not so much of Benthamism as of practical exigencies, that 'administrative momentum' to which reference has already been made earlier.[65] Moreover, so far as Benthamism was an ambivalent doctrine compatible with anti-statist views, it was clearly capable of being an impediment to the development of collectivism. Other contributors to the discussion have, however, sustained the traditional views of J. S. Mill, Dicey, and Halévy that utilitarian ideas made a major contribution to the growth of the positive state in particular as they affected the attitudes of people crucially concerned in the legal and public administration of the day such as Colquhoun, Chadwick, Southwood Smith, and Simon.[66] It is a view which in its extreme version holds that Benthamite proposals 'were the principal inspiration of half the English reforms of the nineteenth century'.[67] This whole discussion raises in a very interesting form the complex issue of the impact of ideas on events and behaviour and how it may be traced and assessed. Probably a wise summary of the matter is that there were areas in which state intervention increased where Benthamism was probably of no account (e.g. the regulation of emigrant traffic); but there were, equally, others (such as prison and law reform) where it may have been an important factor often operating through the actions of particular individuals like Colquhoun and Chadwick. Even in these cases, however,

---

65   *Historical Journal*, i (1958), pp. 52–67; and see above pp. 221–8. A similar view was put forward by D. Roberts, 'Jeremy Bentham and the Victorian Administrative State', *Victorian Studies*, ii (1958–9), pp. 193–210, in B. Parekh (ed.), *Jeremy Bentham: Ten Critical Essays*, ch. 10. An interesting and much earlier statement of the case for diluting claims of supposed Benthamite influence is M. Oakeshott, 'The New Bentham', *Scrutiny*, i (1932–3), pp. 114–31.

66   A list of contributors to this debate is to be found in Parekh, op. cit., p. 187. To this list should be added: S. E. Finer, 'The Transmission of Benthamite Ideas, 1820–50', in G. Sutherland, *Studies in the Growth of Nineteenth-Century Government* (London, 1972), pp. 11–32; U. Henriques, 'Jeremy Bentham and the Machinery of Social Reform', in H. Hearder and H. R. Loyn (eds), *British Government and Administration* (Cardiff, 1974), pp. 169–86; G. Himmelfarb, 'Bentham Scholarship and the Bentham "Problem"', *Journal of Modern History*, xli (1969), pp. 189–206; H. Perkin, 'Individualism Versus Collectivism in Nineteenth-Century Britain: a False Antithesis', *Journal of British Studies*, xvii (1977–8), pp. 105–18; E. T. Stokes, 'Bureaucracy and Ideology: Britain and India in the Nineteenth Century', *Trans. R. Hist. S.*, xxx (1980), pp. 131–56; and A. Heeson, 'The Coal Mines Act of 1842, Social Reform, and Social Control', *Historical Journal*, xxiv (1981), esp. pp. 79–81, 87–8.

67   B. Keith-Lucas, *The English Local Government Franchise: a Short History* (Oxford, 1952), p. 5.

the Benthamite influence was never exclusive and it is necessary to give due weight to practical or empirical considerations of different kinds, as in Chadwick's sanitary proposals.[68]

Comteian positivism

Whenever the word 'positivist' is used to describe a particular way of thinking, it can be assumed that the mode of thought concerned excludes from the realm of true knowledge any supposed understanding (the truths of logic and mathematics apart) which is not based on experience or matter of fact. What is thus rejected may be pejoratively called (as it was in the early-modern period) false or vain philosophy or (as in more recent times) mere speculative metaphysics or 'non-sense'. In this general way positivism may broadly be equated with empirical philosophy as a whole or especially with the attempt to apply causal scientific analysis to as wide a range of data as possible. J. S. Mill defined the basic doctrine seen in this way in the following broad terms:

> We have no knowledge of anything but Phaenomena; and our knowledge of phaenomena is relative, not absolute. We know not the essence, nor the real mode of production, of any fact, but only its relations to other facts in the way of succession or of similitude. These relations are constant; that is, always the same in the same circumstances. The constant resemblances which link phaenomena together, and the constant sequences which unite them as antecedent and consequent, are termed their laws. The laws of phaenomena are all we know respecting them. Their essential nature, and their ultimate causes, either efficient or final, are unknown and inscrutable to us.[69]

But there is also an attribution of the term which refers it specifically to that version of this intellectual manner reflected by Auguste Comte and his followers.

'La philosophie positive' was a concept first enunciated by Henri St-Simon with whom Comte was for a time associated and by whom he was much influenced; nor were the similar and earlier ideas of Condorcet

---

68 Cf. W. C. Lubenow, *The Politics of Government Growth: Early Victorian Attitudes toward State Intervention, 1833–1848* (Newton Abbot, 1971), pp. 76–7. And see, too, the judicious summary in Henriques, loc. cit., pp. 179–86.

69 J. S. Mill, 'Auguste Comte and Positivism' (1865), *Collected Works*, x. 265–6. Cf. D. G. Charlton, *Positivist Thought in France during the Second Empire 1852–1870* (Oxford, 1959), pp. 5–7; also the essay on 'The Meaning of the Word "Positive"', in J. H. Bridges, *Illustrations of Positivism* (1907; new edn, London, 1915), pp. 199–209.

without effect.[70] It was the name Comte gave to his own system of philosophy which he developed from 1820 onwards. Condorcet's and St-Simon's doctrine was based on the application of scientific concepts and methods to every aspect of human experience. Like the Bentham of the *Constitutional Code*, they envisaged a completely rationalized or planned social organization and political structure under technocratic control in order to achieve the maximum satisfaction of human needs. Comte's system of positive philosophy was in the same general style. He believed that 'social phenomena are subject to natural laws, admitting of rational prevision'.[71] And once knowledge had been made definitive on a proper scientific basis, it was necessary that those who had this knowledge and understood the laws which governed it should deal with social and political questions, for advance in the direction of positive science would always be accompanied by social reconstruction carried through under appropriate intellectual auspices.[72] Indeed, in the title of his first sketch of the Positive Philosophy (which appeared in 1822), Comte made this purpose quite apparent: it was called a *Plan of the Scientific Researches Necessary for the Reorganization of Society.*[73] The implications were not Socialist in the sense that Comte did not, for instance, argue for the abolition of private property, but he rejects the libertarian concept of individuality and thinks not in terms of private persons but of state functionaries of various units and grades. A central characteristic of his political ideas was a feeling that wise direction from above was essential: 'la subordination sociale' was to be the crucial basis of the new society.[74] Moreover the 'ruling function' will 'become more, instead of less, as human development proceeds'.[75]

Comte's Positive Philosophy was introduced into this country in the late 1830s and subsequently had a considerable influence on British

70 See the extremely full account in K. M. Baker's recent *Condorcet* (Chicago, 1975). There is a good summary of the scientistic doctrines of St-Simon and Comte in D. Germino, *Modern Western Political Thought: Machiavelli to Marx* (Chicago, 1972), ch. 11.

71 A. Comte, *The Positive Philosophy* (1830–42; trans. and abr. H. Martineau, London, 1896), ii.218 in J. H. Abraham, *The Origins and Growth of Sociology* (Penguin, 1973), p.103.

72 Charlton, op. cit., pp.25–6, 29–32; W. M. Simon, *European Positivism in the Nineteenth Century: an Essay in Intellectual History* (Ithaca, N.Y., 1963), p.6; F. A. Hayek, *The Counter-Revolution of Science: Studies on the Abuse of Reason* (1955; London, 1964), p.183; R. Harrison, *Before the Socialists: Studies in Labour and Politics 1861–1881* (London, 1965), p.260. Cf. J. S. Mill, op. cit., x.302.

73 H. B. Acton, 'Comte's Positivism and the Science of Society', *Philosophy*, xxvi (1951), pp.292–3. Cf. ibid., pp.304–5.

74 Charlton, op. cit., p.48; Hayek, op. cit., pp.183–4; E. Barker, *Political Thought in England 1848–1914* (1915; 2nd edn, London, 1947), p.177; Germino, op. cit., pp.293–5.

75 Abraham, op. cit., p.120.

thought, for instance on such figures as H. Buckle, J. S. Mill, G. H. Lewes, and J. Morley. There was also a specific and organized Comteist school among the leading members of which were people such as H. Crompton, J. H. Bridges, R. Congreve and, probably more well-known, E. S. Beesly and F. Harrison.[76] Professor Royden Harrison has said that 'No one who wants to understand England during the second half of Victoria's reign can afford to ignore the Positivists.'[77] And if the Comteian secular 'religion of humanity' received fervent and often rather weird institutional expression, some of his British disciples were a kind of intellectual pressure group (akin in some respects perhaps to the Utilitarians and Fabians) that was not always without practical influence. Sidney Webb noted that among the factors which exerted 'a potent disintegrating force' on the dominance of bourgeois ideals were the denunciations of 'the small but persistent band of Positivists'.[78] Certainly this band had Socialist connexions: it was Beesly, for instance, who presided in 1864 at the meeting at which the First International was founded and who later joined with H. Hyndman in establishing the Marxist Social Democratic Federation after 1880. Harrison had a special interest in the condition of the working class and was an effective supporter of trade unionism: the Positivists, it has been argued, played a crucial part in securing an effective legal basis for the unions and in turning them towards political commitment.[79] The Positivists followed their Master in believing that the new society which was emerging would be based not on individualistic competition but a planned central control dependent on the authority of intellect: Comteist sociology was firmly related to *étatisme*.[80] Geddes and Branford, both disciples of Comte, wanted to create a genuinely empirical science of sociology, to conduct social experiments on scientific lines, as the basis of civic and social planning.[81]

76 On these people, see R. Harrison, *Before the Socialists*, ch. VI; C. Kent, *Brains and Numbers: Elitism, Comtism, and Democracy in Mid-Victorian England* (Toronto, 1978), esp. chs.4–9; W. M. Simon, 'Auguste Comte's English Disciples', *Victorian Studies*, viii (1964–5), pp.161–72, and his *European Positivism*, chs. VII–VIII. Lord Annan's *The Curious Strength of Positivism in English Political Thought* (London, 1959) contains some curious not to say perverse judgements.
77 In *Victorian Studies*, vii (1963–4), p.397.
78 S. Webb, *Socialism in England* (London, 1890), p.20. Cf. B. Webb, *My Apprenticeship* (Penguin, 1938), i.173.
79 R. Harrison, *Before the Socialists*, pp.277–306 describes this specific process of influence in considerable detail. Cf. Kent, op. cit., pp.80–2.
80 R. Harrison, op. cit., p.272; A. Harrison, *Frederic Harrison: Thoughts and Memories* (London, 1926), p.21; Kent, op. cit., *passim*.
81 L. Mumford, 'Patrick Geddes, Victor Branford, and Applied Sociology in England: the Social Survey, Regionalism, and Urban Planning', in H. E. Barnes (ed.), *An Introduction to the History of Sociology* (1948; abr. edn, London, 1969), ch. XVI, esp. pp.371, 376; H. E. Meller, 'Patrick Geddes: an Analysis of his Theory of Civics, 1880–1904', *Victorian Studies*, xvi (1972–3), pp.294–5, 298–9.

Social evolution

The next naturalistically oriented schools of thought which contributed to a frame of mind congenial to the growth of collectivism are those associated with the idea of evolutionary change. The concept as such is very old and in various forms was well-established before Darwin himself came to write about it.[82] If a literary reference may be allowed to illustrate common knowledge of the theme in the first half of the last century, it will be recalled that in Disraeli's novel *Tancred* (1847) the clever young lady who endeavoured to ensnare the hero nevertheless failed to fascinate him with the latest, all-embracing work which explained everything 'scientifically'. What was most interesting about it, she said, was the way it showed 'man has been developed.'

> You know, all is development. The principle is perpetually going on. First, there was nothing, then there was something; then, I forget the next, I think there were shells, then fishes; then we came, let me see, did we come next? Never mind that; we came at last. And the next change there will be something very superior to us, something with wings. Ah! that's it: we were fishes, and I believe we shall be crows. But you must read it . . . . You understand, it is all science; . . . . Everything is proved: by geology you know.[83]

Lord Montacute, a sensitive mystic, is hardly convinced and does not believe he ever was a fish (or will be a crow); and no doubt the bluestocking summary hardly does justice to the famous *Vestiges of the Natural History of Creation* (1844) which so impressed Darwin himself. But it is apt if not sufficient evidence that the ideas were already fashionably in the air and well enough known to form the credible basis of such a drawing-room conversation.

What was largely new in the mid-century and what gave fresh impact to the idea was a detailed understanding of the mechanism by which the evolutionary process proceeded in the living world: the notion of natural selection, of competitive response to environmental change. Of course, a major immediate source of this idea was Malthus's essay. But before Darwin published *The Origin of Species* it was Spencer who had

---

82 For a brief but comprehensive review of the different phases and versions of the idea, see K. E. Bock, 'Darwin and Social Theory', *Philosophy of Science*, xxii (1955), pp.123–34. See also B. Glass *et al.* (eds), *Forerunners of Darwin: 1745–1859* (Baltimore, Md, 1959); and J. W. Burrow, *Evolution and Society: a Study in Victorian Social Theory* (Cambridge, 1966). For the related concept of progress, there is J. B. Bury, *The Idea of Progress: an Inquiry into its Origin and Growth* (1920; New York, 1955); and more recently S. Pollard, *The Idea of Progress: History and Society* (1968; Penguin, 1971) with a full bibliography.

83 B. Disraeli, *Tancred*, II.ix, in *Collected Edition of the Novels and Tales* (London, 1879–81), iv.109–10.

popularized the concept in a phrase that has since become famous: the survival of the fittest. And it was he who explored the theme most elaborately in the many volumes of his 'Synthetic Philosophy' and did so to argue an extreme libertarian case. But this was not the only set of political implications it was possible to draw from evolutionary theory and many social Darwinists took a very different view of the principles of social progress to be derived therefrom. For (as with utilitarianism) the doctrines built on the basis of a theory of evolution and natural selection could differ rather radically in emphasis. As one commentator asked at the end of the last century, 'Individualism or Collectivism? Which Way Does Evolution Point?'[84] H. G. Wells commented wryly: '"Trust Evolution", said the extreme Socialist and the extreme Individualist, as piously as the Christians put their trust in God.'[85]

The initial point to be made, therefore, is twofold. First that the theory of evolution or natural selection – the development hypothesis as it was sometimes called – had a very considerable impact. Social and political thought of all kinds had to come to terms with it if the esteemed patina of scientific authority was to be acquired by the viewpoint concerned. There was thus 'scarce a party in Europe' that did not claim for its policies the sanction of the creed: it constituted a 'vast and shadowy Colossus' beneath which thinkers and writers of all kinds had perforce to creep about.[86] Thus secondly it followed that exponents of a variety of libertarian and collectivist views would expound their doctrine in this scientistic context using its arguments and jargon. In this section, however, some indication will be given only of the way in which certain brands of statist thought were expressed in evolutionary or cognate terms. The examples to be used are: hyper-Darwinism, Marxism (most briefly), and eugenics.

Hyper-Darwinism

There is a certain tendency to suppose that the political and related implications of evolution (so-called Social Darwinism) are necessarily anti-statist. But though often true this is not always the case. Thus one commentator urged that 'the law underlying the evolutionary process makes for collectivism, and . . . there is a deeper significance in the old saying that man is a "social animal" than we have as yet realised.'[87] The writers adopting this interpretation of the biological tendency have been

---

84 Title of an article by R. Didden, in *Westminster Review*, cxlix (1898), pp. 655–66.
85 H. G. Wells, *The Shape of Things to Come* (1933; Corgi, 1967), p. 43.
86 The image is culled from E. Wingfield-Stratford, *The History of English Patriotism* (London, 1913), ii. 458, 493.
87 Didden, art. cit., p. 661.

called 'hyper-Darwinists' or 'collectivist Social Darwinians'.[88] They stressed the growing complexity and significance of the whole social organism and used this to argue the need for equally enhanced control mechanisms.

To some like T. H. Huxley (who had once been an ardent Spencerian) this was a matter for rational decision. He held that if the organism was to survive then there was need for deliberately adopted means of co-ordination in place of individualist competition and 'administrative nihilism'; and he repudiated (specifically in the case of educational provision) 'the dogmatic assertion that State interference, beyond the limits of home and foreign police must, under all circumstances, do harm.'[89] He wanted to avoid both extremes – anarchic individualism as well as 'regimental socialism' – but was quite definite that, as he wrote in 1888, the 'history of civilisation – that is, of society – is the record of the attempts which the human race has made to escape' from a condition of Hobbesian savagery. 'And of all the successive shapes which society has taken, that most nearly approaches perfection in which the war of individual against individual is most strictly limited.'[90] Again Karl Pearson, while acknowledging the importance of the 'self-asserting instinct of the individual', felt that (by the time he was writing) it had been excessively stressed and was increasingly less appropriate. In the face of a growing and severe international competition, it is vital, he wrote, 'if we as a nation are to be among the surviving fit', to recognize the importance of social organization, of the efficiency that can only come from control making the individual subservient to the whole: he thus expounded a 'veneration of the State', even thinking in terms of the desirability of dictatorship.[91] Equally, in a famous paper L. T. Hobhouse urged that the tendency of the evolutionary process involved the recognition of human interdependence and an increasingly rational 'attempt to shape our social customs and institutions in this spirit': this was 'the aim and principle of Collectiv-

---

88 The terms are used by R. Mackintosh, *From Comte to Benjamin Kidd: the Appeal to Biology or Evolution for Human Guidance* (London, 1899), Part IV; and J. D. Y. Peel, *Herbert Spencer: the Evolution of a Sociologist* (London, 1971), pp.234–7.

89 T. H. Huxley, 'Administrative Nihilism', *Fortnightly Review*, x (1871), p.529.

90 T. H. Huxley, 'The Struggle for Existence: a Programme', *The Nineteenth Century*, xxiii (1888), pp.165–6. Huxley's views and his commitment to (a limited) paternalism are analysed by M. S. Helfand, 'T. H. Huxley's "Evolution and Ethics": the Politics of Evolution and the Evolution of Politics', *Victorian Studies*, xx (1976–7), pp.159–77.

91 K. Pearson, *The Grammar of Science* (1892; Everyman, 1951), pp.307–10. Cf. his 'Socialism and Natural Selection' in *The Chances of Death and other Studies in Evolution* (London, 1897), esp. i.121, 129–32, 138; also the citations in B. Semmel, *Imperialism and Social Reform: English Social-Imperial Thought 1895–1914* (London, 1960), pp.39, 42–3.

ism.'[92] Other authors also used evolution theory to show the necessity of state interference.[93]

To writers of this type, therefore, an excessive stress on individual liberty of action, on *laissez faire*, free competition, and the like was quite inappropriate. It would not do in the context of a highly evolved and complex society in which there was a manifest and growing need for social peace and order and the avoidance of disruption or unrest. At the least, substantial educational and other social provision was vital; and this could only come from government. A. R. Wallace was one scientist who came to adopt such a view, thereby helping him to turn upside-down the libertarian versions of Social Darwinism. He accepted that for man, as for the lower animals, the only method of advance was 'some form of selection'; but this could only effectively occur once the inequalities and other circumstances which marred existing social arrangements had been eliminated by reform thereby creating a state of affairs which would permit mental and cultural development of a higher kind. As he put it in 1912, 'Improvement of social conditions must precede improvement of character; and only when we have so organised society as to abolish the cruel and debasing struggle for existence and for wealth that now prevails, shall we be enabled to liberate those beneficial natural forces which can alone elevate character.'[94]

A writer of particular interest in this connexion is Benjamin Kidd. After some years as a minor civil servant he was able (through the success of his book *Social Evolution*) to resign and devote himself to sociological study. He had a taste for bolstering his ideas with fashionable scientific notions and used arguments of an evolutionary kind for a purpose broadly similar to, though in some respects different from, that of Huxley. In his Herbert Spencer lecture in 1908 on the subject 'Individualism and After', Kidd acknowledged that evolutionary ideas appeared at the apogee of individualism but denied that there was any necessary association. He pointed to the increase in the functions of the state that had been occurring and argued that Spencer's more optimistic expectations about the nature and direction of progress were thus being falsified in fact.[95] In contrast the evolutionary future lay in the direction of an organic society in which the individual unit would become more

92 L. T. Hobhouse, 'The Ethical Basis of Collectivism', *International Journal of Ethics*, viii (1897–8), pp.150–1.

93 e.g. H. Seal, *On the Nature of State Interference* (London, n.d. [1893]).

94 Wallace, 'Evolution and Character', in P. Parker (ed.), *Character and Life* (London, 1912), pp. 49–50. I take this citation from J. R. Durant, 'Scientific Naturalism and Social Reform in the Thought of Alfred Russel Wallace', *British Journal for the History of Science*, xii (1979), p. 50; pp.48–51 of this paper deal with Wallace's fusion of naturalism and social reform.

95 B. Kidd, *Individualism and After* (Oxford, 1908), pp.13, 14–16.

subordinate to corporate interests.[96] The problem was how to achieve the necessary degree of regulation required. And he thought this was a matter of religion and thus of obedience through faith.[97] On this view the quality which gave superiority to a race or species in the struggle for existence was not a competitive individualism from which a natural harmony of interests emerged but a willingness to subordinate the person and his particular concerns to those of the group. Yet this altruism required not a rational submission but one in which another element is paramount:

> On the one side we have the self-assertive reason of the individual necessarily tending to be ever more and more developed by the evolutionary forces at work. On the other, we have the immensely wider interests of the social organism, and behind it those of the race in general, demanding, nevertheless, the most absolute subordination of this ever-increasing rational self-assertiveness in the individual. We find, in fact, if progress is to continue, that the individual must be compelled to submit to conditions of existence of the most onerous kind which, to all appearance, his reason actually gives him the power to suspend – and all to further a development in which he has not, and in which he never can have, *qua* individual, the slightest practical interest. We have, it would now appear, henceforth to witness the extraordinary spectacle of man, moved by a profound social instinct, continually endeavouring in the interests of his social progress to check and control the tendency of his own reason to suspend and reverse the conditions which are producing this progress.[98]

This tension between individual reason and communally oriented religious belief and the emerging dominance of the latter as a socially integrative influence is 'the central feature of human history'. According to the 'law' of human development, as Kidd sees it, there is a conflict of these two opposing forces:

> the disintegrating principle represented by the rational self-assertiveness of the individual units; the integrating principle represented by a religious belief providing a sanction for social conduct which is always of necessity ultra-rational, and the function of which is

96　ibid., pp. 23–4.
97　ibid., p. 27.
98　B. Kidd, *Social Evolution* (1894; WEA, London, 1921), pp. 83–4. Cf. the explicit repudiation of the natural harmony ideas of the utilitarians and Spencer, ibid., pp. 293–9; also the discussion of the two crucial 'counter-principles' in *Individualism and After*, pp. 33–4.

to secure in the stress of evolution the continual subordination of the interests of the individual units to the larger interests of the longer-lived social organism to which they belong.[99]

The implication is that a collectivist tendency, that 'requiring the increasing subordination of the individual to society', is the dominating principle of a 'healthy and progressive' social organism. Not state management simply but 'state interference and state control on a greatly extended scale' is what evolution implies.[100] Kidd's works were extremely popular and widely read. For instance, within a dozen years of its publication in 1894 Social Evolution had gone through three editions and seventeen reprints. It was still in print as late as 1921 and, an important indication of the kind of appeal it had, appeared in a cheap paperback especially produced for classes run by the Workers' Educational Association. Science plus religion equals state control was a sum of ideas that seems to have exercised an irresistible fascination for many people in the Labour movement. Noah Ablett, prominent in the affairs of the South Wales miners, published in 1919, under the aegis of the Plebs League, a primer in economics in which he asserts quite bluntly that 'in the 20th century every system of thought which makes any pretence at being scientific must have an evolutionary basis.'[101] Another reflection of this Socialist absorption of evolutionary theory is provided by one popular ideological catechism. In a section on 'The Socialist Conception of the Universe' it is stated that 'Socialism primarily accepts the theory of evolution in its fullest extent. It bases its view of the universe upon positive science and reasoned conclusions.' It is then asserted that 'the discoveries and teachings of Darwin are not in opposition to Socialism.' There is certainly a struggle for existence but it is not exclusively between individuals; nor is it true 'to suppose that competition alone has at any time brought out the highest qualities of humanity.'[102]

In fact many of the scientistic notions so far described coalesced in the theories of the Fabians. These were indeed a sort of heady mixture of utilitarianism, positivism, and hyper-Darwinist evolutionary ideas, though the leading Fabians – with the possible exception of Mrs Webb – did not see the matter precisely in Kidd's way as one depending on religious belief. There was rather a more secular emphasis to their opinions. Thus G. B. Shaw held that the 'Life Force' would produce a race of supermen and women to solve all the apparently insuperable

99 Social Evolution, p.104 (this entire passage is italicized in the original).
100 ibid., pp.238–9, 240–1 (these phrases are also italicized).
101 N. Ablett, Easy Outlines of Economics (Sheffield, 1919), p.7.
102 E. B. Bax and H. Quelch, A New Catechism of Socialism (6th edn, London, 1909), pp.33–4.

problems that bedevilled history.[103] H. G. Wells continually argued that whatever progress was possible to humanity demanded a greater technocratic control of natural and social forces. It was clear to these people that competitive individualism would not alone lead to desirable advance and that the social dimension must come to the fore. In his contribution to the original *Fabian Essays*, Sidney Webb wrote of the organic view of society and, in that context, of social control over the individual. Society is something more than 'an aggregate of so many individual units'; indeed it creates the individual and what he is and knows; moreover, where individual action is 'inimical to the social welfare, it must sooner or later be checked by the whole'. Seen in the context of the theory of biological evolution, Webb says, the units concerned are not individuals but whole societies with their different forms of organization. There is, therefore, more need to improve 'the social organism' than to pursue merely 'individual development'. Or rather, he adds (using, in typical confusion, the language of mechanism as well as that of biology),

> the perfect and fitting development of each individual is not necessarily the utmost and highest cultivation of his own personality, but the filling, in the best possible way, of his humble function in the great social machine. We must abandon the self-conceit of imagining that we are independent units, and bend our jealous minds, absorbed in their own cultivation, to this subjection to the higher end, the Common Weal. Accordingly, conscious 'direct adaptation' steadily supplants the unconscious and wasteful 'indirect adaptation' of the earlier form of the struggle for existence . . . . Man is seen to assume more and more, not only the mastery of 'things', but also a conscious control over social destiny itself.[104]

Consequently complete individual liberty with unrestrained private ownership of the instruments of wealth production is irreconcilable with the common weal: 'the free struggle for existence among ourselves menaces our survival as a healthy and permanent social organism' so that for 'blind anarchic competition' must be substituted 'consciously regulated co-ordination among the units of each organism'. And this irresistible evolution into collectivism is, says Webb, clear for all to see in the steady increase in government regulation of private enterprise, the

---

103   There is a fascinating account of this doctrine of 'heroic vitalism' in Eric Bentley's *The Cult of the Superman* (London, 1947) which discusses, among other exponents, Carlyle, Nietzsche, Wagner, and Shaw.

104   S. Webb, 'The Basis of Socialism: Historic' in G. B. Shaw *et al.*, *Fabian Essays* (1889; Jubilee edn, London, 1950), pp. 53–4. Cf. Webb's *The Difficulties of Individualism*, Fabian tract no. 69 (London, 1896), pp. 4–6.

growth of municipal administration, and the rapid shifting of the tax burden directly to rent and interest.[105]

Nor were such theories only invoked by Fabian intellectuals. In a pamphlet entitled *Socialism and the Survival of the Fittest* J. Connell argued that it was individualism that was opposed to the laws of science and nature. The struggle for existence has itself improved man's mind and understanding of things which has led him to realize that, at the level of the struggle which has now been reached, it is competition between groups which is crucial and not that between individuals (which is appropriate to a lower stratum of existence). The current question is, therefore, What form of social arrangement conforms most closely to these conditions? And the answer is, of course, the Socialist society.[106] In a nice inversion of the argument of Herbert Spencer (who is nevertheless frequently cited in these matters) it is urged that there can be no effective improvement of the species where there is no equality of opportunity; if every man's reward is to depend on his own exertions merely then inheritance of privilege or wealth is an impediment. Similarly, in terms of sexual selection, possibilities will improve when female choice can be cast in terms of superior morality rather than of wealth. Undoubtedly capitalist individualism exists but it is one of nature's failures; it must be replaced, therefore, in the natural evolutionary course of events.[107] Another pamphlet issued by the ILP which uses *inter alia* the same kind of language to collectivist purpose and which cites both Spencer and Kidd, urges that the principles of social science are biological in form because there is an essential similarity between the evolutionary process in nature and in individual and society: each unit must serve the development of the whole of which it is a part.[108]

Marxism

This is perhaps the obvious point at which to say a very few words about this subject. Marxist doctrine might, it is true, be seen in other contexts, that of utilitarianism, for instance. Thus in a witty (and perceptive) epigram, Lord Keynes once characterized the creed as 'the final *reductio ad absurdum* of Benthamism'.[109] By this remark I take him to be referring not only to Marx's acknowledged indebtedness to bourgeois political economists of the classical school and to the ideas of exploitation and class struggle latent in their work (as in the implications of Ricardo's

105 *Fabian Essays*, pp. 55–6.
106 J. Connell, *Socialism and the Survival of the Fittest* (4th edn, London, n.d.), pp. 1, 11–12.
107 ibid., pp. 12–16.
108 T. D. Benson, *Socialism & Service* (London, n.d. [1906]), pp. 3, 6–7, 9.
109 J. M. Keynes, 'My Early Beliefs' (1938), in *Two Memoirs* (London, 1949), p. 97.

theory of rent) but also, and above all, to the rationalist manner which assumes that scientific laws of human action may be established and knowledge of them used completely to remake society and the relations of its members. Yet if this is the crucial aspect of Marxist thought in view then the evolutionary parallel is uppermost. For in these naturalistic terms Marx's contribution as a scientific sociologist was to reveal the ineluctable laws of human history, in particular of course 'the special law of motion' governing the capitalist mode of production, an achievement specifically seen by his followers in tandem with Darwin's discovery of the principles underlying the development of organic nature.[110] In this context Marx is thus a sort of exotic, collectivist Spencer, even in some respects sharing the latter's sense of the ultimate triumph of libertarian anarchism as with the notion that the state would, in the last outcome, wither away. Yet the Marxist themes are indeed ambiguous. For if it must definitionally be the case that the state as an instrument of class oppression will necessarily disappear with the revolutionary triumph of the workers and so the end of the class struggle and of classes themselves, it is also true that this need not be so with that aspect of the political apparatus seen as a parasitic body, both administrative and military, before which all fall in submission on their knees.[111] This possibility presents an awesome collectivist spectacle indeed, revealed, for Marxist dissidents, in the terrors actual or potential of modern totalitarian society. These are all theoretical prospects, perhaps of little fascination in any case, which I cannot explore here.[112] I must simply note that, to many if not most of its adherents and critics alike, what might be called vulgar Marxism is a social and political doctrine premeditated in a naturalistic way: the Marxist study of society is supposed to proceed just as the scientist studies the working of nature, and Socialism is to be built on this basis (as in the USSR as the older documents always used to say).[113] I know that, especially of late, other emphases of Marxist thought have come often to the fore. But the stress that was long dominant was that which relied on the naturalistic aspects of the creed; and it is one which is clearly (though not exclusively) compatible with a high view of the state.

And this is all – no doubt to the contempt or scorn of those who believe the whole truth lies here – that I care to say about these obscure matters.

110 The *locus classicus* is F. Engels, 'Speech at the Graveside of Karl Marx' (1883), in K. Marx and F. Engels, *Selected Works* (Moscow, 1951–8), ii. 153–4.

111 K. Marx, 'The Eighteenth Brumaire of Louis Bonaparte' (1852), ibid., i. 332; F. Engels, 'The Origin of the Family, Private Property and the State' (1884), ibid., ii. 290–1.

112 Though some aspects of latter-day Trotskyite (or cognate) activity are touched on in *The Ideological Heritage*, ch. 12.

113 On all these points, may one minor instance stand for many? See the Communist Party pamphlet by T. A. Jackson, *Socialism: What? Why? How?* (London, 1945), esp. pp. 6–7, 8, 62.

Eugenics

Another scientistic field that sometimes issued in policy proposals of a startling and intimate kind is eugenics. The word was coined in 1883 by Sir Francis Galton (Darwin's cousin) who defined it as 'the study of agencies under social control that may improve or impair the racial qualities of future generations either physically or mentally'.[114] Its scientific pretensions lay in its association with evolutionary and genetic theories and its application of the biological principles of breeding to improve the quality of the human stock. The difference was that instead of the blind process of natural selection a deliberate effort was to be made to improve the species by attending to the regulation of the production of offspring.[115] And it was seen by its exponents not simply as a genuine science but also as a system of values involving a concept of an ideal society made up of individuals with desirable biological qualities.[116] It did not necessarily look unfavourably on environmental change as a means of advance: indeed many eugenicists saw this as crucial and argued that the rational reorganization of man's natural and social context was a vital key to progress. But a more characteristic eugenic concern (and what so appealed to quite a number of social reformers) was with planned genetic improvement of the human material itself through breeding from the best stocks and controlling the fertility of the worst, in opposition, therefore, to the actual tendencies of the day which intimated a likely degeneration of the race.[117] And this was seen as entailing a varying degree of detailed legal supervision. For 'social hygiene' and the elimination of the unfit might involve quite extensive and minute control of human propagation.[118] Sidney Webb, who preferred rather to stress the manipulation of the environment to produce a higher type of being, nevertheless brought out well the collectivist aspects of the creed: 'No consistent eugenist', he wrote, 'can be a "Laisser Faire" individualist unless he throws up the game in despair. He must interfere, interfere, interfere!'[119] Galton himself described a eugenic utopia called 'Kantsaywhere' which was 'amiably paternalistic'. And, although he affirmed his abhorrence of anything approaching the despotic, he was all the same prepared to countenance a quite notable degree of 'stern compulsion' in order to limit the breeding

---

114 F. Galton, 'Eugenics: Its Definition, Scope and Aims', *Nature*, lxx (1904), p.82.

115 G. R. Searle, *Eugenics and Politics in Britain 1900–1914* (Leyden, 1976), p.4.

116 C. P. Blacker, *Eugenics: Galton and After* (London, 1952), p.13.

117 Searle, op. cit., pp.6–7, 25–8. The differences of emphasis in the eugenic camp are examined *inter alia* by M. Freeden, 'Eugenics and Progressive Thought: a Study in Ideological Affinity', *Historical Journal*, xxii (1979), pp.645–71.

118 Cf. Searle, op. cit., pp.68–9.

119 S. Webb, 'Eugenics and the Poor Law: the Minority Report', *Eugenics Review*, ii (1910–11), p.237.

of dysgenic undesirables.[120] A variety of legislative policies in human stirpiculture was envisaged: changes in the marriage laws; the issue of 'eugenic certificates' to those who would make good mates; family allowances for suitable parents who should also be benefited by changes in the tax system; custody of the defective, that is, the insane, the feeble-minded, confirmed criminals, even paupers; improved education and associated facilities; spread of knowledge about birth control; compulsory sterilization or even castration and spaying. In some places, this last policy was actually implemented, in a dozen or so states of the USA for example.[121] Other recent instances are those coming from Nazi Germany and Mrs Gandhi's India. Occasionally it was even suggested that the unfit should be painlessly killed.[122]

Nowadays some of this literature might seem not so much advanced as distasteful in the extreme but, at the beginning of the century, notions of this sort were not at all uncommon and were widely accepted in professional and progressive circles concerned with the avoidance of racial degeneracy.[123] Liberals, Conservatives, and Socialists alike, people such as Wells, Wallas, Laski, Keynes, Balfour, and the young Neville Chamberlain looked to this branch of biology to achieve that qualitative improvement in human beings necessary for the advancement of national efficiency.[124] Examples of this kind of thinking and the degree of state control envisaged are easily given. For instance, William Beveridge, discussing on one occasion the problem of the unemployed, argued that those who through 'general defects' were unable to fill the social role of a complete person ought to be regarded as 'unemployable' and so as the dependants of the state; they should be maintained in public institutions and lose all their rights as citizens including the franchise, civil freedom, and fatherhood.[125] Similarly the Glaswegian educationalist, H. Dyer, in an article in the *Westminster Review*, proposed the usual array of eugenic controls (including the sterilization of the unfit) to prevent the propagation of the diseased, the mentally defective, those convicted of

---

120 Blacker, *Eugenics: Galton and After*, pp.122–3; F. Galton, *Memories of My Life* (1908; 2nd edn, London, 1908), p.311.

121 M. H. Haller, *Eugenics: Hereditarian Attitudes in American Thought* (New Brunswick, N.J., 1963), ch.IV; Searle, op. cit., ch.8, esp. pp.93–5.

122 Searle, op. cit., pp.92–3.

123 ibid., ch.2 describes the notable range of support the movement received.

124 See e.g. A. White, 'Eugenics and National Efficiency', *Eugenics Review*, i (1909–10), esp. pp.107, 109–11; H. G. Wells, *Anticipations* . . .(1901; London, 1914), pp.299–302, 304; Freeden, art. cit., pp.670–1; Searle, op. cit., pp.11–14, 34ff.

125 W. Beveridge, 'The Problem of the Unemployed. Report of a Conference held by the Sociological Society . . . on April 4, 1906', *Sociological Papers*, iii (1907), p.327. But cf. J. Harris, *William Beveridge: a Biography* (Oxford, 1977), pp.117–19 for Beveridge's change of view.

heinous crime, and so on.[126] For his part J. A. Hobson asserted that to 'abandon the production of children to unrestricted private enterprise is the most dangerous abnegation of its functions which any Government can practise', adding that society had the 'right to insist that worthless, or even noxious, lives shall not be thrust upon it for support by reckless or unfit parents.'[127] One review of the relationship between eugenics and Socialism held that they should be combined so that the 'socially fit would find free scope for the full development of their faculties, while the unfit would be dealt with according to eugenic methods'.[128] And if Havelock Ellis hesitated on the verge of advocating a policy of actual sterilization, Mrs Stopes was not at all inhibited in this respect: she believed this ought to be done compulsorily to prevent the reproduction of 'innumerable tens of thousands of stunted, warped and inferior infants'.[129] A. C. Pigou, the economist, recommended 'violent interference' with individual liberty when dealing with the 'wreckage of society'.[130] The later writings of Karl Pearson, works which he himself described as Socialist, associated these eugenic notions and policies with specific attacks on the lower orders who were seen as breeding inferior stock like rabbits to the detriment of the race: his attitude was statist, 'a regimented socialism, subservient to a racial definition of welfare and morality'.[131] One later and extreme example of this genre traced contemporary ills to 'a process of national impoverishment, which destroyed the great civilizations of the past and which threatens to destroy our own.' Civilization is assumed to depend on 'superior racial stocks', yet the 'under-man' threatens their emergence. The solution lies in applied biology by, for example, 'the prevention of all obvious degenerates from having children' and by encouraging the procreation of a new aristocracy to form *an ever-perfecting super race*' in the society of the future.[132] Another work in the

126 H. Dyer, 'The Future of Politics', *Westminster Review*, cxlv (1896), p.10.
127 J. A. Hobson, *The Social Problem: Life and Work* (London, 1909), pp.214–15; and see pp.213–17 *passim*. Cf. H. J. Laski, 'The Scope of Eugenics', *Westminster Review*, clxxiv (1910), p.34.
128 S. Herbert, 'Eugenics and Socialism', *Eugenics Review*, ii (1910–11), pp.119, 121–2.
129 H. Ellis, 'Sterilization of the Unfit', *Eugenics Review*, i (1909–10), pp.203–6; M. Stopes, *Radiant Motherhood* (1920), p.231, in R. Hall, *Marie Stopes, a Biography* (1977; Virago, 1978), pp.180–1. See also Mrs Stopes's letter cited in L. Hudson, 'From Anguish to Arithmetic', *TLS* (6 October 1978), p.1106; and Searle, op. cit., pp.93ff.
130 A. C. Pigou, 'Some Aspects of the Problem of Charity', in C. F. G. Masterman (ed.), *The Heart of the Empire* (London, 1901), p.246, in M. Freeden, *The New Liberalism: an Ideology of Social Reform* (Oxford, 1978), p.179.
131 Freeden, 'Eugenics and Progressive Thought', art. cit., p.668. On Pearson, see also Semmel, op. cit., pp.48–9; Haller, op. cit., pp.12–14.
132 L. Stoddard, *The Revolt against Civilization: the Menace of the Underman* (London, 1922), esp. pp.v, 19, 220–1, 228, 242–3 (italics in original).

same style stressed the need to tackle the eugenic problem by segregating the unfit and, if possible, sterilizing them.[133] Such issues as these had earlier come to a head in public over the Mental Deficiency Bill of 1912 and similar legislative proposals which were based on the belief that the community had to be protected from this threat of racial degeneration by appropriate state action including the compulsory detention of the mentally deficient. In this case the debate in and out of Parliament centred on the question whether justice to the individual should give way to the scientific protection of the welfare of the community.[134] There were indeed those of libertarian mind who refused to accept the degree of bureaucratic control the pursuit of social hygiene in this manner might entail, and who held it was unacceptable because there would be an alteration of the motives and characters of citizens which would in itself have a deleterious eugenic effect.[135]

Interestingly, many of the sort of questions that arose in the course of eugenic discussion have of late been revived by the development of so-called 'biomedicine' and the possibility of 'genetic engineering' which seem to make feasible at least the elimination of inherited defects and, as well, the controlled production of an improved human breed. And if the former seems to entail no more than an extension of the kind of supervision already involved in compulsory vaccination or X-ray screening, the latter seems indubitably to raise the spectre of Huxley's brave new world.[136] And, to whatever degree, either requires an extension of public supervision. Something of the passions still aroused by discussion of the 'degeneration' of the race brought about (as it is suggested) by the 'rising proportion of children being born to mothers' of inferior education and moral quality is reflected, too, in the furore that followed Sir Keith Joseph's remarks on this matter in 1974. He was certainly outspoken; but all he advocated in effect (and in the manner of the advanced radicalism of a generation or more ago) was the extension of birth-control facilities and education.[137] Yet the resulting outcry at these mild neo-eugenic remarks was loud, vituperative, and not a little astonishing. If they really want to be shocked progressive critics should study the views of a genuine, old-fashioned, Socialist eugenicist like Karl Pearson.

133 R. A. Freeman, *Social Decay and Regeneration* (London, 1921), esp. chs. XI–XIII.
134 See the account in Searle, op. cit., ch.9; and Freeden, *The New Liberalism*, pp.190–3. For one instance of official consideration, see Churchill's 1910 memorandum on the feeble-minded as a social danger in PRO, CAB 37/108/189.
135 W. C. Dampier Whetham, 'Eugenics and Politics', *Eugenics Review*, ii (1910–11), pp.242–3; F. C. S. Schiller, *Eugenics and Politics* (London, 1926), pp.15–16, 22, 99.
136 Cf. Huxley's own remarks, in S. Bedford, *Aldous Huxley: a Biography* (London, 1973–4), i.244–5.
137 Report of Sir Keith Joseph's speech in *The Times* (21 October 1974), p.3.

Psychological theory

I am not sure whether it is proper to regard developments under this head as a form of scientism; in many respects perhaps not. Collingwood for one held that, far from being the 'science of mind' it claimed to be, psychology was merely 'the fashionable scientific fraud of the age.'[138] But certainly in the late nineteenth century 'psychology . . . modelled itself on those successful natural-science neighbours in whose district it had decided to build its mansion'.[139] Nor has the pretension subsequently diminished. In any case it is the intention rather than any valid achievement that is significant in the consideration of those aspects of the study of mind and behaviour bearing on the antithesis between the individual and the collective. And in this context certain facets of psychological theory are indeed relevant, their significance lying in the way each appears to cast grave doubt on a number of the basic assumptions about human nature underlying libertarian political thought, in particular the belief in the rationality of mankind. The ground is thus prepared, albeit indirectly, for the acceptance of some kind of collective control. Obviously it is not that this anti-rationality has developed only in the wake of the psychological themes in question; but these themes, claiming a scientific foundation, have (because of this presumed basis and the authority it brings) given a considerable impetus to this tradition of anti-intellectualism.

Libertarian political and social ideas with their emphasis on the importance of individuality and freedom from external restraint necessarily rested on the supposition that human beings were essentially creatures of reason. In many if not most people this was perhaps a potential rather than an actual capability. Yet, in all but a few, education and experience could mould and develop the rational faculty so that, in due course, men and women would attain to a clear understanding of their own interests and possibilities of development, the means to achieve this end, and its relation to common social concerns. Some such assumption of human rationality invariably provided the foundation of individualist thought from at least early-modern times onwards. It was, too, a crucial part of the libertarian view of government, that is, that the state should leave well alone and that the individual should act rationally in the realm of freedom thereby sustained. Thus the judicious Locke had assumed that 'we are *born Free*, as we are born Rational'; and the freedom man has of acting according to his own will 'is *grounded on* his having *Reason*, which is able to instruct him in that Law he is to govern

138 R. G. Collingwood, *An Autobiography* (1939; Oxford, 1964), pp. 94–5.
139 J. Bruner's Herbert Spencer lecture, 'Psychology and the Image of Man', *TLS* (17 December 1976), p. 1589.

himself by'.[140] Crucial as it was to the libertarian position, it was precisely this kind of presupposition which came under critical fire from certain trends of thought which stressed rather the non-rational elements in human life and behaviour. Of course, this was not at all new: what else was meant by the symbolic story of the Fall of man? And was not one of the eternal themes of literature the dominance of passion over the human will? Goya, inscribing a title on one of his *Caprichos*, wrote 'El sueño de la razón produce monstruos'. In the very recent past, specific scepticism about the role of reason in politics has often been expressed, as by Burke and Disraeli for instance.[141] Carlyle, after chronicling one of the more repugnant sides of the French Revolution, had asked, 'Is Man's civilisation only a wrappage, through which the savage nature of him can still burst, infernal as ever?'[142] It was not an unusual question to pose. And it was one increasingly put after the arrival of the idea of the unconscious mind and of the psycho-analysis of Freud and others with which this idea came to be closely associated. With specific reference to 'a subconscious region', Bishop Gore wrote in 1930 that recent psychology 'has reacted strongly against the older rationalism'; while a decade later the Socialist MP and theorist, E. F. M. Durbin, held that one general conclusion to be derived from 'the evidence of analytical psychology' was 'the importance of the *irrational* and the *unconscious* in social life.'[143]

Of course, Freud himself did not invent this central notion of the unconscious. As reflecting basic, powerful, and untoward aspects of human nature associated with the passions the idea is age-old. And even in its specific form it can be traced back at least to Leibniz.[144] By the mid-nineteenth century it was fashionably in the air. *Philosophy of the Unconscious* was the title of a well-known book published in 1869 by the German philosopher, Eduard von Hartmann, the doctrine of which was referred to in the pages of the *Westminster Review* a few years later.[145]

140 Locke, *Two Treatises of Government*, ed. Laslett (Cambridge, 1960), II, §§61, 63 (pp. 326, 327) (italics in original).
141 e.g. E. Burke, *The Works* (World's Classics, 1925), iv. 95–6; Disraeli, *Coningsby* (1844), in *Collected Edition of the Novels and Tales* (London, 1878–81), ii. 239–40.
142 T. Carlyle, 'The French Revolution' (1837), in *Works* (People's edn, 1871–4), iv. 210.
143 C. Gore, *The Philosophy of the Good Life* (1930; Everyman, 1963), pp. 291–2; E. F. M. Durbin, *The Politics of Democratic Socialism: an Essay on Social Policy* (London, 1940), p. 70 (italics in original).
144 Leibniz, 'New Essays on the Human Understanding' (written 1702–3), in *Philosophical Writings* (Everyman, 1934), pp. 147–8. On the historical background of the notion, cf. R. W. Clark, *Freud: the Man and the Cause* (London, 1980), pp. 114–17.
145 See the references in *OED*, *sub* 'unconscious', §2. Hartmann reviews previous discussion of the subject, *Philosophy of the Unconscious* (trans. edn, London, 1884), i. 16–42.

Again Samuel Butler had, in the 1870s and 1880s, begun to develop a theory of evolution based not on Darwinian natural selection of chance variations but on 'unconscious memory' transmitted as habit from generation to generation. The pastor in Strindberg's *The Father* (1887) refers to the 'Unconscious' and adds, 'what a beautiful idea'.[146] The cognate concept of a 'subliminal' self or memory also appeared in the 1880s and 1890s.[147] Freud was thus building on a notion already familiar but, of course, he extended and systematized it very substantially indeed in much the way that Darwin or Spencer had developed the pre-existing ideas they took over, welding these into a comprehensive scheme. Specifically Freud sought to explain the dynamic mechanisms which restrained the unconscious mind and also to create techniques for examining it.[148] Moreover, vital therapeutic possibilities seemed to derive from this knowledge. A new method of diagnosing and treating neuroses was thus involved.

Sigmund Freud produced an extensive and influential series of books and papers from the 1890s on, all in pursuit of his youthful ambition to be a natural scientist and, like Darwin, to change the world. Above all he wanted to relate mental processes to measurable entities like those found in the sciences of chemistry and physics.[149] His first work to be published in Britain – and the one he himself always regarded as the most important – was *The Interpretation of Dreams* (1900), which appeared in English translation in 1913 with a popular edition the following year. It was somewhat esoteric but its influence was less confined than might have been the case because there were cognate tendencies afoot in other fields (art and literature, for example) and because the book was taken up by Orage's periodical *The New Age*, notice in which helped to spread its ideas among the intellectual laity.[150] But the two works of Freud that are perhaps of most note in the present context, because they deal with some of the social implications of his theories, are *The Future of an Illusion* (1927) – the 'illusion' being religion or the desire for a heavenly Father – and *Civilization and its Discontents* (1930). Sociology is there presented as a form of applied psychology.

In the terms Freud has made familiar, man is not seen simply as the

146 A. Strindberg, *Three Plays* (Penguin, 1976), p.63.
147 Cf. *OED* which cites the first usage in 1886.
148 L. S. Hearnshaw, 'Psychology', in C. B. Cox and A. E. Dyson (eds), *The Twentieth-Century Mind: History, Ideas and Literature in Britain* (London, 1972), i.236.
149 R. W. Clark, op. cit., pp.28–9, 36, 41, 96–7, 117, 121.
150 See e.g. the series of articles by M. W. Robieson, 'Psycho-analysis and Conduct', *The New Age* (5–26 October 1916), pp.543–4, 560–2, 585–6, 607–9. Jung's *Psychology of the Unconscious* was also reviewed, ibid. (20 June 1916), pp.284–5. Of course, Freud's reputation was already spreading in professional circles: see Clark, op. cit., chs.11–12 and pp.373–6, 384–6.

stable, responsible, and rational individual of enlightenment or libertarian convention consciously pursuing the attainment of pleasure or
well-being, but as motivated, even dominated, by inner forces he cannot
direct and of which he is not even aware. He could no longer be regarded,
even potentially, as autonomous and in charge of himself; and his reason
was (in the Humeian phrase) the slave of his passions and impulses. All
the mature achievements of the human spirit in morals, art, religion, and
so on are simply compensations man creates for himself to sustain that
rigorous control of his unconscious desires and instincts that is necessary
for social living. In this sense 'civilization has to be defended against the
individual, and its regulations, institutions and commands are directed
to that task.' Because there are present in all men 'destructive, and
therefore anti-social' propensities, 'every civilization must be built up on
coercion and renunciation of instinct'.[151] Morality is thus not the
outcome of the rational understanding but a restraint which holds in
place those forces which, if released, would render society impossible.[152]
It is because we unconsciously or really hate other people and are in
aggressive competition with them that we are ethically constrained to act
honestly, love our neighbour, and treat him equitably. Conscience is a
sort of social censor or policeman made necessary by the need to regulate
these inner drives and not the embodiment of a deliberately achieved
moral rule. Similarly the masses will necessarily be controlled by a
minority of leaders and, above all perhaps, by such psychological
restraints as those imposed by religion.[153] The decisive step towards
civilization is indeed the 'replacement of the power of the individual' by
that of the community.[154] Rationality itself is thus not the instrument of
truth but the reflection or sublimation of our instinctive needs by which
the will is dominated: so a man's judgements about ethics are 'an attempt
to support his illusions with arguments.' One is reminded of Bradley's
aphorism that 'Metaphysics is the finding of bad reasons for what we
believe upon instinct, but to find these reasons is no less an instinct'.[155]

Thus two levels of mental functioning are discerned and the basic
process is one very different from that so often supposed. It is revealed
not in reason but in dreams, fantasies, desires, myths, mental disorders,

151 S. Freud, 'The Future of an Illusion' (1927), in *The Complete Psychological Works*
      (standard edn, London, 1953–74), xxi.6–7. Cf. ibid., xxi.15.
152 On the Burkeian overtones of this view, see P. Roazen, *Freud: Political and Social
      Thought* (London, 1969), pp.209–10; cf. ibid., p.271–3; also the remarks on Jung's
      concept of the 'Collective Unconscious' in F. W. Matson, 'The Political Implications
      of Psychoanalytic Theory', *The Journal of Politics*, xvi (1954), pp.715–16.
153 Freud, op. cit., in *The Complete Psychological Works*, xxi.7–9, 21.
154 Freud, 'Civilization and its Discontents' (1930), ibid., xxi.95.
155 Freud, ibid., xxi.145; F. H. Bradley, *Appearance and Reality: a Metaphysical Essay*
      (1893; 2nd rev. edn, Oxford, 1959), p.x.

and other such manifestations of the psychically fundamental. Of course, the shattering impact of the Great War seemed to confirm this Hobbesian sense of the savage, irrational forces in human nature and the need for their control. After that revelation of the primeval, it could never be glad, confident morning again. If ever, wrote Wells's Hugh Britling under the stress of his war experiences, 'if ever there was a bigger lie . . . than any other, it is that man is a reasonable creature'. The hopelessness and loss felt in the face of such shock is reflected, too, in a poem of Herbert Read's written at an early climax of the Second World War:

> . . . we who have put our faith
> in the goodness of man
> and now see man's image debas'd
> lower than the wolf or the hog –
>
> Where can we turn for consolation?[156]

L. T. Hobhouse, an arch-apostle of rationality, held that whereas the 'Victorian age believed in law and reason' the Great War showed its 'sons have come in large measure to believe in violence, and in impulse, emotion, or instinct.' Again, Aldous Huxley asserted in this fashion in 1925 that the 'horrors and squalors' of so-called civilization 'arise from men's lack of reason – from their failure to be completely and sapiently human.'[157] If Freud's theory of the subconscious is true then, as W. H. R. Rivers said, it must be taken into account by every one 'concerned with the study of human conduct'. He himself denied the more extravagant claims made in its behalf but had found Freudian theory of immense practical and clinical value in his work on war-neurosis.[158] Its political implications in respect of the possibility of realizing a rational society of free individuals were no less crucial.

Nor was Freudian theory the only view with these perhaps unseemly social and political consequences. The behaviourist school of psychology, otherwise totally different from that of Freud, seemed similarly to imply that human conduct was not really a sequence of rationally considered choices. In its pursuit of the deepest possible causal understanding, behaviourism seemed to place men entirely in the grip of

156 H. G. Wells, *Mr. Britling Sees It Through* (1916; London, 1933), p.224; H. Read, 'Ode Written During the Battle of Dunkirk, May, 1940' in P. Fussell, *The Great War and Modern Memory* (1975; London, 1977), p.295. Cf. H. G. Wells, *The Secret Places of the Heart* (London, 1922), p.16.

157 L. T. Hobhouse, *The World in Conflict* (London, 1915), p.29; A. Huxley, *Those Barren Leaves* (1925; Penguin, 1951), p.84.

158 W. H. R. Rivers, 'Freud's Psychology of the Unconscious' (1917), in *Instinct and the Unconscious: a Contribution to a Biological Theory of the Psycho-Neuroses* (Cambridge, 1920), Appendix I, pp.160, 166, 168–9.

fully determined events. It is a dilemma posed by all forms of scientistic analysis, the acute consciousness of which was revealed in J. S. Mill's remarks about the general doctrine of 'Philosophical Necessity'. It weighed on my existence, he wrote, 'like an incubus. I felt as if I was scientifically proved to be the helpless slave of antecedent circumstances; as if my character and that of all others had been formed for us by agencies beyond our control'.[159]

Behaviourist psychology found its origin in late-Victorian times in studies of animal behaviour. The danger of anthropomorphism was always present and led, therefore, to a stress (as in the work of C. L. Morgan) on both objective, empirical inquiry and the avoidance of reference to forms of higher mental activity.[160] It was, however, the American psychologist, J. B. Watson, who founded the doctrine specifically called 'Behaviourism' by extending these two tenets to the study of man: that is, the rigid use of empirical method and the repudiation of consciousness as the basic subject-matter of analysis. Behaviourism is thus a kind of zoological, materialist approach to human conduct, man being studied like any other member of the animal kingdom: 'it is a purely objective experimental branch of natural science' with as its goal 'the prediction and control of human behaviour'.[161]

The term itself is no older than Watson's paper in the *Psychological Review* in 1913, his book which appeared the following year being the first complete statement of the doctrine.[162] The key viewpoint was that human conduct is in principle a series of responses (so-called 'conditioned reflexes') to various physical stimuli, there being no knowable role for the conscious, that is rational, determination of action by the individual. This sort of approach dominated American psychology for two or three decades and had a notable influence in some quarters elsewhere. Among experimental psychologists it stimulated fresh interest in the physiological foundations of behaviour and especially in the brain as one of its instruments, in the question of the relative importance of inborn and acquired factors, and in the nature of the learning process

159 J. S. Mill, *Autobiography* (1873; World's Classics, 1963), p.143. For Mill's way out of the dilemma, ibid., pp.143–4, and 'A System of Logic' (1843), *Collected Works*, ed. J. M. Robson *et al.* (London, 1963ff), viii.836–43.

160 Cf. B. D. Mackenzie, *Behaviourism and the Limits of Scientific Method* (London, 1977), ch.III.

161 Watson, 'Psychology as the Behaviorist Views It', *The Psychological Review*, xx (1913), pp.158, 176–7. The first full life recently appeared in D. Cohen, *J. B. Watson: the Founder of Behaviourism. A Biography* (London, 1979).

162 *Behavior: an Introduction to Comparative Psychology* (New York, 1914). I. P. Pavlov's *Lectures on Conditioned Reflexes* had been published in 1910 but does not appear to have much influenced Watson's own work: see his article in *Encyclopaedia Britannica*, 14th edn (1947), iii.328.

especially in its relation to Pavlovian conditioning.[163] Not unrelated is the influence of medical discoveries which seemed to show the mastery of the body over the mind as through the effect of hormones on mental activity and personality. One systematic version of this sort of approach is William Sheldon's classification of human types which depends on relating certain physiques to differences of mind and character.[164] Another recent restatement of the behaviourist viewpoint is Dr William Sargant's *Battle for the Mind* which created rather a furore when it appeared a few years ago.

For both these extremely significant schools of psychological theory, free and rational will seemed a delusion: man was determined either by unconscious psychical forces or by automatic bodily responses to outside influences. Freedom is thus a figment; morality is simply the way in which we justify or attempt to regulate non-ethical impulses; rational purpose is an illusion. It seemed that much of the intellectual paraphernalia of libertarian thought was assailed and cast aside by notions such as these.

These ideas seemed particularly to condemn the pretensions of popular democracy dominated as it was by the 'mass man'. What hope was there for a collectivity swayed by emotion and impulse, haunted (in Wells's phrase) by 'the ghosts of apes and monkeys that suddenly come out from the darkness of the subconscious'.[165] Psychologists and those interested in the social implications of the genre were not slow to analyse the nature of the dominant new species, to examine (as the title of Wilfrid Trotter's famous study has it) the *Instincts of the Herd in War and Peace* (1916).[166] Not unusually, the conclusions were anti-democratic and élitist involving a rejection of the infallibility of majorities and repudiating the claims of the liberal or radical tradition, as in Sir Martin Conway's slightly earlier *The Crowd in Peace and War* (1915).[167] Aldous Huxley once likened 'the collective will' to 'a gigantic monkey' with 'the mentality of a delinquent boy'.[168] All this echoes, of course, de Tocqueville's insight about the tendency of a democratic society to

163 O. L. Zangwill, 'Psychology', in Cox and Dyson, op. cit., ii.176–7.
164 See the account in G. A. Harrison *et al.*, *Human Biology: an Introduction to Human Evolution, Variation, Growth and Ecology* (1964; 2nd edn, Oxford, 1977), chs.23–4.
165 Wells, *The Secret Places of the Heart*, p.40.
166 The early development of group psychology is described in W. R. Dennes, *The Method and Pre-suppositions of Group Psychology* (Berkeley, Calif., 1924).
167 On the scientific credentials and élitist purpose of the early social psychologists, see R. A. Soffer, 'New Elitism: Social Psychology in Pre-War England', *Journal of British Studies*, viii (no.2, 1968–9), pp.111–40, esp. p.114. The implications of group psychology were not always deployed to anti-individualist ends: see e.g. M. Ginsberg, *The Psychology of Society* (1921; 4th edn, London, 1933).
168 A. Huxley to V. Ocampo (10 August 1945), in S. Bedford, *Aldous Huxley: a Biography* (London, 1973–4), ii.61.

impose uniformity on its citizens so that each 'having grown like the rest, is lost in the crowd, and nothing stands out conspicuously but the great and imposing image of the people itself.'[169]

A key figure in these early developments of psychological thought was Gustave LeBon whose seminal analysis *Psychologie des foules* appeared in 1895. It was immediately noticed by review in this country and was continuously available in English translation for many years. The genesis of LeBon's concern with the psychology of the masses was twofold: it derived, first, from the scientistic context of much contemporary French thought and, secondly, from the French defeat in the war of 1870, especially collective behaviour as revealed in the Paris Commune. LeBon wanted to show, in a fashion he took to be irrefutable, the nature of democracy and the crowd which dominated it as being, in effect, a major source of social dissolution.[170] Specifically, he stated in his preface that the 'substitution of the unconscious action of crowds for the conscious activity of individuals is one of the principal characteristics of the present age.'[171] LeBon's own subsequent concern was to determine how these mass social forces might be held in check by an élite and made use of in the service of a patriotic nationalism.[172] But the immediately obvious lesson and one that continued to be drawn was the gullibility and irrationality of this dominating social entity, the mass man, and his 'extreme mental inferiority'.[173] The crowd demonstrated characteristics quite different from those of the individuals composing it: it was more impulsive and volatile, credulous and suggestible, and so on. In fact, all the 'unconscious' (and less desirable) qualities gain the upper hand.[174] It is the rule of barbarism and instinct that prevails.[175] Freud was a great admirer of LeBon's work and sought to assimilate it to the analysis of individual psychology he had himself elaborated.[176] And he, too, found the characteristics of the group to be 'lack of independence and initiative in their members, . . . the weakness of intellectual ability, the lack of emotional restraint, the incapacity for moderation and delay, the inclination to exceed every limit in the expression of emotion and to

169 A. de Tocqueville, *Democracy in America* (1835–40; Fontana, 1968), ii.868.
170 An excellent study is R. A. Nye, *The Origins of Crowd Psychology: Gustave LeBon and the Crisis of Mass Democracy in the Third Republic* (London, 1975). See e.g. ibid., pp.44–5, 60.
171 G. LeBon, *The Crowd: a Study of the Popular Mind* (1895; trans., London, 1952), p.6.
172 e.g. Nye, op. cit., pp.106, 112, 167–8, and ch.6 *passim*.
173 LeBon, op. cit., pp.7, 33; also I.iii.2, II.ii.4. It is important to note that LeBon was discussing what he called 'the psychological crowd' rather than a mere group of people collected together in one place, ibid., pp.23–5, and III.i.2, III.iv.
174 ibid., pp.27, 29 and I.ii *passim*.
175 ibid., p.32.
176 In his *Group Psychology and the Analysis of the Ego* (1921).

work it off completely in the form of action', and so on; that is, all the features and qualities contrary to those of the rational individual or group of libertarian theory.[177]

Other contemporary studies of the group mind tended in the same direction, as the work of William McDougall exemplifies. In his early *Introduction to Social Psychology* (1908) McDougall had, in exposition of the so-called hormic analysis, in effect repudiated the Benthamite notion that human action can be viewed as based on a rational calculation of consequences and self-interest; rather the prime mover of human activity was such a force as instinct (which might, of course, be quite selfless). And, in later work, the collectivity, the group, was stressed rather than the individual: 'the social aggregate has a collective mental life, which is not merely the sum of the mental lives of the units [and] it may be contended that a society not only enjoys a collective mental life but also has a collective mind or . . . soul.'[178] In the various types of collective context, the individual is raised to a higher plane of life above all as a member of a nation.[179] It is, McDougall explains, the task of 'Group Psychology' to explore this concept of the collective or group mind and examine its various types and, as well, especially 'to display the general principles of collective mental life which are incapable of being deduced from the laws of the mental life of isolated individuals'.[180] And there is no doubt of McDougall's opinion of the 'mental life of the crowd': it is basically impulsive, emotional, inconsistent, fickle, suggestible, careless in deliberation, and so forth.[181]

Perhaps the key text in the specifically political exploration of these ideas in Britain was Graham Wallas's *Human Nature in Politics*. As early as 1898 he had begun to lose his old faith in democracy and its psychological basis.[182] The book he brought out ten years later was an analysis of this apostasy and what it involved. In the interim, Wallas had also been much influenced by the ideas of Ostrogorski who confirmed in his mind the need to direct attention away from the formal façade of democratic politics.[183] While stressing the desirability in principle of rational control, Wallas acknowledged and emphasized that, in politics, emotion, impulse, habit, suggestion, instinct, and the like were in fact the

177 ibid., as cited in J. Rickman (ed.), *A General Selection from the Works of Sigmund Freud* (London, 1937), p.225.
178 W. McDougall, *The Group Mind: A Sketch of the Principles of Collective Psychology with some Attempt to Apply them to the Interpretation of National Life and Character* (1920; 2nd edn, Cambridge, 1927), p.7.
179 ibid., pp.20, 299–301.
180 ibid., pp.7–8.
181 ibid., pp.44–5.
182 B. Webb, *Diaries, 1924–1932* (London, 1956), p.74.
183 H. G. Wells, *Experiment in Autobiography* (London, 1934), ii.599–600.

primary motivating factors, and this had to be taken into account in a realistic understanding of political thought and behaviour. For example, he suggested that 'most of the political opinions of most men are the result, not of reasoning tested by experience, but of unconscious or half-conscious inference fixed by habit.'[184] A democracy was gullible and its politics might become no more than the exploitation of emotion by skilled governmental or other manipulation. Reflecting on these matters, Mrs Webb later wrote how, having staked everything on a belief in the essential goodness of humankind, she realized looking back 'how permanent are the evil impulses and instincts in man' and 'how little you can count on changing some of these', such as 'the greed of wealth and power', by altering political and social institutions.[185] It seemed that original sin was to dominate after all.

Of course, such views were strengthened by other continental influences than LeBon's. Nietzsche (who became something of a cult figure in some circles in Britain early this century) was taken to urge that man was not primarily a thinking creature at all, reason being not of his essence but a mere surface phenomenon. More basic was the will to power.[186] And Sorel's work stressed that men were moved to action not by reason but by myth, that is, 'a body of images which, *by intuition alone*, and before any considered analyses are made, is capable of evoking as an undivided whole the mass of sentiments' involved.[187] In politics immediate action without rational reflection was vital: 'il s'agit, et voilà tout.' Pareto equally stressed the importance of 'non-logical conduct' and saw political principles as the rationalization of 'residues', his term for the complex of qualities, instincts, and desires in people.[188]

Nor has interest in these facets of the group mind failed since that time nearly a century ago when such themes seemed perhaps new and startling. In different ways, but continually, the point has been pressed home about the fragility of those rational capabilities presupposed by the principles of democracy and individualism, coupled with the assertion that mass man is more swayed by emotion, more subject to adventitious pressure, and more likely to succumb to the lure of the demagogue. It is not surprising that Conservatives have often found this sort of thing congenial. One tract of the 1920s, for instance, said that the appeal of a political party is never likely to be merely a matter of rational argument, for all political experience goes to show that 'reason plays only a limited

184 G. Wallas, *Human Nature in Politics* (1908; 4th edn, London, 1948), p.103.
185 B. Webb, op. cit., p.79.
186 W. J. Dannhauser, 'Friedrich Nietzsche', in L. Strauss and J. Cropsey (eds), *History of Political Philosophy*, 2nd edn (Chicago, 1972), p.797.
187 A. Sorel, *Reflections on Violence* (1906; trans. Hulme, London, 1925), p.130.
188 See the passages from Pareto's *The Mind and Society* (1916), in J. H. Abraham, *The Origins and Growth of Sociology* (Penguin, 1973), pp.471 ff.

part in the formation of human convictions', 'semi-conscious' and 'sub-conscious sentiments and instincts' being by far more important.[189] William Beveridge apparently shared a similar distrust in democracy.[190] And even very staid forms of radicalism, like Fabianism, have been linked with curious and hardly rational sorts of spirituality.[191] The Webbs' rather scornful view of 'l'homme moyen sensuel' is notorious.

The rise of Fascism and Communism, in particular, led to a rash of speculation which is best seen in the context described here. Political commentators and analysts suggested that far from wanting (as the libertarian might suppose) greater freedom of choice and action, most people abhor the stress and responsibility entailed. In 1935 F. W. Hirst wrote of modern militarism as having 'a psychological root not only in fear of disorder but in a not uncommon liking for disciplined servitude' which was all too easily implanted.[192] Somewhat earlier and from the opposite end of the political spectrum, Wyndham Lewis had, as part of his biting criticism of Parliamentary democracy, asserted that the modern public did not want to think for itself, make up its own mind, or accept responsibility: it wanted rather to withdraw from the problems posed by individuality and freedom and to fall back on the safety of the herd and dependence on its leader.[193] This is a line of argument more usually associated perhaps with Erich Fromm who, in a famous book *The Fear of Freedom* (1942), analysed in such terms the development of modern destructiveness and authoritarianism in particular the rise of the Nazi movement. But many years before, Spencer had urged an interestingly similar theme. Writing in 1890 to Auberon Herbert, the fervent and extreme individualist, he discussed the psychology of the populace rapidly acquiring political power. Men are, he said, capable only of a certain amount of freedom and if they are given more they lose it to new forms of tyranny. Thus if men are granted the vote before they are capable of bearing this responsibility effectively, they will (through its use) organize for themselves 'the tyrannies of trade unionism, and socialism, and socialistic legislation' and, as a result, will be in as much if not more bondage than before.[194] Certainly libertarian democracy based on the ideas of the rational citizen and the implied need for only very

189 Rt Hon. E. Wood (later Viscount Halifax), *Conservative Beliefs*, NUA no. 2311 (London, 1924), p.3.
190 J. Harris, *William Beveridge: a Biography* (Oxford, 1977), p.89.
191 Cf. J. C. N. Webb, *The Flight from Reason: Volume 1 of the Age of the Irrational* (London, 1971), pp.228–34, and ch.ix *passim*.
192 F. W. Hirst, *Liberty and Tyranny* (London, 1935), p.16.
193 D. G. Bridson, *The Filibuster: a Study of the Political Ideas of Wyndham Lewis* (London, 1972), pp.31, 41. Cf. ibid., pp.70–1, 105.
194 H. Spencer to A. Herbert (22 October 1890), in D. Duncan, *The Life and Letters of Herbert Spencer* (London, 1908), pp.301–2.

limited government seemed to be cast under a shadow by all such understandings of the human psyche: the assumed natural, almost anarchic, harmony of individual interests and actions came to appear an illusion.[195]

These are complex and difficult matters and, as often the case, literary observers may (in Freud's own phrase) be 'valuable allies' in opening up our knowledge of relevant aspects of the mind.[196] Certainly they often proceeded in advance of science or everyday understanding, reflecting with increasing sophistication a recognition of the unconscious forces in man's nature. This is so, at one level, in terms of the fictional analysis of character, attention being drawn to the sub-conscious determinants of action in individuals, what Bertrand Russell called 'the various forms of passionate madness to which man is prone'. Conrad reflects this, for instance, and so does Dostoevski whose novels were making such an impact at the beginning of the century. In fact his stress on emotional and irrational motives had much impressed Freud himself.[197] In a similar way it was at the end of the last century that the theme of sexuality began to appear in Victorian literature.[198] Lawrence, above all perhaps, seems to suggest that civilization is at war with the real, unconscious roots of man's being. But this was a view often expressed. A writer so different as Henry James, in his less blunt and much more subtle and devious way, intimates the ambiguities and windings of the unconscious self so that there is, instead of objective reality, only a flow of variable awareness. It is even the case that, in the attempt to give a literary rendering or evocation of unconscious powers, the very form of the novel seemed often to represent their distorted flow. Not, of course, that all this was completely new. Browning in *The Ring and the Book* (1868–9) had tried to realize the multi-faceted nature of truth and reality. But the form of the reality discerned was itself now changing into the amorphous world of the unconscious and uncontrollable. In any event the specific suggestion here is not that these developments in the literary world were caused by the irruption of Freudian doctrine but rather that

195 Among the many similar analyses are e.g. S. Chakotin, *The Rape of the Masses: the Psychology of Totalitarian Political Propaganda* (1939; trans. edn, London, 1940), ch. II; R. Tatham, *Understanding the Mass Mind* (1944; 2nd edn, London, 1945), esp. ch. III, 'Logic and the Mass Mind'; and H. Walsby, *The Domain of Ideologies: a Study of the Origin, Development and Structure of Ideologies* (Glasgow, 1947), esp. chs. 4–5.

196 Freud, in Clark, *Freud*, p. 116.

197 W. Martin, *The New Age under Orage: Chapters in English Cultural History* (New York, 1967), pp. 142–3; Clark, op. cit., p. 116.

198 H. House, 'Man and Nature: Some Artists' Views', in H. Grisewood *et al.*, *Ideas and Beliefs of the Victorians: an Historic Revaluation of the Victorian Age* (1949; New York, 1966), pp. 230–2.

a general direction of intellectual movement was afoot in a number of different fields at roughly the same time. For it is a tendency indicated, too, in the world of art. For instance, the Post-Impressionist exhibition held in London in November 1910 had struck more than one contemporary as a revelation of the deeper levels of consciousness such as the collective or race mind, 'the essential and primitive thing' beneath the flow of ordinary experience.[199] Surrealism and Dada, too, helped substantially to break the rule of reason in art. The stress on the absurd and the deliberately paradoxical became the ideal: the only logic was that of caprice. Breton in the first Surrealist manifesto (1924) referred to 'pure psychic automatism', to the revelation of thought 'in the absence of all control by the reason'.[200] Nor was even the world of science immune to the tendency to abandon the absolute and assert elements of uncertainty.[201]

Perhaps, in the literary context, some of the political implications of Freudian and Behaviourist psychology are best revealed in the writings of Aldous Huxley, grandson of T. H. Huxley the Victorian scientist. He was a student both of psychology and contemporary politics, and his novels reflect a continued concern with the dominance of emotion over reason, the impossibility of realizing a rational state of freedom, and the like. Consider, for instance, the remarks attributed to Francis Chelifer in *Those Barren Leaves* (1925) to the effect that there is little evidence in most people of 'the conscious rational virtues that ought to belong by definition to a being calling himself Homo Sapiens.' Animalism rather than sapience seemed to characterize humankind.[202] Or again there are the more extensive and amusing observations of Mr Scogan (who bears a certain wicked resemblance to Bertrand Russell) in the slightly earlier *Crome Yellow* (1921) in the course of which it is urged that reasonable men never achieve anything because they lack the necessary touch of enthusiastic mania: 'Wherever the choice has had to be made between the man of reason and the madman, the world has unhesitatingly followed the madman. For the madman appeals to what is fundamental, to passion and the instincts; the philosophers to what is superficial and supererogatory – reason.'[203] Nevertheless a remedy to this dilemma was available: it was for the few men of genuine intellect (people like Mr Scogan himself) to take over and direct the forces of passion to proper ends, to 'found the Rational State'. This involved a highly organized,

199 G. Calderon, 'The Post Impressionists', *The New Age*, n.s., viii (1910–11), p.89 (issue of 24 November 1910).

200 Cited by E. Lucie-Smith, 'The Other Arts', in Cox and Dyson (eds), *The Twentieth-Century Mind*, ii. 483.

201 Cf. Professor G. H. A. Cole, 'Physics', ibid., i.250–1, 269, 309; ii.230.

202 A. Huxley, *Those Barren Leaves*, pp.83–4.

203 A. Huxley, *Crome Yellow* (1921; Penguin, 1972), p.126.

hierarchical system subject to totalitarian control. Human beings would be separated by examining psychologists into three main groups according to their ability and temperament. Continuing the Platonic caricature, there were to be those suitable to be 'Directing Intelligences', to be 'Men of Faith' (the maniacal propagandists of the system), or those capable only of belonging to 'the Herd'. For those that do not easily fit in, there is no place save 'the lethal chamber'.[204] A decade later Huxley additionally embroidered his amazing prescience of nastiness in the horrifying *Brave New World* (1932) and did so further still in the post-war *Ape and Essence* (1949) revealing the awful culmination of animalistic madness of which human nature was capable. And if Huxley himself later presented a contrasting picture of the good Utopia in *Island*, published in 1962, his earlier theme is one which has become a literary commonplace with such later examplars of the style as Orwell's *1984*, David Karp's *One*, and Anthony Burgess's *A Clockwork Orange*, each of which either depicts a society run autocratically on behaviouristic principles or intimates this possibility.

✻   ✻   ✻

The concept of a genuine social science has had its ups and downs; and it still survives, though we are as far from its ever-promised achievement as we were when Spencer (or Bacon for that matter) first put pen to paper. Indeed it is all the more likely that the continuous attempts made in this direction serve only to demonstrate both the inherent futility of the enterprise and the dangerous prospect it presents of rational or other political control.

But 'Enough of Science' (if not, in this case, of Art): it is time, at Wordsworth's bidding, to 'Close up those barren leaves' and to turn instead to the 'heart That watches and receives.'[205]

---

204 ibid., pp. 128–31.
205 'The Tables Turned' (1798), ll. 29–32, in *The Poetical Works* (1904; London, 1964), p. 377.

6

PHILANTHROPY AND ITS ROLE

Is it well that while we range with Science, glorying in the Time,
City children soak and blacken soul and sense in city slime?

There among the glooming alleys Progress halts on palsied feet,
Crime and hunger cast our maidens by the thousand on the street.

There the Master scrimps his haggard sempstress of her daily bread,
There a single sordid attic holds the living and the dead.

There the smouldering fire of fever creeps across the rotted floor,
And the crowded couch of incest in the warrens of the poor.

TENNYSON, 'Locksley Hall Sixty Years After', 1886, in
The Works, 1894, p. 566

THE HUMANITARIAN IMPULSE

The more carefully we examine the history of the past, the more reason
shall we find to dissent from those who imagine that our age has been
fruitful of new social evils. The truth is that the evils are, with scarcely an
exception, old. That which is new is the intelligence which discerns, and
the humanity which remedies them.

MACAULAY, *The History of England*, 1889, i.205

IN THE lines that follow those cited as motto to the present chapter, the
Poet Laureate urged the younger generation to help their fellow men, to
serve the poor and build the cottage, raise the school and drain the fen.[1]
And indeed humanitarian sentiment was always at work in the service of
social amelioration whether the outlet was voluntary effort or pressure
on public authority to act. For if industry and technology were achieving
great things there were also many problems created that required
attention, 'the mitigation of poverty, disease, infirmity, and ignorance.'[2]
In the end public authority itself very often assumed responsibility; but

1 Tennyson, *The Works* (London, 1894), p. 567.
2 D. Owen, *English Philanthropy 1660–1960* (London, 1965), p.1. Cf. the excellent
  general account of the eighteenth-century background (with special reference to the
  formation of public opinion against slavery) in F. J. Klingberg, *The Anti-Slavery
  Movement in England: a Study in English Humanitarianism* (New Haven, Conn.,
  1926), chs. II–III.

initially and perhaps for a long time its response might be slow and ineffective so that private charity and voluntary action continued to be important for many years (as indeed they still are). This was, too, not simply because in this way many contemporary difficulties were tackled but also because practical benevolence was regarded as a major component of the moral duty borne by the more fortunate individual. Wesley's dictum is apposite: 'Gain all you can; save all you can; give all you can.' But in the end it was through the collective power of the community that the humanitarian impulse was primarily of effect. Reflecting on the causes of the growth of state interference, G. J. Goschen gave pride of place to 'moral considerations', the 'awakening of public conscience', and 'the assertion of the claims of other than material interests'. He thought that this was certainly the case in respect of the Factory and Education Acts, the 'public imagination' being touched by appeals to its higher nature: it was this which 'supplied the tremendous motive power necessary for passing laws which put the State and its inspectors in the place of father and mother as guardians of a child's education, labour, and health'. It was equally true that the victory of the principle of compulsion over that of natural liberty was a triumph of moral force in other fields of reform also, respecting ships and sailors, preventing accidents in mines and factories, curtailing hours of labour, the state of canal boats, the improvement of unsanitary dwellings, temperance reform, and the like. And if in each case there were powerful arguments for expediency the crucial stimulus was none the less given 'by the sense of moral right'.[3] As Chesterton later observed, too, it was 'the emotion of compassion for misfortune' which simply yet deeply related Christianity and collectivism.[4]

A considerable part was played in nineteenth-century social and administrative change, therefore, by the labours and compassion of 'quite ordinary and often nameless' people who were stirred by 'a new acquaintance with great sufferings and misery' to try to bring about a better state of affairs in society. It was this kind of feeling, for instance, which prompted Stephen de Vere to undertake a voyage to North America on an emigrant ship to see what conditions were like. And what he found was an important factor in the passing of the Passenger Act of 1828.[5] Pity for the young or the defenceless was a feeling often at work in these matters. Consider the official report of Palmerston's statement as Home Secretary on a proposal in 1853 to make effective some control of the hours of work of the factory children:

---

3 G. J. Goschen, . . . *Laissez-Faire and Government Interference* (London, 1883), pp. 6–10.
4 Chesterton's notebook, in M. Ward, *Gilbert Keith Chesterton* (London, 1944), p. 71.
5 O. MacDonagh, 'Emigration and the State, 1833–55: an Essay in Administrative History', *Trans. R. Hist. S.*, 5s., v (1955), pp. 151, 159.

he really thought that to have little children of from eight to twelve years of age brought out on a drizzling winter's morning at five, or half-past five, when they perhaps lived three or four miles distant from the place where they worked, and then in the evening to have them walking back, perhaps alone, to their homes in the dark, with perhaps, snow on the ground, was a practice which must entail such evils that no one could be surprised at the extreme mortality among the children of factory operatives. To limit the number of hours . . . for the employment of children would indirectly be to limit the employment of persons of more advanced age;

– because the children did certain vital work –

but all he could say was, he thought it was so essential to protect these children from being overtasked that he could not consider the results which it might be imagined would flow from it, as a reason why such limitation should not be adopted.[6]

Public opinion was stirred and agitated in a variety of ways and on many issues. The result might be an individual making visits to the poor in their own homes. Very often changes were achieved by local groups working to improve conditions in the district where they lived, perhaps through the adoption of permissive powers already existing or through the promotion of a private Act of Parliament. The persons likely to be concerned were a mixed bag: bankers, merchants, some aristocrats or society gentlemen, industrial entrepreneurs, and so on.[7] There was in addition the continued action of professional groups (such as doctors) and the national campaigns of voluntary associations (like that crusading for health in towns). There were numerous societies 'for the relief of distress', associations 'for the prevention of pauperism and crime', trusts for the building of model dwellings, for establishing hospitals and schools, and many others. In 1860 it was estimated that in London alone there were 640 charitable bodies with an annual income of nearly £2¼ million.[8] In 1869 the Charity Organization Society was formed to try to weld all this effort (and that of similar bodies elsewhere) into a more effective system for combating the advance of Socialism and realizing a better society by a discriminating treatment of poverty.[9] In the 1850s, too, the Charity Commission had been created to oversee all this effort.

Motives varied, then, from a simple sense of pity to a consciousness of sin and guilt at privilege or advantage enjoyed, a sort of solace to the

6 128 Parl. Deb. 3s., 5 July 1853, cols. 1269–70.
7 Owen, op. cit., ch. XV provides 'A Gallery of Victorian Philanthropists'.
8 H. Perkin, *The Origins of Modern English Society, 1780–1880* (1969; London, 1972), p. 122. For a detailed estimate of the range and resources of Victorian philanthropy, see Owen, op. cit., ch. XVII.
9 C. L. Mowat, *The Charity Organisation Society 1869–1913: its Ideas and Work* (London, 1961), pp. 1–2, 15–18; ibid., ch. I reviews the social philosophy at work in the charity movement and some of its major personalities.

wealthy, coupled with a belief that even ragged creatures had the divine image stamped on them and, therefore, merited care and attention.[10] Nor was a certain political prudence absent, the sense that unless the condition of the poor was ameliorated and their feelings assuaged then unrest or worse was inevitable. C. F. G. Masterman suggested the point with a touch of dramatic hyperbole when (at the beginning of the present century) he pictured a member of the middle classes gazing 'darkly from his pleasant hill villa' at 'the huge and smoky area of tumbled tenements which stretches at his feet.' This citizen is (the passage continues),

> dimly distrustful of the forces fermenting in this uncouth laboratory. Every hour he anticipates the boiling over of the cauldron. He would never be surprised to find the crowd behind the red flag, surging up his little pleasant pathways, tearing down the railings, trampling the little garden; the 'letting in of the jungle' upon the patch of fertile ground which has been redeemed from the wilderness.[11]

Because of this fear, they and their predecessors had been only too willing to pay what critics called 'the blood money of charity'.[12] This is, of course, a merely pejorative characterization of what was often a simply and deeply felt sense of humanity, good in its way and certainly better than inactivity – unless it was believed (as it was by some) that relief and palliation were themselves undesirable because they prevented deterioration and so the onset of really radical change. But the charitable movement was nevertheless an impressive and unique phenomenon: the Nathan Committee in 1952 described the attempt to create by private effort a series of universal social services as 'one of the magnificent failures of our history.'[13] For in the end it did prove by itself to be ineffective not least perhaps because of its invariable stress on individual responsibility and self-help and its failure or unwillingness to treat causes rather than symptoms. It may be said, at least, to have served the valuable purpose of directing attention to social problems and, by its own inefficacy, to have revealed their true scale. Increasingly, the state was prompted to intervene to aid, supplement, or (in due course) replace voluntary effort in such spheres as poverty, old age, medical aid, and

---

10 See the citations in B. Harrison, 'Philanthropy and the Victorians', *Victorian Studies*, ix (1965–6), pp. 358–9. This paper is a fascinating and concise review of the motives and manner of Victorian philanthropy. On the sense of burden involved, see also R. Hall, *Marie Stopes: a Biography* (1977; Virago, 1978), pp. 23–4.

11 C. F. G. Masterman, *The Condition of England* (1909; 4th edn, London, 1911), p. 67.

12 E. Townshend, *The Case against the Charity Organisation Society*, Fabian tract no. 158 (London, 1911), p. 3.

13 The Law and Practice Relating to Charitable Trusts, Cttee. Rep. (1952), Cmd. 8710, §44, cited in Owen, op. cit., p. 6.

unemployment relief.[14] Shaftesbury who was, of course, one of the great pioneers of reform and who had (if anyone did) 'the Enthusiasm of Humanity' commented late in life how the state was taking over in spheres previously dominated by voluntary effort. 'Sanitary questions,' he wrote in his journal in 1875,

> of which I saw the dawn, and had all the early labours, are passed into 'Imperial' subjects. Boards are everywhere, laws have been enacted, public attention roused, and Ministers have declared themselves willing to bring to bear on them the whole force of Government . . . . *Social* questions are in the same position.[15]

Like Mrs Cheveley in Wilde's *Ideal Husband*, the age seemed in the end to prefer politics to philanthropy.[16] At the same time it would be true to say that some form of voluntary provision provided the roots of nearly every public social service that has been established; it has moreover continued to have a crucial role even in the age of the welfare state.[17]

Two of the numerous strands of thought and feeling involved in this humanitarian tendency may be taken to illustrate its connexion with the growing call for public acknowledgement and action to deal with the social problems of the day: the religious response and what may be called the aesthetic protest.

THE RELIGIOUS RESPONSE

> The swarms of wretched, filthy, haggard, dissolute, profligate, care-worn, outcast masses who inhabit the dingy courts, dingy cellars, and miserable garrets of our great towns, call loudly upon us to go and carry the message of peace to their benighted homes . . . . Christians! arouse yourselves to work! Thrust in the sickle and reap, for the harvest of the earth is ripe.
>
> J. KNOX, *The Masses Without!*, 1857, pp. 4, 30

At the beginning of his monumental survey of English philanthropy since the seventeenth century, Professor Owen stresses that throughout 'religious motives appear strikingly'.[18] Certainly there was a substantial attempt to awaken the conscience of Christianity and to apply its ethic to the alleviation of contemporary problems: salvation was to be achieved by works. It is to make a profound mistake to accept the Weber-Tawney thesis that Protestantism basically and vitally sustained the commercial

---

14 On the movement of ideas involved, see Mowat, *The Charity Organisation Society*, ch. VI. Cf. Owen, op. cit., chs. XVIII–XIX.

15 Journal entry (11 January 1875), in E. Hodder, *The Life and Work of the Seventh Earl of Shaftesbury, K.G.* (London, 1887), iii. 355 (italics in original).

16 Cf. Harrison, art. cit., p. 371.

17 On the latter point, see Owen, op. cit., pp. 531 ff.

18 D. Owen, *English Philanthropy 1660–1960* (London, 1965), p. 3.

spirit merely. On the contrary there were major elements of conflict between the two (as Halévy saw well enough). An obvious early instance is the force of the evangelical revival which, asserting a doctrine of responsibility toward the underprivileged, was a major element in the attack on the slave trade and on child labour and in the movement for prison and factory reform as well as in the agitation to maintain morality by the condemnation of Sabbath-breaking, blasphemy, drunkenness, cruel sports, and the like.[19] To cite a specific example of the extensive pastoral activity that might be involved, there is the case of William Champneys, rector of Whitechapel from 1837 to 1860. He built three churches, founded schools, established a provident society, and started a scheme of relief for vagrant boys including a refuge and an industrial home; he also introduced a local association for the health and comfort of the working classes and was instrumental in providing a hiring office for the men who unloaded coal from ships in the London docks (so they did not as before have to hang about in public houses). This kind of work was obviously not at all unimportant given the general absence or low standard of public provision at the time.[20] And at its best it was reflected in the activities of men and women of all denominations and forms of belief from Catholics and Tractarians to Christian Socialists, the Salvation Army, and other radical Nonconformists. 'Dirt and drains', as Mrs Ward's Robert Elsmere said, 'are the foundations of a sound religion.'[21] The 'State Puseyites' asserted the right of the poor to protection and even discovered, in the primitive origins of the Church, an egalitarian spirit that involved a rejection of riches and the pursuit of wealth, seeing the poor as the blessed of God. In many ways the church or chapel became a kind of informal friendly or aid society, the priest or rector acting as doctor and almoner.[22] One mid-century pamphleteer called Christians to action in stirring terms. When, he said, we look at London and see all the manifest evidence of its wealth and greatness, 'surely we mourn that such a city has so much wickedness, degradation, infidelity, heathenism, and profligacy'. And he went on in the passionate way indicated in the epigraph to this section.[23] The effort envisaged perhaps put social reform in second place to the pursuit of eternity and

---

19 See E. M. Howse, *Saints in Politics: the 'Clapham Sect' and the Growth of Freedom* (1952; London, 1971), esp. ch.6, 'An Industry in Doing Good'. Cf. R. C. K. Ensor, *England, 1870–1914* (1936; Oxford, 1968), pp.137–9.

20 This example is taken from G. K. Clark, *Churchmen and the Condition of England 1832–1885: a Study in the Development of Social Ideas and Practice from the Old Regime to the Modern State* (London, 1973), p.72.

21 Mrs H. Ward, *Robert Elsmere* (1888; London, 1889), p.170.

22 Cf. B. Harrison, 'Philanthropy and the Victorians', *Victorian Studies*, ix (1965–6), p.356; H. J. Dyos, 'The Slums of Victorian London', ibid., xi (1967–8), p.17.

23 J. Knox, *The Masses Without!* . . . (London, 1857), pp.4, 30.

the saving of souls. But the former (if in this spiritual way incidental) was a significant practical dimension; and as Hell lost credibility as a place, its imagery remained: 'The damned were alive and living in Seven Dials.'[24]

And very often, indeed increasingly, the state was involved in a variety of ways to aid this voluntary effort or pursue its aims more effectively. For instance, a lot of public money, over £20 million, was spent buying out the slave owners, that is, in pursuit of a humanitarian measure of social improvement, sponsored by the religious conscience, and which involved legislative action in a crucial and sensitive area. As Maitland confirms: 'in 1833 by an act of the parliament of the United Kingdom . . . slavery was abolished throughout the colonies; and though compensation was provided for the slave owners, this of course was a vast interference with the rights of property.'[25] As well the process of Church reform itself seemed to invite parallel state action elsewhere. If government could interfere with the ecclesiastical polity, for instance to control tithes, abolish pluralities, and otherwise act to secure the proper use of Church property and endowments, why should it not similarly regulate other corporate rights and properties to good social and moral purpose? And, of course, the initial religious effort to establish schools through the voluntary societies was (as has been seen already) aided from 1833 on by an increasing state dole. The Christian Socialist movement urged that religion involved more than a theological doctrine: it was a way of life that required a sense of collective responsibility for the welfare of all and the replacement of competition by co-operation. And if its supporters looked primarily to individual effort and responsibility, to a moral change in the human spirit, they were never averse in principle to the invocation of the public power as a means of dealing with contemporary problems where this seemed the only possible course as in the case of water and gas supply, sewerage, the railroads, or, indeed, 'everything . . . which everybody uses, and must use.'[26] Canon Scott Holland, the friend of T. H. Green, urged the extension of state intervention on the grounds that (as G. K. Chesterton reports) the commonwealth ought to be seen in a positive and not merely negative light, 'the State exists to provide lamp-posts and schools, as well as gibbets and jails.'[27] Consider, too, the radical sentiments of another

24 J. W. Burrow, reviewing G. Rowell, *Hell and the Victorians*, in *TLS* (2 August 1974), p. 822.
25 F. W. Maitland, *The Constitutional History of England* (1908; Cambridge, 1974), pp. 338–9.
26 C. Kingsley, 'The Air-Mothers' (1869), in *Sanitary and Social Lectures and Essays* (1880; new edn, London, 1889), pp. 148–50, 154, 156. For recognition of the interests that stand in the way of sanitary reform by government, see '"A Mad World My Masters"' (1858), ibid., pp. 289–297.
27 G. K. Chesterton, *Autobiography* (1936; London, 1937), pp. 168–9.

churchman, J. N. Figgis, who believed that the 'evils of capitalism' were gross, 'huge as mountains', and that 'the oppression of the poor cries to heaven'. He asserted in one of his sermons that 'the state of our cities, the lives of the vast masses among the workers, are a disgrace to any civilisation, and that in so far as this civilisation calls itself Christian, it is a lie'. In this context the invitation to both Church and state to be remedially active is most clear but what he especially urged was the Christian's own duty in regard to the charitable use of his wealth.[28] Equally, the official doctrine of the Catholic Church was that, while there were clear limits to legitimate state action, public authorities had an undoubted responsibility under the law of God to sustain social justice, control the use of property, ensure a just wage, promote worker participation, and the like.[29] Naturally, in the characteristic style of the churchmen, the state was often transformed when its positive role became thus acceptable. In a revival of the language of the 'two swords', F. D. Maurice said its part was by no means humble and subordinate; nor was it,

> a vulgar earthly institution, which might do the dirty work of the Church, paying its ministers, persecuting its foes or determining its teachings, but a sacred and divine institution bearing a witness for law and justice which the Church under no condition has borne or can bear.[30]

And to take one latter-day instance among many, William Temple urged during the early 1940s that a Christian programme of social reform might entail more government intervention than hitherto in respect of housing and land values, family allowances, the supply of milk and meals to schoolchildren, a 'national minimum' of social provision, public works, employee participation, more economic planning, and so on.[31]

In this way, then, the Christian spirit which was first moved in the sphere of voluntary action came to realize the need for substantial public help. Personal philanthropy could never by itself be enough and had to be supplemented or supplanted by an extensive system of charity by state proxy.

28 J. N. Figgis, *Churches in the Modern State* (1913; 2nd edn, London, 1914), pp. 128–9; idem, *Antichrist and Other Sermons* (London, 1913), p. 191.
29 See e.g. the extracts from the encyclicals *Rerum Novarum* (1891), *Quadragesimo Anno* (1931), and *Mater et Magistra* (1961) in H. Bettenson (ed.), *Documents of the Christian Church* (1943; 2nd edn, London, 1963), pp. 387–95.
30 F. Maurice, *Life of F. D. Maurice* (1884), ii. 584–6, in Clark, op. cit., p. 318.
31 W. Temple, *Christianity and Social Order* (1942; Penguin, 1943), Appendix, pp. 77–93.

I put forward a claim . . . which . . . would put . . . Social order instead of
Individualist anarchy . . . . That system which I have called competitive
Commerce, is . . . of its very nature destructive of Art, that is to say of the
happiness of life.
W. MORRIS, 'Art and Socialism', 1884, in A. L. Morton (ed.),
Political Writings of William Morris, 1973, pp. 111, 123

A cognate movement of criticism took the form of what may be called the
aesthetic protest, the power of literature of various sorts being in particular able to stir the conscience and provoke concern to a considerable
degree. It has indeed been said that the 'first revolt' against the spirit and
deeds of industrialism came from 'the artistic side', as from the 'nest of
singing birds' at the Lakes who would have none of it.[32] This cultural
attack on the ill-effects of industrial change was often extreme and
vituperative but was, too, often all the more effective because it was so
one-sided and so skilfully expressed. The gravamen of the criticism
varied. Sometimes it was purely aesthetic: 'Art and Grace are less and
less', 'Beauty dwindles' with 'roofs of slated hideousness'.[33] William
Clarke, the Fabian, wrote that 'the true artist is at war with commercial-
ism', with the notion that anything, however ugly or abominable, may
be produced so long as it makes a profit.[34] There was also concern with
the impact of industrialism on the moral status of human beings: the
effect of long hours of work, poor housing, and the like; a sense of the
wrongness entailed by human degradation and wastage. There was, in
association with these feelings, a consequential stress on the need to
redress such conditions. This often took the form of insisting on the right
of the community to interfere for this purpose, even to replace the
existing social and economic arrangements with a completely different
and more humane system. And, while this reforming tendency could lead
to pressure for state action, there was often, too, a diffidence about the
overweening power of collectivism: it was seen, for instance, as
incompatible with the freedom of spirit and action necessary for artistic
endeavour and as likely to leave no room for the independent craftsman.

All this rested, certainly, on a scathing repudiation of the shibboleths
of the day, those associated with *laissez faire*. Carlyle put the point in his
inimitable way in *Past and Present* and did not hesitate to draw the
interventionist implication:

32 S. Webb, 'The Basis of Socialism: Historic', in G. B. Shaw *et al.*, *Fabian Essays* (1889;
Jubilee edn, London, 1950), p. 42.
33 Tennyson, 'Locksley Hall Sixty Years After' (1886), in *The Works* (London, 1894),
p. 567.
34 W. Clarke, 'The Fabian Society and its Work' (1893), in *Socialism: the Fabian
Essays* (Boston, 1894), p. xxxiii.

all this Mammon-Gospel, of Supply-and-Demand, Competition, Laissez-faire, and Devil take the hindmost, begins to be one of the shabbiest Gospels ever preached; or altogether the shabbiest.... Leave all to egoism, to ravenous greed of money, of pleasure, of applause:– it is the Gospel of Despair!... All this dire misery, therefore; all this of our poor Workhouse Workmen, of our Chartisms, Trades-strikes, Corn-Laws, Toryism and the general downbreak of Laissez-faire in these days, – may we not regard it as a voice from the dumb bosom of Nature, saying to us: 'Behold! Supply-and-demand is not the one Law of Nature; Cash-payment is not the sole nexus of man with man, – how far from it! Deep, far deeper than Supply-and-demand, are Laws, Obligations sacred as Man's Life itself: these also . . . you shall now learn and obey.

And he goes on from this to note what, he says, all men are beginning to see, 'that Legislative interference, and interferences not a few are indispensable', to supervise factories and mines, the sanitary condition of manufacturing towns, to provide an 'effective "Teaching Service"', and so on.[35] He is quite clear, therefore, that (as he put it elsewhere) the state 'exists here to render existence possible, . . . desirable and noble, for the State's subjects'; and as it gets to work it will find an expanding array of responsibilities to undertake.[36]

The poets themselves were in the vanguard of protest both in their lyrics and other works. One of Wordsworth's comments on the 'Manufacturing spirit' and the growth of towns has already been mentioned.[37] He went on to observe 'the darker side of this great change' and waxed indignant at the outrage thereby done to nature. He spoke of men, women, and little children being sacrificed in factories 'To Gain, the master-idol of the realm'. He was not blind to the great achievement and power involved in the new mastery over nature but paints a picture of a child in a cotton mill, a 'pale Recluse', warped, deadened, and deprived.[38] There is, too, his famous rejection of change in the form of the projected Kendal and Windermere railway (1844):

> Is then no nook of English ground secure
> From rash assault?

And he writes with scorn of 'the Thirst of Gold, That rules o'er Britain like a baneful star' and calls on people to 'protest against the wrong' and 'To

---

35 T. Carlyle, 'Past and Present' (1843), in *Works* (People's edn, 1871–4), xiv. 158–60, 226–9. Cf. 'Chartism' (1839), ibid., xi. 174–5; 'Sartor Resartus' (1831), ibid., i. 160–2.
36 Carlyle, 'The New Downing Street' (1850), in 'Latter-Day Pamphlets', ibid., xx. 139.
37 See p. 80 above.
38 *The Excursion*, VIII. 152–4, 180–5, 199ff, 297ff.

share the passion of a just disdain'. He thus repudiates 'a false utilitarian lure' and 'that idol proudly named "The Wealth of Nations"'.[39] Wordsworth's view was shared by other romanticists, Robert Southey, for instance, who in his famous *Colloquies on the Progress and Prospects of Society* (1829) spurns wealth brought by manufactures as being a delusory prosperity built on the degradation of labourers and the corruption of children, and so on.[40] It is hardly surprising that he was so sympathetic to the proposals of the Socialist, Robert Owen. Matthew Arnold's attack on those aspects of British life usually associated with its greatness is well-known. He was willing to concede that the love of liberty, the development of trade, and the like were of great significance in the process of human expansion. But these were by themselves incomplete and defective. They created industrial 'hell holes' for the working classes and even the life of the prosperous bourgeoisie was really 'singularly dull and mean'. In the outcome England was devoid of comeliness and its appearance revealed no sense of the outward dignity of things, of civilization made pervasive and general. The instinct for conduct, for intellect and knowledge, for beauty, and for a fit and pleasing form of social life and manners was starved. And Arnold was not at all sure that politicians in either of the main parties of the day understood what was necessary to achieve the humanizing goals in view: he was, in fact, pretty certain they did not. And no few tinkering or merely palliative Acts of Parliament would do it.[41] Similarly his specific ridicule of bourgeois philistinism is famous: the state of the country and its great wealth of which people were so proud was no more than 'anarchy' because it confused these things – mere means or machinery – with the proper end of life which was a disinterested endeavour to learn and to propagate 'the best which has been thought and said in the world'. Here production is not to be equated with real improvement or economic growth with 'culture'. And the remedy to the contemporary chaos was the state which might embody the right reason of the community.[42] Of course, Arnold was himself his own model of an enlightened bureaucrat. And there are, naturally, many poems of protest from others: from Thomas Hood's 'The Song of the Shirt' (1843), an indictment of the sweating system, to Mrs Browning's 'Bitter Cry of the Children' of the

39 'Miscellaneous Sonnets', xlv, xlvi, in *Poetical Works* (Oxford, 1964), p.224; *The Prelude* (1850 text), ibid., p.580 (XIII.77–8).
40 See the summary and citations, in L. Stephen, *The English Utilitarians* (1900; London, 1950), ii.111–12 *et seq.*
41 All this is expressed very clearly, for instance, in Arnold's 'The Future of Liberalism', *The Nineteenth Century*, viii (1880), 1–18.
42 Arnold, *Culture and Anarchy* (1869; Cambridge, 1960), *passim*: the phrase cited is at p.6.

same year and which, inveighing against the evils of child labour, was occasioned directly by official reports which had been published about such employment in mines and factories. And there are phrases from both these poems echoed more than a generation later in Tennyson's 'Locksley Hall Sixty Years After' (1886), like the lines already cited.

Equally a powerful and realistic school of novelists began to affect people's views on social matters. The authors were naturally a varied group but their work helped to create the feeling from which acceptance of state action could grow. It seems likely that the fictional embodiment of the aesthetic and literary protest may have had the widest and sharpest impact. It could be more graphic and would appeal to a larger public. At the same time it is wise not to exaggerate either the number of these people or the extent of their period of production. They were a few great figures mainly active in the two decades after the mid-1830s.

Dickens is the obvious and foremost example. Only *Hard Times* (1854), which was dedicated to Carlyle, dealt exclusively with the harshness of industrial conditions, but as well many incidents and characters in other works reveal the sufferings of the poor as in the descriptions of slum life in *Bleak House* (1853) and *Oliver Twist* (1838). Similarly characters such as Bounderby and Gradgrind reveal Dickens's low opinion of the merchant and manufacturing classes; and Mr Podsnap is a classic caricature of the smug and self-satisfied middle class. It is very clear why it should have been suggested that their creator was for so long the inspirer and embodiment of English radicalism.[43] Among other such authors there was, for instance, Mrs Gaskell who dealt directly with the evils of the factories. Thus *Mary Barton* (1848) gives a vivid account of the lives and struggles of the textile operatives as does *North and South* (1855). Disraeli, too, attacks the evils of the manu-facturing system and the commercial classes in such novels as *Sybil* (1845) and urges there and in *Coningsby* (1844) the ideals of Toryism as he sees it: that the cause of the common people should be espoused by the traditional landed classes or by the enlightened among their mercantile successors. Charles Kingsley, the Christian Socialist, wrote two novels well-known in this connexion, *Yeast* (1848) which deals with the agricultural aspect of the Chartist revolt and depicts the poverty and squalor of rural life, and *Alton Locke* (1850) which describes Chartism through the eyes of a London journeyman tailor and gives a gloomy picture of living conditions among sweated workers. Both novels were quite popular. Such fictional examples might be multiplied by reference, for instance, to the work of William Morris and George Gissing; and the

43 e.g. M. Muggeridge, *Chronicles of Wasted Time* (London, 1972–3), i.26.

twentieth century can provide counterparts in, say, D. H. Lawrence and George Orwell.[44]

Something of the detailed manner of the aesthetic protest may be briefly conveyed by two other examples. First by reference to the criticism of John Ruskin and secondly by giving some account of the medievalist reaction to the development of urban industrialism.

Perhaps no one did more to elaborate and spread an anti-commercialist attitude in the latter part of the nineteenth century than John Ruskin. He was then the country's major figure in the field of aesthetic criticism; one, moreover, whose attitude to art and literature was by no means unrelated to his wider views. As Lord Clark has observed, Ruskin applied to social conditions the same analytical processes and the same moral standards he used in judgement of landscape painting.[45] And for all that he appreciated the economic and even artistic potentiality of industrialism, Ruskin was also always aware of its dark side: thus the railway crowded more and more people into abominable towns; its 'ferruginous temper' was clamping Merrie England solid in an iron mask.[46] And for the time Ruskin held to a strong public line:

> 'I hold it for indisputable, that the first duty of a State is to see that every child born therein shall be well housed, clothed, fed, and educated, till it attain years of discretion. But in order to the effecting this the Government must have an authority over the people of which we now do not so much as dream.'[47]

His sentiments at large may be exemplified by some well-known sentences – they are one slight instance among many – from *The Stones of Venice*. Man, he says, cannot remain true to his real nature and also be required to work with the accuracy and perfection of a machine. If he is, 'so soul and sight' will be 'worn away, and the whole human being be lost at last'. Yet this is what has happened with the industrial system in the mechanical age. There follows a famous rhetorical passage:

> And now, reader, look round this English room of yours, about which you have been proud so often, because the work of it was so good and

44 A most useful symposium that came too late to hand is K. Gross (ed.), *Der Englische Soziale Roman im 19. Jahrhundert* (Darmstadt, 1977) which reprints numerous studies (most of them in English) on the relation between novels and novelists on the one hand and social and political criticism on the other. There is also an extensive bibliography.

45 K. Clark, introduction to Ruskin's *Praeterita* (1885–9; Oxford, 1978), p. xv.

46 J. Ruskin, 'The Seven Lamps of Architecture' (1849), in *The Works* (London, 1903–12), viii. 66 note † (added in 1880). And cf. the apostrophe to Carlyle (by whom he was above all influenced), in 'Munera Pulveris' (1872), §158, ibid., xvii. 280–1.

47 J. Ruskin, 'Time and Tide' (1867), letter xiii, ibid., xvii. 377 (citing 'Stones of Venice', ibid., xi. 263).

strong, and the ornaments of it so finished. Examine again all those accurate mouldings, and perfect polishings, and unerring adjustments of the seasoned wood and tempered steel. Many a time you have exulted over them, and thought how great England was, because her slightest work was done so thoroughly. Alas! if read rightly, these perfectnesses are signs of a slavery in our England a thousand times more bitter and more degrading than of the scourged African, or helot Greek. Men may be beaten, chained, tormented, yoked like cattle, slaughtered like summer flies, and yet remain in one sense, and the best sense, free. But to smother their souls with them, to blight and hew into rotting pollards the suckling branches of their human intelligence, to make the flesh and skin which, after the worm's work on it, is to see God, into leathern thongs to yoke machinery with, – this is to be slave-masters indeed; and there might be more freedom in England, though her feudal lords' lightest words were worth men's lives, and though the blood of the vexed husbandman dropped in the furrows of her fields, than there is while the animation of her multitudes is sent like fuel to feed the factory smoke, and the strength of them is given daily to be wasted into the fineness of a web, or racked into the exactness of a line.[48]

He goes on to write of 'this degradation of the operative into a machine', this feeling men have that they 'cannot endure' their labour because it makes them less than men: this is the cause of the unrest of the time. Men will willingly and nobly sacrifice themselves for others, yet

to feel their souls withering within them, unthanked, to find their whole being sunk into an unrecognized abyss, to be counted off into a heap of mechanism numbered with its wheels, and weighed with its hammer strokes – this, nature bade not, – this, God blesses not, – this, humanity for no long time is able to endure.... [The] great cry that rises from all our manufacturing cities, louder than their furnace blast is ... that we manufacture everything there except men; we blanch cotton, and strengthen steel, and refine sugar, and shape pottery; but to brighten, to strengthen, to refine, or to form a single living spirit, never enters into our estimate of advantages. And all the evil to which that cry is urging our myriads can be met only in one way: not by teaching nor preaching, for to teach them is but to show them their misery, and to preach to them, if we do nothing more than preach, is to

48 'The Stones of Venice' (1851–3), ibid., x.192–3, §§12–13. For similar sentiments expressed by one of Ruskin's Guild Socialist disciples, see A. J. Penty, *Towards a Christian Sociology* (London, 1923), pp.178–9. Cf. H. Spencer, 'What Knowledge Is Worth Most' (1859), in *Essays on Education and Kindred Subjects* (Everyman, 1966), p.16.

mock at it. It can be met only by a right understanding, on the part of all classes, of what kinds of labour are good for men, raising them, and making them happy; by a determined sacrifice of such convenience, or beauty, or cheapness as is to be got only by the degradation of the workman; and by equally determined demand for the products and results of healthy and ennobling labour.[49]

And so on and on, through many passionate volumes of criticism and protest, inveighing against the destruction and pollution of the natural landscape by industry, the false material values built into the economic orthodoxy then current, and the rest. Ruskin (who regarded himself as 'a violent Tory of the old school') had, of course, interventionist sympathies which appear at large in his works of political and social commentary and in which he insists that the welfare of the community is more important than individual profit-seeking.[50] Nor was the effect of his ideas short-lived either intellectually or on practical affairs. As to the latter, reference may be made simply to A. J. Penty's comment that he was surprised to note the extent to which Ruskin's name and authority were invoked by both sides in the discussions after the Great War about the organization of the building industry and the degree to which both employers and workers were familiar with his publications. 'I never realized before', he wrote, 'how far the influence of Ruskin had penetrated.'[51]

Another aspect of the contemporary repudiation of the ugliness and depravity associated with industrialism was the renewed interest of the time in the spirit and institutions of the Middle Ages: one version simply of the tendency to escape the evils of the day by looking back to a supposed Golden Age, a past in terms of which present degeneration could be assessed and criticized. This was a varied reaction and took many forms from Young England to the Oxford Movement and the Gothic revival. Nor was it merely intellectual: it appealed in some ways, for instance, to William Cobbett who often idealized the medieval period and spoke of the Reformation as the beginning of all the untoward features of his own day; in similar nostalgic mood he frequently regretted the loss of the intimate feudal relationships of those distant times.[52] There was a sense that solutions to current problems should be sought in the older heritage thus invoked. Carlyle gave this view great force as in

49 'The Stones of Venice, *The Works*, x.193–6, §§15–16.
50 Especially 'The Political Economy of Art' (1857); 'Unto This Last' (1862); 'Munera Pulveris' (1872); and 'Fors Clavigera' (1871–84). For his confession of Toryism, see *Praeterita* (edn cit.), pp. 5, 153, 169.
51 A. J. Penty, *Post-Industrialism* (London, 1922), p. 92. Cf. ibid., pp. 144ff.
52 L. Melville, *The Life and Letters of William Cobbett in England and America* (London, 1913), ii.218–21 (letter V).

Past and Present where he contrasts unfavourably the current condition of workers and the manner of their employment with the ways of the earlier world from which so much could be learned, in particular the need for wise and moral leadership by 'Real-Superiors' (such as the Middle Ages at their best had). Ruskin also proposed a deliberate turning back to medieval customs and institutions. For instance, he stressed the importance of the idea of a 'just price', thought trade unions should be converted into craft guilds, and was himself involved in the attempt to establish a sort of rural feudal colony.[53] He also influenced artistic reaction in favour of the medieval as with the Arts and Crafts Movement and the Pre-Raphaelite Brotherhood. Burne-Jones, Dante Gabriel Rossetti, and William Morris were the leading members of the Brotherhood (the name itself has significance in this context) which tried to recreate through art 'the forgotten world of old romance – that world of wonder and mystery and spiritual beauty which the old masters knew'.[54] Morris for his part wanted more than some aesthetic link with the spirit of the medieval past and wished to infuse this spirit into a practical reform movement based on the crafts system of the Middle Ages. He founded a 'Guild of Handicraft' the members of which lived on communal and co-operative lines; he revived a number of medieval crafts (such as glass-making, weaving, and bookbinding) in which the old careful standards of hand production, thoroughness, and beauty in workmanship were given key importance. Art was a necessity in life and so far as modern industrialism made this impossible then so far was the contemporary world to be repudiated and if feasible reformed. The chief accusation, he said, that he brought against the modern state of society was that 'it is founded on the art-lacking or unhappy labour of the greater part of men'; and all the 'external degradation of the face of the country' was 'hateful' because it was not only a cause of unhappiness to those who love art but 'a token of the unhappy life forced on the great mass of the population by the system of competitive commerce.'[55] Like Ruskin, Morris believed that good art could only come as *the expression of pleasure in the labour of production*': life was, therefore, a time to be passed in enjoyable work. Industrial division of labour turned men into machines, destroyed their individuality, and enslaved them hopelessly to their 'profit-grinding masters'. Throughout, in his literary and artistic work as well as in his political and social agitation, Morris continually

---

53 'Fors Clavigera', letter 89 in *The Works*, xxix, 398 ff; 'Time and Tide' (1867), ibid., xvii. 384–7, §§78–80; J. Hobson, *John Ruskin, Social Reformer* (1898; 2nd edn, London, 1899), ch. XII.

54 W. T. Watts-Dunton, 'D. G. Rossetti', *Encyclopaedia Britannica*, 11th edn (1910–11), xxiii. 749.

55 W. Morris, *Art, Labour & Socialism* (1884; London, 1962), p. 22.

dwelt on the superiority over the modern period of the Middle Ages. It was his main source of inspiration and constituted what was probably the most enthusiastic and successful example of the medieval reaction in nineteenth-century Britain.[56]

Of course, this nostalgic ethos was of some influence in other radical quarters: the Fabian Society and the Guild Socialist movement must be mentioned in this connexion. And a leading member of the latter, one who shared this sense of the loss of the medieval ethos, may be left with a final, summary word:

> the secret of the great intellectual and scholastic activity of the nineteenth century [was] its aim . . . to enable men to regain that grip on reality which they had lost. To talk about the nineteenth century as being an age of enlightenment is nonsense. It was perhaps the darkest period in history, when the great traditions were dead; when great men groped for the light and ordinary men were saved from despair by the hypnotism of the machine.[57]

And if, in this context of criticism, there was often a feeling that political reform might achieve little, might even tighten the grip of the state to deadening effect, there was also a recognition of the positive role that public authority could play in the limited task of creating the conditions of fulfilment and, specifically, of supporting culture and the arts, so resisting the philistinism of the day.

56 Morris, 'The Socialist Ideal', *The New Review*, iv (1891), pp.2, 6 (italics in original). On the aesthetic basis of Morris's ideas, cf. S. Ingle, 'Socialist Man', in B. C. Parekh (ed.), *The Concept of Socialism* (London, 1975), pp.73–83.
57 A. J. Penty, *A Guildsman's Interpretation of History* (London, 1920), p.250. Penty specifically placed Guild Socialism in the context of the nineteenth-century medieval revival, *Post-industrialism*, pp.154–6.

CODA

For all the reasons, then, that have been reviewed in the preceding chapters (and no doubt for others, too, that I have not discerned or have otherwise omitted) the tendency to increase the range and intensity of state involvement has grown substantially in strength over the past century and a half. It remains to consider specifically the ways in which this great change has been reflected in (and, of course, been assisted or hindered by) our political ideas and institutions and in respect of Britain's foreign and imperial policies and relationships. These aspects of our affairs will be examined in detail in the volumes which follow.

INDEX

An index is less useful than it ought to be if it is too sparse. Equally the entries are not so helpful as they might be if insufficiently specified: too many long strings of page numbers can be merely irritating. I have tried to avoid such obvious deficiencies without going to excessive length overall (though it is better to err on the side of fullness) and without being too concerned about a strict consistency in the lay-out adopted. For example, titles of nobility are always a bother; but I have used my discretion about the degree of detail given and the extent of cross-referencing attempted. Again, where it seemed to me interesting and likely to be useful, I have broken down quite short entries into sub-headings though in other, not dissimilar, cases I have left the bare page references. Nor have I bothered to be uniform about the use of people's initials and forenames; or about the precise alphabetical ordering of cognate entries. It is amateur work and no doubt the Society of Indexers is unlikely to commend such cavalier treatment of its subtle rules and principles. All I hope is that what I have done is helpful to the reader in practice.